*Encyclopedia of Giants
and Humanoids in Myth,
Legend and Folklore*

Encyclopedia of Giants and Humanoids in Myth, Legend and Folklore

Theresa Bane

McFarland & Company, Inc., Publishers
Jefferson, North Carolina

ISBN (print) 978-1-4766-6351-7
ISBN (ebook) 978-1-4766-2338-2

LIBRARY OF CONGRESS CATALOGUING DATA ARE AVAILABLE

BRITISH LIBRARY CATALOGUING DATA ARE AVAILABLE

Front cover illustration © 2016 iStock

Printed in the United States of America

McFarland & Company, Inc., Publishers
Box 611, Jefferson, North Carolina 28640
www.mcfarlandpub.com

To Don Shelor

A twenty-eight-year veteran in our country's military,
father of nine, and grandfather to twenty.

Thank you for your service, sir!

Table of Contents

Preface

This volume takes as its subject matter folkloric, legendary, and mythological humanoids. Interestingly, as this project's research was undertaken I discovered while there are anthropomorphic beings, creatures, deities, and the like in the fables, religions, and stories of many cultures there was no book available that covered the subject. True, there are a few books that cover GIANTS, both biblical and historically tall individuals, as well as some works that detail the VALKYRIES of Norse mythology. However the primary foci of these works were not solely humanoids, no matter how thoroughly they covered their subject matter. Again, I found myself writing the very book I wished I could purchase.

Typically when I begin working on one of my encyclopedias, I swivel my chair and begin consulting the books in my personal library, a large collection that has been amassed over the years. This time there was no need. Prior to this book, I wrote an encyclopedia of mythological creatures that I intended to be the be-all, end-all of creature reference books. Normally it takes me about a year to write an encyclopedia, but the creature book was such rich subject matter, even with the considerable exclusions I placed on potential entries, it took a lengthy extension and two years to complete. I was working, on average, eight hours a day, six days a week. When it was finished I had written over 500,000 words and just fewer than 4,000 entries including everything I wanted from rare entries of well-known mythologies to exotic creatures in lore and religions. It was large and impressive to behold but perhaps too unwieldy to be of practical use. When the publisher approached me with the idea of dividing it up into a few smaller but more tightly focused books, I had to side with them (as soon as I recovered from the apoplexy).

I consulted with my beta-readers, librarian friends, and fellow researchers for their best brainstormed ideas. The colossus would be divided into three encyclopedias: one of creatures, one of humanoids, and one of spirits. Once I had devised criteria for each and reworked the material as three manuscripts, I found I was most pleased with the results.

This book, like my other books, does not contain fictional creations from the imaginations of authors for the purpose of creating a fictional work. No mythology includes such characters in its pantheon. No legends of their exploits are told and retold around campfires. Although many of them are well known, these fictional characters are not candidates for inclusion in this work.

Also omitted were those hominids, simian-like cryptids living, allegedly, wild and unchecked in the wildernesses throughout the world. Bigfoot and swamp apes alike are not herein. Whether or not such creatures do or ever did exist, their realm is that of cryptozoology, not myth, legend or folklore.

Indigo children as well as human and grey alien hybrids were not counted among the potential entries for this book, the trope of "aliens among us" being outside the intended scope.

If readers are interested in that subject, *Barlowe's Guide to Extraterrestrials* (1979) is an excellent book.

Unaccustomed as I am to accepting purported and unsubstantiated facts as being true, I also avoided speculations as to what any given being "may have actually been" or how it could have been misidentified by an ancient eyewitness and is in truth a creature any modern reader would now recognize. Is it possible Marco Polo was looking at a Thompson gazelle and not a unicorn? Yes, it is. Was I there to witness what he was looking at and under what conditions the sighting took place? No, and for that that reason, I will not attempt to correct him or any other long-ago writer or observer whose work does fall within my criteria and was accepted for inclusion.

The objective here is to fully document as many of the folkloric, legendary, and mythological beings as possible into one work so other researchers may have a historically accurate and reliable resource not polluted with personal opinion and speculation. It is my dearest hope for academics, authors, researchers and the like to possess a copy of each of my books, so that they may find all reliable and legitimate information on an entry in one location.

Every effort was made to include for each entry all of the available information on a being as well as the name of the myth or story for which it is best known. Included is the creature's country of origin, a physical description, what it hunts and how it pursues its prey. If the being is sentient, its personality and moral alignment was also included. Some beings are clearly defined as "good" or "evil" whereas others are fickle in their intent, susceptible to flattery, easily offended by even the slightest of transgressions, and prone to random acts of either charity or devastation. Occasionally there is a pronunciation guide which I was able to provide, but sadly not as often as I would have liked. As always, some entries are longer and more detailed than others, but this is only because the people who originated the being fleshed out its history; a short entry exists not because I chose to make it brief but rather because the information available to discover was limited. A quick glance at the bibliography will prove it was not from lack of trying.

The entries are presented in alphabetical order in a single sequence for ease of reference. I have provided a thorough index, which I consider the very life blood of a book. I have been told time and again by authors and fellow researchers they often do not know exactly what they are looking for but have "an idea." For instance, if they wanted to know the name of a specific JOTUN who had once shared an adventure with Thor they could look up the words "JOTUN" and "Thor" in the index and see what pages each entry had in common to narrow their search. If an author was looking to add a monster to their story but all they knew for certain was it had to be a nocturnal predator, they could look up the word "NOCTURNAL" rather than scan through the pages of the book in search of a creature that would fit their needs.

Older and more developed societies tend to have mythologies and folklore more complete and detailed than newer societies that have not had the opportunity to develop their own. Greek, Hindu, and Norse mythologies tend to be detail-rich with many named characters possessing magical items that are also detailed in both their creation and abilities; therefore it is logical to assume there will be a great many entries originating from these cultures. With complicated storytelling involved in these and other such cultures, where characters tend to appear in many stories, I have employed the use of SMALL CAPS signaling to the reader there is more information available on this being and to take advantage of the cross-referenced work embedded in the book.

In my research I made use of the books and academic articles written by my predecessors—the older the better. There is something special about using information taken from older documents; perhaps it is because they were written by people with what a modern audience would consider to be a "traditional classical education." But there is also something special about the language they employed; it is more precise, more exacting, unadulterated, and written for an audience of their peers, never watering-down the information.

I would like to thank all of the people who made this book possible: Amedeo C. Falcone, my morale officer who asked daily for progress reports; Jeanie Bone, Angela McGill, Traci McGill and Pam Parisi, beta-readers and index assistants; my publisher McFarland, for initially suggesting dividing my colossal work into smaller and more concise books. And thanks most of all to my devoted and supporting husband, T. Glenn Bane, who enables me to pursue this vocation. Without this devoted cadre of overworked individuals, this book could not have happened.

Introduction

When I began writing this book and pulling information together, I knew there was interest in the subject matter as my reader base and I communicate frequently with one another via social media. I did initially wonder if there would even be enough mythological and folkloric humanoids to justify making a book, but it did not take long to quell my fear, as the number of entries to be considered for inclusion accumulated at an alarming rate. To be successful, the book had to include those humanoids from all cultures and mythologies, all geographic regions, and delve into traditional folklore as well as considering some of the more prevalent fairy-tales that were based on regional lore. As always, once the "easy" entries were added to the collection, I delved deeply into the subject matter and began to dig, looking for the most obscure and forgotten humanoids I could find in the works available to me.

Humanoids, those beings that have the appearance or characteristics of a human, are an accustomed staple in fantasy and science fiction genres as well as in the folklores and mythologies of mankind. Not as large or powerful as the gods but clearly more than human, these beings are markedly different from mankind yet are able to cohabit and interbreed with them, producing (oftentimes) monstrous hybrids.

Humanoid is a word which has been heavily adopted and eagerly embraced by the science fiction community, appearing regularly in those narratives. Alien races are described in books and regularly depicted in film as being more or less humanoid or human-like in their appearance—never the other way around. A person from Earth is never said to be Venusian in general size and shape; even when the story is told from the alien point of view, the word *humanoid* is employed.

Aliens notwithstanding, the fabled GIANTS of European lore and the GIGANTE and TITANS from ancient Greek mythology are likely the first sort of humanoids that come to mind—tall, powerfully built individuals with near divine strength, a booming voice, and a rather terrifying, if not horrific, visage to behold. More often than not these beings are driven by lust and hunger and make their most important life decisions in a fit of rage. As this is the image that is most frequently imagined when the word humanoid is heard, there are more of these beings in this book than any other species; those beings were also quite popular with ancient man. There are a large number of VALKYRIES from Norse mythology as well as GANA from Hindu lore, but in both cases it is interesting to note that as important a role as each plays in their respective myths, they are seldom thoroughly defined or fleshed out as individual characters; their names are all we know of them.

I am not aware of any culture in which humanoids do not appear, whether they pass for humans or interbreed with them. Such is the case with the VALKYRIES of Norse mythology or when humanoids were used as ancient heavy artillery; an example would be LAHMI, the brother

5

of the biblical GOLIATH OF GATH, who performed this function for the Philistine army. Interaction between their kind and ours was entirely dependent on the social role the being was originally assigned to perform, such as an angelic celestial messenger or a NURSERY BOGIE.

The word *humanoid* is a rather broad term. According to my favorite Merriam-Webster's dictionary, the word only came into being in 1918 and simply means "looking or acting like a human"; this is not the best definition to act as my foundation for deciding what beings and creatures should be included in this book. It simply does not work. My beloved dog Athena, for example, could never be passed off as a human being but at certain times her behavior is distinctly similar to that of a person. Clearly Merriam-Webster's definition leaves much to be desired.

The Oxford dictionary did little to help: "the appearance or character resembling that of a human." The Collins dictionary added to the definition by contributing "human rather than anthropoid characteristics" and "in science fiction, a robot or creature resembling a human being." Truth be told, the most helpful source to actually give the breadth and scope of the word came from—of all places—Wikipedia. It became apparent to me I needed to use a more holistic method of defining what a humanoid is for the purposes of entry admission into this book in such a way that my dog would not make an appearance. It was more difficult than you might think.

Naturally, I first relied on individual cultures to see if they considered the being to be a humanoid or not. Also of importance are bipedalism and a human level of intelligence as opposed to highly developed animal cunning. If the being was able to interbreed with mankind, it was included, as this indicated to me it was apparently human enough to achieve a hybrid. Oftentimes I found myself wondering about the entity's skeleton, a morbid prospect; nevertheless, if its physical description lent itself to having a human-like skeleton, it too was included, so long as it was not a mythological anthropotheism of a deity but rather a species, race, or individual. This process allowed me to exclude the divine and semi-divine offspring of the ancient gods. This application seemed to be a far better foundation upon which to make decisions than Merriam-Webster's six words.

In a world filled with humanoids, Man sat in a delicately balanced position; he may one day be allied with GIANTS, fighting together against a common enemy or living side-by-side raising children together in a peaceful community. However, at any moment, for any reason, the scales of equality could tip and the companionable humanoids could instantly become a most dangerous adversary and the bane of the countryside, pillaging the populace and slaughtering the livestock.

It seems to be the case, no matter the country of origin or the time period the story originates from, that human and humanoid communities or cooperations were never permanent arrangements. No matter how long standing their arrangements were, at some point, they dissolved either by miscommunication, a base desire allowed to develop unchecked, or by social taboos being broken. Perhaps this is a reflection or evidence of ancient or racial memory (memories, feelings, and ideas inherited from our ancestors) during a time when *Homo sapiens* coexisted with *Homo neanderthalensis*.

We know it is true there was interbreeding between the two species, as Neanderthal DNA is still present in our own; and as prevalent as the DNA is, it cannot simply be written off as an anomaly or the occasional unwanted coupling. It may be that the very reason humanoids and humans eventually had a falling out in our folklore and mythology was because of an ancient ripple making its way to us. Perhaps these stories were, in fact, prehistoric cautionary tales originating from a time when two similar but decidedly different species attempted to survive by living and commingling together. If this is true, it must have ended with disastrous results—particularly for the Neanderthal, the humanoid.

Many of the tales involving humanoids begin with the intrusion of mankind. Violence is perpetrated eventually, if not immediately, and only after the loss of life does the situation resolve, even if only resulting in both parties retreating to their neutral corners. If the Jungian idea of racial memory can be upheld as being true, perhaps these are cautionary tales that are advising against allowing foreigners into your land for any length of time: trade should only be permitted as a necessary evil but never allowed to develop into familiarity as only bloodshed and suffering will result.

Interestingly, like the fairies of the world, humanoids are neither wholly "good" nor entirely "evil" by design (as is the case with demons and many species of vampires) but have the propensity for either, depending on the inclination of the individual or collective race. Not all of the JOTUN of Norse mythology were the enemy of the Aesir; in fact, not only are there many tales in which the gods and the JOTUN are close friends, hunting companions, and fighting side-by-side as if brothers, they intermarried and had many children together. More than one Aesir had a JOTUN lover of whom their spouse was unaware. Perhaps these beings are the most like us, as they live in communities similar to our own where they have a king or some powerful individual they answer to as a species; they also marry and provide for their families. Perhaps this is the very reason they are called humanoid (a combination of the English word human and the Latin, *oid*, "resembling"). Like us they have desires, hopes, secrets, and roles to play in their society.

Even after the introduction of organized religion, we clung to these beings, choosing to include them when we evolved socially and spiritually. There are many tales of GIANTS converting to Christianity, as in the case of CHRISTOPHERUS. Some GIANTS joined the army of Charlemagne and thwarted the enemies of not only the Church but the country they loved and lived in as a citizen, a true patriot.

Regarding traditional and regional fairy tales, it was difficult to disregard so many of the familiar European tales involving the commonly-told Jack the Giant Slayer stories. I made this decision firm in the instances where the GIANT itself or the city it was distressing was not named. There are hundreds of such Jack stories similar in structure, moral lesson, and outcome but there are only a handful where the oppressor is even named, as if he was not even an important character, factor, or obstacle in the story. A compilation of Jack the Giant Slayer stories would be a wonderful book by itself, but including the nameless and repetitively slain giants was not appropriate for inclusion in this work.

It is not required of the reader to believe in the existence of ASYNJR, GIANTS, or the PANOTTI to garner some entertainment, if not knowledge, from this work. As a mythologist I feel it is more important to understand the message of the legend or story of the creature than to demand proof of its existence. Oftentimes these beings are symbolic of an undesirable or maligned aspect of human nature, such as avarice and lasciviousness, weather events, or other natural phenomena.

The purpose envisioned for this work was to collect, identify, and thoroughly detail all humanoids and alleged races described in ancient texts by long-ago mythologists and travelers alike. These descriptions contain all of the collected information I was able to gather and deposit in one place; it includes, when appropriate, a brief summary of the folktale or myth in which the being or race originated. When such tales were constructed to teach a moral lesson I did not offer my opinion on the subject, as ancient customs are very different from our own and future generations are likely to be even more changed. To ensure the purity of the original myth, I only retold the tale rather than try to interpret it.

A comprehensive cross-referencing system allows readers and researchers to follow the flow of additional information as they choose throughout the book without ever having to reference an outside source for additional details. All words appearing in SMALL CAPS are also entries to be found in the book.

A particular humanoid may be known by many different names or a variety of spellings as a result of translations and attempts to modernize the word. In these instances, I did my best to choose the most common word or name used among the listed references and the most familiar version of its spelling to be the boldfaced named entry. All additional spelling variants immediately follow in a heading entitled "Variations."

THE ENCYCLOPEDIA

A-Mi-Kuk

Variations: Amekak, Amiguk ("wolf"), Amikuk, Amorak

A creature from Inuit mythology, the large, human-looking a-mi-kuk is said to live in the ground and has the ability not to leave a hole as it emerges. Disliking mankind, it attacks, passing through the human body leaving no tell-tale mark behind; soon thereafter the victim lies down and dies. As the creature moves, it is said to make a thumping sound.

Some versions of the folklore describe the creature as being large with thick, slimy skin, four legs and wide-spread arms, a naturally fierce animal living in the sea and hunting those Inuit it happens upon as they kayak. Wrapping its arms and legs it drags the vessel under water, drowning its victim before consumption. Should the person manage to escape and swim to some floating ice, it will break up the ice and finish the attack. In this version of the folklore no one ever survives an a-mi-kuk attack.

The a-mi-kuk has the ability of therianthropy and uses it to shape-shift into other forms when it grows weary of being an a-mi-kuk. On occasion it will take a human form and will be seen pulling a sled; when it assumes this visage it is called a *qamungelriit*. Should a person see this, they are advised to sit directly in the creature's path as it does not have the ability to move around them. The a-mi-kuk turned qamungelriit will offer the person sitting in its way a gift to move out of its way but it is said not to reply. The creature will become more and more frantic offering more and better gifts, hoping to entice the person to move. Folklore tells tales of individuals becoming wealthy in this fashion.

Source: Fienup-Riordan, *Boundaries and Passages*, 80–2; Judson, *Myths and Legends of Alaska*, 27–8; Robisch, *Wolves and the Wolf Myth in American Literature*, 239; Zell-Ravenheart, *Wizard's Bestiary*, 18

A-senee-ki-wakw

In the Abenaki mythology of the Algonquian speaking Native American tribes of northeastern North America, the A-senee-ki-wakw were a race of stone GIANTs as well as the first race created by the mythical and cultural hero Gluskab. Sadly, because the A-senee-ki-wakw were so large they crushed many animals and did damage to the earth when they moved; for this, Gluskab had them destroyed.

Source: Books, *Native American Legendary Creatures*, 127

Abaasy, plural abassylar

Variations: Abaahy, Abassi, Abasy, Chebeldei

An Underworld being from Yakut mythology, the abassylar ("black") are described as one-eyed beings (CYCLOPS) with seven iron teeth; the abassylar, like all Underworld beings, are composed in some part of iron. The abassylar, spirits of sickness capable of driving men mad, are under the dominion of the god Ulu Tojon or Arson Duolai, the ruler of the dead. The cultural hero Njurgun Bootur was sent to earth to confront and destroy the abassylar, consumers of both animal and human souls.

Source: Coulter, *Encyclopedia of Ancient Deities*, 6; Meletinskiĭ, *Poetics of Myth*, Volume 1944, 413–14, 243–44

Abarimon

The Greek ethnographer and explorer Megasthenes (350 BC–290 BC) as well as Pliny the Elder, the Roman author and natural philosopher, each said the abarimon were a race of forest-dwelling men who lived in Scythia near the uncharted north. The singular distinguishing feature of these people was their backward-facing feet, enabling them to run as fast as woodland animals. According to Baeton, the road-surveyor of Alexander the Great, the abarimon people were unable to breathe in any other environment.

Source: Friedman, *Monstrous Races in Medieval Art and Thought*, 9; Lemprière, *Bibliotheca Classica*, 3

Abatwa

According to South African and Zulu folklore, the Abatwa are a tiny race of insect-sized cooperative-hunting people living peacefully alongside ants; at night they sleep in their colonies, occasionally occupying an ant hill. The abatwa do not have villages of their own but rather live wherever they kill game, moving only when the carcass is consumed. When it is time to move, they mount up upon a horse sitting one behind another from the length of its neck and all the way down its back to the top of its tail. If they cannot find game in a reasonable amount of time the abatwa will slay and consume the horse. They ambush game from hidden positions in the tall grass.

Typically, the abatwa are indifferent to mankind as they wander the forest and mountains following the migration patterns of animals, but if they are disturbed or stepped upon they are quick to vengeance, attacking the offender in the heel with a poison barb; they are also known to abduct children although it is considered to be a sign of good luck for a child to report seeing one. On occasion the abatwa reveal themselves but only to children, pregnant women, and wizards. It is believed if a pregnant woman sees an Abatwa during her seventh month it will ensure the birth of a male child. As bothersome as fleas, the abatwa will harass and torment a man, keeping him awake at night by giving him chest palpitations.

Source: Callaway, *Nursery Tales, Traditions, and Histories of the Zulus*, 352–5; Illes, *Encyclopedia of Spirits*, 6; Maberry, *Vampire Universe*, 1–2

Abgal

Variations: Apkallu

In Sumerian mythology the abgal ("chief," "leader," "ruler from heaven") were a race of seven merfolk (see MERMAID and MERMAN) who were considered to be guardians and teachers of the arts and sciences. Described as having the head of a man and the body of a fish, the abgal were believed to have been part of the entourage of the god of wisdom, Enki; the king of the abgal was named Dagon.

Source: De Lafayette, *Sumerian-English Dictionary*, 75; Lurker, *Dictionary of Gods and Goddesses, Devils and Demons*, 1; Zell-Ravenheart, *Wizard's Bestiary*, 15

Abiku

Variations: Ogbanje

In Dahomey mythology the abiku ("one who is born, dies") is a type of otherworld being, part human and part spirit, which is locked into a continuous cycle of life, death, and rebirth. This belief is particularly strong in southern Nigeria where it is said the abiku begins the cycle in the spirit world; there, among its companions, it makes a pact to leave but sets a date on when it will return. The abiku enters the world via a woman's womb and is given birth to after which it lives a short life, willing its own death before it can complete a full and natural life-cycle; the cycle is then repeated with the abiku often returning to the world by use of the same mother.

While it is alive in our world the cantankerous abiku has great power over its parents, who live in constant fear of its too early demise. Typically, this creature is seen as having a mental state somewhere between eccentric and insane as it is often observed having long conversations with its invisible spirit companions. Prone to fights and unpredictable, this creature is also perennially sick and in need of ongoing medical attention. Should the creature die within days of its birth the body must be whipped into a mutilated condition in order to prevent it from returning—especially to the same mother.

It is possible to sever the link the abiku has with the spirit world and permanently bind it to its earthly home if its magic token is found and destroyed; it is said to be buried in a secret location in a remote area. Another method is to find the abiku's "sealed words," its secret oath containing the circumstances, method, and time of its return to the spirit world. If a *babalawo* (witch doctor) can discover this item he will be able to break the abiku of its death wish. There are some tales of an abiku choosing to break its own sacred oath in order to remain in the world of the living; when this occurs its spirit world companions will try to lure it back, first by means of persuasion and then by force.

The West African Yourba translation for abiku means "children born of the spirit world" or "ancestral soul being reborn." Here the belief is an abiko is the returning soul of a child who died prematurely. Mothers will cut a notch in the ear of a child so if it should die they will have an easier time finding it upon its return.

Source: Falola, *Historical Dictionary of Nigeria*, 4; Lim, *Infinite Longing for Home*, 63–4; Matthews, *Element Encyclopedia of Magical Creatures*, 2

Abnuaanya

Variations: Alboost, Almast, Altaic ("WILD MAN"), Bekk-Bok, Biabin Guli, Golub Yavan, Gul Biavan, Guli Avan, Habisun mortu ("edge going wise"), Kaptar, Khun Goruessu, Kra Dhan, Ksy Giik, Mirygdy, Mulen, Nuhni Almas ("burrow almas"), Voita, Zagin Almas ("saxaul almas"), Zagitmegen ("old woman of the saxaul thicket")

A yeti-like WILD MAN living in the Caucasus Mountains of Central Asia, the abnuaanya is described as having coarse body hair, deep chest, long arms, short legs, simian (ape-like) facial features, sloping brow, sloping muscular shoulders, and clothing made of animal fur and pelts. Only attacking humans in the coldest of winters, the shy and timid abnuaanya has been sighted since 1420.

Source: Eberhart, *Mysterious Creatures*, 12–13; Khatri, *Mysterious Monstors of the World*, 36; Maberry, *Vampire Universe*, 2–4

Abu Rigl Maslukha

A NURSERY BOGIE from Egyptian folklore, the Abu Rigl Maslukha ("man with the burnt leg/skin") is a monster used by parents to coerce their children into good behavior. The story says when Abu Rigl Maslukha was a child he did not listen to his parents and because of it was badly burned; now he kidnaps children who will not obey their parents, taking them to his home and cooking them.

Source: 'Abd al-Raḥmān Ismā'īl. *Folk Medicine in Modern Egypt*, 70

Acamas (ak-a-DEE-mus)

In classical Greek mythology, Acamas, POLYPHEMUS and PYRACMON are, according to Homer's *The Iliad*, a new breed of CYCLOPS born from the union of the original CYCLOPES and the women who lived upon Mount Etna. Acamas was a companion to the god Hephaistos (Vulcan), working at his forge beneath Mount Etna.

Source: Daniels, *Encyclopædia of Superstitions, Folklore, and the Occult Sciences of the World*, 1375; Rose, *Giants, Monsters, and Dragons*, 2, 91; Schmidt, *Larousse Greek and Roman Mythology*, 295

Acephali, singular, Acephalos

Variations: Acephalites (plural), Akephalos

The ancient Greek historian Herodotus (484– 425 BC) described the Acephali as a savage race of people living in Libya who have no head; their eyes rest upon their chests but Herodotus makes no mention of the placement of their ears, mouth, or nose. At one time the Acephali had a normal appearance but after losing an altercation with the gods, were, as a people, beheaded. In some versions of the myth, the Acephali are described as carrying their heads with them. In medieval folklore the Acephali have huge eyes and a gaping mouth in the middle of their chest, the very sight of it causing terror.

Source: Avant, *Mythological Reference*, 1; Herodotus, *Ancient History of Herodotus*, 240; Rose, *Giants, Monsters, and Dragons*, 2–3

The Actorione

Variations: Actorid, the Moliones

The Actorione is the collective name of the monstrous humanoid twins, Cteatus and Eurytus, from classical Greek and Roman mythology. Born of Molione and her husband, Actor, their actual father was the god of the sea, Poseidon (Neptune). In later traditions, the Actorione were said to have been born out of an egg and over time their bodies fused together, having one torso but two heads, four arms, and four legs.

Source: Pausânias, *Pausanias's Description of Greece*, Volume 3, 466; Rose, *Giants, Monsters, and Dragons*, 3; Smith, *New Classical Dictionary of Greek and Roman Biography*, 524

Adamastor, the Giant

According to the French Renaissance doctor, Greek scholar, humanist, monk, and writer François Rabelais (AD 1494–1553), who compiled the lineage of the GIANTS, Adamastor was listed as the father of Anteus, who "*begot* AGATHO; *who begot* PORUS, *against whom Alexander the Great fought; who begot* ARANTHAS, *who begot* GABBARA, *who invented drinking to one's health; and from his descendants begot* GRANGOUSIER; *who begot* GARGANTUAN; *who begot* PANTAGRUEL."

Source: Brewer, *Character Sketches of Romance, Fiction and the Drama*, Volume 3, 80; Daniels, *Encyclopædia of Superstitions, Folklore, and the Occult Sciences of the World*, 1376; Rabelais, *Hours with Rabelais*, 80

Adlet

Variations: Erqigdlit

According to Inuit mythology in Alaska and Canada the adlet are the five monstrous and unholy offspring from the sexual union between an Inuit woman and a demonically possessed red-haired dog. The woman, recognizing her children as the embodiment of all evil, set them adrift on a raft made of animal hide and whale bone. The adlet landed on the European shore and were the progenitors of the European race of people. One of the adlet managed to return to its homeland after which it hunted down and killed all the descendants of its mother's family line. Described as having the upper body of a dog and the lower body of a man, confrontations between the adlet and mankind are always vicious and bloody, and usually end in the death of the creature.

Source: Boas, *Race, Language, and Culture*, 512; Lynch, *Native American Mythology A to Z*, 2; Maberry, *Vampire Universe*, 5–6

Aegir

Variations: Æge, Æger, Ægir, Ägir, Eagor ("destruction"), Egir, Hler, Oegir

Aegir ("sea" or "the frightening, the terrible"), a JOTUN in Norse mythology, was called the Lord of the Sea. Born one of the three sons of FORNJOTR the storm personified, he was married to his sister, Ran (Ran-Gullveig) and together they had nine daughters, WAVE-MAIDENS BEYLGJA, Blodughadda, DROFN, DUFA, HEFRING, HIMINGLAEVA, HRONN, KOLGA, and UDR, who collectively were the mother to the god Heimdall. Aegir and (Ran-Gullveig) had two other brothers, KAARE (KARI, "air"), the lord of the wind, and LOGE (Logi), the lord of the fire. Aegir also had two servants, Eldir and Fimageng. Aegir and his wife lived on the island of Hlessey (also known as Kattigut); their hall was located in a cave there. Described as being gaunt, green-haired, tall, and having a long flowing white beard, he with his wife was a frequent visitor to Asgard. He was the owner of a gigantic kettle used for brewing mead taken from fellow JOTUN HYMIR and given to him by the gods Thor and Tyr.

There is another character from Norse mythology named Aegir, a magician skilled in the black arts and one of the main characters in the Icelandic historian, poet, and politician Snorri Sturluson's (1179–1241) *Prose Edda*.

Source: Anderson, *Norse Mythology*, 445; Daly, *Norse Mythology A to Z*, 1; Grimes, *Norse Myths*, 253; Lindow, *Handbook of Norse Mythology*, 47; Norroena Society, *Asatrii Edda*, 25

Aello

Variations: Aellopus ("storm foot"), Nicothoe

One of the four named harpies from ancient Greek mythology, Aello ("rainstorm," "storm wind," "stormy," "squall," or "whirlwind") was originally a storm or nature spirit associated with the weather and was accordingly blamed for storms and undesirable winds (see HARPY).

According to the ancient Greek poet Hesiod in his work *Theogony* ("*Theogonía*," circa 700 BC), which describes the genealogy of the gods, there were only two harpies, Aello and OCYPETE, the winged daughters of ELECTRA and Thaumas. Hesiod he commented only on how swiftly the sisters could fly. The Roman poet Valerius Flaccus said there were three harpies, adding CELAENO to the list. Homer, the greatest of ancient Greek epic poets, rounded off the list of named harpies with OCYPETE and PODARGE.

Lore tells us the gods plagued Phineus, a seer who had lost his sight, with two harpies, Aello and OCYPETE, who would without fail swoop down from the sky and steal his every meal leaving only just enough food for him to survive. Two of the Argonauts, Calais and Zetes, were the sons of the god Boreas and, having wings, volunteered to pursue and slay the creatures in exchange for Phineus' assistance. In the chase Aello grew exhausted and fell, crashing into the Tigres River; OCYPETE managed to fly as far as the Strophades Island where she swore to never return nor bother Phineus again in exchange for her life.

Source: Apollodorus, *Gods and Heroes of the Greeks*, 56; Littleton, *Gods, Goddesses, and Mythology*, Volume 10, 611, 614; *London Encyclopaedia*, Volume 11, 53; Murray, *Classical Manual Being a Mythological, Historical, and Geographical*, 160

Ænotherus

Variations: Aenotherus

In French medieval folklore Ænotherus was a GIANT said to have been the body guard to Emperor Charlemagne; the Bavarian author, humanist, historian, and philologist Johannes Aventinus (1477–1534) described the GIANT in his work *Annals of Bavaria* (1523) as being large enough to lay low entire battalions as easily as mowing grass. Ænotherus was said to have come from a region near the Lake of Constance called Turgan.

Source: Thompson, *History and Lore of Freaks*, 132

Aepir (AIP-ir)

In Norse mythology Aepir ("to bellow," "to cry," or "roarer") was a JOTUN of the sea; beyond a name, there is nothing else known.

Source: Carlyle, *Complete Works*, Volumes 1–2, 252; Norroena Society, *Asatrii Edda*, 336

Aeti (AIT-i)

In Norse mythology Aeti ("eaten") was the JOTUN of grain; beyond this, there is little if anything else known.

Source: Norroena Society, *Asatrii Edda*, 336

Agatho

François Rabelais (AD 1494–1553) compiled the lineage of the GIANTS. Born the son of the GIANT ANTEUS, Agatho was the father of PORUS who "*begot ARANTHAS, who begot GABBARA, who invented drinking to one's health; and from his descendants begot GRANGOUSIER; who begot GARGANTUAN; who begot PANTAGRUEL.*"

Source: Brewer, *Character Sketches of Romance, Fiction and the Drama*, Volume 3, 80; Daniels, *Encyclopædia of Superstitions, Folklore, and the Occult Sciences of the World*, 1376; Rabelais, *Hours with Rabelais*, 80

Agathodemon (AH-gath-oh-de-mon), plural: Agathodemons

Variations: Agathodaemon, Agathodaimon, Agathos Daimon

The history of the agathodemon begins in

ancient Egyptian mythology; however, *agathodemon* is a Greek word which translates to mean "the good god" or "good divinity." It was believed every person was born with two personal, invisible guardian spirits, the agathodemons and the CACODAEMON. Agathodemons were said to be their good-natured protectors and CACODAEMONS were their evil counterparts. Each demon encouraged its own impulses. Agathodemons are most often depicted as a snake with a human head, but on occasion they have been shown as a young man holding a basket full of ears of corn.

Agathodemons are most powerful on the first day after a new moon, a time when they are to be remembered for the duty they perform. They are given tribute daily and it is shown by the consumption of a glass of wine after a meal has been eaten. Agathodemons are the symbolic reminder to live a moral life and to always seek to improve oneself. The only time one of them would ever attack a person is if they were attempting to destroy a vineyard under their protection.

Source: De Claremont, *Ancient's Book of Magic*, 106; Osburn, *Monumental History of Egypt*, 289–91; Vaughan, *British Quarterly Review*, Volume 7, 236

Aglaope

One of the three SIRENS from ancient Greek mythology, Aglaope ("beautiful face") was described as being the most beautiful of her kind; although ancient writers do not agree on their lineage, names, or numbers she is typically one of a trio of sisters, grouped with PEISINOË and THELCHTEREIA, born the daughters of Achelous and Thelxiepia.

Source: Apollodorus, *Library*, Volume 2, 290; Leland, *Unpublished Legends of Virgil*, 37; Sardi, *Psychological Activity in the Homeric Circe Episode*, 28; Smith, *Dictionary of Greek and Roman Biography and Mythology*, Volume 3, 840

Aglaophone

A SIREN from ancient Greek mythology, Aglaophone was said to have a most enchanting voice. She was one of a trio of Sirens, typically grouped with her two sisters; however in the case of Aglaophone, they remain unnamed.

Source: Grant, *Who's Who in Classical Mythology*, 27; Leland, *Unpublished Legends of Virgil*, 37

Aglaophonos

Variations: AGLAOPE, Aglaopheme ("illustrious of voice")

According to the ancient Greek poet Cherilus of Samos, Aglaophonos ("beautiful voice"), MOLPE, and THELXIOPE were the three SIRENS of ancient Greek mythology, a species of injurious NYMPH born the offspring of the ancient god of the sea,

PHORCYS. Described as being half bird and half woman, she and her sisters would perch on the rocky Sicilian coastline and lure sailors in with their melodious song; once caught, their prey were eaten alive. Although they hunted along the coastline Aglaophonos and her sisters lived inland in a meadow.

Source: Leland, *Unpublished Legends of Virgil*, 37; Rose, *Spirits, Fairies, Leprechauns, and Goblins*, 6; Smith, *Dictionary of Greek and Roman Biography and Mythology*, 817

Agogwe

Variations: Kakundakari, Ngogwe ("little men of the trees"), Sehit

Rarely encountered, the agogwe of East Africa is a bipedal humanoid creature or nature spirit which will tend a person's garden in exchange for an offering of food and millet beer; this is similar to the elves of Europe, doing household chores in exchange for offerings of food and drink. Described in folklore as looking like furry men and standing less than four feet tall (1.22 meters), the tailless agogwe are known to chant a strange song as they travel. For humans they like, the agogwe will produce meat, milk, or porridge from a stone and leave it for their favored person to find. If ever a child should go missing and blood is discovered at the scene, it is said the agogwe has taken it.

Source: Forth, *Images of the Wildman in Southeast Asia*, 218, 227, 307; Maberry, *Vampire Universe*, 10–11; Zell-Ravenheart, *Wizard's Bestiary*, 15

Agrios

Variations: Agrios, AGRIUS

A GIGANTE from ancient Greek mythology, Agrios ("wild," as in "rustic") was born the son of the TITAN Uranus ("heaven") and the Earth, Gaea. He and his siblings were extremely large, immensely strong, and absolutely fearsome to behold as they had dense beards, a thick head of hair, and feet covered with drakon (a species of Greek dragon) scales; they threw flaming oak trees and rocks at the heavens.

Agrios was slain during the ten year war against the Olympian gods, the Gigantomachy, when the Fate Parcæ (Parcae) beat him and THOON to death with a bronze cudgel.

In very old writings, Agrios was the name of a Centaur (a creature from Greek mythology, half equine and half human entangled with issues of sexual boundaries and promiscuity), symbolic of the force of nature.

Source: Apollodorus, *Library of Greek Mythology*, 34–5; Daniels, *Encyclopædia of Superstitions, Folklore, and the Occult Sciences of the World*, 1375–8; Room, *Who's Who in Classical Mythology*, 33

Agrius

Variations: Agreus, AGRIOS, Agrotes, Agroueros

An anthropophagous (man-eating) GIGANTE from the mythology of the ancient Greeks, Agrius and his twin brother OREUS were Thracian by birth and the children of the NYMPH Polyphonte and a bear. Described as being half-bear and half-human the cannibalistic brothers had a ferocious temper and would not only insult but attack and consume travelers. The twins were an affront to Zeus (Jupiter) who ordered Hermes (Mercury) to destroy them; however Ares (Mars) intervened on their behalf as their mother was the daughter of Thrassa, one of his own daughters. Rather than be utterly destroyed, the twins were transformed into birds of prey as punishment for their crimes.

There were many other individuals from ancient Greek and Sumerian mythologies bearing the name Agrius; among them was a Centaur (a creature from Greek mythology, half equine and half human entangled with issues of sexual boundaries and promiscuity) who attempted to kill the demi-god and hero Hercules (Heracles) but failed and was in turn slain by him. Another Agrius was a GIGANTE born of the goddess Gaea who took part in the Gigantomachy; he and THOAS were slain by the FATES, beaten to death with bronze clubs.

Source: Coulter, *Encyclopedia of Ancient Deities*, 26–7; Dixon-Kennedy, *Encyclopedia of Greco-Roman Mythology*, 138; Lemprière, *Classical Dictionary*, 36

Aguane

The aguane were a type of female fairy or nature spirit found in the Austrian Alps in northern Italy near the Slovenian border; they live in the hills and in the rivers and streams crossing them. These creatures are said to be very beautiful with long, luxurious hair, and large breasts, but some sources say they also have either the feet of a goat or those of a horse. Expert shape-shifters, the aguane act as protectors of mountain streams and rivers, much like the sub-species of NYMPH known as NAPAEAE. Before entering into a body of water it is advised to ask for their permission, as the aguane have been known to eat trespassers. In spite of their harsh treatment of intruders, the aguane are said to be fond of children and will carry them safely across water.

Aguane were said to be able to successfully mate with the SILVANI thereby producing offspring known as SALVANELLI.

Source: Arrowsmith, *Field Guide to the Little People*, 103–4; Euvino, *Complete Idiot's Guide to Italian History and Culture*, 274; Grimassi, *Hereditary Witchcraft: Secrets of the Old Religion*, 83; Illes, *Encyclopedia of Spirits*, 11

Ahiman

A GIANT from Hebrew Scriptures, Ahiman was so great in stature he terrified ten of the spies Moses sent to Canaan into returning and persuading the army not to attack. Ahiman, son of ANAK, was the most feared of his people, the ANAKIMS; however, his brothers, SHESHAI and TALMAI, ruled their people and the country of Hebron (Kirjath-Arba). Ahiman and his brothers were, according to the Book of Judges, slain by Judah.

Source: DeLoach, *Giants*, 12; Taylor, *Calmets Great Dictionary of the Holy Bible*, 10

Ai (AH-i)

A DVERG (DWARF) from Norse mythology created by DURINN, Ai ("great-grandfather") was one of DVALIN'S HOSTS who lived in Juravale's Marsh; his horse was Hrafn. Ai, like the other DVERGAR created, paid particular attention to his leadership.

Source: Grimes, *Norse Myths*, 253; Lindow, *Norse Mythology*, 260

Aigmuxab, plural: aigamuxa, aigamuchas

An anthropophagous (man-eating) monster from the mythology of the Khoisin people of South Africa, the humanoid-looking aigamuxa can be found in the sand dunes of the Kalahari Desert. Described as having their eyes located in their instep or on their heels, they must stop and lift up their feet every few steps or lie down to see where they are going and reposition themselves if necessary. Anthropomorphic in appearance and naturally curious, their huge bodies and heads give them a fearsome appearance; unlike the OGRE of European folklore, the cannibalistic aigamuxa are easily avoided, fooled, or otherwise tricked.

Source: Chopra, *Academic Dictionary of Mythology*, 15; Cotterell, *Dictionary of World Mythology*, 239; Lynch, *African Mythology, A to Z*, 85

Aku

Variations: Aku-Aku, Akuaku

According to the beliefs of the people of Easter Island, the aku ("devil," "ghost" or "spirit") are indistinguishable from humans. Considered to be spirits of the dead, some of which were deified, the aku can be of either sex and are associated with particular areas of the island. Although they are not worshiped or left offerings, traditionally they are acknowledged before a meal is taken; this may be how the aku survive, living off of the aroma of the meal. If the aku is well fed and likes a particular person it may be inclined to do some of their daily household chores, such as weed the garden. Interestingly, the aku are not immortal and tales of employing an *ivi-atua* to dispose of violent ones abound.

Source: Bello, *Dictionary and Grammar of the Easter Island Language*, 696; Williamson, *Religion and Social Organization in Central Polynesia*, 34–35

Akuan

Akuan was a GIANT in Persian mythology that was slain by Roostem (Rustam).

Source: Reddall, *Fact, Fancy, and Fable*, 20

Al

Variations: Elk

A race of hairy anthropoids of Armenian, Libyan, and Persian folklore, the Al were described as having boar-like tusks protruding from their mouth, brass claws, fiery eyes, iron teeth, and shaggy serpentine hair; they lived in dark and damp places such as in the corners of stables, wet houses, and in swamps. The Al, one of the KHRAFSTRA, attack humans who enter into their territory; they are especially fond of women who are incapacitated by childbirth as infants are their favorite food; they are even said to carry scissors on them to cut the umbilical cord. The Al will also steal the woman's liver and consume it back in its lair.

In the folklore of Afghanistan the Al is said to be a ghoul-like female creature, having long floating hair and talons for fingernails; they consume human corpses.

Source: Zell-Ravenheart, *Wizard's Bestiary*, 16

The Alaisiagae

The Alaisiagae was the collective name of two VALKYRIES from Norse mythology who were known in ancient Britain as their names are carved onto Hadrian's Wall; their names were BAUDIHILLIE ("ruler of battle") and Friagabi ("giver of freedom").

Source: Coulter, *Encyclopedia of Ancient Deities*, 34, 490; Monaghan, *Encyclopedia of Goddesses and Heroines*, 282

Alan

Variations: Balbal, Manananggal, Mananggal, Wak Wak

A species of winged creatures from Filipino folklore, the alan live in the deep forest and spend much of their time hanging upside down from trees; some tales say they have homes constructed on the ground made of pure gold. Described as being human in appearance, half bird and half man, they also are said to have a long tongue, scaly arms, curved claws, and fingers on their feet and toes on their hands; all their digits also point backward. The alan are generally benign toward humans but there are tales of them acting both maliciously and mischievously. Typically they assist heroes on their quests.

Source: Eberhart, *Mysterious Creatures*, 8; Rose, *Giants, Monsters, and Dragons*, 11; Worcester, *Philippine Islands and Their People*, 109; Zell-Ravenheart, *Wizard's Bestiary*, 17

Alarabi

A nature spirit of the mountains, Alarabi is a TÁRTALO ("CYCLOPS") or evil spirit from Basque mythology in the region of Marquina; it is said to live in a cave.

Source: Miguel de Barandiarán, *Selected Writings of José Miguel De Barandiarán*, 92

Albadan

Variations: Famangomadan

A brave, fierce, and strong GIANT from Spanish folklore, Albadan lived on the Rock of Galtares; he was described as wearing a large shining helmet and plated armor, and carrying a heavy iron mace. Albadan was slain and beheaded in one-on-one combat with the heroic knight Galaor. Albadan was the lifelong enemy of the good GIANT GANDALUE and the previous owner of the Rock of Galtares.

Source: Rodríguez de Montalvo, *Amadis of Gaul*, 125–26; Spence, *Legends and Romances of Spain*, 100

Albastor

Variations: Labasta

A species of fairy from the folklore of the Mari people of Russia, the albastor were believed to live in the bathhouse disguised as an old man or woman; however, these beings could also take on the appearance of a GIANT with long flowing hair. An albastor is created when an illegitimate child died unbaptized; these fairy-creatures have the ability of therianthropy, enabling them to shape-shift into any animal so long as it remains upon the ground. As it travels through the sky it looks like a shooting star.

Like the demonic succubus (sexually driven vampiric demons), the albastor engages in sexual intercourse with humans; it punishes those who overindulge themselves with excessive sex, slowly killing them with exhaustion. Victims of this sort of assault will have a sore on their lips, left there by the albastor's kiss. Any human lover the victim took on would then also become sick and may die as well. An albastor can be defeated by catching it and breaking the fingers of its left hand or by hanging a cross over each doorway of the house to prevent its entry.

Source: Rose, *Spirits, Fairies, Leprechauns, and Goblins*, 9; Sebeok, *Studies in Cheremis*, 51

Albion

Variations: Albion the

Born the fourth son of the Roman god of the sea, Neptune, and the sixth son of Osiris, Albion ("lofty") was a one-time ruler of England. A descendant of Noah's son Ham, he came to the island of England after the flood and was able to easily conquer its then current occupants, the Samotheans. During his rule of tyranny, forty-four years, the island was called "Albion," after himself. Albion was slain by his uncle Hercules Libicus.

Albion's brother BERGION ruled over Ireland and his other brother LESTRIGO ruled Italy.

Source: Kewes, *Oxford Handbook of Holinshed's Chronicles*, 162; Roof, *Popular History of Noble County Capitals and Greater Albion*, 13

Albjofr (AL-thyohv-r)

In Norse mythology, Albjofr ("all thief") was one of the many named DRAUGR about whom, beyond a name, there is nothing else known.

Source: Norroena Society, *Asatrii Edda*, 336

Alcyoneus

Variations: Alcion, Alkyoneos, Alkyoneus, Sithon

A GIGANTE from ancient Greek mythology, Alcyoneus ("brayer") was born the son of the TITAN Uranus ("heaven") and the Earth, Gaea. He and his siblings were extremely large, immensely strong, and absolutely fearsome to behold as they had dense beards, a thick head of hair, and feet covered with DRAKON scales; they threw flaming oak trees and rocks at the heavens. Of all the GIGANTES, he and his brother PORPHYRON were considered to be the mightiest. As long as he fought on the land, he was immortal. He was slain in the ten year war against the gods, the Gigantomachy, when the demi-god Hercules (Heracles) dragged him from his homeland and slew him beyond its borders.

Source: Apollodorus, *Library of Greek Mythology*, 34–5; Daniels, *Encyclopædia of Superstitions, Folklore, and the Occult Sciences of the World*, 1375–8; Hard, *Routledge Handbook of Greek Mythology*, 89

The Alcyonii

Variations: Alcyonides, Alcyonis, Alkyonides, Alkyonides, Alkyonis

In ancient Greek mythology, the GIGANTE ALCYONEUS was the father of the Alcyonii, the collective name for his numerous daughters. Although the numbers vary with the ancient authors, both Aristoteles, a philosopher and scientist, and Simonides, a Greek poet, place their number at eleven; Philochorus, an Atthidographer and Greek historian,

said there were nine; Demagoras claimed seven. In *Commentaries* (*Hypomnemata*) written by Hegesander, he names seven daughters and lists them as ALKIPPA, ANTHE, ASTERIA, DRIMO, METHONE, PALLENE, and PHOSTHONIA. According to him, after the death of their father during the Gigantomachy, they leapt to their demise from Kanastraion into the sea where Amphitrite transformed them into ice-birds; thereafter the sisters were collectively known as the Alcyonii.

Source: Blunck, *Solar System Moons*, 83

Alf

A rock DVERG (DWARF) from Norse mythology created by DURINN, Alf is listed as being one of DURINN's KIN. He like the others created paid particular attention to DURINN's leadership.

Source: Grimes, *Norse Myths*, 260

Alfarinn (AHLV-ar-in)

Variations: Alfarin, Alfgeirr, Alfarin

In Norse mythology, Alfarinn ("fire-ELF" or "well-traveled"), son of Vali, was one of the many named Jotnar (see JOTUN) about whom, beyond a name, there is little else known.

Source: Norroena Society, *Asatrii Edda*, 336

Alfrig

A rock DVERG (DWARF) from Norse mythology created by DURINN, Alfrig is listed as being one of DURINN's KIN. He like the others created paid particular attention to DURINN's leadership. Alfrig, along with DVALIN, BERLING, and GRER, collectively known as the four Brisingamen DWARFS, constructed the golden necklace of the goddess Freyia.

Source: Grimes, *Norse Myths*, 260; Thorpe, *Northern Mythology*, Volume 1, 32

Algebar

Variations: Al'gebar ("the giant"), ORION

The GIANT Algebar of Arabic folklore is also known as ORION from ancient Greek mythology.

Source: Brewer, *Character Sketches of Romance, Fiction and the Drama*, Volumes 1–2, 28; Daniels, *Encyclopædia of Superstitions, Folklore, and the Occult Sciences of the World*, 1375

Alifanfaron the Giant

Variations: Aliphraon, Alipha-Ron

A fictional GIANT with a furious temper, Alifanfaron the Giant, a pagan and the emperor of Trapoban, was in love with the daughter of Pentapolin, a beautiful and gracious Christian lady. In the Spanish novel, *The Ingenious Gentleman Don Quixote of La Mancha* (1505–15), by Miguel de Cervantes Saavedra, Quixote attacked a flock of sheep imagining them to be the standing army of Alifanfaron.

Source: Daniels, *Encyclopædia of Superstitions, Folklore, and the Occult Sciences of the World*, 1375; Saavedra, *History of Don Quixote de la Mancha*, 44–5

Alii Menehune

Chief of the FAIRY-folk from Hawaiian folklore, Alii Menehune ("highest Menehune") is described as wearing a cloak and shorts; his favorite food is the *maiʻa* (banana).

Source: Avant, *Mythological Reference*, 413; Polynesian Society, *Journal of the Polynesian Society*, Volume 68, 241

Alkippa

Variations: Alcippa, Aleippe

Born the daughter of the GIGANTE ALCYONEUS, Alkippa ("strong horse") was, according to the ancient Greek historian Hegesander, one of the ALCYONII; she and her sisters, ANTHE, ASTERIA, DRIMO, PALLENE, and PHOSTHONIA, are named in his six-volume work *Commentaries* (*Hypomnemata*).

Source: Blunck, *Solar System Moons*, 83; Smith, *Dictionary of Greek and Roman Biography and Mythology*, 108

Almas

Variations: Albasty, Alboost, Albnuaaya, Almast, Almasti, Bekk-Bokk, Habisunmortu ("edge going wise"), Khar Baavgai ("black bear"), Khun Goroos ("man antelope"), Mongolian Wildman, Nuhni almas ("burrow almas"), Zagin almas ("sexual almas"), Zagitmegen ("old woman of the sexual thickets")

Mongolian folklore described the almas ("to kill animals") as a WILD MAN, or a tribe of wild men, for centuries; however, there are some references to it as being a female demon. The almas is said to live in the uppermost parts of high mountain ranges, such as in the Altai, Pamir, and Tien Shan peaks.

Although alleged sightings of this creature are very rare it has been depicted in old manuscripts and is shown as having a coat of dark red hair, a cone-shaped head, and protruding jaw; stories of it say this creature walks stooped over.

Source: Eberhart, *Mysterious Creatures*, 12; Sanders, *Historical Dictionary of Mongolia*, 45; Shuker, *Beasts That Hide from Man*, 37; Zell-Ravenheart, *Wizard's Bestiary*, 17

The Aloadae

Variations: Aloades, ALOEOS, Aloidai, Aloids

In ancient Greek mythology the Aloadae ("sons of Aloeus") was the collective name for the handsome twin GIGANTE brothers, EPHIALTES and OTOS. According to Latin author Gaius Julius Hyginus (64 BC–AD 17) in his work *Fabulae* ("*Fables*") the father of the twins was ALOEUS; however, other sources claim they were born of the union between Triops' daughter Iphimedia and the god of the sea, Poseidon (Neptune). By the age of nine years, the twins were said to be nine cubits tall (54 feet); upon reaching adulthood the aloadae decided to storm the heavens and stacked Mount Pelion upon Mount Ossa and then topped it off with Mount Olympus. Although they did manage to imprison the god of war, Ares (Mars), in a brazen vessel for 13 months they were otherwise unsuccessful in their assault. Ephialtes attempted to seduce the goddess Hera (Juno) while Otus attempted to seduce the goddess Artemis (Diana). In the telling of the myth by the ancient Greek historian and mythographer Apollodorus in his work *The Bibliotheca* ("*Library*") the goddess Artemis (Diana) transformed herself into the guise of a deer and when the aloadae hunted her, she placed herself in-between them where they accidentally killed one another. According to Hyginus, the brothers were punished by the Olympian gods by being sentenced to Hades where they were bound back-to-back by serpents to a column.

Source: Daniels, *Encyclopædia of Superstitions, Folklore, and the Occult Sciences of the World*, 1375–8; Grant, *Who's Who in Classical Mythology*, 390; Roman, *Encyclopedia of Greek and Roman Mythology*, 55; Rose, *Giants, Monsters, and Dragons*, 13

Aloeus

A GIGANTE from ancient Greek mythology, Aloeus ("the planter") was born of the great goddess Gaea and the TITAN Uranus ("heaven"). He and his siblings were extremely large, immensely strong, and absolutely fearsome to behold as they had dense beards, a thick head of hair, and feet covered with *drakon* (a species of Greek dragon) scales; they threw flaming oak trees and rocks at the heavens. Aloeus was married to Iphimedia who had two sons from Poseidon (Neptune), EPHIALTES and OTUS, but after her marriage the boys were collectively known as the ALOADAE.

Source: Coulter, *Encyclopedia of Ancient Deities*, 37; Daly, *Greek and Roman Mythology, A to Z*, 8

Alom-bag-winno-sis

Variations: Alom-begwi-no-sis

In the mythology of the Abenaki Indians of New England, Alom-bag-winno-sis were a race of injurious aquatic DWARF living in deep pools, rivers, and lakes. In areas where the water was particularly turbulent they came up underneath canoes and capsized them in the hopes of drowning their occupants. Powerful fay, they had the ability to increase their size at will, becoming either extremely large or incredibly small. Generally the Alom-bag-winno-sis lived in underwater communities but there were stories of an isolated individual living on its own.

They possessed a magical pot; when a few grains of maize were added to it, the pot inflated to a huge size, making more than enough food for the community. They were described as being about three feet tall and having incredibly black and straight hair growing down past their waist; they did not wear clothing of any sort. Normally these fay preferred to remain hidden and avoided contact with mankind, but to see one of the Alom-bag-winnosis was considered a psychopomp (death omen), a prediction of one's death by drowning.

Source: Maberry, *They Bite*, 192

Alpos

A Sicilian GIGANTE who terrorized the countryside from ancient Greek mythology, Alpos, a son of the Earth, was described as having many arms, one-hundred vipers on his head in place of hair, and being tall enough to pull down the moon and touch the sun. Alpos, likely one of the HECATONCHEIRES, was slain by the god of ecstasy, grape harvest, ritual madness, wine, and winemaking, Dionysos (Bacchus).

The Greek epic poet Nonnus of Panopolis of the late fourth century is best known for his work *Dionysiaca*, where he tells the tale of the god Dionysos. As Alpos appears nowhere else in Greek mythology it is quite possible the GIANT was an invention of Nonnus.

Source: Damsté, *Propertiana*: Volume 53, 196; Grimal, *Dictionary of Classical Mythology*, n.pag.; Nonnus, *Dionysiaca*, Volume 2, 269

Alseid

Variations: Alsea, Alseides

The alseids ("groves") of ancient Greek mythology were a sub-species of the LIMONIAD; they were the NYMPHS of sacred groves but they also appeared in glens, lightly forested areas, and meadows. These fairies had a reputation as being pranksters and enjoyed playing tricks on travelers.

Source: Custer, *Treasury of New Testament Synonyms*, 76; Hesiod, *Hesiod, the Homeric Hymns, and Homerica*, 413; Homer, *Iliad of Homer, Books 1–6*, 9; Illes, *Encyclopedia of Spirits*, 161; Littleton, *Gods, Goddesses, and Mythology*, Volume 4, 440

Alsvartr

In Norse mythology, Alsvartr ("all black" or "coal black") was one of the many named Jotnar (see JOTUN) about whom, beyond a name, there is nothing else known.

Source: Norroena Society, *Asatrii Edda*, 336; Vigfússon, *Court Poetry*: Volume 2, 425

Alta

An ASYNJR from Norse mythology, Alta ("fury") was one of the WAVE MAIDENS who were mother to the god Heimdall; she was the daughter of the god of the sea, Aegir. She, like her sisters, was said to have snow-white skin, blue eyes, and billowing blond hair; in one hand they carried a golden goblet filled with mead and in the other seashells filled with the finest foods. They wore long transparent robes of green or blue trimmed in white. When not serving food in the hall, they played on the shore in groups of three.

Source: Daly, *Norse Mythology A to Z*, 47

Alvit

Variations: Hervor ("host warder"), Hervor Alvit

A VALKYRIE from Norse mythology, Alvit ("all white") was once married to Volund the Smith but after nine years of marriage left her husband to return to Valhalla and rejoin ranks. At some point in their relationship she had gifted him with a ring he adored; after she left he made seven-hundred copies of it and tied them all together with the original. Nidud, the King of Sweden, abducted Volund, stole his band of rings, and forced him to forge weapons. Volund made a pair of wings similar to Alvit's so he could escape and when the opportunity came, slew Nidud's sons, took back his band of rings, and flew up to Valhalla where he rejoined Alvit.

Source: Coulter, *Encyclopedia of Ancient Deities*, 500; Puryear, *Nature of Asatru*, 206

Amala

In Tsinshian mythology, Amala was a GIANT who, while lying on his back, held a pole atop which the earth sat spinning. Amala's great strength came from wild duck oil rubbed onto his back annually. There is a finite amount of this oil and when ducks have been hunted to extinction the supply will run out and Amala will die, dropping the pole, and destroying the planet.

Source: de Rijke, *Duck*, 163; Lynch, *Native American Mythology A to Z*, 2

Amalanhig

In the Filipino mythology from the western Visayan Islands, the amalanhigs ("the stiff one") are ASWANG witches who did not pass along their power before they died.

Source: Ramos, *Creatures of Midnight*, 81

Amchi-malghen

A class of guardian NYMPH of Chilean folklore, the amchi-malghen are believed to be a force of feminine, invisible power. The expression "I keep my amchi-malghen still" is commonly said at the beginning of any undertaking.

Source: Alexander, *Latin-American [Mythology]* Volume 11, 330; Hastings, *Encyclopaedia of Religion and Ethics*, Volume 3, 548

Amerant

A cruel GIANT of British folklore, Amerant was slain by the gallant champion, hero, and monster slayer Guy of Warwick in hand-to-hand combat.

Source: Daniels, *Encyclopædia of Superstitions, Folklore, and the Occult Sciences of the World*, 1375; Wiggins, *Guy of Warwick*, 164, 165

Amnisiades

Variations: Amnisides

In classical Greek mythology, the Amnisiades were specifically the NYMPHS of the river Amnisus on the island of Crete in the Aegean Sea; these devotees of the goddess Artemis (Diana) cared for her sacred deer.

Source: Bell, *Bell's New Pantheon*, 56; Smith, *New Classical Dictionary of Greek and Roman Biography, Mythology and Geography*, Volume 1, 561

Amr (AHM-r)

In Norse mythology, Amr ("darkness") was one of the many named Jotnar (see JOTUN) about whom, beyond a name, there is little else known.

Source: Norroena Society, *Asatrii Edda*, 336

An

In Norse mythology An was one of the rock DVERG (DWARF) created by DURINN.

Source: Grimes, *Norse Myths*, 260

Anak

Variations: Anok

Anak, son of Arba, lived about the time when Canaan was invaded by the Israelites. According to the book of Deuteronomy Anak had three sons, AHIMAN, SHESHAI, and TALMAI, who were descendants of the REPHAIM and became the progenitors of a specific species of GIANTS known as the ANAKIM or the B'ne Anak. According to the Book of Numbers (13:33) the three sons of Anak were a particular kind of NEPHILIM.

Source: DeLoach, *Giants*, 47, 57; Hengstenberg, *Dissertations on the Genuineness of the* Pentateuch, Volume 2, 153, 195; Taylor, *Calmets Great Dictionary of the Holy Bible*, n.pag.

Anakim

Variations: ANAK, B'ne Anak

In the Old Testament Book of Numbers Moses explains the Anakims ("people of the necklace"), a species of GIANT, are the descendants of the NEPHILIM. These fierce and wild beings were prone to acts of violence and considered war and warfare to be a normal way of life. When there was no enemy to fight they would wage war upon one another. The Anakims have been described as being pale skinned, golden haired, lightly bearded, and wore striped cloaks; upon their necks they wore torques. The progenitor of the Anakim was called ANAK, the son of Arba.

Source: DeLoach, *Giants*, 47, 57; Hengstenberg, *Dissertations on the Genuineness of the* Pentateuch, Volume 2, 153, 195; Taylor, *Calmets Great Dictionary of the Holy Bible*, n.pag.

Anansi

Variations: Ananse-Sem, Ananse, *Anansi*-Tori, Aunt Nancy, Kweku Ananse

Portrayed intermittently as both a human and a creature, Anansi ("spider") of West African folklore is a cultural hero depicted as an atypical trickster. In Caribbean island folklore as in the akan-speaking tribes of West Africa Anansi is associated with spiders and is often described as such. In these tales he is described as being a large and long-legged husky crab-spider. Tales of the wise and wily Anansi are popular in spite of the fact he is a treacherous liar, a murderer, and a thief. In most of his folktales Anansi is pitted against Canary, Lion, and Turtle, and in these tales he is portrayed as a spider. His most dangerous enemy is Tiger. Other animals he is pitted against are Agouti, Ass, Boa Constrictor (*Abona*), Caiman, Cat, Cock, Cockroach, Cow, Cricket (*Sen-Sen*), Deer, Dog, Elephant, Fly, Goat, Hen, Horse, Howling Monkey, Rat, Snail, Snake, Toad, Vulture, Whale, and Wren. However, when he is dealing with people, Anansi is humanoid in appearance.

Born as the son of the god of the sky, Nyame, mortal Anansi often acts as an intermediary between his father and the earth. He taught mankind how to sow grain, married a princess, possessed endless resources, and was the owner of a magical stone whose name, if ever said aloud, would kill the person who spoke it. He also has the ability to decrease or increase his size whenever he chooses.

Source: Haase, *Greenwood Encyclopedia of Folktales and Fairy Tales*, 31; Penard, *Journal of American Folk-lore*, Volume 7, 241–42

Anar

In Norse mythology Anar was one of the rock DVERG (DWARF) created by DURINN.

Source: Grimes, *Norse Myths*, 260

Anax

In ancient Greek mythology the GIGANTE Anax ("lord") was born the son of the TITAN Uranus ("heaven") and the Earth, Gaea; he was the king of the city of Anactiria and the father of the GIGANTE ASTERIUS. It was during the reign of his son that Anactiria was conquered by the Cretan Miletus who then renamed the city after himself.

Source: Graves, *Greek Myths*, 88; Smith, *Dictionary of Greek and Roman Biography and Mythology*, 162

Anaye

Variations: Alien Gods, Child of the Waters

In the Navajo folklore of the United States of America, the anaye ("evil gods" or "monsters") is the collective name for four types of supernatural beings, the limbless BINAYE AHANI, the feathered TSANAHALE, the headless THELGETH, and an unnamed fourth. The chief of the anaye was the scaly GIANT YEITSO. Anaye are the product of evil women, conceived without a human father; folklore says all anaye are the progeny of the god Sun Bearer. These gigantic and monstrous beings cause fear, misery, and wickedness throughout the world. According to the folklore the anaye were eventually defeated by the two sons of the sun and water, Nayanezgani ("slayer of alien gods") and Thobadzistshini ("child born of water"); however, their siblings, Cold, Famine, Lice Man, Old Age, Poverty, and Sleep, continue to plague mankind.

Source: Cotterell, *Dictionary of World Mythology*, 220; Coulter, *Encyclopedia of Ancient Deities*, 51; Leviton, *Encyclopedia of Earth Myths*, n.pag.; Rose, *Giants, Monsters, and Dragons*, 18

Andandara

From the sixteenth century Spanish folklore comes the folklore of the andandara, a race of evil were-cats who would seek out women to rape in order to produce a line of feline-human offspring. In addition to having deadly claws and teeth, the andandara were said to have the ability to kill with their intense stare. The presence of one of these creatures can cause crop failure, disease, and ill fortune.

The Azande people of Africa describe the andandara as a race of malevolent wild cat described as having bright bodies and gleaming eyes; these creatures have intercourse with women who then will give birth to both a child and a kitten. Similar to the Spanish folklore, the African version of this monster has the Evil Eye; its presence can cause misfortune and to hear its cry in the bush is considered to be an unlucky omen.

Source: Bharati, *Agents and Audiences*, Volume 1, 43; Guiley, *Encyclopedia of Vampires, Werewolves, and Other Monsters*, 5; Maberry, *Vampire Universe*, 17

Andaokut

In the folklore of the Tsimshian, a people who live along the Pacific Northwest Coast of Alaska and British Columbia, Andaokut ("mucous boy"), is homunculus-like being created from the accumulation of mucus a woman created mourning the loss of her child who was stolen by the Great Woman of the Wood, Malahas. This witch was well known for abducting children and smoking them alive over a fire pit so she could eat them at her leisure. The creation grew very fast and soon asked its new parents for a bow and an arrow. After discovering why his foster mother cried so often Andaokut set out to find Malahas. Through a series of carefully played tricks he managed to kill the old witch the only way she could be killed—by finding her small black heart where she hid it and piercing it with an arrow. Once Malahas was destroyed, Andaokut gathered up the bodies of the children, laid them out on the ground, and urinated all over them which brought them back to life.

Source: Boas, *Tsimshian mythology*, 903–07

Andumbulu

In Dogon mythology, the andumbulu were believed to be the first humans created; they were described as being pygmies. The andumbulu did not die but rather were transformed into snakes; some of them are said to still live among the rocks, invisibly. By the use of wooden masks the andumbulu have the ability to gain power over others.

Source: Eliade, *Encyclopedia of Religion*, Volume 4, 254; Ezquerra, *Romanising Oriental Gods*, 120

Andvari (AND-var-i)

A rock DVERG (DWARF) from Norse mythology created by DURINN, Andvari ("careful one") is listed as being one of DURINN's KIN. He like the others created paid particular attention to DURINN's leadership. Andvari is the DWARF whose hoard of gold the god Loki robs in order to pay the magician Hreidmar the death price for having slain his son, Otr. The treasure was guarded by the dragon Fafnir.

Source: Daly, *Norse Mythology A to Z*, 4–5; Grimes, *Norse Myths*, 260; Sturluson, *Prose Edda*, 26

Angerboda (ahng'-gur-boh-du)

Variations: Angurboda, Angrboða ("harm-foreboding")

In Norse mythology Angerboda ("anguish-creating" or "one who warns of [bodes] danger") was an ASYNJR and the mistress of the trickster god Loki with whom she gave birth to Fenrir, Hel the goddess of death, and Jormungandr, the Midgard Serpent.

Other than living in Jotunheim, little else is known about her.

Source: Macdowall, *Asgard and the Gods*, 53, 250; Monaghan, *New Book of Goddesses and Heroines*, 47; Oehlenschläger, *Gods of the North*, xxxvii

Angeyja (ANG-ay-ya)

In Norse mythology Angeyja ("she who makes the islands closer"), the personification of the waves, was an ASYNJR, one of the WAVE MAIDENS who gave birth to the god Heimdall. Angeyja was also one of the maids who turned the mill Grottimill ("mill of the skerries") which created land from Jotnar's limbs.

Source: Anderson, *History and Romance of Northern Europe*, Volume 5, 1014; Norroena Society, *Asatrii Edda*, 25

Angoulaffre of the Broken Teeth

A descendant of GOLIATH, the French GIANT Angoulaffre of the Broken Teeth was said to stand eighteen feet tall and had a face three feet wide with a nine-inch-long nose upon it; his hands sported six-inch-long fingers; and his arms and legs were six feet long each. Assuming the title of the Governor of Jerusalem, having the strength of thirty men, and sporting a mace made from the trunk of a 300-year-old oak tree, Angoulaffre had an enormous mouth filled with sharp and pointed yellow teeth. There is a legend that the Tower of Pisa leans because Angoulaffre rested against it one day when he was tired. The hero Roland slew Angoulaffre in one-on-one combat at the Fronsac.

Source: Brewer, *Dictionary of Phrase and Fable*, 49; Daniels, *Encyclopædia of Superstitions, Folklore, and the Occult Sciences of the World*, 1375–8

Anitsutsa

Variations: The PLEIADES, the Seven Boys, Unädatsügl ("the group")

In Cherokee mythology Anitsutsa is the collective name for a group of seven boys, preeminent dancers, who would rather practice target shooting with their bows and arrows than do anything else; they were believed to have power over the harvest and the rain. One day their mothers, annoyed they were shooting at corn cobs rather than hunting for food, told the boys to practice where they did not have to look at them. The anitsutsa obeyed and went to the other side of the hill. Many hours later their parents worried where they were and went looking for them; they discovered the boys doing the feather-circle dance and ascending into the air. The parents tried to reach their children and pull them back down to earth but it was too late.

The anitsutsa became the seven stars of the Pleiades and their favorite drum became the nearby nebula. The seven stars possess great magic and must be propitiated with the feather-dance for the anitsutsa may cause cold weather and destroy the crops.

Source: Boas, *Anthropological Papers*, 358–59; Hail, *Cherokee Astrology*, 6–7

Ankou (Ahn-koo)

Variations: Death, Father Time, Grim Reaper

In the Breton folklore tradition Ankou ("reaper of the dead") is the personification of Death; it is described as looking like a tall, thin, white-haired person carrying a scythe, wearing a felt hat, and dressed in either black clothing or a shroud. Sometimes he is said to look like a skeleton. Ankou's head can rotate three-hundred-sixty degrees; he drives *karrigell an Ankou* ("carriage of Ankou") pulled by skeletal horses and has a servant called *mevel an Ankou*. In some parts of Brittany, it is believed the last person who died in the previous year is the current year's Ankou.

Ankou is said to travel the countryside collecting the souls of the dead and dying, although there is some confusion over what he does with the souls once he has them. Some tales say he delivers them to Anaon, the king of the Underworld, or takes them across the sea, or delivers them to face their Final Judgment.

Source: Koch, *Celtic Culture*, 67; McCoy, *Witch's Guide to Faery Folk*, 175; Van Scott, *Encyclopedia of Hell*, 19

Annis (An-eez)

Variations: Agnes, Ana, Annan, Annowre, Ano, Anoniredi, Anu, Befind, Benie, Bheur, BLACK ANNIS, Blue HAG, Bric, Cailleach, Caillech, Cethlann, Cethlionn, Danu, Don, Donu, Gray HAG, Gry, Gyre Carlin, HAG of Beare, Saint Anna

A singular being, the vampiric sorceress Annis ("pure, as in virginal") has legends of her dating back to the founding of both Ireland and Scotland, a country named in her honor. The name *Scota* from where Scotland originates, was originally called *Caledonia*, which means "lands given by Caillech," as Annis was then called.

Annis is known in Arthurian folklore as Annowre. She is so ingrained in the minds of the people she has even been converted into Christendom as Saint Anna, the daughter of Saint Joseph of Arimathea. Annis has had so many names throughout history and in different regions it would be impossible to list them all.

Annis is reportedly able to shape-shift, most notably into an owl. There are also stories in which she has the ability to control the weather, conduct initiation ceremonies, dispense wisdom to those who seek her out, and heal the wounded. She has in the past been worshiped as a goddess, revered as a saint, and cursed as a demon. Hills, rivers, and even countries have been named in her honor, but despite her long and varied history, she has always had one common thread—she regularly consumed the blood of children.

Source: Barber, *Dictionary of Fabulous Beasts*, 33; Briggs, *Nine Lives*, 57; Spence, *Minor Traditions*, 29, 93–94, 133, 173; Spence, *Mysteries of Celtic Britain*, 174; Turner, *Dictionary of Ancient Deities*, 55

Anog Ite (an-og ee-day)

Variations: Double Woman, Iktomi, Two-Faced

In Lakota mythology, Anog Ite attempted to seduce Wi and steal him away from his wife, Hanwi. For her crimes of arrogance, flouting her husband Tate, neglecting her children, and vanity she was cursed to immortality. Additionally, one of her two faces remained beautiful but the other became repulsive and she was known thereafter as Anog Ite ("double face woman"); her last child was born prematurely and sent to live with its father and she was banished to live in isolation upon the earth. She is the cause of fighting, gossip, and lightning.

Source: Dooling, *Sons of the Wind*, xiv, 40; Knudson, *Beginning Dakota*, 43

Antaeos (an-tee'-uhs)

Variations: Antaeus, Anteaus, Antaios

In Greek mythology Antaeos was a GIGANTE of immense strength said to stand about eighty-five feet tall; living in a Libyan wasteland, he killed anyone who dared to travel into his domain. Born the son of the god of the sea, Poseidon (Neptune), he drew his strength from his mother, Gaea, the earth. He was defeated in a wrestling match by the demigod and cultural hero Hercules (Heracles) who lifted him off the ground, cutting him off from his source of strength.

Source: Daniels, *Encyclopædia of Superstitions, Folklore, and the Occult Sciences of the World*, 1375–8; Roman, *Encyclopedia of Greek and Roman Mythology*, 211; Westmoreland, *Ancient Greek Beliefs*, 682

Antero Vipunen

In Finnish folklore, Antero Vipunen was a GIANT said to be so large he used the earth as his blanket when he lay down in the underworld, Tuonela, to sleep; he knows all the secrets of the earth including its folklore, magic, and songs; he was also renowned throughout the land for his wisdom in spite of having the reputation for being a man-eater. He is mentioned in song seventeen of the *Kalevala*, the national saga of Finland, compiled and written in the nineteenth century by Elias Lönnrot.

Source: Honko, *Religion, Myth and Folklore in the World's Epics*, 168; Lönnrot, *Kalevala*, 103–04; Rose, *Giants, Monsters, and Dragons*, 20

Anteus

François Rabelais (AD 1494–1553) compiled the lineage of the GIANTS. Born the son of ADAMASTOR, Anteus was the father of AGATHO who *"begot PORUS, against whom Alexander the Great fought; who begot ARANTHAS, who begot GABBARA, who invented drinking to one's health; and from his descendants begot GRANGOUSIER; who begot GARGANTUAN; who begot PANTAGRUEL."*

Source: Brewer, *Character Sketches of Romance, Fiction and the Drama*, Volume 3, 80; Daniels, *Encyclopædia of Superstitions, Folklore, and the Occult Sciences of the World*, 1376; Rabelais, *Hours with Rabelais*, 80

Anthe (AN-thee)

Variations: Authe, Anthos ("flower")

Born the daughter of the GIGANTE ALCYONEUS, Anthe ("bloom") was, according to the ancient Greek historian Hegesander, one of the ALCYONII; she and her sisters, ALKIPPA, ASTERIA, DRIMO, PALLENE, and PHOSTHONIA, are named in his six-volume work *Commentaries* (*Hypomnemata*).

Source: Bell, *Bell's New Pantheon*, 110; Blunck, *Solar System Moons*, 83; Groves, *Baby Names that Go Together*, 168; Smith, *Dictionary of Greek and Roman Biography and Mythology*, 108

Anthropophagi

Variations: Anthropohagi, Anthropophagi

A legendary race of humanoids from ancient Greek mythology, the cannibalistic Anthropophagi ("eaters of humans") were described as not having a head; their mouth was located in their chest, their eyes were in their shoulders, and their very small brain was found in their groin. Their lack of a nose allowed them to consume human flesh, as they did not have to smell it. The cultural hero Odysseus escaped them only by a small margin.

In British fairy folklore the anthropophagi preyed upon humans when hungry. They were made popular by their appearance in William Shakespeare's plays *The Merry Wives of Windsor* and *Othello*.

Source: Manser, *Facts on File Dictionary of Classical and Biblical Allusions*, 20; McCoy, *Witch's Guide to Faery Folk*, 176; Shakespeare, *Merry Wives of Windsor*, 186; Shakespeare, *Othello*, 38

Antiphates

In classical Greek and Roman mythology Antiphates was a GIGANTE and the king of LAESTRYGONES, a land of fierce and cannibalistic GIGANTES. The herald of Odysseus was captured and eaten by him. Antiphates then ran to the shoreline with his entourage and began to hurl large boulders at Odysseus' fleet; they managed to sink eleven of them, taking all hands with them. It was only the ship Odysseus commanded and was on that survived the attack.

Source: Berens, *Myths and Legends of Ancient Greece and Rome*, 228; Rose, *Giants, Monsters, and Dragons*, 21

Anxo

Variations: Ancho, Antxo

A nature spirit of the mountains, Anxo is a CYCLOPS or evil spirit from Basque mythology in the region of Marquina; it is said to live in a cave.

Source: Miguel de Barandiarán, *Selected Writings of José Miguel De Barandiarán*, 92

Anxo Torto

An evil spirit of the mountains, Anxo Torto is a TÁRTALO ("CYCLOPS") from Basque mythology in the region of Marquina; it is said to live in a cave.

Source: Miguel de Barandiarán, *Selected Writings of José Miguel De Barandiarán*, 92

Ao Bing

Variations: Ao Ping

In ancient Chinese mythology, Ao Bing was a dragon and the third son of the dragon king Ao Kuang; he was described as having the head of a fish and the body of a human. Ao Bing was slain by the violent cultural warrior Nezha (Nazha, Nuozha) while trying to retrieve an apology from him for his having slain two of his father's messengers. Nezha had Ao Bing's tendons removed and woven into a belt to commemorate his great victory.

Source: Roberts, *Chinese Mythology, A to Z*, 3, 4, 36

Aobōzu

In Japanese folklore the aobōzu ("blue priest") is a yōkai (a creature of Japanese folklore) possibly created by the eighteenth century artist Toriyama Sekien in his book *Gazu Hyakki Yakō*; it was depicted as a one-eyed Buddhist priest standing next to a thatched hut. It is possible the aobōzu was the inspiration for the one-eyed yōkai (a creature of Japanese folklore) priest Hitotsume-Kozō.

Source: Murakami, *Yōkai Jiten*, 3–4, 164; Tada, *Edo Yōkai Karuta*, 18

Apci'lnic

The apci'lnic were a species of fairy or DWARF from the folklore of the Montagnais of Labrador, Canada. Living in the mountainous wilderness these little people stood only a foot or two tall but their presence was associated with danger. The apci'lnic had the ability to appear anyplace at will and were known to steal human children.

Source: Blackman, *Field Guide to North American Monsters*, 123; Rose, *Spirits, Fairies, Leprechauns, and Goblins*, 17

Apopa

In the folklore from the Inuit and Ihalmiut people of North America the apopa were dwarflike creatures, deformed and hideously ugly. They behaved much like the kobold of Europe and Puck from classical mythology, mischievous, never benevolent, but relatively harmless. Some sources claim Apopa was a single entity and not a species of fay.

Source: Mowat, *People of the Deer*, 254; Rose, *Spirits, Fairies, Leprechauns, and Goblins*, 17

Apsaras (Ap-sa-rahs)

Similar to the alp of German folklore, the apsaras ("from the water") of India is a female vampiric celestial creature. They were created when Vishnu used Mount Mandara as a churning rod in the *Churning of the Ocean* folklore. As he did so, aside from the other fabulous treasures and creatures he created, 35 million apsaras came forth.

They are known for their goddess-like beauty and charms, artistic talents, excessive love of wine and dice, as well as their love of dance. Apsaras are sent to earth to defile virtuous men, particularly those seeking to become even more virtuous. The creature will seduce a victim off his path, causing him to use up the merit he had accumulated.

An apsaras has a wide array of talents and abilities to assist it in carrying out its tasks, such as the ability to cause insanity, having complete control over the animals of the forest, inspiring a warlike fury in a man, making frighteningly accurate predictions, shape-shifting into various forms, and sending inspiration to lovers. Although apsaras can also perform minor miracles, they do not have the power to grant a boon like the Devas or the gods.

Occasionally, an apsaras will enjoy the task it has been sent on. Should it succeed in breaking the man's will and find him to be a pleasurable lover, it may offer him the reward of immortality. However, if despite its best efforts the apsaras cannot make the man succumb, it will either cause him to go insane or have his body torn apart by the wild animals of the forest.

Collectively, the apsaras are mated to the gandharvas, who can play music as beautifully as the apsaras can dance; however, there have been times when an apsaras has fallen in love with the man it was sent to seduce. Rather than cause his ruin, she would marry him. Stories say they make for an excellent wife and mother.

When not seeking to undo righteous men, the apsaras fly about the heads of those who will be great warriors on the battlefield. If one of these warriors dies with his weapon still in hand, the apsaras will carry his soul up and into Paradise.

Source: Bolle, *Freedom of Man In Myth*, 69, 74–75; Dowson, *Classical Dictionary*, 19; Hopkins, *Epic Mythology*, 28, 45, 164; Meyer, *Mythologie der Germanen*, 138, 142, 148; Turner, *Dictionary of Ancient Deities*, 63

Apuku

Fairy spirits from the Afro-South American Suriname folklore, the apuku lived in clearings found naturally in the bush and jungle. Described as looking like DWARFS from European mythologies, the apuku had a frightening appearance and were powerfully built.

Source: Jones, *Encyclopedia of Religion*, Volume 1, 126; Rose, *Spirits, Fairies, Leprechauns, and Goblins*, 18

Aqueous Devils

In Francesco Maria Guazzo's book *Compendium Maleficarum* (*Compendium of Witches*, 1628), he described seven different types of demons, one of which is the aqueous, or aquatic devil. He writes as a species they appear as generally beautiful and seductive women who prey upon mankind, striking whenever an opportunity presents itself. They have the ability to drown swimmers, cause storms at sea, and sink ships. Naturally, one would encounter such a creature in lakes, oceans, and other bodies of water where they must live.

Source: Kipfer, *Order of Things*, 255; Paine, *Hierarchy of Hell*, 69; Simons, *Witchcraft World*, 78; Summers, *Witchcraft and Black Magic*, 77

Aranthas

François Rabelais (AD 1494–1553) compiled the lineage of the GIANTS. Born the son of PORUS, Aranthas was the father of GABBARA whose "*descendants begot GRANGOUSIER; who begot GARGANTUAN; who begot PANTAGRUEL*."

Source: Brewer, *Character Sketches of Romance, Fiction and the Drama*, Volume 3, 80; Daniels, *Encyclopædia of Superstitions, Folklore, and the Occult Sciences of the World*, 1376; Rabelais, *Hours with Rabelais*, 80

Argeak

Variations: Argenk

In ancient Persian folklore the GIANT Argeak created a gallery on Mount Kaf which contained statues of ancient men in their various forms, seventy-two wise men from the east known as *Sulimans* (Solomons) as well as paintings of the animals which roamed the earth before the creation of Adam.

Source: Blavatsky, *Secret Doctrine*, 396; Brewer, *Reader's Handbook of Allusions, References, Plots and Stories*, 49

Arges

Variations: Ardes ("lightning"), Pyracmon

From classical Greek mythology, Arges ("flashing" or "thunderbolt"), BRONTES ("thunder"), and STEROPES ("thunder-clouds") are the three elder CYCLOPES, born the sons of the TITAN Uranus ("heaven") and the Earth, Gaea. Arges and his brothers were all born with a single eye in the middle of their forehead and were exceedingly strong. Their siblings were the HECATONCHEIRES and the TITAN. After the rise of the Olympian gods, Arges and his brothers were slain by the god Apollo because they created the thunderbolt which killed his son, Asclepius.

Source: Daly, *Greek and Roman Mythology, A to Z*, 39–40; Daniels, *Encyclopædia of Superstitions, Folklore, and the Occult Sciences of the World*, 1375–8

Argus Panoptes (ahr-gus pan-op'tez)

Variations: Argos, Argus, Argos Panoptês, Argus Panoptes, Hundred-Eyed, Panoptes

A GIGANTE from ancient Greek mythology whose entire body was covered with eyes, Argus Panoptes ("Argus who sees everything") had been appointed by the goddess Hera (Juno) to watch over Io who had been transformed into a heifer by her husband, the god Zeus (Jupiter). While he slept, half his eyes closed and rested while the other half kept watch. Hermes lulled the GIGANTE to sleep with a tune so beautiful from his lyre every one of his eyes closed. Once Argus Panoptes was fast asleep Hermes cut off his head to prevent him from reviving and informing Hera (Juno) what occurred; this allowed Zeus (Jupiter) to have his tryst. Hera (Juno), to honor the death of her favorite guardian, placed Argus Panoptes' eyes in the tail of her favorite bird, the peacock.

Source: Manser, *Facts on File Dictionary of Classical and Biblical Allusions*, 26; Rose, *Giants, Monsters, and Dragons*, 25

Ari, Norse (AR-I or aa-ree)

Variations: Are, HRIMGRIMNIR

In Norse mythology, Ari ("eagle" or "fast one") is a JOTUN who appears as an eagle; he has a perch in Nefhel. It is the wings of Ari which create the winds.

Source: Norroena Society, *Asatrii Edda*, 25

Ari, Sumerian

Variations: Akkad

The deified kings from ancient Sumerian mythology, the Ari ("the shining ones") were a race of GIANTS depicted on seals as being very large in stature; even when seated, they are still the largest person depicted.

Source: De Lafayette, *New de Lafayette Mega Encyclopedia of Anunnaki* , 560; De Lafayette, *Sumerian-English Dictionary*, 176

Ariels

In the King James interpretation of the Bible, the ariels were leonine (lion-like) men, humans whose faces were similar to a lion's because they were descendants of the NEPHILIM. Behaiah, one of the thirty mighty men of King David, was said to have slain two from Moab.

Source: Comay, *Who's Who in the Old Testament*, 57; DeLoach, *Giants*, 17, 77

Arimaspi

According to the fifth century Greek historian Herodotus, the Arimaspians were a race of people from Scythia who had only one eye in the middle of their forehead, much like a CYCLOPS; they were in a constant war against the *grypes* (griffins) who viciously guarded the vast quantities of gold they habitually dug free from mines.

Source: Anthon, *Classical Dictionary*, 195; Pliny the Elder, *Natural History of Pliny*, Volume 2, 123

Arinnefja (AR-in-ehv-ya)

One of the hrymthursars (FROST GIANTS) from Norse mythology, Arinnefja ("cooking maid" or "hearth nose") was born one of the daughters of THRAEL and THIR. Arinnefja, her parents, and siblings all lived a hard life of labor performing thankless tasks, such as cleaning, herding goats and swine, placing dung in the fields, and other varied unskilled labor. She and her family became the progenitors of the serving folk and thrall.

Source: Grimes, *Norse Myths*, 27, 255; Norroena Society, *Asatrii Edda*, 334

Arioch (AHR-ee-ahk)

Named in the *Targum of Palestine* (also known as the *Targum of Jonathan Ben Uzziel on the Book of Genesis*), the GIANT King Arioch ("tall among GIANTs") of Ellasar was one of the Babylonian kings who joined in with Chedorlaomer King of Elam in his war against Sodom, Gomorrah, and their neighboring cities. The story, as told in the Old Testament's Book of Genesis, names King Amraphael of Shinar and King Tidal of Goiym also siding with Chedorlaomer. The battle, which took place in the Valley of Siddim, was fought in waves; Arioch and his army were last in the battle order.

Source: Boulay, *Flying Serpents and Dragons*, 198–9; DeLoach, *Giants*, 19; Mandel, *Ultimate Who's Who in the Bible*, 62

Arrach

Variations: Arachd

In Scottish folklore the arrach ("manikin") is a grotesque GIANT which disappears so quickly no one has ever been able to see it long enough to get a more thorough description of it. The arrach is said to live in the high moors and mountains of the Highlands.

Source: Rose, *Giants, Monsters, and Dragons*, 26

Asa-Loki

Variations: Asa-Loke, Ása-Loki

In Norse mythology the name Asa-Loki is sometimes used to differentiate the god Loki from the JOTUN Utgardr-Loki.

Source: Anderson, *Norræna*, 1014; Grimes, *Norse Myths*, 255

Asanbonsam (Ah-san-bon-some)

Variation: Asambosam, Asanbosan, Asasabonsam, SASABONSAM

Similar to the YARA-MA-YHA-WHO of Australia, the asanbonsam terrorizes mankind from southern Ghana in Togo and along the Ivory Coast of Africa. Although rarely encountered, it is said to look like a human with hooks of iron for its hands and feet. The preferred method of hunting employed by the asanbonsam is to patiently sit in a tree and wait for an individual to pass directly underneath it. When this happens, the asanbonsam will use its hooks to snatch up its prey and drain them dry of blood. When times are lean, it will venture into a village at night and sip blood from a sleeping person's thumb. Fortunately, the regular sacrifice of a goat and the spilling of its blood on the ground will keep the asanbonsam satisfied enough to not hunt within the village.

Source: Bryant, *Handbook of Death*, 99; Bunson, *Vampire Encyclopedia*, 11; Masters, *Natural History of the Vampire*, 47; Volta, *The Vampire*, 152

Ascapart

Variations: Ascupart

In British folklore Ascapart was a GIANT said to stand thirty feet tall, twelve feet wide, and having a foot of distance in between his eyes. He once carried Sir Bevis of Southampton, his horse Arundel, the sword Morglay, and Sir Bvis' wife Josian all under one arm. Bevis eventually subjugated Ascapart and turned him into a docile servant made to jog alongside his horse.

Source: Brewer, *Character Sketches of Romance, Fiction and the Drama*, Volumes 1–2, 75; Daniels, *Encyclopædia of Superstitions, Folklore, and the Occult Sciences of the World*, 1375–8; Walsh, *Heroes and Heroines of Fiction, Classical Mediæval, Legendary*, 34

Asiman (Ass-ah-min)

Variations: Azeman

From Dahomey folklore of Africa comes the asiman, a living vampiric witch. She gained her evil powers originally by casting a specific magical spell and is now forever changed, no longer considered to be human; she can remove her skin and transform into a corpse candle, giving her the ability to fly through the sky. From the air she hunts for suitable prey and after feeding, she is able by use of therianthropy to shape-shift into an animal. Only when the asiman is in its animal form can the creature be destroyed.

Source: Davison, *Sucking Through the Century*, 358; Farrar, *Life of Christ*, 467; *Melbourne Review*, Volume 10, 225; Folklore Society of Great Britain, *Folklore Society*, Volume 61, 71; Stefoff, *Vampires, Zombies, and Shape-Shifters*, 17

Asin

From the Alsean folklore of the Pacific Northwest comes the legend of the asin, a being described both as a demon in human form and as a monstrous creature of the woods, feminine in form but covered in hair with claw-like hands and wolf-like teeth. Common to the folklore of the NURSERY BOGIE, the asin hunts children who stray too far from home, snatching them up, and disappearing into the woods with them, moving at incredible speeds. It also has the magical ability to enchant the huckleberry bush so any child who eats its fruit will fall under the asin's enchantment and wander off into the woods. Although this cannibal prefers to consume children, it will eat whoever it can catch. Often before it strikes, its laughter can be heard. It is believed if a medicine man dreams of the asin a great misfortune is about to occur in the community.

Source: Maberry, *Vampire Universe*, 24; Rose, *Giants, Monsters, and Dragons*, 27

Asmegir

Variations: Asasynir

In Norse mythology the Asmegir ("god might") are those living humans who will reside in Mimiur's Grove ("Odinsaker") with Baldur, Leifthrasir, and Lif; this enclosed area and citadel, Breidablik, was constructed by five architects, Bare, Ire, Ore, Une, Ure, and Vegdrasil, and three DVERG (DWARF) architects named Dore, Ore, and VAR. The gate to this realm is guarded by the extremely cunning DVERG (DWARF) Dellingr. The Asmegir are to be the progenitors of the next race of humanity and their children will be the ones to repopulate the earth.

Source: Rydberg, *Our Fathers' Godsaga*, xiv, 163; Rydberg, *Teutonic Mythology*, 239, 248, 306

Assiles

A GIANT of Arthurian folklore, Assiles, strong enough to move mountains, lived upon a desert island. With the assistance of his foster son, the GIANT GALAAS, Assiles routinely raided the lands of King Flois of Effin. The king, ultimately unable to resolve the situation on his own, enlisted the assistance of Sir Gawain to act as his champion; the knight slew Assiles but solicited an oath of fealty from GALAAS.

Source: Bruce, *Arthurian Name Dictionary*, 48; Thomas, *Diu Crône and the Medieval Arthurian Cycle*, 3–4

Asteria (ah-STEER-ee-yah)

Variations: Asterie

Born the daughter of the GIGANTE ALCYONEUS, Asteria ("starry") was, according to the ancient Greek historian Hegesander, one of the TITANS as well as one of the ALCYONII; she and her sisters, ALKIPPA, ANTHE, DRIMO, PALLENE, and PHOSTHONIA, are named in his six-volume work *Commentaries* (*Hypomnemata*).

Source: Blunck, *Solar System Moons*, 83; Groves, *Baby Names That Go Together*, 168; Smith, *Dictionary of Greek and Roman Biography and Mythology*, 108

Asterion

Variations: Asterius

In ancient Greek mythology Asterion ("starry") was the name of the MINOTAUR born from the wife of King Minos, Pasiphae; it was made to inhabit the labyrinth constructed by the great inventor Daedalus on the island of Cnossus.

Source: Coulter, *Encyclopedia of Ancient Deities*, 76

Astomi

Variations: Apple-Smellers, Gangines

The astomi ("mouthless") were a race of mouthless beings who survived on the sustenance of the odor of apples and flowers rather than eating. Pliny the Elder in his work *Natural History* (AD 77) described them as being covered with hair and living near the top of the Ganges River in the eastern part of India; they were said to wear clothing made from a soft cotton-like down collected from trees. Should an astomi come upon a particular foul-smelling scent, it may die. In some accounts of the astomi, they were an all-male race and it is assumed because of their lack of mouth are incapable of speaking.

Source: Friedman, *Monstrous Races in Medieval Art and Thought*, 11, 19, 29; Pesznecker, *Gargoyles*, 47

Astraeus

A TITAN from ancient Greek mythology, Astraeus was born one of the three children of the first generation TITAN CRIUS, a god of leadership. The siblings of Astraeus were PALLAS and PERSES. By EOS, TITAN and goddess of the Dawn, Astraeus was the father of the winds Boreas (north), Eurus (east), Notus (south), and Zephyrus (west), as well as various astral bodies.

Source: Daly, *Greek and Roman Mythology, A to Z*, 51, 141; Dixon-Kennedy, *Encyclopedia of Greco-Roman Mythology*, 14–5, 52

Asynjr (AHS-en-yur)

Variations: Asynja, Asynjur, Gygr ("ogress," "troll wife"), GYGUR, Jettinde

In Norse mythology asynjr is the generic word used to refer to a female JOTUN or a troll wife; in many instances, beyond a name, there is little else to nothing known: Ama ("nuisance"), Amgerdr ("creator of darkness"), Atla ("the awful-grim maiden"), Bakrauf ("robber-bitch"), Brana ("the hastening"), Bryja ("troll"), Buseyra ("big-eared"), Eisurfala ("fire-giantess"), Elli ("old age"), Fala ("immoral"), Fjolvor ("glutton"), Forad ("ruiner"), Geitla ("goat"), Gestilja ("guest-maiden"), Geysa ("storm-bringer"), Glumra ("din"), Gneip ("cliff-dweller"), Gnepja ("hunchback," "the stooping"), Gnissa ("screamer"), Goi ("winter month"), GREIP ("the grasping"), Gridr ("greedy," "violence"), Grima ("the masked"), Grottintanna ("gap-toothed"), GRYLA ("nightmare"), Guma ("earthy"), Hala ("large"), Hardgrepa ("the hard-grasping"), Hengjankjapta ("hanging-chin"), Herkja ("noisy"), Holgabrudr ("holy-bride"), Horn ("horn"), Hriiga ("the excessive"), Hrimgerdr ("rime-producer"), Hryggda ("the sad"), Hsera ("grey-haired"), Hundla ("hound," "dog"), Hvedna ("roarer"), Hvedra ("roarer"), Hyndla ("bitch"), Hyrja ("slattern"), Ima ("sooty"), Imdr ("embers from the Grotti-mill"), Imgerdr ("producer of conflict"), Imrbord ("arrow-shield"), Jarnglumra ("iron-din"), JARNSAXA ("she who crushes the iron"), Keila ("vixen"), Kjallandi ("the feminine"), Kleima ("the filthy"), Kraka ("screamer," "crow"), Leirvor, Ljota ("the ugly"), Lodinfingra ("shaggy-finger"), Mana ("moon"), Margerdr ("maker of wounds"), Morn ("agony"), Munnharpa ("witch"), Myrkrida ("murk-rider"), Nefja ("nose"), OFLUGBARDA ("strong-beard"), Rifingafla ("mighty-tearer"), Rygr ("the bellowing"), SELA ("woman"), Simul ("brewing ale," "mead"), Sivor ("burnt-lip"), Skrikja ("the screaming"), Sveipinfalda ("the veiled"), Svivor ("the mocking," "the shameful"), Vardriina ("protective rune"), Vigglod ("willing to travel"), Yma ("the screaming")

Source: Grimm, *Teutonic Mythology*, 525; Monaghan, *New Book of Goddesses and Heroines*, 57; Norroena Society, *Asatrii Edda*, 333–398; Puryear, *Nature of Asatru*, 201

Athos (ATH-thohss)

In ancient Greek mythology Athos, a GIGANTES and an illegitimate son of the god of the sea, Poseidon (Neptune), became angry with his father during a family argument. While standing in Thrace he picked up the mountain where the gods originally dwelt and hurled it at his father, where it landed in the Aegean Sea; after this event the gods then resided atop Mount Olympus. In another version of the tale Poseidon (Neptune) trapped Athos beneath a peninsula, entombing him there.

Source: Daniélou, *Gods of Love and Ecstasy*, 133; Middleton, *Broken Hallelujah*, 12

Atla

An ASYNJR from Norse mythology, Atla ("the awful-grim maiden") was one of the WAVE MAIDENS who were mother to the god Heimdall; she was the daughter of the god of the sea, Aegir. She, like her sisters, was said to have snow-white skin, blue eyes, and billowing blond hair; in one hand they carried a golden goblet filled with mead and in the other seashells filled with the finest foods. They wore long transparent robes of green or blue trimmed in white. When not serving food in the hall, they played on the shore in groups of three.

Source: Anderson, *Norse Mythology*, 440; Lindow, *Norse Mythology*, 63

Atlantes

Mentioned by Pliny the Elder in his work *Natural History* (AD 77), the Atlantes were a race of people who live in the interior of Africa with two interesting customs: they did not have individual names and they cursed rather than worshiped the sun, each morning calling out insults at it because it burned both them and the land.

Source: Pliny the Elder, *Natural History of Pliny*, Volume 6, 405; Sprague de Camp, *Lands Beyond*, 221–22

Atlas

In classical Greek mythology, Atlas was one of the second generation TITANS, born one of four sons to the TITAN IAPETOS and the second generation TITAN and OCEANID CLYMENE. Atlas had seven daughters (Alcyone, Asterope, CELAENO, ELECTRA, Maia, Merope, and Taygete) with his wife PLEIONE, and one son, Hyas. By Hesperis he was also the father of Hesperides.

His brothers EPIMETHEUS, MENOETIUS, and PROMETHEUS sided with the Olympians in the Titanomachy. For his punishment in the war against the Olympian gods Zeus (Jupiter) did not condemn Atlas to Tartarus as he did the other TITANS but rather forced him to hold the bronze dome of the heavens on his shoulders and back.

François Rabelais (AD 1494–1553) compiled the lineage of the GIANTS. Born the son of NEMBROTH,

Atlas was the father of GOLIAH whose *"descendants begot* BRIAREOS, *who had a hundred hands; who begot* PORPHYRIA; *who begot* ADAMASTOR; *who begot* ANTEUS; *who begot* AGATHO; *who begot* PORUS, *against whom Alexander the Great fought; who begot* ARANTHAS, *who begot* GABBARA, *who invented drinking to one's health; and from his descendants begot* GRANGOUSIER; *who begot* GARGANTUAN; *who begot* PANTAGRUEL."

Source: Brewer, *Character Sketches of Romance, Fiction and the Drama*, Volume 3, 80; Daly, *Greek and Roman Mythology, A to Z*, 22; Daniels, *Encyclopædia of Superstitions, Folklore, and the Occult Sciences of the World*, 1375–8; Rabelais, *Hours with Rabelais*, 80; Roman, *Encyclopedia of Greek and Roman Mythology*, 92

Atshen

Variations: Acten, Atce'n

In the Inuit mythology of the Innu people, the atshen was once a member of the tribe who became a "wild person" and then a cannibalistic monster; the more human flesh it devoured the larger it became. A small atshen is known as an *athsheniss*. Stories about the atshen are not considered by the Innu to be myth (*atanukans*) but rather the retelling of actual events within contemporary memory (*tipatshimuns*). To destroy an atshen it needs to be captured and held in a secure location, deprived of food and water until it dies; then, the body must be burned.

Source: Henriksen, *I Dreamed the Animals*, 27, 157–8

Augeia

Variations: ANGEYJA, Anheyja, Aurgeia, AURGIAFA, EGIA ("whelmer")

An ASYNJR from Norse mythology, Augeia ("sane strewer") was one of the WAVE MAIDENS who were mother to the god Heimdall; she was the daughter of the god of the sea, Aegir. She, like her sisters, was said to have snow-white skin, blue eyes, and billowing blond hair; in one hand they carried a golden goblet filled with mead and in the other seashells filled with the finest foods. They wore long transparent robes of green or blue trimmed in white. When not serving food in the hall, they played on the shore in groups of three.

Source: Daly, *Norse Mythology A to Z*, 47; Grimes, *Norse Myths*, 255

Augilae

Described by the Roman author and natural philosopher Pliny the Elder in his work, *Natural History* (AD 77), the Augilae were a race of people who worshiped only the gods of the lower world; they lived in a land twelve days' journey beyond the borders of the GARAMANTES.

Source: Pliny the Elder, *Pliny's Natural History*, 52; Sprague de Camp, *Lands Beyond*, 221–22

Auloniad

Variations: Napææ

The Auloniad ("ravine" or "valley") were a subspecies of the NAPAEA; they were the NYMPHS of mountain pastures and vales. Oftentimes they were seen in the company of Pan (Faunus), the god of nature. Eurydice, for whom Orpheus traveled into the underworld Hades, was a beloved and lovely auloniad.

Source: Bechtel, *Dictionary of Mythology*, 152; Maberry, *Cryptopedia*, 112; Murray, *Manual of Mythology*, 183

Aunyaina

In Brazilian folklore, especially from the Tupari people, the aunyaina was believed to be a gigantic, cannibalistic sorcerer and monster; it was described as being humanoid in appearance, with boar tusks protruding from his mouth. Although it would hunt and consume anyone it was particularly fond of preying on children who wandered just outside of camp and into the forest.

Source: Dixon-Kennedy, *Native American Myth and Legend*, 28; Rose, *Giants, Monsters, and Dragons*, 32

Aurboda

Variations: HAG of Eastern Winds, HAG of Ironwood, Mother of Evil

In Norse mythology, Aurboda ("gravel-offerer") was an ASYNJR, a maid servant in Asgard to Freyja, and by Gymir was the mother of GERDR, the wife of Frey. She is an evil and powerful sorceress or *valas* who practiced witchcraft and used her magic to whip up storms at sea. It was said in the poem *Hyndlujoth* her heart was "primeval cold."

Source: Anderson, *Norræna*, 213; Lindow, *Handbook of Norse Mythology*, 64; Rydberg, *Teutonic Mythology*, 157–8, 164

Aurgelmer

Variations: Aurgelmir, Ymer, YMIR

According to the Icelandic historian, poet, and politician Snorri Sturluson (1179–1241), in Norse mythology Aurgelmer ("gravel yeller") was a JOTUN, the father of THRUDGELMIR, and the grandfather of Bergelmer.

Source: Anderson, *Norse Mythology*, 174, 194, 441; Sturluson, *Prose Edda*, 24, 123

Aurgiafa

Variations: ANGEYJA, Anheyja, AUGEIA, Aurgeia, EGIA

An ASYNJR from Norse mythology, Aurgiafa ("sorrow whelmer") was one of the WAVE MAIDENS who were mother to the god Heimdall; she was the daughter of the god of the sea, Aegir. She, like her sisters, was said to have snow-white skin, blue eyes, and billowing blond hair; in one hand they carried a golden goblet filled with mead and in the other seashells filled with the finest foods. They wore long transparent robes of green or blue trimmed in white. When not serving food in the hall, they played on the shore in groups of three.

Source: Daly, *Norse Mythology A to Z*, 47; Grimes, *Norse Myths*, 255

Aurgrimnir (OUR-greem-nir)

In Norse mythology, Aurgrimnir ("mud-grimnir") was one of the many named Jotnar (see JOTUN) about whom, beyond a name, there is little to nothing else known.

Source: Norroena Society, *Asatrii Edda*, 336

Aurnir

Variations: Aumir, Aurinir, Aurnir-Egil, Gdngr, Ornir ("eagle" or "quick")

In Norse mythology, Aurnir ("wild boar"), along with IDI and THJAZI, is the son of the storm JOTUN Olvalde; their mother was the ASYNJR GREIP. In the *Younger Edda* he is known as Gangr.

Source: Norroena Society, *Asatrii Edda*, 380; Rydberg, *Norroena*, 951; Rydberg, *Teutonic Mythology*, 643, 645, 672

Aurvandill

Variations: Aurvandil, The Brave

The newly wed husband of the ASYNJR seer GROA, Aurvandill was a brave warrior and a friend of the god Thor. Aurvandill was rescued from the Jotnar (see JOTUN) by Thor and carried across Elivagar in a basket; when his toe, which had been poking out of the basket, froze, Thor snapped it off and threw it into the heavens creating a new star.

Source: Grimes, *Norse Myths*, 111–12; Guerber, *Hammer of Thor*, 52

Aurvangr (OUR-vang-r)

In Norse mythology, Aurvangr ("mud-field") was one of the many named DRAUGR about whom, beyond a name, there is little to nothing else known.

Source: Norroena Society, *Asatrii Edda*, 336

Austre

Variations: Austri

In Norse mythology Austre was one of the four DVERGAR (DWARFS) who were appointed by the gods to hold up the sky which they constructed from the skull of YMIR. Austre held up the East, NORDRE held the North, SUDRE held the South, and VESTRE held the West.

Source: Anderson, *Norse Mythology*, 183; Grimes, *Norse Myths*, 9; Norroena Society, *Asatrii Edda*, 336; Sturluson, *Prose Edda*, 26

Auvekoejak

Variations: Havstrambe

A species of Merfolk (see MERMAID and MERMAN) from the folklore of Greenland, the Auvekoejak, rather than having Piscean scales covering their body, have fur.

Source: Meurger, *Lake Monster Traditions*, 218; Rose, *Giants, Monsters, and Dragons*, 32; Zell-Ravenheart, *Wizard's Bestiary*, 20

Avvim

According to the Bible, Joshua 13:3 (English Standard Version), the Avvim and Hurrians were the two tribes of GIANTS which first occupied Canaan; the Avvim lived on the plains around Gaza and were nearly annihilated by the Caphtorim. Those Avvim who survived the assault founded a city which later fell to the tribe of Benjamin.

Source: DeLoach, *Giants*, 20; McClintock, *Cyclopaedia of Biblical, Theological, and Ecclesiastical Literature*, Volume 1, 570

Azrail

Azrail was a GIANT in Armenian folklore who lived on Mount Djandjavaz. According to folklore, the GIANT captured and took into slavery the brother of three fairies. Although many tried no one was able to rescue him. One day, a young man known only as "the apprentice" told the king for the price of eleven goblets he would slay Azrail. In addition to the goblets the king gave "the apprentice" a mace, a suit of armor, and a warhorse. The slayer first killed the two serpents guarding Azrail's castle before confronting the GIANT himself. A terrific battle ensued and "the apprentice" managed to land two decisive blows. Azrail begged to be finished off but the youth previously learned a third strike would magically restore the GIANT to full health and vigor. Rather than striking his opponent, he left Azrail to bleed to death.

Sources: Dixon-Kennedy, *Encyclopedia of Russian and Slavic Myth and Legend*, 22; Rose, *Giants, Monsters, and Dragons*, 33

Baba Yaga

Variations: Бáба-Ягá ("Baba Yaga"), Баба Яга ("Baba Yaga"), Баба Яга ("Baba Yaga"), Babba Yagga, Baba Yaga Kostianaya Noga ("bone-legs"), Grandmother Bony-shanks, Grandmother in the Forest, Iron Nosed Witch, Iron Nosed Woman, Jaga Baba, Ježibaba, Jezi-Baba

Originally from Hungarian folklore, Baba Yaga

("old woman Yaga" or "old woman Jadwiga") was a kind and benevolent FAIRY; over time her stories changed and she became a cannibalistic old crone or witch, small and ugly; in some stories Baba Yaga was a race of evil fay and not an individual. The name and character of Baba Yaga appeared in a number of eastern European and Slavic myths.

As an evil individual, Baba Yaga is described as being old, short, skinny, and ugly with a particularly distorted and large nose and long, crooked teeth. Her behavior has earned her the reputation of being the Devil's own grandmother.

In instances where Baba Yaga was a fairy race rather than a singular individual, such as in the fairy tale of "The Feather of Finist the Falcon," the hero was met by not one but three baba yagas. In these instances, the baba yagas were commonly benevolent, gifting the hero with both advice and magical presents he would later need to succeed in his quest.

Baba Yaga, as a character, was hardly set in her ways; she was used seemingly to fulfill a storyteller's need. There were numerous stories of her kidnapping children and threatening to eat them; in fact, many versions of cruel and evil witches living in houses of cake and candy were named Baba Yaga. In some stories heroes would make the brave and dangerous decision to seek out Baba Yaga for advice or assistance in completing a quest; in these stories there was always an emphasis placed on the hero's level of politeness, his need for proper preparation, and purity of his spirit. Sometimes she played the role of an antagonist while other times she was a necessary source of guidance. No matter what role she was fulfilling, she drove a hard bargain, and was the one who set the conditions and terms of the agreement; it mattered not to her if the hero accepted or refused the deal. All of her verbal contracts allowed her the right to eat anyone who was later unable or unwilling to fulfill their end of the deal.

By use of a gigantic mortar Baba Yaga could fly amazingly fast through the forest, steering by use of the accompanying pestle in her right hand while with her left she uses her magical broom made out of silver birch to sweep away any sign of her having passed through the area. As she traveled it was believed a host of spirits trail behind her.

Source: Dixion, *Encyclopedia of Russian and Slavic Myth and Legend*, 23–8; Evans-Wentz, *Fairy Faith in Celtic Countries*, 247; Lurker, *Routledge Dictionary of Gods and Goddesses*, 29; Rose, *Spirits, Fairies, Leprechauns, and Goblins*, 29; Rosen, *Mythical Creatures Bible*, 234

Babamik

In the Arapesh mythology of New Guinea, Babamik was a female OGRE and a cannibal; she was lured to her death, tricked into crossing a river on a narrow plank and then beaten with canoe paddles until she fell off. Once in the water, she and her spirit were consumed by an anthropophagous (man-eating) crocodile.

Source: Chopra, *Academic Dictionary of Mythology*, 46; Mead, *Mountain Arapesh*, 270

Babaroga

Variations: Aga, Ajshir-Baba, Egaboua, Egga, Egibishna, Egibitsa, Gnishna, Iga, Igaya, Indzi-Baba, Jagok, Jedibaba, Jedubaba, Jezibaba, Lyaga, Oga, Yagaba, Yagabaka, Yagabova, Yaga-Bura, Yaganishna, Yagichina- Bibichina, Yagishna, Yagivouna, Yagushna, Yaza, Yega, Yegiboba, Yeza, Yuga

From the folklore of Bosnia, Croatia, Herzegovina, Macedonia, and Serbia, the NURSERY BOGIE babaroga ("old woman with horns") and her level of involvement varies from household to household. Sometimes she is said to snatch up naughty children in a sack and then take them to her cave where she will eat them. In another home the story may say she grabs up disobedient children through a hole she punches through the roof. The babaroga, like her Russian counter-part BABA YAGA, has innumerable name variants.

Source: Ugresic, *Baba Yaga Laid an Egg*, 247; Krensky, *Bogeyman*, 43

Badabada

Humanoids from Melanesian folklore, the Badabada ("largest") are said to have only one leg and must move about with the assistance of a staff; larger than the natives, they usually live in the tree branches from where they can safely throw projectiles at anyone who gets too near to their location. It is unknown what the Badabada eat and it is suspected they may not require any food.

Source: Seligman, *Melanesians of British New Guinea*, 649

Bafurr (BAHV-ur)

Variations: Bafur

In Norse mythology, Bafurr ("bean") was one of the many named rock DVERG (DWARFS) who, along with BIFUR, BOMBOR, DAIN, NAIN, NAR, NIPING, NORI, and "hundreds of others," worked together to create the fetter Gleipnir to bind Fenrir; beyond a name, there is little to nothing else known.

Source: Crossley-Holland, *Norse Myths*, 35; Grimes, *Norse Mythology*, 7; Norroena Society, *Asatrii Edda*, 336

Baginis

Variations: Diba, Ngakoula-Ngou

In Australian aboriginal folklore the baginis are a species of beautiful hybrid women, part human and part animal; they are described as having claw-like fingers and toes; sometimes they are considered to be spirits and beings from the Dreamtime. The baginis are known for abducting, raping, and then releasing men, or consuming them as food.

Source: Coleman, *Dictionary of Mythology*, 122; Zell-Ravenheart, *Wizard's Bestiary*, 21

Bakhtak

A humanoid ursidae (bear-like) KHRAFSTRA from Iranian mythology, the bakhtak ("nightmare") would creep into a person's room at night and settle upon a person's chest, pressing down, causing the sleeper to have nightmares, similar to the alp of German folklore; in extreme cases, the bakhtak kills its victim and then eats the remains.

Source: Guppy, *Blindfold Horse*, 82

Bakru

A race of evil fairies or DWARFS living in the Paramaribo and coastal region of Suriname, the bakru were described as being half flesh and half wood, with black skin and hair, and having very large black eyes set in their very large heads on their child-like bodies. Some sources claim they were the constructs of evil magicians. Always appearing in twos, one male and one female, the bakru were similar to the APUKU of West African folklore.

If one wishes to have a bakru as a servant the person must agree to a pact with the being, signing away their soul for whatever riches the bakru will bring them, much like the AITVARAS of European folklore. Other sources claim they can be created and purchased from evil magicians and kept as servants. If someone strikes their master, the bakru dashes in the way, taking the shot with the wooden side of their body; later they will kill the assailant. When the owner of a bakru dies the fairy is then free and will wander the roads looking for children to tease; if a child should ever accept a drink from a bakru, it will die.

Source: Begley, *Faith of Legacy*, 420; Herskovits, *Myth of the Negro Past*, 254–5; Rose, *Spirits, Fairies, Leprechauns, and Goblins*, 31

Balan

The bravest and the strongest of the GIANTS from the literature of medieval France, Balan was renowned for his courage. He was the father of the GIANT FIERBRAS and, according to folklore, ultimately defeated by the cultural hero Emperor Charlemagne.

Source: Brewer, *Character Sketches of Romance, Fiction and the Drama*, Volumes 3, 80; Daniels, *Encyclopædia of Supersti-* tions, Folklore, and the Occult Sciences of the World, 1375–8; Rose, *Giants, Monsters, and Dragons*, 37–8

Bali

Variations: Balin, Mahabali

In Hindu mythology in India there are at least two supernatural creatures with the name Bali.

The first Bali (also known as Mahabali) was a malicious GIANT, one of the DANAVAS, and the grandson of an incarnation of Ravana. Bali seized control of the earth and the heavens, temporarily ousting the gods who lost their power when they lost their domain. Vishnu took an incarnation as a DWARF called Brahmin and visited Bali as a guest of his home where he requested to become ruler of all the land he could cover in the span of three paces. No sooner had the GIANT granted the odd request than the guise of the DWARF was dropped; Vishnu took two paces which covered the entire universe and used his third to banish Bali to the underworld. In a different version of the tale, Indra defeated Bali in battle; when the GIANT was slain rather than blood, he bled out a cascade of jewels. Curious, Indra chopped up the body: crystals from his flesh, diamonds from his bones, emeralds from the marrow, pearls came from his teeth, rubies from his blood, and sapphires from his eyes.

The other Bali in Hindu mythology was also a GIANT and was created from the *bala* (hair) of his mother; he was described as resembling a human who was completely covered in hair and had an extremely long tail. Bali was the Prince of Apes and Monkeys and the step-brother of the King of Apes and Monkeys, Surgriva. When he overthrew his sibling he angered the gods and was consequently slain by Rama.

Source: Dowson, *Classical Dictionary of Hindu Mythology and Religion, Geography, History, and Literature*, 42; Rose, *Giants, Monsters, and Dragons*, 38

Bapet

In Ute folklore and legends in the Great Basin region of the United States of America there was a race of monstrous humanoids known as the SIATS; the females of the species were known as bapets. These cannibals would kidnap children to consume but were also known to suckle a child with their enormous breasts filled with poisonous milk. Under normal conditions, the bapet were immortal but could be killed only if fatally shot with an obsidian tipped arrow.

Source: Rose, *Giants, Monsters, and Dragons*, 39

Bara

Variations: DROFN

An ASYNJR from Norse mythology, Bara ("foam fleck" or "wave") was one of the WAVE MAIDENS who were mother to the god Heimdall; she was the daughter of the god of the sea, Aegir. She, like her sisters, was said to have snow-white skin, blue eyes, and billowing blond hair; in one hand they carried a golden goblet filled with mead and in the other seashells filled with the finest foods. They wore long transparent robes of green or blue trimmed in white. When not serving food in the hall, they played on the shore in groups of three.

Source: Grimes, *Norse Myths*, 122; Sturluson, *Prose Edda*, 137

Barbegazi

In Swiss folklore the rarely seen barbegazi ("frozen beards") were small GNOME-like humanoid creatures living in the mountains between France and Switzerland; described as looking like a man frozen in ice or sculpted of ice they are nimble and quick, moving with perfect ease through the snow. They wore white clothing and the beards of the males were made of icicles. Hibernating all summer long, they only leave their subterranean caves in the dead of winter and only when the temperature is below zero Fahrenheit (or -17.77 Celsius). Generally the barbegazi will warn travelers of an imminent avalanche by making a hooting call and assist lost travelers by making a fire or luring them to safety. However if anyone ever attempted to follow one back to its lair the otherwise benign barbegazi would toss them off a cliff.

Source: Conway, *Ancient Art of Faery Magick*, 128–9; Maberry, *Vampire Universe*, 35

Barong

In Balinese mythology Barong is the antagonist to the ferocious female folk demon witch and queen of the leyaks (a type of vampiric witch), RANGDA ("widow"). A benevolent spirit king, Barong is portrayed in dance drama as a boar, dragon, lion, serpent, and a tiger. By use of his magic, Barong is able to drive off the evil RANGDA but he is never able to truly defeat her, just as she is never able to completely defeat him. The story of Barong is told with slight deviations from region to region but generally he is depicted as a grandiose, playful narcissist.

Source: Beers, *Women and Sacrifice*, 53; Rosen, *Mythical Creatures Bible*, 353

Baudihillie

Variations: Beda, Boudihillia

A VALKYRIES from Norse mythology, Baudihillie ("ruler of battle") was one of the two ALAISIAGAE; she and her companion FRIAGABI ("giver of freedom") had their names carved on Hadrian's Wall and were likely worshiped by the soldiers stationed there as goddesses of Fate.

Source: Coulter, *Encyclopedia of Ancient Deities*, 34, 490; Monaghan, *Encyclopedia of Goddesses and Heroines*, 282

Baugi (BOUG-i)

Variation: Bauge ("ring")

As a character in Norse mythology, Baugi ("bowed" or "ring-shaped") only exists in Snorri Sturluson's (1179–1241) version of the *Prose Edda*. Baugi, brother of Suttung, was the JOTUN from whom the god Odin obtained the Mead of Poetry. According to *Skaldskaparmal*, Snorri tells a tale where Odin, calling himself Bolverk ("evil deed"), happens upon nine slaves who are cutting hay. Odin lets them borrow his whetstone and the slaves, impressed with how much sharper it makes their blades, all begin to bid for its purchase. Odin throws the stone into the air and in the scramble the slaves cut each other's throats. The slaves belonged to Baugi and in compensation Odin promises to do the work of nine men in exchange for a drink of mead. Baugi does not actually have the mead, which is in his brother's care, but he is sure Suttung would agree to the terms so he accepts on his behalf. At the end of the season when Odin asks for his drink Suttung learns of the transaction and flatly refuses payment. Odin enlists Baugi's assistance in stealing what is owed but while drilling their way into the mountain Hnitbjorg the god discovers the JOTUN is attempting to deceive him. Odin transforms himself into a snake and quickly slithers into a hole; Baugi strikes at the snake, but misses and thereafter disappears from the mythology.

Source: Daly, *Norse Mythology A to Z*, 11; Grimes, *Norse Mythology*, 52–56; Lindow, *Handbook of Norse Mythology*, 72–3; Oehlenschläger, *Gods of the North*, xxxviii

Baykok

In the Great Lakes region of the United States of America, the Ojibwa people have in their folklore a being known as the Baykok ("skin draped bones" or "skeletal decomposed remains"); it is undead and wanders the woods at night compelled by an undead hunger, attacking only lone travelers, and eating their livers. Wielding a bludgeoning club and invisible spirit arrows, the Baykok will incapacitate his victims before consuming them. According to folklore a highly skilled and proud hunter became hopelessly lost in the woods while tracking a large buck. Unable to find his way home or catch any food to eat, the hunter began to die of starvation. Just before he died the hunter swore with his last breath his spirit would never leave his body. Sometime after his death a hunting party passed by his remains and roused his spirit. The Baykok rose and attacked the group, eating them; thereafter he wandered the woods, continuing his hunt for more to eat.

Source: Brown, *Complete Idiot's Guide to Zombies*, n.pag.; Ingpen, *Ghouls and Monsters*, 43

Bebhionn

Variations: Vivionn

A GIANT from Celtic mythology known for her beauty; she kept her long, wavy golden hair done up in seven braids and wore a gilded helm inlaid with jewels and golden rings upon each of her fingers. Bebhionn was the daughter of Treon; she was said to reside in the Land of Women (Tir na mBan, the Otherworld). Bebhionn was engaged to marry the DWARF king Aeda, but displeased with the match she fled and sought the protection of Fianna, the famous warrior of Fionn McCumhal. Her jilted husband-to-be gave chase and as she reached the Fianna, threw his spear and fatally wounded her; with her dying breath she bequeathed her wealth to the Fianna; they placed an ogham over her burial site and the area became known as the Ridge of the Dead Woman.

Source: McCoy, *Celtic Myth and Magick*, 243, Mountain, *Celtic Encyclopedia*, Volume 2, 352

Begdu San

A GIANT from Chinese folklore, Begdu San was born in Korea; there his appetite was so great he consumed all of the vegetation as far as the eye could see; this resulted in him growing so tall as to block out the sun. The villagers forced him to leave and go live in the mountains to the north. Begdu San complied but soon consumed all of the vegetation there as well as having drunk the rivers dry; he began grazing his way towards eastern China. Upon arrival Begdu San was thirsty and began to drink up the sea; fortunately the salt water made him ill and as he fell to the earth, his body transformed into a mountain range.

Source: Knudsen, *Giants, Trolls, and Ogres*, 31; Rose, *Giants, Monsters, and Dragons*, 43

Beinvidr (BAYN-vith-r)

In Norse mythology, Beinvidr ("big-bone") was one of the many named Jotnar (see JOTUN) about whom, beyond a name, there is little to nothing else known.

Source: Norroena Society, *Asatrii Edda*, 341

Beitr (BAYT-r)

In Norse mythology, Beitr ("the caustic") was one of the many named Jotnar (see JOTUN) who, beyond a name, there is little else to nothing known.

Source: Norroena Society, *Asatrii Edda*, 341

Beli (BEHL-i)

Variations: Bele, BILLINGR

A JOTUN in Norse mythology, Beli ("bellower" or "roarer") was born the son of the JOTUN Gymir. After Beli won GERDR who was loved by Frey as his wife, Frey killed him with a deer horn. This story is little known as it only appears in *Gylfaginning* by the Icelandic historian, poet, and politician, Snorri Sturluson (1179–1241).

Source: Daly, *Norse Mythology A to Z*, 11; Grimm, *Teutonic Mythology*, Volume 2, 530; Lindow, *Handbook of Norse Mythology*, 73

Belle

In British folklore there once was a GIANT named Belle; at a place known as Mount Sorrel he mounted upon his sorrel horse and they leapt a mile. The place where they landed was then called Wanlip ("One Leap"). Belle then leaped another mile but in doing so burst all of his girths, therefore the place where he landed this time was named Burstall. The third time Belle leapt, he died from exertion and the place where he fell dead and was buried was called Bellegrave.

Source: Brewer, *Dictionary of Phrase and Fable*, 81; Daniels, *Encyclopædia of Superstitions, Folklore, and the Occult Sciences of the World*, 1375–8

Bellerus

In British folklore Bellerus was a GIANT from Bellerium, a holding of the Roman Empire; this place is now known as Cornwall, England.

Source: Daniels, *Encyclopædia of Superstitions, Folklore, and the Occult Sciences of the World*, 1375; Rose, *Giants, Monsters, and Dragons*, 45

Ben Varrey

Variations: Ben-Varrey

On the Isle of Man, England, *ben varrey* was the Manx word for MERMAID, a beautiful sea creature with long golden hair enchanting fishermen with their laughter and voice and then luring them to their deaths. The ben varrey had the same general description and disposition as other mermaids, luring fishermen to their death, but in Manx tales they tend to be generally kinder. There are more than a few folktales where the ben varrey was benevolent, such as in Dora Broome's *Fairy Tales from the Isle of Man* where a grateful MERMAID told a fisherman where to find a treasure hoard. In another tale a ben varrey rose up from the water and called out "shiaull er thalloo" ("sail to land") just as a violent storm was about to roll up; those who heeded its warning lived, and the rest were lost to the sea forever.

Source: Briggs, *Encyclopedia of Fairies*, 22–3; Conway, *Magical, Mystical Creatures*, 156; Maberry, *Vampire Universe*, 38; Rose, *Spirits, Fairies, Leprechauns, and Goblins*, 38

Berg Folk

Variations: Berg People, Bjerg-Trolds, Hill-Men, Skovtrolde ("wood TROLL")

Said to resemble DWARFS, the berg folk of Dutch folklore were a species of fairly benign TROLL often appearing to humans as a toad. The god Thor was particularly hostile to them.

Source: Briggs, *Vanishing People*, 195; Gray, *Mythology of All Races*, Volume 2, 224; Keightley, *Fairy Mythology*, 106; Rose, *Spirits, Fairies, Leprechauns, and Goblins*, 39

Bergbui

In Norse mythology the berbui ("cliff dweller") were a species of GIANT, a type of mountain dwelling JOTUN. The JOTUN HRUNGNIR who fought against the god of thunder, Thor, with a horn or stone hammer was one of the berbui.

Source: Dickens, *Icelandic Runic Poem*, 29; Rose, *Giants, Monsters, and Dragons*, 46; Selbie, *Encyclopædia of Religion and Ethics*, Volume 12, 253

Bergelmir

Variations: Bergelmer

In Norse mythology, Bergelmir ("bare-yeller," "bear-yeller," "mountain roarer," or "mountain-yeller"), a wise JOTUN, was the oldest of the Aesir, born many years before the earth was even formed; his father was named THRUDGELMIR and his grandfather was called AURGELMER. Bergelmir and his wife were the only survivors of the deluge of blood which swept the land when YMIR died. The couple were the parents of all the FROST GIANTS; in the war against Odin and the Aesir, again only Bergelmir and wife survived the assault, escaping and creating a new home for themselves in Jotunheim where they became the progenitors of a new race of FROST GIANTS.

Source: Coulter, *Encyclopedia of Ancient Deities*, 97; Lindow, *Handbook of Norse Mythology*, 74; Oehlenschläger, *Gods of the North*, xxxv

Bergion

Born one of the sons of the god of the sea, Neptune, Bergion was a one-time ruler over Ireland. One of his brothers, ALBION, once ruled over the island of England and another brother, LESTRIGO, ruled over Italy. The demi-god Hercules (Heracles) once fought Albion and Bergion on the stony field of Craus between Marseilles and Rhone.

Source: Roof, *Popular History of Noble County Capitals and Greater Albion*, 13; Stubbs, *Origines Celticae*, 18

Bergrisar (BERG-ris-ar), plural: Bergrisi (BERG-ris-i)

Variations: Berg-risar, Bergjarlar ("mountain rulers"), Bergthursar

In Norse mythology there are several species of Jotnar (see JOTUN); the bergrisi are the mountain JOTUN, whereas the FROST GIANTS were called the HRIMPURSAR and the FIRE GIANTS were the ELD-JOTNAR. At the time of Ragnarok they will gather with the others of their kind and wage war against the gods on the Plain of Vigdir. The bergrisi were well known for causing earthquakes and landslides.

Source: Grimes, *Norse Myths*, 257; Halpin, *Manlike Monsters on Trial*, 52; Maberry, *They Bite*, 344

Berling

Variations: Bari ("the bearing") Berlingr ("builder"), Bjar, Berlingr

A rock DVERG (DWARF) from Norse mythology created by DURINN, Berling ("handspike") is listed as being one of DURINN'S KIN. He like the others created paid particular attention to DURINN's leadership. Berling was also the name of one of the four Brisingamen DWARFS, ALFRIG, DVALIN, and GRER, who created the prized necklace for the goddess Freyr. Berling was an uncommon name for a DWARF; it only appeared in the *Sorla Thattr* in the *Flateyjarbok* manuscript.

Source: Daly, *Norse Mythology A to Z*, 2, 11, 32–3; Grimes, *Norse Myths*, 131–2, 254, 260

Bernardo Carpio

Variations: Hari ng mga Tagalog (King of the Tagalogs)

Bernardo Carpio is a GIANT in the folklore of the Tagalogs, Philippines, who was rebuked by the gods for his insolence, chained for eternity in Montalban Gorge in Rizal Province and cursed to keep two mountain walls from colliding. Each time he pauses to recoup his strength, the walls begin to close in, crushing him between them, forcing him to push them back. This is the explanation for earthquakes.

Source: Guillermo, *Historical Dictionary of the Philippines*, 73; Halili, *Philippine History*, 17

Bestla (Best-lah)

Variations: Betsla

An ancient FROST GIANT from Norse mythology, Bestla was, according to Snorri Sturluson's (1179–1241) *Prose Edda*, born the daughter of the JOTUN BOLTHORN and married the god Bor (BURI); together they were the parents of three sons, the gods Odin, Ve, and Vili.

Source: Anderson, *Norse Mythology*, 441; Lindow, *Hand-*

book of Norse Mythology, 77; Oehlenschläger, Gods of the North, xxxv

Beylgja (BELG-ya)

Variations: BYLGJA

An ASYNJR from Norse mythology, Beylgja ("billow") was one of the WAVE MAIDENS compiled by Snorri Sturluson (1179–1241), the Icelandic historian, poet, and politician, who were mother to the god Heimdall; she was the daughter of the god of the sea, Aegir. She, like her sisters, was said to have snow-white skin, blue eyes, and billowing blond hair; in one hand they carried a golden goblet filled with mead and in the other seashells filled with the finest foods. They wore long transparent robes of green or blue trimmed in white. When not serving food in the hall, they played on the shore in groups of three.

Source: Grimes, Norse Myths, 122, 253, 258; Rydberg, Our Fathers' Godsaga, 194

Bi-Blouk

Folktale of the Khoikhoi people of south Africa tell of the bi-blouk, a dangerous female creature; it is described as having only one half of a human body—one arm and leg and one half of a head with one eye and half a nose and mouth. The bi-blouk is a cannibal and hunts for its prey by jumping and leaping with its extremely powerful leg. The male version of this creature is called HAI-URI.

Source: Knudsen, Fantastical Creatures and Magical Beasts, 28

Bidadari

Variations: Jayadeva

A type of NYMPH from Javanese mythology, a bidadari is a beautiful creature with magical knowledge; in stories involving a bidadari they have been known to rescue the hero of the story and even to marry him.

In one story of a bidadari several are bathing in a pool when the hero Jaka Tarub sees them; he steals the winged garment of one of the bidadari, Nawangwulan, to fly away with the others. The two marry and have a daughter they name Nawangshi. Each day the bidadari is able to magically feed her family by placing only a single grain of rice into the pot but is only able to do this on the condition her husband never takes a peek inside of it. Naturally, the day comes when the husband looks into the pot and the magic is lost. Nawangwulan then looks for and finds her hidden winged clothing and flies off, abandoning her family.

Source: Leeming, Dictionary of Asian Mythology, 89–90

Bifurr (BIV-ur)

Variations: Bifur, Bivor

In Norse mythology, Bifurr ("quaking one") was one of the many named DVERG (DWARFS) who, along with BAFURR, BOMBOR, DAIN, NAIN, NAR, NIPING, NORI, and "hundreds of others," worked together to create the fetter Gleipnir to bind Fenrir.

Source: Crossley-Holland, Norse Myths, 35; Grimes, Norse Mythology, 7, 258; Norroena Society, Asatrii Edda, 337

Bildr (BEELD-r)

In Norse mythology, Bildr ("plowman") was one of the many named DVERGAR (DWARFS) about whom, beyond a name, there is little to nothing else known.

Source: Norroena Society, Asatrii Edda, 337

Bildur

Variations: Bíldur

A rock DVERG (DWARF) from Norse mythology created by DURINN, Bildur is listed as being one of DURINN's KIN. He like the others created paid particular attention to DURINN's leadership.

Source: Auden, Norse Poems, 247; Grimes, Norse Myths, 258

Billingr

Variations: Billing

A DVERG (DWARF) in Norse mythology, Billingr ("twin") was one of the many DWARFs named in the Voluspa, the first and best known poem of the Poetic Edda, a collection of Old Norse poems dating back to about AD 985.

As Billing, he is the father of a young woman who caught the attention of the god Odin but was thwarted before he could seduce or rape her. "Billing's girl," as she is known in the poem Hávamál, is notable because she is one of the very few female dwarfs mentioned. He is also listed as one of DURINN's KIN, created by the DWARF Durinn; he was said to have paid particular attention to DURINN's leadership.

Source: Lindow, Norse Mythology, 79; McKinnell, Meeting the Other in Norse Myth and Legend, 168; Wilkinson, Book of Edda called Völuspá, 12

Binaye Ahani

Variations: Ahani, Binaye Albani

In the folklore of the Navajo people of the United States of America, the binaye ahani ("the people who slay with their eyes") were one of the ANAYE, the four races of gigantic and monstrous supernatural beings causing fear, misery, and wickedness throughout the world. Binaye ahani are described as being limbless twins conjoined at the torso, full of hate, and related to the feathered TSANAHALE and the headless THELGETH; these creatures are similar to the HARPIES of Greek mythology.

Source: Cotterell, *Dictionary of World Mythology*, 220; Dixon-Kennedy, *Native American Myth and Legend*, 23; Rose, *Giants, Monsters, and Dragons*, 49; Zell-Ravenheart, *Wizard's Bestiary*, 15

Bird Man

A creature in Japanese folklore and mythology, bird man is described as being humanoid with a bird shaped head, a beak and cock's comb, human ears, wattles, and human hands on the tips of its wings. It dresses in traditional Japanese clothing.

Source: Rose, *Giants, Monsters, and Dragons*, 49

Birsha (Buhr-shuh)

The biblical king of the city of Gomorrah, Birsha ("evil-doer" or "large man"), a GIANT, fought a war against the king of Elam and conqueror of Canaan, Chedorlaomer.

Originally a vassal of King Chedorlaomer, after twelve years rebelled and joining four other kings met with their armies in the valley of Siddim. During the battle Birsha and King Bera of the city of Sodom fled and each fell into a pit of tar, presumably dying.

Source: DeLoach, *Giants*, 27; Jackson, *Mystical Bible*, 492; Mandel, *Ultimate Who's Who in the Bible*, 102

Bisimbi Bi Masa

The bisimbi bi masa are a species of water NYMPH from African mythology.

Source: Knappert, *African Mythology*, 181

Bixhimin

Bixhimin ("something or other") is a dwarflike figure from Albanian folklore.

Source: Elsie, *Dictionary of Albanian Religion, Mythology, and Folk Culture*, 40

Bjorgolfr (BYURHG-ohlv-r)

In Norse mythology, Bjorgolfr ("mountain-wolf") was one of the many named Jotnar (see JOTUN) about whom, beyond a name, there is little to nothing else known.

Source: Norroena Society, *Asatrii Edda*, 338

Black Annis

Variations: Black Agnes

Black Annis is a blue-faced HAG who was well known in the Dane Hills region near Leicester, England. Described as having long claws and yellow fangs, this powerful fairy lives in a cave called by locals Black Annis' Bower. Folklore has it she made the cave herself by hewing out the stone with her own talon-tipped fingers. Her antithesis is a being named GENTLE ANNIS. Black Annis catches children and lambs who linger in the Dane Hills near twilight, removing the skin from their bodies, devouring their flesh and scattering their bones over the land.

As late as the eighteenth century, on Easter Monday, a dead cat soaked in aniseed was dragged past the opening of Black Annis' Bower with a pack of hunting hounds in pursuit. It was hoped she would follow suit and be exposed to purifying sunlight. In modern times she is considered to be little more than a NURSERY BOGIE although she is associated with sightings of monstrous cats and Alien Big Cats.

Source: Briggs, *Encyclopedia of Fairies*, 24; Monaghan, *Encyclopedia of Goddesses and Heroines*, 335; Rose, *Spirits, Fairies, Leprechauns, and Goblins*, 41

Black Tamanous (tah-mah-no-us)

Variations: Dzunkwa, Tsonokwa, Tsonoqoa

A cannibalistic monster from the mythology of the Pacific Northwest Indians of North America, the terrifying Black Tamanous ("black spirit") would hunt for humans in the wilderness. When the Great Transformer cleansed the earth of all the evil GIANTS he somehow managed to miss Black Tamanous, leaving him to continue to plague the people.

Source: Rose, *Giants, Monsters, and Dragons*, 51; Underhill, *Indians of the Pacific Northwest*, 189

Blainn (BLAH-in)

In Norse mythology, Blainn ("dark-hued") was one of the many named DVERGAR (DWARFS) about whom, beyond a name, there is little to nothing else known.

Source: Grimes, *Norse Mythology*, 4; Norroena Society, *Asatrii Edda*, 338

Blappvari (BLAP-thvar-i)

In Norse mythology, Blappvari ("chattering weapon") was one of the many named Jotnar (see JOTUN) about whom, beyond a name, there is little to nothing else known.

Source: Norroena Society, *Asatrii Edda*, 338

Blapthvari

In Norse mythology Blapthvari ("smiter") was one of the many named Jotnar (see JOTUN) named in the *Asatrii Edda*. Beyond a name, there is little to nothing else known.

Source: Norroena Society, *Asatrii Edda*, 25

Blemmyae

According to Pliny the Elder as well and many medieval bestiaries, Blemmyae country is home of the cannibalistic Blemmyae, a race of people who have no heads, their face being located upon their chest. They subsist on a diet of human flesh. Few people travel through this region of Africa near Ethiopia and Namibia.

Source: Manguel, *Dictionary of Imaginary Places*, 83; Pliny the Elder, *Natural History of Pliny*, Volume 1, 405; Sprague de Camp, *Lands Beyond*, 221–22

Blodughadda (BLOHIH-ug-had-a)

An ASYNJR from Norse mythology, Blodughadda ("bloody hair") was one of the WAVE MAIDENS who were mother to the god Heimdall; she was the daughter of the god of the sea, Aegir. She, like her sisters, was said to have snow-white skin, blue eyes, and billowing blond hair; in one hand they carried a golden goblet filled with mead and in the other seashells filled with the finest foods. They wore long transparent robes of green or blue trimmed in white. When not serving food in the hall, they played on the shore in groups of three.

Source: Grimes, *Norse Myths*, 122, 253; Sturluson, *Prose Edda*, Volume 5, 219

Blunderbore

Variations: Blunderboar, Blunderbus, Blunderbuss, Thunderbore

A GIANT in Cornish and British folklore, Blunderbore is most often recognized as the obstacle character in the popular *Jack the Giant Killer* and *Tom the Tinkeard* (or *Tom the Tinkard*) stories or "Tom Hickathrift" as he is known in England.

Source: Daniels, *Encyclopædia of Superstitions, Folklore, and the Occult Sciences of the World*, 1375–8; Matthews, *History of the Parishes of St. Ives*, 380–81

Boginki (Bow-gin-key)

A vampiric NYMPH-like demon from Polish mythology, the boginki ("little princess") lives near riverbanks; they were said to have been created by the original deities of life who preyed upon the sky gods. Boginki attack mothers with newborn babies, stealing the children to eat and replacing them with a type of evil CHANGELING called an ODMIENCE ("the changed one"). Making regular ritualistic sacrifices to these creatures will prevent them from attacking.

Source: Georgieva, *Bulgarian Mythology*, 103; Icon Group International, *Sacrificing*, 232; Leary, *Wisconsin Folklore*, 445; Ostling, *Between the Devil and the Host*, 203; Thomas, *Polish Peasant in Europe and America*, 238

Boitatá

Variations: Baetatá, Boi-tata, Boi-tatá

In Brazilian mythology there are two creatures with the name boitatá ("fatuous fire" or "fire thing"), but they are very different from one another.

In one version of the myth the boitatá is the manifestation of an evil soul with the ability to assume the form of a monster capable of walking upright; its head is bull-like, its eyes glow red and its nostrils flare with fire. The boitatá is said to hunt and eat humans.

The other boitatá is created when a person who has made a deal with the devil then tries to cheat his way out of its near death; he is transformed into a fiery snake for all eternity. This creature preys nocturnally only upon animals with one eye by draining them of their life force to feed its own; it only hunts at night as it is blind during the daylight hours. Sometimes the boitatá is said to appear as a glowing ball of light similar to a will-o'-the-wisp.

Source: Blayer, *Latin American Narratives and Cultural Identity*, 6; Maberry, *Vampire Universe*, 48–49; Redfern, *Most Mysterious Places on Earth*, 91

Bokwus

Bokwus ("WILD MAN of the woods") is a nature spirit found in the folklore of the Kwakiutl people of Native Americans of northwest America. Described as a skeletal being and wearing fearsome war paint, it uses the sound of rushing water to mask its movement through the spruce wood forest, then, sneaking up on an unsuspecting fisherman it pushes him in the water and tries to drown him. If he succeeds, Bokwus captures his soul. If ever Bokwus offers a person a piece of dried salmon they should not accept it, as in truth it is a piece of dried tree bark; if it is eaten, it will transform the person into a ghost under his control.

Source: Avant, *Mythological Reference*, 497; Eason, *Complete Guide to Faeries and Magical Being*, 197; Ingpen, *Ghouls and Monsters*, 43

Bolay

Variations: Boley

A GIANT from Indian mythology, Bolay was said to have conquered Earth, Heaven, and Hell.

Source: Brewer, *Wordsworth Dictionary of Phrase and Fable*, 103

Bolster

A GIANT from British folklore, Bolster was exceedingly large, as it was said he could stand with one foot on Saint Agnes' Beacon and the other on Carn Brea, six miles apart. There are a great number of ancient earthworks in the region which in some part are named after him. Tyrannical by nature, Bolster had a wife whom he tormented; whenever he was inclined he would compel her to gather up stones and carry them in her apron to the top of Saint Agnes' Beacon; there to this day are grouped masses of small stones. Other evidence of her fruitless labor is that the surrounding area is surprisingly free of stones in its fields.

Bolster, in spite of the fact he was married, was in love with Saint Agnes; he would follow her around and profess his love to her. Saint Agnes, a singular beauty and the very model of womanly virtue, was not only uninterested in his love or his attention but did everything in her power to dissuade this attention. Unable to be rid of the GIANT by act, prayer, or word, she resolved to take drastic measures. Saint Agnes asked Bolster to prove his love to her by filling a small hole in the cliff face at the valley base near Chapel Porth with his blood. Confident he would succeed, Bolster cut his wrist deeply and bled into the hole; soon he began to feel weak and then fell to one knee. Before he could rise to his feet and bind the wound, Bolster passed out. Lying upon the ground and still bleeding into the hole, the GIANT died. Unbeknownst to Bolster the hole, albeit small at its opening, opened up into the ocean below.

Source: Bottrell, *Traditions and Hearthside Stories of West Cornwall*, 47–8; Hunt, *Popular Romances of the West of England*, 73–5

Bolthorn

Variations: Bölthor, Bölthorn

A FROST GIANT of Norse mythology, Bolthorn ("evil thorn") was the father of the wise JOTUN MIMIR and the grandfather of Odin, Vili, and Ve, the ancestors of the Aesir. His daughter BESTLA was the wife of the god Bor (BURI). In the *Hávamál*, a single poem in the *Poetic Edda*, Bolthorn is also the father of the nameless JOTUN who taught Odin the nine magical songs or charms as well as protected a sacred well.

Source: Anderson, *Norse Mythology*, 441; Coulter, *Encyclopedia of Ancient Deities*, 104; Rydberg, *Teutonic Mythology*, 224

Bombor (BUHM-bur)

Variations: Bomburr

A DVERG (DWARF) from Norse mythology, Bombor ("drummer") is named in the *Voluspa* part of the *Poetic Edda*. He, along with BAFURR, BIFURR, DAIN, NAIN, NAR, NIPING, NORI, and "hundreds of others," worked together to create the fetter Gleipnir to bind Fenrir.

Source: Crossley-Holland, *Norse Myths*, 35; Daly, *Norse Mythology A to Z*, 22; Norroena Society, *Asatrii Edda*, 338

Bonito Maidens

The MERMAIDS of the Melanesian people of southeastern Solomon Islands, the bonito maidens are the protectors and guardians of the sacred bonito fish. These fish will seek out the bonito maidens in the deep waters so they may remove the hooks from their mouth, having escaped the fisherman's line. Bonito maidens are seldom seen but exceedingly beautiful, adorned with the jewels of the ocean, ivory, pearls, and shells.

Source: Knight, *Goth Magick*, 132; Oliver, *Oceania*, 683

Boomasoh

Similar to the HAMADRYADS of classical Greek mythology, the boomasoh are tree spirits or NAT from Burmese folklore. They live in the roots of the trees.

Source: Porteous, *Forest in Folklore and Mythology*, 125; Scott, *Burman: His Life and Notions*, Volume 1, 286

Boraro

Humanoid monsters in Tukano mythology in the Amazon, the boraro ("white ones") are hairy-chested, pallid, tall beings with backward facing feet, an enormous phallus, glowing red eyes, protruding ears, and no knees. They also have a powerful sounding jaguar-like roar. These cannibals use stone weapons when hunting and tracking unwary humans. To subdue its prey the boraro will urinate on them or beat them severely with its stone weapon; once the person is incapacitated, it will suck out the person's insides through a hole it chews in the top of the victim's head.

Source: Rose, *Giants, Monsters, and Dragons*, 56; Smith, *Enchanted Amazon Rain Forest*, 55

Borbytingarna

Variations: TROLL

In Norse mythology and Scandinavian folklore the borbytingarna was once believed to be a regional species of OGRE or TROLL roaming the forests and mountains and living in caves and fissures. In more modern times, this regional name is all but forgotten.

Source: Rose, *Giants, Monsters, and Dragons*, 56; Warner, *Monsters of Our Own Making* 25

Bouda

Variations: Buda, Bultungin ("I turn into a hyena")

Created through magic, the bouda of Ethiopian, Moroccan, and Tanzanian folklore is a sorcerer who, through a magical talisman, has the ability of therianthropy, enabling it to shape-shift into a hyena; should he ever lose this charm the man will be permanently changed into the animal, lose all of its humanity, and become particularly fierce. Any means which would kill a human or hyena will kill a bouda.

Source: Fanthorpe, *Mysteries and Secrets of Voodoo, Santeria, and Obeah*, 68; Maberry, *Vampire Universe*, 51; Steiger, *Werewolf Book*, 146–7

Bouders

Variations: Boudons

A tribe of evil DJINN and GIANTS from Indian mythology, the Bouders are the guardians of the god Shiva.

Source: Brewer, *Dictionary of Phrase and Fable*, 167; Wildridge, *Grotesque in Church Art*, 66

Brandingi (BRAND-ing-i)

One of the JOTUN from Norse mythology, Brandingi ("burner") was, along with EIMNIR, ELDR, and LOGI, the personification of fire.

Source: Norroena Society, *Asatrii Edda*, 339; Taunton, *Northern Traditions*, 31

Briareos (bree-AH-rooss)

Variations: Ægeon, Aegaeon ("sea goat"), Aigaion, Briareus, Briareus the Vigorous, Ombriareos

A GIGANTE in ancient Greek mythology, Briareos ("he is enormously powerful" or "mighty one") as he was known to the gods, was born one of the three sons of the TITAN Uranus ("heaven") and the Earth, Gaea; the mortal world knew him as Aigaion. He, along with his brothers COTTOS and GYGES, was said to have fifty heads and one hundred arms, and collectively they would eventually become known as the HECATONCHEIRES. The brothers with their unimaginable strength were important allies to the god Zeus (Jupiter) in his war against the TITANS; after winning the war the brothers were sent to Tartarus to be the guards of the defeated TITANS.

Braiareos was married to Kymopoleia ("wave walker"), the daughter of the god Poseidon (Neptune); together, they lived in the sea. Once he was summoned to Olympus by the NYMPH Thetis to assist Zeus (Jupiter) in the revolt being thrown against him by the gods Athena (Minerva), Hera (Juno), and Poseidon (Neptune). Once, at a contest in Corinth he acted as an arbitrator, awarding the isthmus to his father-in-law but the acropolis of the city to the god of the sun, second generation TITAN HELIOS (Sol).

François Rabelais (AD 1494–1553) compiled the lineage of the GIANTS. A descendant of GOLIAH, Braiareos was the father of PORPHYRIA who *"begot* ADAMASTOR; *who begot* ANTEUS; *who begot* AGATHO; *who begot* PORUS, *against whom Alexander the Great fought; who begot* ARANTHAS, *who begot* GABBARA, *who invented drinking to one's health; and from his descendants begot* GRANGOUSIER; *who begot* GARGANTUAN; *who begot* PANTAGRUEL."

Source: Brewer, *Character Sketches of Romance, Fiction and the Drama*, Volume 3, 80; Daniels, *Encyclopædia of Superstitions, Folklore, and the Occult Sciences of the World*, 1376;

Hard, *Routledge Handbook of Greek Mythology*, 66–7, 103; Rabelais, *Hours with Rabelais*, 80

Brontes

From classical Greek mythology, Brontes ("thunder"), ARGES ("flashing" or "thunderbolt"), and STEROPES ("lightning") are the three elder CYCLOPS, born the sons of the TITAN Uranus ("heaven") and the Earth, Gaea. He and his brothers were all born with a single eye in the middle of their forehead and were exceedingly strong. Brontes was the personification of the blacksmith. Their siblings were the HECATONCHEIRES and the TITANS. After the rise of the Olympian gods, Brontes and his brothers were slain by the god Apollo because they created the thunderbolt which killed his son, Asclepius.

Source: Daly, *Greek and Roman Mythology, A to Z*, 39–40; Daniels, *Encyclopædia of Superstitions, Folklore, and the Occult Sciences of the World*, 1375–8

Brown Man of the Muirs

Variations: Brown Man of the Moors, Brown Man of the Moors and Mountains

The Brown Man of the Muirs is a square and stout DWARF with red hair wearing clothes made of bracken; he is a nature spirit and a guardian spirit of the animals living in the border country of Scotland. A strict vegetarian surviving solely on apples, nuts, and whortleberries, this fairy is particularly injurious to those who hunt for sport and not for food. There are many stories of this SOLITARY fairy enacting his own brand of justice on greedy sportsmen; however according to Skamble's *Fairy Tales*, an angered Brown Man may be appeased and calmed by chanting the phrase "Munko tiggle snobart tolwol dixy crambo"; afterward, the red-eyed DWARF will not only be civil but courteous and helpful.

Source: Briggs, *Encyclopedia of Fairies*, 44–5; Moorey, *Fairy Bible*, 388; Rose, *Spirits, Fairies, Gnomes, and Goblins*, 51; Skamble, *Fairy Tales*, 152–3

Bruja (Brew-ha)

Variations: Brujavampyre, Bruxa, Bruxae, Bruxas, Cucubuth, Jorguinas, Xorguinae

In Spain there is a living vampiric witch known as a *bruja* ("witch"). By day she is a beautiful woman living an ordinary life, but by night, through the use of her magic, she hunts for children and lonely travelers to attack and drain of blood. The bruja is most powerful between the hours of midnight and 2 a.m. She also regularly meets with others of her kind every Tuesday and Friday at a predetermined crossroad. Once gathered together, they will worship the devil and develop their various evil powers such as use of the evil eye ("*mal occhio*") and by use of therianthropy, shape-shifting into various animals like ants, doves, ducks, geese, and rats.

Before the introduction of Christianity to Portugal, it was believed the bruja could be warded off with iron. Keeping some nails under a child's bed or a pair of scissors in a pocket was protection enough. After the arrival of Christianity, talismans of protection against the evil eye could be purchased. There were various incantations which could be recited as well, but the simplest means of protection was to regularly consume garlic. Some folks even went as far as to sew garlic into their clothes.

Should a child actually survive an attack from a bruja, the mother must boil the infant's clothes and jab them with sharp iron instruments. By doing so, she is actually inflicting harm upon the witch, ensuring the witch will leave her child alone, but the retaliatory assault will not kill her. There is no known method of destruction for a bruja.

There are a few regional bits of folklore which tie the bruja with lycanthropy and the demonic succubus (sexually driven vampiric demons), but this is most likely due to the witch's shape-changing ability and her beauty.

If the witch is a male, then it is called a brujo (or bruxo). Like his female counterpart, he can cause the evil eye but by use of therianthropy shape-shifts into a barn owl, cat, coyote, or turkey. He is also something of a supernatural matchmaker, causing one person to fall madly in love with a seemingly randomly chosen person. Only by having a priest offer up prayers and masses can a victim of a brujo be saved.

Source: Bryant, *Handbook of Death*, 99; Kanellos, *Handbook of Hispanic Cultures*, 228; Ramos, *The Aswang Syncrasy*, 5; Shoumatoff, *Legends of the American Desert*, 234

Brunhilde

Variations: Brunhilt, Brünnehilde, Brynhilde, Brynhild, Brynhilda

In Nordic and Teutonic mythology Brunhilde was one of the named VALKYRIES; she was one of a handful of her kind who were not only named but had adventures apart from her cohorts. In the *Poetic Edda*, Brunhilde is strong-minded and strong willed with super-human abilities; she goes against Odin's will and is punished for it by being placed in a magical sleep and surrounded by a wall of fire. In the story, Brunhilde and the great hero Sigurd exchange oaths of fidelity as well as promise rings. Sigurd is later tricked into drinking a potion which makes him forget Brunhilde and instead he marries GUDRUN. Sigurd shape-shifts into his bride's brother, King Gunnar, and completes difficult quests in order to win the love of Brunhilde in the hope she will want to marry the real Gunnar. Although the shape-shifted Sigurd never had intercourse with Brunhilde she tells Gunnar they did as her anger against Sigurd has overshadowed her love for him. By the time the story ends, Brunhilde is an embittered shrew of a woman but nevertheless, lies atop Sigurd's funeral pyre in an attempt to unite within the grave.

Source: Doty, *Mythosphere: Issue 4*, 529–30; Rose, *Spirits, Fairies, Leprechauns, and Goblins*, 325

Bruni

Variations: Brúni

A rock DVERG (DWARF) from Norse mythology created by DURINN, Bruni ("brown") is listed as being one of DURINN's KIN. He like the others created paid particular attention to DURINN's leadership. Bruni appears in the *Voluspa*, the first and best known poem of the *Poetic Edda* (AD 985).

Source: Auden, *Norse Poems*, 247; Daly, *Norse Mythology A to Z*, 22; Grimes, *Norse Myths*, 260; Wilkinson, *Book of Edda called Völuspá*, 12

Buarainech

In Irish mythology Buarainech ("bull faced man") was the father of the king of the FORMORIAN Balor.

Source: Skyes, *Who's Who in Non-Classical Mythology*, 29; Squire, *Celtic Myths and Legend Poetry and Romance*, 48

Bungisngis

In Filipino folklore Bungisngis ("showing his teeth") is a club wielding GIANT with acute hearing as well as a cannibal who will relentlessly track and consume anyone who enters into his territory. He is described as having only one eye and a top lip so large he can wrap it over the top of his head and use it like a hat. He is always smirking and has boarlike tusks protruding out of either side of his mouth. The grip of Bungisngis is unbreakable due to his limitless strength; anyone who is grabbed by him will soon become a meal. The cultural hero Suac stole Bungisngis's mighty club and, using it for himself, fought the enemies of his people.

Source: Ramos, *Creatures of Midnight*, 59; Rose, *Giants, Monsters, and Dragons*, 61

Buri

Variations: Bori, Bur, Bure

In Norse mythology, Buri ("son") existed at the time of the creation and came to life when AUDHUMLA, the cosmic cow, brought him to life. He had a son named Bor who went on to marry the ASYNJR BESTLA and together they fathered the gods Odin,

Vili and Ve. In the war against the FROST GIANTS Buri and his sons defeated YMIR and all of the FROST GIANTS except for BERGELMIR.

Buri is also the name of a DVERG (DWARF) created by DURINN; Buri is listed as being one of DURINN's KIN. He like the others created paid particular attention to DURINN's leadership.

Source: Coulter, *Encyclopedia of Ancient Deities*, 82, 98; Daly, *Norse Mythology A to Z*, 12; Grimes, *Norse Myths*, 260; Oehlenschläger, *Gods of the North*, xxxvi

Buringcantada

In Filipino folklore Buringcantada is a GIANT and a CYCLOPES; he is described as having a single eye in the middle of his forehead and long tusks which protrude out from either side of his mouth. Malevolent and cruel, treasure hoarding Buringcantada is not very intelligent and is easily outsmarted.

Source: Fansler, *Filipino Popular Tales*, Volume 12, 46–7; Ramos, *Creatures of Philippine Lower Mythology*, 84

Burryman

Variations: Birleyman, Brugh-Law-Man, Burghman, Burry Man

An ancient, mythical, and traditional figure in Scottish folklore, the Burryman dates back some seven hundred years to the last Battle of Falkirk. Although the true purpose and origin of the Burryman has been lost to antiquity the practice of the tradition is still carried out to this day. Each year in South Queensferry, Scotland, a local man who is also a native born resident is selected to act as the nature spirit. He collects by hand hundreds of boughs of flannel and burdock burs (*Aretium cardana*) and sews them onto a suit covering his entire body. On August 3 the Burryman then walks the seven mile boundary of the town followed by others who are dressed in costumes as they make merry and collect money. It has been speculated the Burryman is acting as some sort of SCAPEGOAT, letting the sins of the town stick to him as he walks through. Another theory says the Burryman is related to an ancient custom having to do with fishing and a means of collecting all the lingering bad luck to ensure a good herring season.

Source: Hallen, *Scottish Antiquary*, Volumes 13–14, 109; Varner, *Mythic Forest*, 108–09

Busaw

A cannibal from the folklore of the Bagobos, Bukidnons, and Mandayas people of the Philippines, the busaw looks like a human by day, even keeping a farm and raising animals; however, at night it takes on an OGRE-like appearance and goes hunting for human flesh. It is described as having hooked claws, a long tongue, and pointed teeth; some versions of the tale say the females of the species have only one eye centered CYCLOPS-like in the center of their forehead. This monster is said to live in trees near cemeteries, in caves or in isolated farms in the wilderness. The busaw is usually a carrion eater, preferring to steal human corpses from cemeteries rather than hunting for live prey. To keep it from exhuming the deceased the bodies are washed with vinegar and interred with strong smelling herbs and salt. There are also wide arrays of amulets, charms, medicines, and rituals which can be purchased to keep the busaw away.

Source: Ramos, *Creatures of Midnight*, 75; West, *Encyclopedia of the Peoples of Asia and Oceania*, 811

Buschfrauen

Variations: Buschweiber ("wild maidens"), Dziwozony, Moosfraulein (Moss-damsels)

The German NYMPH–like nature spirits known as the buschfrauen ("bush women") live communally in the hollows of trees but they only appear alone. Standing a little taller than a DWARF, they have golden hair and are most likely to be seen when bread is baking. The white-haired and mossy-footed fairy Queen of the buschfrauen is named Buschgrossmutter ("grandmother of the bushes"); she is both respected and feared.

Source: Elliott, *Modern Language Notes*, Volume 16, 65; Monaghan, *New Book of Goddesses and Heroines*, 76

Buto

In Javanese folklore buto ("giant") is a GIANT or TROLL-like creature with a voracious appetite; there are three species of buto in Javanese folklore: BUTO CAKIL ("fanged GIANT") is symbolic of rage, BUTO IJO ("green GIANT") is symbolic of corruption and thievery, and BUTO KALA ("time GIANT") is symbolic of lust.

Source: Torchia, *Indonesian Idioms and Expressions*, 51–3

Buto Cakil

In Javanese folklore Buto Cakil ("fanged GIANT") is symbolic of rage and is depicted as having two large teeth protruding from its bottom jaw. In most stories involving this species of GIANT it is confronted by a knight who ultimately defeats it.

Source: Torchia, *Indonesian Idioms and Expressions*, 53

Buto Ijo

In Javanese folklore Buto Ijo ("Green Giant") is symbolic of corruption and thievery; he is the villain in the tale *Timun Mas*. In the story Buto Ijo gives a magical cucumber to an elderly couple, telling them if its seeds are planted it will yield them a child, but the gift is conditional. If the couple accepts, they must then allow the GIANT to consume the child on her seventeenth birthday. The lonely old couple agree and following the GIANT's directions plant the seeds and soon find themselves the parents of a beautiful baby girl they name Timun Mas. True to his word Buto Cakil returns when the girl is of age, but the parents have prepared a bag of magical tricks for her to employ during her escape from the GIANT. Eventually, she is able to defeat and kill Buto Cakil and return home to her parents.

Source: Torchia, *Indonesian Idioms and Expressions*, 51–2

Buto Kala

In Javanese folklore Buto Kala ("time giant") is representational for lust. In one story he overheard the gods talking about *amerta*, the Elixir of Immortality, and desired to have some for himself. By use of a disguise he was able to steal a drink when the gods gathered to enjoy some for themselves. Angered, they cut off his head, but Buto Kala had fallen in love with the goddess of the moon, Dewi Ratih, and insisted on having her. She refused his advances so the GIANT grabbed her and swallowed her up whole; fortunately she was able to escape through his decapitated neck. Buto Kala would not give up and chased the goddess. Javanese folklore says whenever there is a lunar eclipse Buto Kala has caught and consumed Dewi Ratih, but they know her imprisonment will not be for long.

Source: Torchia, *Indonesian Idioms and Expressions*, 51–2

Byleistr (BEE-layst-r)

Variations: Byleist ("wind lightning from the East")

The lesser known brother of the trickster god Loki from Norse mythology, Byleistr ("lame"), his parents FARBANTI and LAUFEY, and other brother HELBLINDI, are Jotnar (see JOTUN) and not divine entities. Other than his name, there is no other surviving information of this being.

Source: Daly, *Norse Mythology A to Z*, 14–15; Norroena Society, *Asatrii Edda*, 25; Rooth, *Loki in Scandinavian Mythology*, 170

Bylgja (BELG-ya)

An ASYNJR from Norse mythology, Bylgja ("billow") was one of the WAVE MAIDENS who were mother to the god Heimdall; she was the daughter of the god of the sea, Aegir. She, like her sisters, was said to have snow-white skin, blue eyes, and billowing blond hair; in one hand they carried a golden goblet filled with mead and in the other seashells filled with the finest foods. They wore long transparent robes of green or blue trimmed in white. When not serving food in the hall, they played on the shore in groups of three.

Source: Grimes, *Norse Myths*, 122, 253; Sturluson, *Prose Edda*, Volume 5, 219

The Caberi

Variations: Cabeiri, Caheiri, Cahiri, Kabeiroi, Kabris

The Caberi of Samothrace was the collective name for the children born of the god Zeus (Jupiter) and the NYMPH Calliope of ancient Greek mythology; in some parts of the ancient world they were interchangeable with the CYCLOPES.

Source: Coulter, *Encyclopedia of Ancient Deities*, 111

Cabezudo, plural cabezudos

In Catalan, Spain, the cabezudos ("big heads") are a type of GIANT described as having bulbous piercing eyes, overly large heads, and clothing reminiscent of the seventeenth or eighteenth century. Effigies of these town GIANTS are made and marched about in parades during festivals.

Source: Rose, *Giants, Monsters, and Dragons*, 63

Cabrakan

Variations: Kab'raqan

Born the son of the Mayan GIANTS and gods VUCUB CAQUIX and his wife CHIMALMAT, arrogant Cabrakan ("earthquake"), the younger brother of ZIPACNA ("one who throws up the earth"), would cause great and powerful earthquakes every day in order to destroy the mountains his brother constructed daily. Because he was so dangerous, the Hero Twins, the cultural heroes of the Mayans, decided he needed to die. They caused the loss of the strength in his arms and legs when they tricked him into eating a bird coated with poisoned earth; he was then buried alive in the ground. Without his great strength Cabrakan was trapped but his ongoing attempts to escape are said to be the cause of earthquakes.

Source: Bingham, *South and Meso-American Mythology A to Z*, 18; Spence, *Popol Vuh*, 12–16

Cacodaemon (kak-oh-DEE-mon)

Variations: Cacodemon, Kakadaimon, Kakodaimon, Kakos Daimon

A Greek word meaning "bad demon" or "bad spirit" which crossed over into the Enochian language sometime in the sixteenth century, cacodaemons were said by some sources to be the fallen angels. Banished from Heaven and unable to find a place of their own to call home, they settled down to live in the space between the earth and the stars. They have been described as being large and powerfully built humanoids with dark-hued skin and also as a swirling black mass.

Cacodaemons are attracted to a particular person at birth; the demon attaches itself to a person and follows them through their life, controlling their impulses and personalities from time to time. They also act as a messenger between their charge and the gods.

Hostile by nature, they take pleasure in acting out revenge and causing injury. Some demonologists placed them under the command of the god Hades (Dis). Inferior demons, they have dominion over the twelfth house of the Zodiac. The opposite of a Cacodaemon is an agathodaemon (AGATHODE-MON) or eudemon.

Source: Hyatt, *Book of Demons*, 60; Russell, *Lucifer, the Devil in the Middle Ages*, 249; Wray, *Birth of Satan*, 25

Cacos

Variations: Cacus, Kakos

A monstrous, fire-breathing GIGANTE and son of the god Hephaistos (Vulcan), Cacos ("evil one") lived in a cave on Aventine Hill. Cacos was, in the classical Greek telling of the Labors of Hercules (Heracles), one of the ten robbers who rustled the Erytheian cattle. The ancient Roman annalist Gnaeus Gellius said Cacos was a lieutenant of the Phrygian Marsyas, an individual identified with the god Pan. Cacos stole the cattle while Hercules was overcome with too much food and wine and hid the herd in his cave. CACA, the sister of the GIGANTES, betrayed her brother to the demigod in return for his love; Hercules favored her and left her with a son, Latinus.

Source: Daniels, *Encyclopædia of Superstitions, Folklore, and the Occult Sciences of the World*, 1375–8; Fontenrose, *Python*, 339, 340; Smith, *Dictionary of Greek and Roman Biography and Mythology*, 523

Cacy Taperere

Variations: SACI, Sasy Perere

In southern Brazilian fairy folklore cacy taperere is a dwarflike spirit; it is described as having fiery eyes and one leg, smoking a pipe, and wearing a red cap. A household fairy similar to the brownie (a species of domestic fairy or HOUSE-SPIRIT from Scottish fairy folklore), when not being helpful the cacy taperere enjoys playing little pranks, such as hiding objects or moving belongings.

Source: Leach, *Funk and Wagnalls Standard Dictionary of Folklore, Mythology, and Legend*, n.pag.; Rose, *Spirits, Fairies, Gnomes, and Goblins*, 58

Calanget

Variations: Caranget, Carango

Tiny dwarflike beings in Filipino folklore, the calanget are said to live in mounds in the fields and woods; it is considered bad luck to dig up these mounds as the calanget are considered to be the true owners of the land and will inflict harm upon anyone who disturbs their home.

Source: Paraiso, *Balete Book*, 63; Ramos, *Creatures of Philippine Lower Mythology*, 401

La Calchona

Variations: Chiludo

A species of WILD MAN from South American folklore, la calchona ("bogey" or "ghost") is described as looking like a large bearded man whose body is covered with sheep-like wool. A nocturnal creature living in the fields and hills of the countryside, it is reported as doing little more than scaring horses and travelers. In Chile the calchona is described as looking like a large wooly dog with a tangled coat; said to live in the mountains where it frightens travelers and their horses, it occasionally steals their food.

Source: Eberhart, *Mysterious Creatures*, 82; Rose, *Giants, Monsters, and Dragons*, 65; Zell-Ravenheart, *Wizard's Bestiary*, 27

Caligorant

A GIANT and a cannibal, Caligorant, an Egyptian by birth, had a magical net he would use to entrap people. The net was made by the Greek god Hephaistos (Vulcan) in order to catch Ares (Mars) and Venus; the god Hermes (Mercury) stole it to capture Chloris and when finished left it in the temple of Anubis where it was taken by Caligorant. Astolpho, one of the fictional paladins of Charlemagne, blew upon his magical horn causing the GIANT to run in fear and in his haste trip himself up in his own net. Once captured, Caligorant was deprived of the magical net and until his conversion to Christianity was used as a beast of burden.

Source: Daniels, *Encyclopædia of Superstitions, Folklore, and the Occult Sciences of the World*, 1375–8; Reddall, *Fact, Fancy, and Fable*, 82

Camenae

Variations: Carmenae, Carmentis, Casmenae, Muses

The collective name for the prophetic NYMPHS of classical Roman mythology who were once worshiped as goddesses, the camenae lived in the freshwater spring which supplied water to Rome, specifically to the temple of the Vestal Virgins; their names were Antevorta, Carmenta (or Carmentis), and Postvorta.

Source: Avant, *Mythological Reference*, 436; Daly, *Greek and Roman Mythology, A to Z*, 31

Canotila (can-oh-tee-la)

Nature spirits of the trees from the Lakota and Sioux mythology, canotila are said to be NYMPH-like creatures which live in the woods and act as messengers.

Source: Brokenleg, *Yanktonai Sioux Water Colors*, 27

Caraculiambo

A GIANT from the Spanish novel *The Ingenious Gentleman Don Quixote of La Mancha* (1605), by Miguel de Cervantes Saavedra, Caraculiambo, the Lord of the island of Malindrama, was expected to kneel at the feet of the peasant woman Dulcinea del Toboso by the book's tragi-comical hero Don Quixote.

Source: Brewer, *Character Sketches of Romance, Fiction and the Drama*, Volumes 5–6, 80; Daniels, *Encyclopædia of Superstitions, Folklore, and the Occult Sciences of the World*, 1376; Saavedra, *History of the Renowned Don Quixote de la Mancha*, 9

Cawr

Variations: Gwyr

In Welsh folklore the Cambrian GIANT Cawr ("Giant"), lived with his family in prehistoric times in a cave upon a hill; as a clan leader he was known to give excellent advice to goat, sheep, and swineherders about their care and protection from wolves. He was driven to increase his holdings, protect his family and servants, and while conducting successful raids against his neighbors to also be able to repel such attacks. Cawr was a peer and rival of the Loegrian GIANT BRAN, who saw him as a tight-fisted, selfish and self-serving tyrant. BRAN challenged Cawr to battle in personal combat; when they met it was a long and brutal battle as both were immensely strong and brutal, but with a mighty blow BRAN knocked Cawr into the Severn Sea where the waters covered him up and pulled him down to his death.

Source: Pughe, *Dictionary of the Welsh Language*, 377; Rowse, *In and Around Swansea*, 14, 96

Ceasg

Variations: Maighdean Mhara ("maid of the sea"), Maighdean na Tuinne ("maid of the wave")

In the Scottish Highlands the ceasg ("tuft") is a MERMAID, having the upper body of a woman and the lower body of a salmon, and injurious by nature. The only way to kill this creature is to discover where it has hidden its soul, usually in an egg or shell, and then destroy it. To see one while out on the sea is considered to be an ill omen. Fishermen would take the chance of confronting this fairy ANIMAL for if they were successful in capturing one it was compelled to grant its captor three wishes. If the fisherman is kind hearted and good looking and can convince the ceasg to live with him, his luck would be perpetual; the ceasg will shape-shift into a beautiful woman and be his wife. There are some Scottish families who claim to be descendants of a male fisherman and a ceasg mother.

Sources: Conway, *Magickal Mermaids and Water Creatures*, 60; Evans-Wentz, *Fairy Faith in Celtic Countries*, 25; Monaghan, *Encyclopedia of Celtic Mythology and Folklore*, 80; Snow, *Incredible Mysteries and Legends of the Sea*, 112

Cecropes

Variations: Athenians

A race of evil people from classical Greek mythology, the Cecropes ("deceitful") were said to have once lived in Lydia. After the heroic demi-god Hercules (Heracles) defeated them, the god Zeus (Jupiter) transformed them all into apes and banished them to live on Pithicusae, the Island of the Apes.

Source: Bower, *Historia Litteraria*, 515; Rzach, *Sibylline Oracles*, 246

Celaeno

Variations: Kelaino ("dark," "like a storm cloud"), Thyella

One of the named harpies from ancient Greek mythology, Celaeno ("storm cloud") was originally a storm or nature spirit associated with the weather and, accordingly, blamed for storms and undesirable winds (see HARPY).

According to the ancient Greek poet Hesiod in his work *Theogony* ("*Theogonia*," circa 700 BC) where he describes the genealogy of the gods, there were only two harpies, AELLO and OCYPETE, the winged daughters of ELECTRA and Thaumas; therein he commented only on how swiftly the sisters could fly. The Roman poet Valerius Flaccus said there were three harpies, adding Celaeno to the list. Homer, the greatest of ancient Greek epic poets, rounded off the list of named harpies with PODARGE.

Source: Bell, *Bell's New Pantheon or Historical Dictionary of the Gods*, 112; Littleton, *Gods, Goddesses, and Mythology*, Volume 10, 611, 614; *London Encyclopaedia*, Volume 11, 53; March, *Penguin Book of Classical Myths*, 37

Cethlenn

Variations: Cethleann, Cethlion, Kehlen

One of the FORMORIANs of Irish mythologies, Cethlenn, a prophetess, was the wife of Balor of the Mighty Blows, and together they were the parents of Ethniu. It was she who delivered the fatal blow to Dagda, the king of the TUATHA DE DANANNs.

Source: Avant, *Mythological Reference*, 507; Joyce, *Origin and History of Irish Names of Places*, Volume 1, 156

Ceto

Variations: Keto

Born one of the 3,000 daughters of the TITANS OCEANUS and TETHYS, Ceto ("whale") was one of the named OCEANIDS in classical Greek mythology; Ceto was also the name of one of the children of Gaea and the ancient god of the sea, Pontus. By her brother, a god of the sea, PHORCYS, she begot the GORGO GRAEAE, the Hesperian dragon, and the Heaprides; because of this the word *ceto* came to refer to any sort of SEA SERPENT.

Sources: Day, *God's Conflict with the Dragon and the Sea*, 388; Daly, *Greek and Roman Mythology, A to Z*; 34; Smith, *New Classical Dictionary of Biography, Mythology, and Geography*, 571; Trzaskoma, *Anthology of Classical Myth*, 18

Chahnameed

A GIANT from Pequot tribal folklore, Chahnameed ("one who eats to excess") was a renowned glutton; it was said he lived in a house upon an island in a cove near Massapeag, Connecticut, United States of America, where he owned two canoes. He had a beautiful Mohegan wife (unnamed) who knew magic. Chahnameed was accustomed to being alone and would be gone for long periods of time. Deciding to leave her husband the wife made her escape using one of the canoes but Chahnameed, in the other, gave chase. By use of her magic she was able to keep ahead of him for a little while but eventually knew if she was ever to make it to the shore she would have to kill him. She plucked a hair from the top of her head and held it straight, making it hard and stiff and into a weapon and throwing the nearly invisible spear. Chahnameed did not see the attack coming at him; he was struck directly in the middle of his forehead and fell dead into the water.

Source: Fawcett, *Medicine Trail*, 48–50; Speck, *Journal of American Folklore*, Volume 7, 104–07

Chalbroth

François Rabelais (AD 1494–1553) compiled the lineage of the GIANTS. He listed Chalbroth as the progenitor of the race and the lineage as follows:

"*Chalbroth who begot* SARABROTH; *who begot* FARIBROTH; *who begot* HURTALI, *a brave eater of pottage (soup) who lived in the time of the Flood; who begot* NEMBROTH; *who begot* ATLAS, *who with his shoulders keeps the sky from falling; who begot* GOLIAH; *and from his descendants begot* BRIAREOS, *who had a hundred hands; who begot* PORPHYRIA; *who begot* ADAMASTOR; *who begot* ANTEUS; *who begot* AGATHO; *who begot* PORUS, *against whom Alexander the Great fought; who begot* ARANTHAS, *who begot* GABBARA, *who invented drinking to one's health; and from his descendants begot* GRANGOUSIER; *who begot* GARGANTUAN; *who begot* PANTAGRUEL."

Source: Brewer, *Character Sketches of Romance, Fiction and the Drama*, Volume 3, 80; Daniels, *Encyclopædia of Superstitions, Folklore, and the Occult Sciences of the World*, 1376; Rabelais, *Hours with Rabelais*, 80

Chaneque (chah-neh-keh)

Variations: Chanekos, Chanques

Dwarflike beings with the face of a young child, the chaneque of Aztec mythology had a reputation for chasing women and generally bothering people. These little poltergeist-like beings live in waterfalls and cause illness and dominate fish and wild animals. The chaneque were known to eat human brains and had the ability to cause illness and foresee the rain. In order to appease these beings people would throw buckets of water into the air, as it was considered to be their "magic food." Chaneque would carry a cane with them presumably used to break up the clouds.

Source: Bernal, *Olmec World*, 100–01; Maberry, *Cryptopedia*, 231; Varner, *Mysteries of Native American Myth and Religion*, 137–38

Changeling

Variations: Callicanzaris, Changeling Child ("plentyn newid"), Crimbil, Gremlin, Hosentefel, Kontsodaimonas, Leurre, Sibhreach

A changeling is, in brief, the being left behind by a fairy when it steals a human child; this being looks at best like a sickly version of the stolen child. Only a child who has not been christened can be taken. In some traditions, a log rather than a changeling is left behind to punish the mother. The changeling is believed to be the deformed child of a DWARF or ELF, a senile, or old and withered FAIRY.

The reason for stealing human babies and replacing them with a fairy changeling are numerous; some sources claim this is done because the fairies are a real race of hidden people who need to replenish their bloodlines due to years of their own inbreeding. Other possible explanations include taking a human child to deliver to the Tithe, a seven year tribute paid to the Devil; fairies see human babies as wonderfully beautiful and desire to have one, be it as a lover, plaything, or slave. Changeling folklore may have originated to explain why a child is born with a physical or mental defect. This belief exists in the mythology and folklore of China, France, Germany, Great Britain, Greece, Ireland, the Native Americans, Scotland, and the Scandinavian countries.

Common to the changeling fairy folklore is a means by which the being can be exposed for what it is and a method for the return of the human child. To expose a changeling may be as simple as making it laugh or doing something so amazing it shocks the fairy into leaving of its own accord, but usually the process involves some sort of torture. Common methods employed to expose a changeling in folklore include abandoning it on a hillside, bathing it in scalding water, chasing after it with a red-hot poker, dropping it into a racing river, dumping it in a dung heap, dunking it into a well, forcing foxglove tea down its throat and waiting for it to immolate, placing it in a pot over a roaring fire, stabbing the suspected babe with a knife, threatening it with a sword, or tossing it into a chimney fire. There are many reports of women killing infants by trying to drive out the changeling and have their own child returned to them. For example, in 1826 a woman was acquitted of the murder of her son by drowning because she was trying to compel the changeling to leave.

In Great Britain, changelings are described as looking like a baby having some sort of physical deformity, noticeable intellectual disabilities, an overly large head, and pale skin. They are known to play little tricks, such as breaking sentimental or valuable objects, playing music which forces people to dance against their will, and stealing items when no one is looking.

In some parts of Germany it was believed when a child did not thrive it was a changeling. The fairy being was then taken to Cyriac's Mead, a place near Neuhausen, and was forced to drink from Cyriacc's well. Then, the child was left there unattended for nine days where it would either die from exposure or recover. Jacob Ludwig Carl and Wilhelm Grimm, noted German academics, authors, cultural researchers, and linguists who collected folklore, recorded a story how a woman suspected her child to have been swapped out with a changeling. She had been advised to brew beer in an acorn where the child could watch. The changeling was so amazed at the spectacle it exclaimed *"I am as old as any oak in the wood but never have I seen beer brewed in an acorn"* and then disappeared.

In Ireland, it is sometimes thought left handed people are changelings. Although the belief in the folklore of fairy changelings is older than recorded history as recently as 1894, a woman named Bridget Cleary of Clommel, Ireland, had been accused of being a changeling by her husband and family when she recovered from a case of phenomena. Nine members of her family had been charged with her murder; they burned her to death trying to drive the changeling away. Although they were arrested on murder charges the most severe charge pressed was manslaughter; most other charges of "wounding" were dropped.

In Welsh folklore it is not immediately apparent when a changeling has been placed; only after a period of time does its natural behavior reveal it for what it is by gradually becoming deformed, ill-tempered, ugly, and having fits of uncontrollable biting and crying. In addition to its difficult behavior, the child will also show cunning and wisdom more appropriate to an adult. As a sort of payment for caring for the changeling, the fay will leave some money to be found every day in the same place. So long as the family cares for the changeling and does not reveal the source of the money, they will continued to be paid but if the secret is revealed, the money will cease to appear. To discover if a child has been replaced for a changeling Welsh folklore says to bathe it in foxglove, hold it over an open fire, or place it in a hot oven. Similar to the German idea of brewing beer in an acorn, in Wales it is advised to cook the family's evening meal in an eggshell; this will so confound the fairy it will leave, returning the human child to its family.

In Scandinavian fairy mythology fairies are said to have an extreme aversion to steel, so parents would place a steel item, such as a knife or a pair of scissors, in the bed of an unbaptized child. If the steel deterrent did not work it was believed if the changeling was treated badly the fay would return the human baby; methods employed included whippings and inserting the changeling into a heated oven.

Source: Briggs, *Encyclopedia of Fairies*, 69–74; Evans-Wentz, *Fairy Faith in Celtic Countries*, 58; Keightley *World Guide to Gnomes, Fairies, Elves, and Other Little People*, 227, 418; McCoy, *Witch's Guide to Faery Folk*, 7, 71; Sikes, *British Goblins*, 50–56

Cheeroonear

A race of dog-faced humanoids from Australian folklore, the cheeroonear are described as having arms so long their hands drag along the ground as they walk and a wrinkled dewlap so large it hangs over their distended stomachs. The cheeroonear are known to hunt humans for meat on the arid, flat, and treeless Nullabor Plain, Australia.

Source: Covey, *Beasts*, 34; Rose, *Giants, Monsters, and Dragons*, 77; Zell-Ravenheart, *Wizard's Bestiary*, 30

Chimalmat

A GIANT from Mayan lore, Chimalmat ("netted round shield") was by her husband Vucub Caquix ("seven macaw") the mother of CABRAKAN and ZIPACNA.

Source: Recinos, *Popol Vuh*, 95; Tate, *Reconsidering Olmec Visual Culture*, 224

Chivato

Variations: Encerrados ("captive" or "recluse")

In the mythology of the Araucanian (Mapuchen) people of Chile the chivato ("young goat") is believed to be a monstrous humanoid; once a child this person was kidnapped by witches and over the course of several years was physically transformed into this cannibalistic beast. According to folklore, the chivato was fed by one of the witch's servants, an INVUNCHE or a trelquehuecuve (an octopus-like creature) who captured young girls while they were drawing water. Chivato live in the caverns near the towns of Ancud and Chiloc; there is believed to be a passageway or tunnel on the island lake which goes to the lair of the creatures.

Source: Meurger, *Lake Monster Traditions*, 280–81; Rose, *Giants, Monsters, and Dragons*, 80

Christmas Lads

Variations: Jolasveinar, Yule Lads

A group of GIANTS or TROLLS from Icelandic folklore, the NURSERY BOGIE Christmas Lads (*Jolasveinar*) were the thirteen children born of GRÝLA and her husband LEPPA LUDI. According to the folklore the first brother would leave home thirteen days before Christmas seeking out naughty children to bring home for a Christmas day feast. The Christmas Lads date back as far as the 1600s and were originally every bit as mean and hideous as their parents but over the centuries have become more and more oafish. In the 1920s, Icelandic children began to leave their shoes on windowsills in anticipation of the brothers leaving them filled with candy and treats.

Source: Raedisch, *Old Magic of Christmas*, 91; Simpson, *Icelandic Folktales and Legends*, 90

Christopherus

Variations: Saint Christopher

According to the Christian folklore, Christopherus was a GIANT who once carried Christ across a fjord; the GIANT was borne down by the ever increasing weight of the Son of God.

Source: Brewer, *Character Sketches of Romance, Fiction and the Drama*, Volumes 5–6, 80; Daniels, *Encyclopædia of Superstitions, Folklore, and the Occult Sciences of the World*, 1376

Chronos

Variations: CRONUS

In the Latin narrative poem *Metamorphoses* (2.153) written by the Roman poet Ovid (43 BC– AD 17), the sun god and second generation TITAN, HELIOS (Sol), had his golden chariot, Quadriga, pulled across the sky by the flying horses Aethon, Astrope, Bronte, Chronos, Eous, Lampoon, Phaethon, Phlegon, and Pyrois. All of these horses are described as being pure white and having flaring nostrils which can breathe forth flame.

According to the ancient Greek poet Apollonius of Rhodes, the god Chronos had many extramarital affairs on his wife, RHEA; when caught or when attempting to escape her general anger, he would transform into a horse; one such assignation was with the NYMPH Philyra, who later fathered the scholarly Centaur (a creature from Greek mythology, half equine and half human, entangled with issues of sexual boundaries and promiscuity) CHEIRON. Over time, according to Apollonius, the idea of the god and a horse of the same name merged into one being, a magnificent flying horse.

Source: Breese, *God's Steed*, 86; Hollenbaugh, *Nessus the Centaur*, 159; Shalit, *Will Fishes Fly in Aquarius*, 39

Chrysaor

Variations: Chryseis, Khrysaor

In ancient Greek mythology Chrysaor was a GIGANTE born of the GORGON MEDUSA; his mother, who had recently had sexual relations with the god of the sea, Neptune (Poseidon), was pregnant at the time of her beheading by the cultural hero Perseus. When the blood of MEDUSA hit the ground, both Chrysaor and the winged horse PEGASUS came into being. Chrysaor was born holding a golden sword in his hand; he went on to marry the OCEANID Callirrhoe, one of the daughters of OCEANUS, and together they were the parents of ECHIDNA, the mother of all monsters, and GERYONES.

Source: Hard, *Routledge Handbook of Greek Mythology*, 60–2; Smith, *New Classical Dictionary of Greek and Roman Biography, Mythology and Geography*, 199, 617

Chthonius, the Sown Man

Variations: Chthonios

In classical Greek mythology, Chthonius ("of the soil") was one of the five SPARTI who went on to become the progenitors of the five leading families of the city of Thebes who formed the military caste.

Source: Apollodorus, *Apollodorus' Library and Hyginus' Fabulae*, 22, 47; Dixon-Kennedy, *Encyclopedia of Greco-Roman Mythology*, 86; Hard, *Routledge Handbook of Greek Mythology*, 296

Ch'uan-t'ou

In Chinese mythology, the ch'uan-t'ou were believed to be a race of flying humanoids, having the head of a bird and the wings of a bat. The ch'uan-t'ou were described in a book published in

AD 981 entitled *T'ai P'ing Kuang Chi* ("*Great Records Made in the Period of Peace and Prosperity*"). When seen, it was as they were catching fish from the river and sea.

Source: Borges, *Book of Imaginary Beings*, 102; Eberhart, *Mysterious Creatures*, 176; Rose, *Giants, Monsters, and Dragons*, 82

Ciguapa

In Haitian mythology the ciguapa are said to be a race of tiny people, fiercely loyal, and of perfect beauty; they resemble the local population in every way except for their diminutive size and their being incapable of human speech. Ciguapas are passionately jealous creatures; if ever one was to happen upon a couple engaged in romantic talk it would make its presence known; if the ciguapa is male, then the woman of the couple will die the instant she sees it. Likewise, if the ciguapa is female than it will reveal itself to the man, killing him in the same fashion.

In Dominican Republic folklore the ciguapa is an exquisitely beautiful dark-eyed woman having shining black hair, her only clothing reaching down to her ankles. As cruel and dangerous as she is beautiful, she will use her natural powers of seduction to lure her victims, traditionally men, into the deep wilderness, never to be seen again. As the personification of Death, it is said if one were to stand near the ocean and call out her name, a gigantic wave would come ashore and pull the victim out to sea.

Source: Fanthorpe, *Mysteries and Secrets of Voodoo, Santeria, and Obeah*, 115; Fischer, *Modernity Disavowed*, 335

Circhos

A three-toed humanoid monster from Scandinavian folklore, Circhos is described as having both crusty and soft skin colored black and red; its right foot is very small but its left is long. When Circhos walks it leans on the left side and draws his right foot after itself. It is said when the sky is cloudy and the winds blow, Circhos sits upon the rocks and remains there, unmovable.

Source: Ashton, *Curious Creatures in Zoology*, 247; Rose, *Giants, Monsters, and Dragons*, 83

Cliff Giant

Variations: BERGBUI, Bergriser

In Norse mythology, the cliff giants were a species of JOTUN who were mountain dwellers and lived on the edge of cliffs. All the cliff giants along with the FROST GIANTS (HRIMTHURSAR) swore protection of Fenriswulf (Fenrir), Hela (Hel), and Jormungandr, the Midgard Serpent.

Source: Grimes, *Norse Myths*, 70; Rose, *Giants, Monsters, and Dragons*, 46

Cliff Ogre

A common obstacle to overcome in the tribal folklore of Native American Indians of North American, the cliff ogres were monstrous humanoids who lived in the mountains and were known to kick people off cliffs. After the person had fallen to their death the body was collected and used to feed the cliff ogre's family and pets.

Source: Lowie, *Test-theme in North American Mythology*, 120, 136, 139, 142–3; Rose, *Giants, Monsters, and Dragons*, 84

Clymene

An OCEANID and TITAN from ancient Greek mythology, Clymene was born one of the daughters of the first generation TITAN OCEANIDS and his sister wife TETHYS. Clymene and IAPETUS had four TITAN sons: ATLAS, EPIMETHEUS, MENOETIUS, and PROMETHEUS.

Source: Daly, *Greek and Roman Mythology, A to Z*, 141; Westmoreland, *Ancient Greek Beliefs*, 27–8

Clytios

Variations: Clytius, Klytius

A GIGANTE born of Ouranos from classical Greek mythology, Clytios ("renowned"), like the rest of his kind, was powerful beyond defeat and unsurpassed in bodily size; thick hair hung loose from his chin and head. He and his brothers would hurl flaming trees and rocks into the heavens to attack the gods. Some say this GIGANTE was born in PALLENE but others say it was Phlegrain. During the war against the gods, Clytios was slain by Hecate with a torch.

Source: Apollodorus, *Apollodorus' Library and Hyginus' Fabulae*, 5–6; Daniels, *Encyclopædia of Superstitions, Folklore, and the Occult Sciences of the World*, 1376

Coeus

Variations: Cœos, Koios

A GIGANTE and TITAN from classical Greek mythology, Coeus ("intelligent") was born the son of the TITAN Uranus ("heaven") and the Earth, Gaea; his siblings were CRIUS, CRONUS, HYPERION, IAPETUS, MNEMOSYNE, OCEANUS, PHOEBE, RHEA, TETHYS, THEIA, and THEMIS. Collectively the siblings were known as the Titanides. Coeus was married to the TITAN PHOEBE ("bright") and their daughter, LETO, was the mother of the god Apollo and the goddess Artemis (Diana).

Source: Daly, *Greek and Roman Mythology, A to Z*, 105; Hard, *Routledge Handbook of Greek Mythology*, 37; Rose, *Giants, Monsters, and Dragons*, 85

Colbrand

Variations: Colbrond, Colebrant

A feared GIANT of Danish folklore, the enormous Colbrand was a fighting champion in the Dutch army; he stood relentless guard against the wall of King Aethelstan's castle in Winchester while it was under siege and periodically offered a challenge to the castle to send out its champion to duel him. Sir Guy of Warwick accepted the challenge and the two met at nearby Hyde Mead. The battle ended with Colbrand dead at the knight's feet. The Dutch suffered greatly from the loss and ending their campaign, withdrew from England.

Source: Daniels, *Encyclopædia of Superstitions, Folklore, and the Occult Sciences of the World*, 1376; DeLoach, *Giants*, 65–6; Wiggins, *Guy of Warwick*, 216

Coranians

The Mabinogion, a medieval Welsh manuscript, says three plagues came to the British Islands, the first of which was the invasion of a DWARF race known as the Coranians. According to the text, these people were immune to the effects of weapons against their body; additionally they had the most remarkable hearing, as anything said into the wind could be heard by their ears. The Coranians were also known to freely use fairy money, coins which in every way looked and felt real but a short time later would transform into fungus or leaves. Having come from the country of Pwyl, they settled along the river Humber and the shores of the German Ocean.

Source: Nicholas, *Pedigree of the English People*, 192; Schreiber, *Mabinogion*, 50–1

Corb

One of the FORMORIANs from Irish mythology, Corb was at one point worshiped as a god.

Source: Avant, *Mythological Reference*, 92; Skyes, *Who's Who in Non-Classical Mythology*, 49

Cormoran

A Cornish GIANT from British and Arthurian folklore, Cormoran was said to terrorize the region in and around Saint Michael's Mount. A fierce and hideous savage standing 18 feet tall (5.5 meters) and three feet around (1 meter), Cormoran would wade across the bay each evening and rustle cattle off the mainland. One evening Jack swam across the bay and dug a deep pit he then covered with bracken, earth, grass, gravel, and sticks. At dawn, Jack blew his horn rousing the angry GIANT from his sleep; Cormoran flew from his cave in a fitful rage, yelling obscenities and making threats against Jack for rousing him from his sleep. Before he could reach his brazen opponent, Cormoran crashed down into the pit where Jack finished off the dazed GIANT with his pickaxe. In the Arthurian version of the tale, the popular folk hero is reward with a gift of a belt from the King.

Source: Daniels, *Encyclopædia of Superstitions, Folklore, and the Occult Sciences of the World*, 1376; Jones, *Myths and Legends of Britain and Ireland*, 17

Cottos (KO-tus)

Variations: Cottu, Cottus, Cottus the Furious, Cottus the Striker, Kottos

In ancient Greek mythology the GIGANTE Cottos ("he is conflict") was one of three sons born the son of the TITAN Uranus ("heaven") and the Earth, Gaea; his brothers were named BRAIAREOS and GYGES and collectively they were known as the HECATONCHEIRES ("hundred handers"). The brothers were said to have fifty heads and one-hundred arms; with their unimaginable strength they were important allies to the god Zeus (Jupiter) in his war against the TITANS; after winning the war the brothers were sent to Tartarus to be the guards of the defeated TITANS.

Source: Apollodorus, *Library of Greek Mythology*, 27; Daniels, *Encyclopædia of Superstitions, Folklore, and the Occult Sciences of the World*, 1376; Hard, *Routledge Handbook of Greek Mythology*, 66

Coulin

A belligerent, rebellious Irish GIANT from British folklore, Coulin was pursued by the GIANT DEBON; they both are characters who appear in Spenser's *Faerie Queene*. Coulin died when he fell into a deep chasm.

Source: Brewer, *Character Sketches of Romance, Fiction and the Drama*, Volume 3, 81; Daniels, *Encyclopædia of Superstitions, Folklore, and the Occult Sciences of the World*, 1376; Herron, *Spenser's Irish Work*, 176

Crimbils

Variations: Cryfaglach, Cyrfaglach

In Welsh fairy folklore, crimbils are the offspring born of the fairies known as *bendith y mamau*; these are very often the babes left behind when a human baby has been stolen and a CHANGELING has been left in its place. Crimbils are ugly but have a calm temperament. Because of their appearance they tend to have lonely childhoods. Born with a natural gift for music and song, the crimbil will use it to gain attention and praise.

Sources: Briggs, *Encyclopedia of Fairies*, 81; Page, *Encyclopedia of Things that Never Were*, 54; Rhys, *Celtic Folklore*, 496

Crinaeae

In Greek mythology the crinaeae are a sub-species of the NAIAD; they are the NYMPHS of fountains.

Source: Chopra, *Academic Dictionary of Mythology*, 198; Day, *God's Conflict with the Dragon and the Sea*, 391, 394; Maberry, *Cryptopedia*, 112

Crius

Variations: Ciriu, Kreios, Krius

In ancient Greek mythology the GIGANTE and TITAN Crius ("ram") was born the son of the TITAN Uranus ("heaven") and the Earth, Gaea; by his wife, EURYBIA, he fathered ASTRAEUS, PALLAS, and PERSES. Little is known of him as he is not involved in any particular myths and is only listed in the genealogy of others. Apollodorus, for instance, lists his siblings as COEUS, CRONUS, HYPERION, IAPETUS, MNEMOSYNE, OCEANUS, PHOEBE, RHEA, TETHYS, THEIA, and THEMIS. Collectively the siblings were known as the Titanides. It is possible Crius may have been worshiped as a god of domestic animals and leadership. Crius has no specific myths attached to him.

Source: Apollodorus, *Apollodorus: The Library*, Volume 2, 518; Daly, *Greek and Roman Mythology, A to Z*, 39; Roman, *Encyclopedia of Greek and Roman Mythology*, 120–21; Smith, *Dictionary of Greek and Roman Biography and Mythology*, 100, 1156

Cronus (cro-nus)

Variations: Coelus, Cronos, Kronos, Kronus

In classical Greek mythology, Cronus was the youngest of the first generation of TITANS, the children of Uranus ("heaven") and the Earth, Gaea. Likely, Cronus began as a corn spirit as he is depicted as holding a scythe or a sickle, the very weapon he used against his father. The Roman equivalent of Cronus is Saturn (Saturnus). There are many versions of the story of Cronus but the oldest and the one most often cited is the one written by ancient Greek poet Hesiod.

Uranus and Gaea had many children together, the CYCLOPES, the HEKATONCHEIRES ("hundred handers"), as well as the TITANS, but their father became jealous of the children and banished them all to live beneath the earth. Gaea was distraught over having lost her children and gave to her youngest and most brave child, Cronus, a sickle, along with the encouragement and support to use it against his own father. Empowered, Cronus attacked and disfigured Uranus, the wound leaving him impotent; the blood spilt created the Furies (Erinyes), the GIGANTES, and the Melian NYMPHS. A section of flesh Cronus had cut off and tossed into the ocean rose up as the goddess Aphrodite (Venus). Defeated and disfigured, Uranus abandoned his throne and left it to his conquering son but warned him one day the same fate would befall him.

Cronus married his sister, the TITAN RHEA, and together they had six godling children, three boys, Hades (Dis), Poseidon (Neptune), and Zeus (Jupiter), and three girls, Demeter (Ceres), Hestia (Vesta), and Hera (Juno). Remembering the warning given, Cronus swallowed each child shortly after it was born. RHEA was distressed with the loss of each child and sought the advice of her mother; Gaea advised she take the next child born and hide it away and in its place wrap a stone in cloth and present it to Cronus as the child. RHEA did as her mother counseled when her youngest child, Zeus (Jupiter), was born and as predicted, Cronus ate the stone.

Under his rule humans lived a care-free and toil free life; the earth produced crops in amazing bounty and without any tending. Many years later when the young godling was on the brink of manhood he returned and tricked his father into coughing up the contents of his stomach, releasing his siblings and the stone which replaced him. Reunited, the siblings began a long war against their father but ultimately managed to defeat him. Zeus (Jupiter) and his siblings then founded the Olympian dynasty.

Source: Daly, *Greek and Roman Mythology, A to Z*, 38–9; Edmonds, *Redefining Ancient Orphism*, 169–70; Fox, *Greek and Roman*, 6–8; Roman, *Encyclopedia of Greek and Roman Mythology*, 121–22

Cuegle

A monstrous humanoid from the folklore of Cantabrian, Northern Spain, the cuegle, although an omnivore, preys on anything which can be easily caught as it is a less than adequate hunter, such as nesting chicks, unattended infants, and young animals. The cuegle is described as being small, black skinned, and having arms without hands, five rows of razor sharp teeth, a great horn atop its head, and three eyes, one blue, one green, and one red. The cuegle cannot be slain but its attacks can be prevented by spreading holly and oak leaves around the home and inside an infant's cradle.

Source: Maberry, *Vampire Universe*, 87–88

Cyclopes, Elder

Variations: Kyklopes, Uranian Cyclopes

From classical Greek mythology, ARGES ("flashing" or "thunderbolt"), BRONTES ("thunder"), and STEROPES ("thunder-clouds") are the three elder CYCLOPES, the sons of Uranus ("heaven") and Gaea; each was born exceedingly strong and with a single eye in the middle of their foreheads. They were the siblings of the HECATONCHEIRES and the TITANS. Uranus hated his children and banished them to Tartarus but his wife eventually convinced him to release them. The youngest of the TITANS, Cronus, revolted against his father; once he defeated Uranus he banished the three CYCLOPES back to Tartarus. The Olympian god Zeus (Jupiter), learned from a prophecy he would not be able to defeat CRONUS without the assistance of the three CYCLOPE brothers. He freed them from Tartarus; in return they assisted Zeus (Jupiter) in overthrowing his father and created a great many treasures for the Olympians. The three brothers were slain by the god Apollo because they created the thunderbolt which killed his son, Asclepius.

Source: Daly, *Greek and Roman Mythology, A to Z*, 39–40; Daniels, *Encyclopædia of Superstitions, Folklore, and the Occult Sciences of the World*, 1375–8

Cyclopes, Younger

Variations: Kyklopes

The ancient Greek mythology the younger Cyclopes were, as described by Homer, "overbearing and lawless"; as well as being highly territorial herdsmen, these younger Cyclopes were also cannibals and lived apart from ordered law and religion in a region which had never been settled by humans or plowed in any fashion. These newer generation of CYCLOPES were GIANT nomadic barbarians who raised goats.

Source: Daly, *Greek and Roman Mythology, A to Z*, 40; Homer, *Eight Books of Homer's Odyssey*, 60–61; Roman, *Encyclopedia of Greek and Roman Mythology*, 125–26

Cyclops (si-clops), plural, Cyclopes

Variations: Kyklops

One-eyed GIGANTE from ancient Greek mythology, the Cyclopes ("one-eyed") was the collective name for the three children born the children of the TITAN Uranus ("heaven") and the Earth, Gaea, who had a single eye in the middle of their forehead; the brothers were individually named ARGES ("flashing" or "thunderbolt"), BRONTES ("thunder"), and STEROPES ("thunder-clouds"). When Zeus (Jupiter) and his siblings waged war against CRONUS the Cyclopes, identified as storm spirits, forged the lightning and thunderbolts used by Zeus (Jupiter) and continued to do so after he assumed power and established Olympus. They also forged other weapons for the other gods, such as Hades' (Dis) helmet, which went on to become the symbols of their power. Later legends say they worked at Hephaistos' (Vulcan)'s forge in Mount Aetna.

In *The Odyssey*, the epic Greek poem attributed to Homer, the greatest of Greek epic poets, the Cyclopes (see CYCLOPSE, YOUNGER) were said to be "overbearing and lawless" in addition to being aggressive pastoralists prone to cannibalism. POLYPHEMUS had captured the hero Odysseus and the crew of his ship, but was blinded in his eye when tricked into falling into a drunken stupor and allowed his prisoners to escape. Although Odysseus

managed to flee, he earned the eternal hatred of POLYPHEMUS' father, the god of the sea, Poseidon (Neptune).

Source: Cotterell, *Dictionary of World Mythology*, 136–137; Daniels, *Encyclopædia of Superstitions, Folklore, and the Occult Sciences of the World*, 1376; Grimal, *Larousse World Mythology*, 106, 108, Jordan, *Encyclopedia of Gods*, 285

Cymopoleia

Variations: Kymopoleia ("wave-walker")

In classical Greek mythology, Cymopoleia was a GIGANTE and a daughter of the god of the sea, Poseidon (Neptune); she was the wife of BRIAREOS, one of the HECATONCHEIRES.

Source: Barthell, *Gods and Goddesses of Ancient Greece*, 144; Rose, *A Handbook of Greek Mythology*, 61

Cynnocephalus

Variations: Cynocephali, Cynocephalus

Tales of a race of canine humanoids came from travelers as far back as the fifth century, BC; the Cynnocephalus ("dog head") were described as looking much like a WEREWOLF, as their bodies are very hairy. They have no power of transformation and were believed to be vegetarians, although the 1550 Pierre Descelier world map manuscripts depict an image of one Cynnocephalus butchering another Cynnocephalus in preparation to eat it. Eastern Christian Orthodox church tradition claims Saint Christopher was a Cynnocephalus.

Source: Friedman, *Monstrous Races in Medieval Art and Thought*, 157; Mittman, *Ashgate Research Companion to Monsters and the Monstrous*, 410; Rosen, *Mythical Creatures Bible*, 130

Daidarabochi

Variations: Daidarabo, Daidarabotchi, Daidarabocchi

A species of nature spirit in Japanese folklore, the Daidarabochi are said to appear as GIANTS, and appear in many tales; in one story the Daidarabochi took part in the creation of the world while in another tale a Daidarabochi placed Mount Fuji and Mount Tsukuba on scales to see which was heavier. The Daidarabochi were said to have created many of the country's geographical features including Mount Fuji, which was constructed in a single night.

Source: *Japan Architect*, Volume 42, 16; Kenkyūjo, *Japanese Journal of Religious Studies*, Volume 16, 184; Yoda, *Yokai Attack*, 70

Daitya

A race of hostile GIANTS from Hindu mythology, the nocturnal daitya is the collective name for the gigantic sons of Casyapa by his wife Dita. The term *daitya* is limited to the antediluvian period, as all of the daitya died in the flood. The daitya are similar in Hindu mythology to the TITANS of classical Greek mythology; in the book of Genesis the word *daityas* is denoted by the word NEPHILIM.

After the *Samudra Manthana* ("Churning of the Ocean"), the daitya rose up against Deva when he took possession of the cup of Amritsar but were defeated and driven back to Petala (Hell). Before they returned, the daitya admitted the supremacy of the users of the discus and the mace. Over time, this battle became distorted and was eventually retold as a battle between demons and the gods.

Source: Balfour, *Cyclopædia of India and of Eastern and Southern Asia*, Volume 1, 877; Dalal, *Hinduism*, n.pag.; Taylor, *Hand-book of Hindu Mythology and Philosophy*, 31, 36

Dakini

A species of female OGRE with distorted feet, the dakini are hunch backed and have a hole in their stomach, like in the hollow of a tree; they are associated with death but they are unable to kill even though they are known to eat human hearts. The dakini have their own type of magic they practice and with it they can come to know the names of people who will die within the upcoming six months. In addition to their magic, the dakini have the ability to dominate others, grant any wish, hurt and sicken people, and travel the world in a day.

In Chinese folklore Dakini is a singular individual deity who was named as "the mother who rides in the sky"; she does so astride a white fox, carrying a bushel of rice, and no longer an OGRE but a beautiful woman.

Source: Boscaro, *Rethinking Japan*, 330; Khanam, *Demonology*, 24–25

Damasen

A Mysian GIANT from classical Greek mythology, Damasen ("subdue") was appealed to by the grieving Moera ("fate") to avenge the death of her heroic brother Tylus ("knot" or "phallus") of Lydian who had been attacked and poisoned by a serpent as he walked along the banks of the Hermus. Damasen did as she asked, hunted down the serpent and killed it. The creature's mate discovered the body and using an herb, restored it to life. Moera, who watched this happen, did likewise for her brother and resurrected him in the same fashion.

Source: Frazer, *Adonis, Attis, Osiris*, 153; Graves, *Greek Myths*, 308

Damysus (DAM-uh-sus)

Variations: Damysos

A Thracian GIGANTE from classical Greek mythology, Damysus was the swiftest of all the GIGANTE who warred against the gods. According to legend, when Thetis attempted to test her infant son Achilles for immortality by burning him in a fire, his father Peleus snatched him up just as the child's heel was scorched. To replace the missing section, Peleus exhumed the remains of the Damysus and took the Achilles's ankle bone which was forcibly inserted into the infant's open wound. Next, the child was made to consume a number of elixirs which magically bound the replacement bone perfectly to the body. In some versions of the story, it was the Centaur (a creature from Greek mythology, half equine and half human, entangled with issues of sexual boundaries and promiscuity) CHEIRON and not Peleus who performed this limp replacement surgery.

Source: Apollodorus, *Apollodorus: The Library*, Volume 2, 69; McClintock, *Cyclopaedia of Biblical, Theological, and Ecclesiastical Literature*, Volume 12, 230

Danaid, plural Danaids

Variations: Danaides, Danaïdes, Daughters of Danaus

In ancient Greek mythology a danaid was a water-NYMPH; as the fifty daughters of Danaus, they were known collectively as the Danaids.

In the most popular version of the myth the sisters were each set to marry one of the fifty sons of Aegyptus, a mythical king of Egypt. Their father, King Danaus, not pleased with the arrangement he agreed to, ordered his daughters to murder their respective spouses. On their wedding night, the Danaids did as their father asked save for one, a daughter named Amymone; she chose not to join her sisters in the murderous plot because her husband, Lynceus (Enceladus), respected her desire to remain a virgin. For their crime the Danaids were condemned to spend eternity carrying water in a sieve in an attempt to fill a leaky tub in order to wash away the sin of their crime; they have come to represent the futility of repeating a task which can never be completed.

Apollodorus, a Greek scholar and grammarian, listed not only the daughters and who they married but also the names of the mothers:

Actaea, one of the six daughters of Pieria, was given to Periphas, one of the six sons of Gorgo; Adiante, one of the two daughters of Herse, was given to Daiphron (different one), one of the two sons of Hephaestine; Adite, one of the six daughters of Pieria, was given to Menalces, one of the six sons of Gorgo; Agave, one of the four daughters of Europe, was given to Lycus, one of the four sons of Argyphia; Amymone, one of the four daughters of Europe, was given to Enceladus, one of the four sons of Argyphia; Anaxibia, one of the seven daughters of an unnamed Ethiopian woman, to Archelaus, one of the seven sons of an unnamed Phoenician woman; Antheli, one of the twelve daughters of Polyxo and a NAIAD, was given to Cisseus, one of the twelve sons of Caliadne who was also a NAIAD; ASTERIA, one of the ten daughters of either Atlanteia or of PHOEBE, the Hamadryads, was given to Chaetus, one of the ten sons of an unnamed Arabic woman; Automate, one of the four daughters of Europe, was given to Busiris, one of the four sons of Argyphia; Autonoe, one of the twelve daughters of Polyxo and a NAIAD, was given to Eurylochus, one of the twelve sons of Caliadne who was also a NAIAD; Bryce, one of the twelve daughters of Polyxo and a NAIAD, was given to CHTHONIUS, one of the twelve sons of Caliadne who was also a NAIAD; Callidice, one of the four daughters of Crino, was given to Pandion, one of the four sons of Hephaestine; CELAENO, one of the four daughters of Crino, was given to Hyperbius, one of the four sons of Hephaestine; Chrysippe, one of the three daughters of Memphis, was given to Chrysippus, one of the three sons of Tyria, without the casting of lots since they were namesakes; Cleodore, one of the twelve daughters of Polyxo and a NAIAD, was given to Lixus, one of the twelve sons of Caliadne who was also a NAIAD; Cleopatra (not the Egyptian queen), one of the twelve daughters of Polyxo and a NAIAD, was given to Hermus, one of the twelve sons of Caliadne who was also a NAIAD; Cleopatra, one of the ten daughters of either Atlanteia or of Phoebe, the Hamadryads, was given to Agenor, one of the ten sons of an unnamed Arabic woman; Clite, one of the three daughters of Memphis, was given to Clitus, one of the three sons of Tyria, without the casting of lots since they were namesakes; Dioxippe, one of the six daughters of Pieria, was given to Aegyptus, one of the six sons of Gorgo; Dorion, one of the seven daughters of an unnamed Ethiopian woman, was given to Cercetes, one of the seven sons of an unnamed Phoenician woman; Electra, one of the twelve daughters of Polyxo and a NAIAD, was given to Peristhenes, one of the twelve sons of Caliadne who was also a NAIAD; Erato, one of the twelve daughters of Polyxo and a NAIAD, was given to Bromius, one of the twelve sons of Caliadne who was also a NAIAD; Eurydice, one of the twelve daughters of Polyxo and a NAIAD, was given to Dryas, one of the twelve sons of Caliadne who was also a NAIAD; Evippe (different one), one of the twelve daughters of Polyxo and a NAIAD, was given to Imbrus, one of the twelve sons of Caliadne who was also a NAIAD; Evippe, one of the seven daughters of an unnamed Ethiopian woman, to Argius, one of the seven sons of an unnamed Phoenician woman; Glauce, one of the ten daughters of either Atlanteia or of Phoebe, the Hamadryads, was given to Alces, one of the ten sons of an unnamed Arabic woman; Glaucippe, one of the twelve daughters of Polyxo and a NAIAD, was given to Potamon, one of the twelve sons of Caliadne who was also a NAIAD; Gorge, one of the ten daughters of either Atlanteia or of Phoebe, the Hamadryads, was given to Hippothous, one of the ten sons of an unnamed Arabic woman; Gorgophone, one of the two daughters of Elephantis, was given to Proteus, one of the two sons of Queen Argyphia; Hippodamia (different one), one of the ten daughters of either Atlanteia or of Phoebe, the Hamadryads, was given to Diocorystes, one of the ten sons of an unnamed Arabic woman; Hippodamia, one of the ten daughters of either Atlanteia or of Phoebe, the Hamadryads, was given to Istrus, one of the ten sons of an unnamed Arabic woman; Hippodice, one of the two daughters of Herse, was given to Idas, one of the two sons of Hephaestine; Hippomedusa, one of the ten daughters of either Atlanteia or of Phoebe, the Hamadryads, was given to Alcmenor, one of the ten sons of an unnamed Arabic woman; Hyperippe, one of the four daughters of Crino, was given to Hippocorystes, one of the four sons of Hephaestine; Hypermnestra, one of the two daughters of Elephantis, was given to Lynceus, one of the two sons of Queen Argyphia; Iphimedusa, one of the ten daughters of either Atlanteia or of Phoebe, the Hamadryads, was given to Euchenor, one of the ten sons of an unnamed Arabic woman; Mnestra, one of the seven daughters of an unnamed Ethiopian woman, was given to Aegius, one of the seven sons of an unnamed Phoenician woman; Nelo, one of the seven daughters of an unnamed Ethiopian woman, was given to Menemachus, one of the seven sons of an unnamed Phoenician woman; OCYPETE, one of the six daughters of Pieria, was given to Lampus, one of the six sons of Gorgo; Oeme, one of the four daughters of Crino, was given to Arbelus, one of the four sons of Hephaestine; Phartis, one of the seven daughters of an unnamed Ethiopian woman, was given to Eurydamas, one of the seven sons of an unnamed Phoenician woman; Pirene, one of the seven daughters of an unnamed Ethiopian woman, was given to Agaptolemus, one of the seven sons of an unnamed Phoenician woman; Podarce, one of the six daughters of Pieria, was given to Oeneus, one of the six sons of Gorgo; Pylarge, one of the six daughters of Pieria, was given to Idmon, one of the six sons of Gorgo; Rhode, one of the ten daughters of either Atlanteia or of Phoebe, the Hamadryads, was given to Hippolytus, one of the ten sons of an unnamed Arabic woman; Rhodia, one of the ten daughters of either Atlanteia or of Phoebe, the Hamadryads, was given to Chalcodon, one of the ten sons of an unnamed Arabic woman; Scaea, one of the four daughters of Europe, was given to Daiphron, one of the four sons of Argyphia; Sthenele, one of the three daughters of Memphis, was given to Sthenelus, one of the three sons of Tyria, without the casting of lots since they were namesakes; Stygne, one of the twelve daughters of Polyxo and a NAIAD, was given to Polyctor, one of the twelve sons of Caliadne who was also a NAIAD; and Theano, one of the twelve daughters of Polyxo and a NAIAD, was given to Phantes, one of the twelve sons of Caliadne who was also a NAIAD.

Gaius Julius Hyginus (ca. 64 BC–AD 17), a Latin author and a freedman of Caesar Augustus, has also compiled a list of the Danaids and their husbands. It should be noted his list has little in common with Apollodorus'; he makes only forty-nine pairs, and does not name all the Danaids:

An unnamed Danaid was married to Armoasbus; Acamantis to Ecnomius; Amphicomone to Plexippus; Amymone to Midanus; Arcadia to Xanthus; Arsalte to EPHIALTES; Autodice to Clytus; CELAENO to Aristonoos; Chrysothemis to Asterides; Cleo to Asterius; Cleopatra to Hermus; Cleopatra (a second daughter with the same name) to Metalces; Critomedia to Antipaphus; Damone to Amyntor; Danaïs to Pelops; Daplidice to Pugno; Demoditas to Chrysippus; Demophile to Pamphilus; Electra to Hyperantus; Erato to Eudaemon; Eubule to Demarchus; Eupheme to Hyperbius; Europome to Athletes; Eurydice to Canthus; Evippe, to Agenor; Glaucippe to Niauius; Hecabe to Dryas; Helice to Evidea; Helicta to Cassus; Hero to Andromachus; Hipparete to Protheon; Hippothoe to Obrimus; Hyale to Perius; Itea to Antiochus; Midea to Antimachus; Monuste to Eurysthenes; Myrmidone to Mineus; Oeme to Polydector; Phila to Philinus; Philomela to Panthius; Pirene to Dolichus; Polybe to Itonomus; Polyxena to Aegyptus; Pyrante to Athamas; Pyrantis to Plexippus; Scylla to Proteus; Themistagora to Podasimus; and Trite to Enceladus. Hypermnestra saved her husband, Lynceus.

Throughout Greek mythology there are a few other women who are mentioned in passing as being one of the Danaids: Amphimedusa, the mother of Erythras by the god Poseidon (Neptune); Anaxithea, the mother of Olenus by the god Zeus (Jupiter); Eurythoe was one of the possible mothers of Oenomaus by the god Ares (Mars) (she may also be the mother of Hippodamia by Oenomaus); Hippodamia and Isione, wives of Olenus and Orchomenus or Chryses respectively, who were both seduced by the god Zeus (Jupiter); Isonoe, mother of Orchomenus by the god Zeus (Jupiter); Phaethusa, one of the possible mothers of Myrtilus by the god Hermes (Mercury); Phylodameia, mother of Pharis by the god Hermes (Mercury); Physadeia, who, like her sister Amymone, gave her name to a freshwater source; Polydora, mother of Dryops (Oeta) by the river god Spercheus; and Side, a mythical eponym of a town in Laconia.

Sources: Antoninus Liberalis, *Metamorphoses of Antoninus Liberalis*, 32; Bowlby, *Freudian Mythologies*, 392–3; Parada, *Genealogical Guide to Greek Mythology*, 59

Dark Elves

Variations: Daoi-Sith, Dökkálfar ("dark-elves"), Drow, Obscure Elves, Swartelves ("black elves"), Swarthy-Elves

In Norse mythology the dark elves lived in the subterranean world Svartálfheim. Neither innately benevolent nor injurious, they worked the forges under the deepest root of the world-tree, near the northern gate to the lower world (*iormungrundar i iodyr, nyrdra*). Constantly near the flames and soot covered thereby earning their name, dark elves are considered by some to be synonymous with the DVERGAR ("DWARFS").

In Germanic traditions the Dökkálfar ("dark-elves") are ancestral spirits, always male, protecting their family line. Although not strictly subterranean, they avoid light and can be quite intimidating when provoked.

In fairy mythology from the Orkney Islands the cave and mine dwelling TROW are similar to the DWARFS and TROLLS of Scandinavian folklore. Typically injurious, the TROW can be benevolent or indifferent to mankind.

In the Shetland Islands the drow are essentially the same beings as the TROW except they are exclusively injurious. Like DWARFS, the diminutive drow work their mines and are expert metal-workers. However, in Irish mythology, the drow is more like the TROLL of Scandinavian folklore and is considered to be a creature of stone aligned to the FORMORIANS.

Source: Daly, *Norse Mythology A to Z*, 26; Guerber, *Hammer of Thor*, 174, 237; Lindow, *Norse Mythology*, 54, 110; Maberry, *Cryptopedia*, 104–5; Rydberg, *Teutonic Mythology*, 553

Datagaliwabe

In Huli mythology, Datagaliwabe is a *dama* and a GIANT who oversees the laws of moral transgressions between kinships; whenever one is broken he punishes the offender with death in battle, a fatal accident, or illness. The person who has broken the laws can do nothing to save themselves once Datagaliwabe has passed judgment. Originally in Huli traditions, Datagaliwabe was little more than a NURSERY BOGIE used to frighten children into good behavior, but since the introduction of Christianity, his role has become more dominant in society and his punishments more obvious and frequent.

Source: Chopra, *Academic Dictionary of Mythology*, 81; Frankel, *Huli Response to Illness*, 154

Debon

A GIANT from British folklore, Debon pursued the belligerent, rebellious Irish GIANT COULIN to a pit some eight leagues across; COULIN was unable to make the leap and fell to his death. A character who appears in Spenser's *Faerie Queene*, Debon was one of the companions of Brute, the mythological first king of England.

Source: Brewer, *Character Sketches of Romance, Fiction and the Drama*, Volume 3, 250; Daniels, *Encyclopædia of Superstitions, Folklore, and the Occult Sciences of the World*, 1376; Herron, *Spenser's Irish Work*, 176

Deer Woman

Variations: Deer Maiden

A shape-shifting deer and human hybrid from the mythology of numerous Native American tribes, the Deer Woman appears in many stories; usually she is taken as a wife and has a son with her husband but leaves him after the husband has offended her, usually by criticizing the way she eats.

According to Lakota folklore, Deer Woman will appear to a hunter when he is hunting far from home, unsuccessfully, and has grown lonely, hungry, and tired; appearing as the most beautiful woman he has ever seen, with long shiny hair and sparkling eyes, she will invite the hunter to her lodge which is nearby. Once in the lodge, the Deer Woman will seduce the man and after a night of passion, he will awake in the morning to discover she and her lodge have disappeared. The hunter is now captivated by the Deer Woman, and some may say he has lost his soul to her, because for the rest of his life he will think of nothing else but looking for her.

Source: Lynch, *Native American Mythology A to Z*, 33; Marshall, *Lakota Way*, 37–40

Dehotgohsgayeh

Variations: Wry Face

A repulsively ugly GIANT from Iroquois and Onondaga folklore, Dehotgohsgayeh ("split face being" or "wry faced") is benevolent towards humans and protects them from harm.

Source: Rose, *Giants, Monsters, and Dragons*, 95, 398

Denbras

In British folklore Denbras is an old GIANT who lived in Towednack Hills with his wives; he was described as a gentle soul who would only on occasion accidentally kill a man while rough-housing with him. Denbras was slain in a fair fight by the famed regional GIANT killer Tom. Denbras was stabbed through with an oak axel-tree and buried respectfully in a barrow.

Source: Cook, *Saturday Review of Politics, Literature, Science and Art*, Volume 31, 267; Williams-Ellis, *Story of English Life*, 12

Devalpa

In Arabic folklore the devalpa is described as appearing as a decrepit and pathetic looking old man who is standing on the side of the road, deeply sighing sadly to himself. He will ask those who pass by to carry him on their shoulders; if anyone should comply, once he is seated, numerous serpentine legs suddenly erupt out from his abdomen and entwine around the body of his would-be helper, demanding they work for him. The only way to be rid of this creature is to trick it into drinking copious amounts of wine. Once it passes out, the devalpa can be shrugged off.

Source: Cronin, *Last Migration*, 201; Mack, *Field Guide to Demons, Vampires, Fallen Angels, and Other Subversive Spirits*, 162–63

Devil-Fish People

In the folklore of the Haida people of the Pacific Northwest Coast of North America, the devil-fish people were one of the many supernatural ocean people who lived in underwater villages scattered up and down the shore. Since the ocean people were in control of a large part of the food supply they not only were held in the highest of regard but were also appealed to for assistance with offerings of rare flicker feathers, grease, and tobacco.

The devil-fish people lived their lives in their underwater village much as humans do but they had the ability to change the state of other beings and shape-shift their own form.

Source: Goldenweiser, *Early Civilization*, 63; Rose, *Spirits, Fairies, Leprechauns, and Goblins*, 84–5

Dhampire (Dom-peer)

Variations: Dhampir, Dhampyr, Dhampyri, Lampijerovics (feminine), Vamphile, Vampijerovic (masculine), Vampir (masculine), Vampirdzhija, Vampiritc, Vampirovitch, Vampuiera (feminine), Vampuira

The Gypsy folklore from Eastern Europe claims if the child of a woman and a male mullo vampire is not stillborn, it will be a dhampire, a natural born vampire hunter. In almost all cases the dhampire is male (females are called *dhampiresa*), but no matter the gender, they tend to have a shorter lifespan than humans. This is because it is believed dhampires do not have any bones in their body but rather a thick rubberlike substance instead. Usually the dhampire has a restless spirit and becomes a wanderer, and it is because of this, and the fact he is also the child of a vampire, he is generally distrusted. Even if he should be an established member of a community, his ability to hunt and destroy vampires will be respected, but he will have no social or political power among his people.

The dhampire does not have any of the vampiric abilities of his vampire father. He has no enhanced senses or regenerative abilities, nor is he a shapeshifter; not only is he not immortal, he does not even have slowed aging. What he can do is see a vampire for the creature it is, even if it is invisible. Dhampires are also able to destroy a vampire without having to use a special weapon. For instance, if a vampire can only be slain by being stabbed through the heart with a stake made of ash, the dhampire can use a stake made of any material. They can even extend this ability to their gun and shoot a vampire while it lies at rest in its grave.

For more stubborn cases of vampiric attacks, a dhampire may be hired. Once he has arrived at the infested town and money has changed hands, the dhampire will go to the center of town and call out a challenge for the vampire to meet him there the next day at a certain time. The next day, the dhampire will show up early and wait for the vampire to arrive, and when it does, it usually does so invisibly. If it is hiding, the dhampire will be able to feel its presence or catch its scent on the wind, allowing him to track it. Usually the dhampire can see a vampire without any assistance, but occasionally he needs to perform a simple magical ceremony to do so. Usually this ritual is as simple as looking through a shirtsleeve, putting his clothes on backward, or whistling. Once the dhampire is ready, he'll physically confront the vampire, grab it, and wrestle with it. Eventually, the dhampire will be able to overcome the creature and manage to stake it or shoot it or even run it out of town with a banishment.

In 1959 there was a dhampire who was still actively working in Kosova. The last time he was ever heard from was when he was performing the last known vampire removal ceremony later that same year.

A dhampire, because of the conditions of his birth, must make arrangements to have a proper funeral held for him when he dies. If not, he will return to unlife as a vampire himself.

Source: Elsie, *Dictionary of Albanian Religion, Mythology, and Folk Culture*, 69; Gypsy Lore Society, *Journal of the Gypsy Lore Society*, 44; MacGillivray, *Stoker's Spoiled Masterpiece*, 518–27; Richardson, *Psychoanalysis of Ghost Stories*, 427–28; Senf, *The Vampire in Nineteenth-Century English Literature*, 165; Twitchell, *Living Dead*, 11–12, 46, 50, 52, 89

Dharmapalas

Variations: Hu Fa

The eight GIANT guardians and warriors of Tibetan Buddhist teachings, the dharmapalas are guardian spirits whose role it is to protect against confusion and false teachings; some of the dharmapalas are recognized as Tibetan national deities. The heads of the dharmapalas stretch from horizon to horizon and their mouths are filled with razor-sharp teeth; their tongues are made of fire and each has a third eye in the middle of their forehead which can sear their enemies with the perfect light of knowledge.

Source: Chopra, *Academic Dictionary of Mythology*, 85; Stevenson, *Complete Idiot's Guide to Eastern Philosophy*, 363

Dheeyabery

According to Australian mythology, the Dheeyabery were a tribe of people who looked like ordinary folks from the front but when viewed from the rear they appeared to be great gobs of flesh. The cultural hero Yooneeara happened upon this tribe as he was journeying to the setting sun. All of the Dheeyabery tried to capture him, but he managed to escape.

Source: Rose, *Giants, Monsters, and Dragons*, 96–7

Dheveshtrues

A humanoid from Albanian mythology, the dheveshtrues ("earth observer") has the ability to put its ear to the ground in the Spring night and detect the sound of running water beneath the earth. Sitting upon the rump of a *dhembesuta* (a traditional deaf and enfeebled mare), he rides across the sea and over the mountains followed by the cold.

Source: Elsie, *Dictionary of Albanian Religion, Mythology, and Folk Culture*, 69

Dhinnabarrada

A monstrous tribe of people from the folklore of the Kamilaroi peoples of Australia, the Dhinnabarrada were described as having the body of a man but the legs and feet of an emu. Never moving anywhere alone but always in at least a small group, the Dhinnabarrada sustained themselves on grubs and made boomerangs from the wood of the gidyer tree.

Source: Rose, *Giants, Monsters, and Dragons*, 97; Woodgate, *Kamilaroi and Assimilation*, 59

Di-Di

Variations: Dai-Dai, Didi-Aguiri, Dru-Didi

On the northern coast of South America, in British Guyana (Guiana) there is the folkloric belief of a species of hairy simian (ape-like) humanoid known as the di-di which are feared although very seldom seen. Legend says these creatures are covered with brown fur and live in pairs. Killing one is very dangerous, as its mate is said to be naturally vengeful and will stalk out its spouse's killer and strangle them one night while they sleep.

Source: Eberhart, *Mysterious Creatures*, 131; Sanderson, *Abominable Snowmen*, 180–81; Zell-Ravenheart, *Wizard's Bestiary*, 35

Digraldi (DIG-rald-i)

One of the hrymthursars (FROST GIANTS) from Norse mythology, Digraldi ("fat") was born one of the sons of THRAEL and THIR. Digraldi, his parents, and siblings all lived a hard life of labor performing thankless tasks such as cleaning, herding goats and swine, placing dung in the fields, and other varied unskilled labor. He and his family became the progenitors of the serving folk and thrall.

Source: Grimes, *Norse Myths*, 27, 261; Norroena Society, *Asatrii Edda*, 340

Dinabuc

Variations: Danibus, Dinabus, Dynabrok, Dynabus

A Spanish GIANT from Arthurian folklore, Dinabuc, a fierce and savage brute, was said to live upon Mount Saint Michel or Saint Bernard's Mount (ballads and sources vary); he terrorized the countryside by destroying houses, kidnapping women, and stealing their children. King Arthur is finally moved to action when Dinabuc abducts the maiden Helen who is crushed to death beneath his weight while he rapes her. With Sir Cai (Kay) and Sir Bedwer by his side, Arthur confronts the GIANT and kills him.

Source: Ackerman, *Index of the Arthurian Names in Middle English*, Volume 10, 70; Cohen, *Of Giants*, 70, 77

Dinny-Mara

Variations: Doinney Marrey ("man of the sea"), Dooinney Marrey, Duny Mara

Dinny-Mara was the amiable MERMAN from the Isle of Man; they were said to be far less fierce than the mermen of England and more easygoing, like the MERROW (a species of merfolk) of Ireland. As benign as this MERMAN may have been, there was the belief if one whistles onboard a sail ship the dinny-mara would send more wind than is needed to the ship. This aquatic fairy animal was described as having large, porcine (piglike) eyes, and a bright red nose from drinking too much brandy salvaged from sunken ships. Their breath smelled like the raw fish they ate.

Source: Briggs, *Encyclopedia of Fairies*, 102; Monaghan, *Encyclopedia of Celtic Mythology and Folklore*, 327; Rose, *Spirits, Fairies, Gnomes, and Goblins*, 86–7

Dione

An OCEANID and TITAN from ancient Greek mythology, Dione was born one of the earliest daughters of the first generation TITAN OCEANIDS and his sister wife TETHYS. Traditionally, she is not listed as one of the TITAN, and there are a number of possible origins of who she was, her lineage, spouses, and possible children.

Source: Daly, *Greek and Roman Mythology, A to Z*, 141; Westmoreland, *Ancient Greek Beliefs*, 86–7

Diwata

Variations: Encantada (female), Encantado (male), Engkantada, Engkanto, Lambana

In Filipino mythology, the diwata were originally seen and worshiped as gods but in modern times they are comparable to fairies, nature spirits, or NYMPHS. Descriptions of their appearance varies, but generally they are said to look human, ageless and beautiful with a singular distinct characteristic; this can be anything from having perfectly smooth, wrinkle-free skin even in places like the knees and elbows to not having a philtrum. Diwata live in large trees, such as acacia and balete; they will bless those who benefit and protect the forest and mountains and will curse those who attempt to exploit or harm them.

A male diwata is called an *enkanto* (also spelt ENCANTO, ENCANTADO, and *ingkanto*) and lives in the sea. Filipino fishermen will make offerings of meat to them after a successful day.

Source: Demetrio, *Myths and Symbols, Philippines*, 346; Olupọna, *Beyond Primitivism*, 257–8

Dodonides

Variations: Dododaean Nymphs

The Dodonides, as they were collectively known, were the seven NYMPHS of the oracles of Zeus (Jupiter) at Dodone, the god's birthplace in classical Greek mythology; their names were Ambrosia, Dione, Eudore, Koronis (Coronis), Phaio (Phaeno), Phaisyle, and Polyxo.

Source: Larson, *Greek Nymphs*, 161; Rigoglioso, *Cult of Divine Birth in Ancient Greece*, 87, 144

Dofri (DUHV-ri)

A JOTUN from Norse mythology, Dofri ("mountain man" or "spear thrower") was described as being stout and tall with the strength of sixty men. He lived in a land named after him, Dovrefjell ("Dofri's Mountains"), and the JOTUN who stole the gold of King Halfdan the Black. Dofri was the foster-father of Prince Harald for five years, teaching him a basic education and many feats of skill.

Source: Craigie, *Scandinavian Folk-Lore*, 72–4; Norroena Society, *Asatrii Edda*, 25

Dogai

In the mythology of the people of the Torres Strait Islands, the dogai is said to be a female, witch-like creature of sub-human intelligence but yet charming and shrewd. Living in stone, trees, or underground, the long-eared and sharp-featured dogai were always on the lookout for a human man to kidnap and keep as their husband. Most dogai were evil by nature and all of them had the ability to impersonate a living woman; their language was a gibberish version of the Islanders' native tongue.

Source: Monaghan, *New Book of Goddesses and Heroines*, 148–49; Ragan, *Fearless Girls, Wise Women, and Beloved Sisters*, 299

Dogirs (Dog-ers)

In the Egyptian village of Dabod there is a species of vampire called a dogirs which normally lives peacefully with its human neighbors. A type of vampiric spirit, it looks just like a human during the day but with a lump on its lower back. This lump is in truth the dogirs's tail hidden under the skin. In its true form, which it can assume at night by rolling in ashes, the vampire looks like a WEREWOLF with glowing eyes.

In 1929 the police of the village were called to conduct an official search for a dogirs. Law enforcement officials cited having a lump on a person's back as grounds for arrest.

Source: American Anthropological Association, *American Anthropologist*, Volume 69, 689; Beshir, *Nile Valley Countries*, 139; Grauer, *The Dogri*, 114–24

Dolgtthrasir (DAWLG-thras-ir)

A DVERG (DWARF) from Norse mythology created by DURINN, Dolgtthrasir ("enemy-combatant") is listed as being one of DURINN's KIN. He, like the others created, paid particular attention to DURINN's leadership.

Source: Grimes, *Norse Myths*, 260

Dondasch

A contemporary of Seth, Dondasch was an Asian GIANT in his service; Dondasch did not use weapons, as he was strong enough to destroy anything he wished with the strength of his own two hands.

Source: Brewer, *Character Sketches of Romance, Fiction and the Drama*, Volume 3, 81; Daniels, *Encyclopædia of Superstitions, Folklore, and the Occult Sciences of the World*, 1376

Dori (DOHR-i)

A DVERG (DWARF) from Norse mythology created by DURINN, Dori ("borer") is listed as being one of DURINN's KIN. He, like the others created, paid particular attention to DURINN's leadership.

Source: Grimes, *Norse Myths*, 260; Young, *Prose Edda*, 175

Doris

An OCEANID and TITAN from ancient Greek mythology, Doris was born one of the daughters of the first generation TITAN OCEANIDS and his sister wife TETHYS; she was described as being fair-haired and by NEREUS was the mother of Thetis and the fifty NEREIDS.

Source: Daly, *Greek and Roman Mythology, A to Z*, 141; Westmoreland, *Ancient Greek Beliefs*, 25, 103

Dragon Maid

Variations: Dragon MERMAID

A creature from Celtic folklore, the dragon maid was described as looking like a monstrous woman, part human and part dragon. It was believed she had the ability to bless childless couples who treated her well with progeny but would curse those who did not show her respect.

Source: Rose, *Giants, Monsters, and Dragons*, 107; Zell-Ravenheart, *Wizard's Bestiary*, 36

Dragua, plural dragonj

In northern Albanian mythology the dragua ("dragon") is a semi-human being born with the instinctual drive to seek out and slay a *kulshedra* (a demonic dragon with faceted silver eyes, four legs, a long, serpentine body, and small wings). Born wearing a caul shirt, the dragua have a set of two or four invisible wings under their armpits. As the arms and wings are the centralized location of their power, dragonj must never hear the phrase "may your arms wither" as this will cause their immediate death. The mother of a dragua must hide the shirt-caul and not tell anyone what her child is, for doing so will also cause the infant to die. In the north of Albania it was said dragonj were born only to those couples whose ancestors had not committed adultery for three consecutive generations. When a dragua dies, if it is dissected it will be discovered its heart is a golden color and a jewel resides within it.

Even as newborn infants, dragonj have developed

supernatural powers; for instance, during lightning and thunder storms dragonj magically assemble, crib in tow, in the dragua gathering place. Infant dragonj protect themselves from the attacks of a *kulshedra* by hiding in their cribs or using it as a weapon. As the goal of a dragua's life is to combat and kill *kulshedra* they spend their childhood developing the skills they need; especially important is to develop their ability to leap long distances quickly in order to avoid the *kulshedra's* spraying attack of milk and urine, its main weapons.

When a dragua finally confronts its natural enemy it goes into a berserker rage, its soul leaving its body for the duration of the conflict. They can sense when a human is being attacked by a *kulshedra* and will, by use of a magical felt hat, fly to their rescue and attack it with cudgels, thrown houses, lances, ploughs, stones, uprooted trees, and yokes; these attacks will look like lightning strikes to the human.

Male animals can also be born as a dragua, particularly black roosters and black rams. In Korca and Pograde, Albania, the dragua can also be a beautiful and strong winged stallion bent on defending civilization. Billy-goats can never be born dragonj.

Source: Elsie, *Dictionary of Albanian Religion, Mythology, and Folk Culture*, 74–5

Draupnir (DROUP-nir)

A DVERG (DWARF) from Norse mythology created by DURINN, Draupnir ("dropper") is listed as being one of DURINN's KIN. He, like the others created, paid particular attention to DURINN's leadership.

Source: Daly, *Norse Mythology A to Z*, 21; Grimes, *Norse Myths*, 260; Young, *Prose Edda*, 175

Drimo (DREEM-moh)

Born the daughter of the GIGANTE ALCYONEUS, Drimo ("piercing," "sharp") was, according to the ancient Greek historian Hegesander, one of the ALCYONII; she and her sisters, ALKIPPA, ANTHE, ASTERIA, PALLENE, and PHOSTHONIA, are named in his six-volume work *Commentaries* (*Hypomnemata*).

Source: Blunck, *Solar System Moons*, 83; Groves, *Baby Names that Go Together*, 168; Smith, *Dictionary of Greek and Roman Biography and Mythology*, 108

Drofn

Variations: Dröfn

An ASYNJR from Norse mythology, Drofn ("foam fleck" or "wave") was one of the WAVE MAIDENS who were mother to the god Heimdall; she was the daughter of the god of the sea, Aegir. She, like her sisters, was said to have snow-white skin, blue eyes, and billowing blond hair; in one hand they carried a golden goblet filled with mead and in the other seashells filled with the finest foods. They wore long transparent robes of green or blue trimmed in white. When not serving food in the hall, they played on the shore in groups of three.

Source: Grimes, *Norse Myths*, 122, 261; Sturluson, *Prose Edda*, Volume 5, 219

Drottr (DRUHT-r)

Variations: Drott, Drotr

One of the hrymthursars (FROST GIANTS) from Norse mythology, Drottr ("lazy" or "sluggard") was born one of the sons of THRAEL and THIR. Drottr, his parents, and siblings all lived a hard life of labor performing thankless tasks, such as cleaning, herding goats and swine, placing dung in the fields, and other varied unskilled labor. He and his family became the progenitors of the serving folk and thrall.

Source: Grimes, *Norse Myths*, 27, 261; Norroena Society, *Asatrii Edda*, 341

Drumba (DRUM-ba)

One of the hrymthursars (FROST GIANTS) from Norse mythology, Drumba ("clumsy" or "log") was born one of the daughters of THRAEL and THIR. Drumba, her parents, and siblings all lived a hard life of labor performing thankless tasks, such as cleaning, herding goats and swine, placing dung in the fields, and other varied unskilled labor. He and his family became the progenitors of the serving folk and thrall.

Source: Grimes, *Norse Myths*, 27, 261; Norroena Society, *Asatrii Edda*, 341

Drumbr (DRUM-br)

Variations: Drumb

One of the hrymthursars (FROST GIANTS) from Norse mythology, Drumbr ("clumsy") was born one of the sons of THRAEL and THIR. Drumbr, his parents, and siblings all lived a hard life of labor performing thankless tasks, such as cleaning, herding goats and swine, placing dung in the fields, and other varied unskilled labor. He and his family became the progenitors of the serving folk and thrall.

Source: Grimes, *Norse Myths*, 27, 301; Norroena Society, *Asatrii Edda*, 341

Dryad

Variations: Dryade, HAMADRYAD

Although originating in the folklore of ancient Greece, the dryads are well known all throughout the Celtic countries. The dryads are one of twelve species of NYMPHS; they are the NYMPHS of the forests and trees, particularly oak trees. They have the power to both punish those who abridge the life of the trees under their protection and reward those who actively extend and protect their trees. The life of the dryad is tied to its tree; it is only as long lived as its tree. Ash, oak, and thorn trees are especially important in the Celtic traditions; when these three species of trees are found together they form what is call a Fairy Triad. The trees in these groves are considered sacred to fairies, more so to the dryads.

Described as looking like the perfection of female beauty and youth, a dryad woman will take a human male as her lover; when it does, it is not uncommon for the dryad to solicit a vow from the man asking him to avoid sexual intercourse with all other women. If the lover breaks the vow, he will be struck blind.

Daphne, the dryad associated with the laurel tree, was loved and pursued by the god Apollo. Another famous dryad was Aegle.

Source: Evans-Wentz, *Fairy Faith in Celtic Countries*, 372; Hansen, *Classical Mythology*, 240–1; Keightley, *World Guide to Gnomes, Fairies, Elves, and Other Little People*, 447; Littleton, *Gods, Goddesses, and Mythology*, Volume 4, 440–42

Duergar

Variations: Deugar, Dvergr ("DWARF")

According to Scandinavian folklore, the duergar were the maggots who consumed the flesh of the dead JOTUN YMIR; as they ate they were gifted with human knowledge and took on the general appearance of mankind but were short, having stubby legs but long arms which almost touched the ground. The name of the very first duergar was MODSOGNER, and the name of the second was Dyrin. Skilled gold-, iron-, metal-, and silversmiths, they forged many magical items for both the Æsar and mortal heroes. They are said to reside in the underground realm of Nidavellir, one of the nine worlds fixed to the world-tree Ygdrasil according to Norse cosmology.

In Norse mythology there was a great number of named Duergar about whom, beyond a name, there is little else to nothing known: ALBJOFR ("all thief"), AURGRIMNIR ("mud-grimnir"), AURVANGR ("mudfield"), BAFURR ("bean"), Bari ("the bearing"), BIFURR ("quaking one"), Biiri ("progenitor"), BILDR ("plowman"), BLAINN ("dark-hued"), Blovurr ("the shining"), Bofurr ("bean"), Bomburr ("drummer"), Dari ("the fortifying"), Diifr ("the crooked"), Diiri ("slumber"), Dolgvari ("enemy-weapon"), Dulinn ("the reserved"), Eikinskjaldi ("oaken shield"), Fair ("the caretaker," "the defender"), Fili ("the one who files"), Gandalfr ("wand-ELF"), Gjolp ("boastful," "braggart"), Gloni ("staring"), Grimr ("the masked one"), Gud ("god"), Hannarr ("the skillful"), HARR ("the high"), Haurr ("the high"), Heptifili ("file-

holder," "filer"), Heri ("host"), Hledjolfr ("Shield-Wolf"), Hlevargr ("grave-mound"), Hljodolfr ("silent-wolf"), Hoggstari ("high-star"), Hornbori ("he who bore horn's hair"), Horr ("the dear"), Hugstari ("battle-thinker," or "strategist"), Ingi ("king"), Iri ("the rumor spreading"), JARI ("the disputing"), Litr ("countenance," or "image"), Moinn ("moor-beast"), Nainn ("corpse"), NALI ("corpse," "death"), NAR ("corpse"), Nid ("new moon"), Nidi ("underworld being"), Nipingr ("the dark"), Siarr ("the panning"), SKAFIDR ("the scraper"), Skavaer ("the good-natured"), SKIRFIR ("skillful artisan"), Sviurr ("the disappearing"), Thekkr ("the welcome one"), Thorinn ("the daring"), THRAINN ("the threatening"), THROR ("inciter of strife"), Uni ("the content"), Uri ("the smith"), Varr ("the cautious"), Vegdrasill ("courageous in battle"), VEIGR ("the defiant"), Viggr ("the toothy"), Vindalfr ("wind-ELF"), Virfir ("the virulent"), Vitr ("wise"), YNGVI, Ynguni ("prince," "warrior")

Source: Briggs, *Encyclopedia of Fairies*, 111–12; Keightley, *World Guide to Gnomes, Fairies, Elves, and Other Little People*, 66–7; McCoy, *Witch's Guide to Faery Folk*, 213; Norroena Society, *Asatrii Edda*, 346–401

Dufa

Variations: Dúfa

An ASYNJR from Norse mythology, Dufa ("the pitching one") was one of the WAVE MAIDENS who were mother to the god Heimdall; she was the daughter of the god of the sea, Aegir. She, like her sisters, was said to have snow-white skin, blue eyes, and billowing blond hair; in one hand they carried a golden goblet filled with mead and in the other seashells filled with the finest foods. They wore long transparent robes of green or blue trimmed in white. When not serving food in the hall, they played on the shore in groups of three.

Source: Grimes, *Norse Myths*, 122, 253; Sturluson, *Prose Edda*, Volume 5, 219

Dufur

A DVERG (DWARF) from Norse mythology created by DURINN, Dufur is listed as being one of DURINN's KIN. He, like the others created, paid particular attention to DURINN's leadership.

Source: Grimes, *Norse Myths*, 7

Dumbr

A handsome GIANT of gentle disposition from the Bdrdar saga of Norwegian folklore, Dumbr ("dumb" or "stupid") was also part TROLL and prone to bouts of moodiness. The king of Helluland, Dumbr, father of the hero Bardur, was killed by his rival Hardverkur.

Source: Hollengreen, *Translatio*, 153; Viking Society for Northern Research, *Saga Book of the Viking Society for Northern Research*, Volume 25, 62

Durinn

According to Norse mythology, after the Aesir created the DVERG (DWARF) MODSOGNER from the squirming maggots eating the flesh of the fallen JOTUN YMIR, they then created the DWARF Durinn ("dripper"). Together the two DWARFS created many more of their kind, the story of which is told in the *Voluspa* part of the *Poetic Edda*. The DWARFS made by DURINN were collectively known as DURINN'S KIN.

Source: Daly, *Norse Mythology A to Z*, 21; Lindow, *Norse Mythology*, 99; Young, *Prose Edda*, 26

Durnir

Variations: Durin, DURINN, DVALINN, Dvalnir, Surt

There are both a DVERG (DWARF) and a JOTUN from Norse mythology sharing the name Durnir ("sleepy"). The father of Suttung-Fjalar and forebear to Suttung's sons, Durnir was at one time a friend and ally to the gods working closely with MIMIR until Odin slew his son. After this child's death he denied the Aesir the mead of Byrgir. Durnir will take part in the battle of Ragnarok, wielding the Volund sword, setting the earth ablaze.

Scholars have speculated the characters of DURINN, Drunir, SOKMIMIR, and SURTR are all the same being as they all have a story where their son is slain by Odin in the same manner.

Source: Rydberg, *Our Fathers' Godsaga*, 169; Rydberg, *Teutonic Mythology*, 443–4

Duwende

Variations: Kama-Kama, Lamang Lapa ("earth beings")

A species of invisible DWARF from Filipino folklore, the duwende, described as looking like little bearded men with short arms and legs but large joints, are believed to cause illness in people who disturb their homes, earthen mounds or trees. These nature spirits are also said to play harmless tricks on people; folklore says a white duwende brings good luck while a black one brings bad luck.

Source: Lee, *Encyclopedia of Asian American Folklore and Folklife*, Volume 1, 393; Ramos, *Creatures of Midnight*, 29; Wiegele, *Investing in Miracles*, 133

Dvalin

Variations: DVALINN

A JOTUN in Norse mythology, Dvalin and his brother, DURINN, were created by Modsoghir at Odin's command. Dvalin had a devoted group of Jotnar (see JOTUN) who were his followers; collectively they were known as DVALIN'S HOST and lived in Juravale's Marsh. Whenever he wished to visit his followers, Dvalin would ride his horse MODNIR, there.

As a DVERG (DWARF), Dvalin, along with ALFRIG, BERLING, and GRER, were all skilled smiths who collectively were known as the four Brisingamen DWARFS, and constructed the golden necklace of the goddess Freyia.

Dvalin ("the dormant" or "unconscious one'") was also the name of one of the harts (male Red Deer) or stags named in Thorgrimr's *Rhymes* and in Snorri Sturluson's (1179–1241) *Prose Edda*; the other stags were Dain, Duneyr, and Durathror. Dvalin was symbolic of the calm winds. The stags all lived in the branches of the World Tree, Ygdrasil, eating its branches and leaves. It was from the antlers of these animals that honey-dew fell to the earth and supplied the water for all of the rivers of the world.

Source: Daly, *Norse Mythology A to Z*, 19; Grimes, *Norse Myths*, 260, Guerber, *Hammer of Thor*, 9; Jennbert, *Animals and Humans*, 50; Thorpe, *Northern Mythology*, Volume 1, 32

Dvalin's Host

The collective name for the dwarfs who were the devoted followers and the creation of the DWARF DAVLIN, Dvalin's Host lived in Juravale's Marsh. The names of these dwarfs were AI (who rode upon the horse Hrafn), ALF, ANDVARI, DOLGTTHRASIR, DORI, DRAUPNIR, DUFUR, EIKINSKAJALDI, FINNR, FROSTI, GINNARR, GLOI, HARR, HAUGSPORI, HLEVANGUR, ORI, SKAFIDUR, SKIRFIR, VIRVIR, and YNGVI. When visiting them, Dvalin would ride his horse MODNIR.

Source: Grimes, *Norse Myths*, 7

Dverg, plural Dvergar

Variations: Svartalf

The black DWARFs of Norse mythology, the dvergar were described as being smaller than men, swarthy and ugly looking; these tumorous creatures, bred from maggots, were expert craftsmen and metal smiths. Like TROLLS, dvergar were unable to withstand direct sunlight, making them cave dwelling nocturnal beings.

Source: Oehlenschläger, *Gods of the North*, xxxviii

Dwarf, plural dwarfs

Variations: Berg-Mänlein ("hill-mannikins"), Dorch, Drerge, DVERG, Dware, Dweeorg, Dwerger, Dwergugh, Dworh, Erd-Mänlein ("ground-mannikins"), Gotho, Härdmandle, Hel-kaplein, Hill TROLLS, Kleine Volk ("little people"), MOSS PEOPLE,

Oennerbanske, Oennereeske, Stele Volk ("still peo-ple"), Tarnkapppe, Tele Volk ("still people"), Tim-ber, Torpek, Trold, TROLL, Unnerorske ("under-ground folks"), Wichtelweib, Wichtlein ("little Wights"), Wild, Zwerge, Zzwerg

The dwarf is a popular and staple figure in folk-lore. Generally these short but powerfully built beings are beneficent and will assist those who treat them with respect; however if injured or offended they will quickly vent their rage on cattle. They appear to be old, reach maturity at three years of age, and the males of the species will have long, grey beards. Dwarfs who live underground do not involve themselves with humans if they can help it, as they would rather mine for their gold and pre-cious gems. If they venture above ground, the dwarf will do so at night. They have the ability to become invisible and can walk through rocks and walls. The folklore varies as to why they do not venture out into the light; sometimes it is said they will turn to stone but other times it is said they spend their day-light hours in the guise of a frog. Because they are such isolationists they are said to be members of the Unseelie Court.

The fairies of England are the dwarfs of Ger-many and the lands to its north.

In Iceland dwarfs are said to wear red clothing. The fullest account of Icelandic dwarfs comes from the learned Bishop of Skalholt, Finnus Johannaeus, in his book *The Ecclesiastical History of Iceland*, but it makes almost no distinction between elves and dwarfs.

In Brenton dwarfs are called KORRIGAN.

In Finland and Lapland it is believed dwarfs live in a magnificent underground land and sometimes mortals are allowed to enter. While a guest, they are spectacularly entertained and given copious amounts of brandy and tobacco.

In Friesland, Netherlands, dwarfs are called oen-nereeske and tend to fall in love with mortal women and steal them away, keeping them for long periods of time. They also steal children and leave CHANGELINGS in their place. Oennereeske will also borrow and lend plates and pots as well as money, sometimes even charging interest. They will assist in the construction of churches and homes, help when a cart is stuck in the mud, and bring field workers pancakes and water.

In Switzerland dwarfs are called DVERG ("spi-der") and are described as being generous, kind and having a joyous nature. Fond of strolling throughout the land, they will randomly take part in acts of kindness, such as driving sheep and leaving berries where poor children can find them. In Scandinavian folklore, the more common word used for the dwarf is TROLL or trold.

The fifteenth century German manuscript enti-tled *The Heldenbuch* (*Book of Heroes*) claims "God created the GIANTs that they might kill the wild beasts, and the great dragons, that the dwarfs might be more secure."

Dwarfs in southern Germany live in large com-munal groups but tend to appear to man alone. They are described as being small, grey and old looking, hairy and covered in moss, standing as tall as a three-year-old child. Female dwarfs in southern Germany have a nicer disposition than their male counterparts; they wear green clothing trimmed in red and cocked hats upon their heads. They live deep back in the woods and will give woodcutters good advice and assist in cooking and washing clothes. They most often appear where people are baking so they can use the fire. A bit of dough is left for them as an offering. The male dwarfs in southern Germany live in mines and dress like min-ers, carrying a hammer, lantern, and mallet. They enjoy throwing stones at miners but unless they have been offended, the assault is harmless.

In Lusatia, Germany, it is believed dwarfs are actually fallen angels.

In some German tales when a dwarf's hat is knocked off of their head it becomes visible. They can also bestow physical strength, curse a family to poverty, foresee future events, gift prosperity upon a family, and shape-shift into any form.

Interestingly, there are no dwarfs in Italian folk-lore.

Source: Bord, *Fairies*, 60; Briggs, *Encyclopedia of Fairies*, 115; Evans-Wentz, *Fairy Faith in Celtic Countries*, 374–75; Keightley, *World Guide to Gnomes, Fairies, Elves, and Other Little People*, 216–17, 229–30, 264, 281, 448; Lindow, *Norse Mythology*, 99–101.

Dynas

Variations: Dan Dynas, Den-an-Dyans

A GIANT of Cornish folklore, Dynas and his wife, An Venna (Aunt Venna), were credited with having built the outer walls of Castle Treen, England. It was said his wife assisted him because Dynas was both deaf and unable to speak; however it was said he had a fierce and resounding roar of anger. Dynas would stand on Carnol and from his perch sink invading ships by hurling stones at them from his sling while they were still far out or, when they drew near, dropping boulders on them as they attempted to pass his post. Like many Cornish GIANTs, Dynas was fond of "old time" games and would play with the local children. However, he was unaware of his own strength and would every now and again accidentally kill one of them.

Source: Bottrell, *Traditions and Hearthside Stories of West Cornwall*, 137–8

Dzoo-Noo-Qua

A giantess from the folklore of the Kwakiutl people of British Columbia, Canada, Dzoo-Noo-Qua was a cannibal who specifically sought out children to enslave and later consume. Living deep in the wilderness, she kept her spirit hidden beneath the floorboards of her lodge thereby making her body indestructible. According to the story, the cultural hero Sky Boy had tracked the GIANT to her home and took a shot at her with his bow and arrow. Although he missed his mark the arrow flew through her home and into a hole in the floorboard landing directly in her hidden spirit, killing Dzoo-Noo-Qua instantly.

Source: Mason, *Indian Tales of the Northwest*, 71; Rose, *Giants, Monsters, and Dragons*, 108

Dzunukwa

Variations: Wild Woman of the Woods

In Kwakwaka'wakw folklore, Dzunukwa was a child-eating cannibal; she is depicted as having large round eyes set in an oversized head; long, thick dark hair; large breasts; facial hair; black skin; and lips stained red from the copious amounts of human blood she has consumed. The skulls of the children she has consumed are used as adornments on her body. Physically she is strong enough to uproot trees and spiritually she is powerful enough to resurrect the dead. She can also call lightning from the sky with her cry of *"Huu, huu, huu!"* Dzunukwa has a great treasure hoard in her possession consisting of items of both wealth and magical properties. Both stupid and vain, she can be tricked by a clever person and have treasures stolen. Typically, she travels underground but when she is above ground she travels with a basket on her back to hold her captives.

Source: Illes, *Encyclopedia of Spirits*, 377; Shearar, *Understanding Northwest Coast Art*, 41–2

Ebu Gogo

According to Flores Island folklore of the Azores, the ebu gogo were a race of diminutive humanoids who once lived in a cave called Lia Ula at the base of the volcano Gunung Ebulobo on the southern edge of Soa Basin. According to legend the ebu gogo, apart from being small, were hairy and had canine teeth, potbellies, overly long arms and legs, and protruding ears; they were said to be very strong and fast runners. The females had breasts so long they would keep them over their shoulders and feed their young from behind. These little creatures, although capable of human speech, would only repeat back exactly the words spoken to them. Fearful of fire, the ebu gogo would normally stand outside of the village and murmur to one another before sneaking in to steal food or livestock. In the legend, they stole a baby which caused the villagers to chase them back to their cave. Unable to make the sheer climb, the locals tied baskets of hot coals to long bamboo sticks and tossed them into the cave, igniting what lay within and killing the ebu gogo to the last.

Source: Forth, *Images of the Wildman in Southeast Asia*, 12–3; Goldenberg, *Little People and a Lost World*, 45

Echion, Gigantes

Variations: Echinades

Not to be confused with the SPARTI of the same name, the blood-thirsty GIGANTE Echion ("snake man" or "viper") was born of the earth and a natural enemy of the gods of Olympus.

Source: Segal, *Dionysiac Poetics and Euripides' Bacchae*, 130

Echion, Sparti

Variations: Echinades

In classical Greek mythology, Echion ("snake man" or "viper") was one of the five SPARTI who went on to become the progenitors of the five leading families of the city of Thebes who formed the military caste. Echion was married to Agave and they were the parents of Pentheus. After dedicating a temple to Cybele in Boeotia, Echion went on to assist Cadmus (Kadmos) in constructing the city of Thebes.

Source: Apollodorus, *Apollodorus' Library and Hyginus' Fabulae*, 22, 47; Dixon-Kennedy, *Encyclopedia of Greco-Roman Mythology*, 86; Hard, *Routledge Handbook of Greek Mythology*, 296

Egia

An ASYNJR from Norse mythology, Egia ("foamer") was one of the WAVE MAIDENS who were mother to the god Heimdall; she was the daughter of the god of the sea, Aegir. She, like her sisters, was said to have snow-white skin, blue eyes, and billowing blond hair; in one hand they carried a golden goblet filled with mead and in the other seashells filled with the finest foods. They wore long transparent robes of green or blue trimmed in white. When not serving food in the hall, they played on the shore in groups of three.

Source: Daly, *Norse Mythology A to Z*, 47; Grimes, *Norse Myths*, 255

Eigi Einhamr

In Iceland and Norway there was a cult of people

who, according to legend, had the ability of theri-anthropy, enabling them to shape-shift themselves into animals and take on the characteristics and powers of the animal they became while retaining their human intellect and reason; these individuals were known as eigi einhamr ("not of one skin") and a man once transformed was called a *hamrammr*. The transformation from man to animal could take place in a number of ways, such as by donning an animal pelt or reciting a magical incantation. The eigi einhamr's body remained in a cataleptic trance while the spirit of the man entered into his animal form.

Source: Guiley, *Encyclopedia of Vampires, Werewolves, and Other Monsters*, 117; Maberry, *Vampire Universe*, 105–107

Eikinskajaldi

A DVERG (DWARF) from Norse mythology created by DURINN, Eikinskajaldi is listed as being one of DURINN's KIN. He, like the others created, paid particular attention to DURINN's leadership; he lived in Juravale's Marsh.

Source: Grimes, *Norse Myths*, 7, 263

Eikintjasna (AYK-in-tyas-na)

One of the hrymthursars (FROST GIANTS) from Norse mythology, Eikintjasna ("gossiper" or "oak peg") was born one of the daughters of THRAEL and THIR. Eikintjasna, her parents, and siblings all lived a hard life of labor performing thankless tasks, such as cleaning, herding goats and swine, placing dung in the fields, and other varied unskilled labor. He and his family became the progenitors of the serving folk and thrall.

Source: Grimes, Norse Myths, 27, 263; Norroena Society, *Asatrii Edda*, 343

Eimnir

One of the JOTUN from Norse mythology, Eimnir ("reeking with blood") was, along with BRANDINGI, ELDR, and LOGI, the personification of fire.

Source: Norroena Society, *Asatrii Edda*, 336; Taunton, *Northern Traditions*, 31

Eir (AYR)

An ASYNJR of Norse mythology, Eir ("clemency," "help," or "peace") was the healer of Aesir; the best of all physicians, she was one of Menglod's attendants.

Source: Grimes, *Norse Myths*, 263

Eistla

In Norse mythology Eistla was an ASYNJR, one of the WAVE MAIDENS who gave birth to the god Heimdall.

Source: Anderson, *History and Romance of Northern Europe*, Volume 5, 1018; Norroena Society, *Asatrii Edda*, 25

Elate

In Greek mythology, the giantess (female GIGANTE) Elate ("fir tree") was the sister of the ALOADAE, as tall as her brothers, and born the daughter of ALOEUS and Iphimedea. After the death of her brothers Elate could not control her grief and wept continuously; the gods took pity on her and transformed her into a spruce tree.

Source: Fontenrose, *Orion*, 116

Elathan

Variations: Elatha

According to Gaelic mythology and described in the *Book of the Dun Cow (Lebor Na H-Uidhri)*, an ancient Irish manuscript compiled around the year 1100 CE, Elathan is a Chief among the FORMORI-ANs, considered by some to be a demon of darkness. Like all FORMORIANs, he has the body of a man and the head of a goat; however, Elathan was said to be very handsome. He and all of his kind were defeated by the TUATHA DE DENANN and driven into the sea.

Source: Knox, *History of the County of Mayo*, 329; Moore, *The Unicorn*, 71, 72; Squire, *Celtic Myths and Legend Poetry and Romance*, 33, 51

Eldjötnar

Variations: Fire Giants

One of the species of JOTUN from Norse mythology, the Eldjötnar were FIRE GIANTS; the BERGRISAR are the mountain GIANTS; the FROST GIANTS were called the Hrimpursar. The Eldjötnar live in the realm of fire, Muspelheim; at the time of Ragnarok they will gather with the others of their kind and wage war against the gods on the Plain of Vigdir.

Source: Maberry, *They Bite*, 344; Mabie, *Norse Mythology*, 88

Eldr

One of the JOTUN from Norse mythology, Eldr ("fire"), along with BRANDINGI, EIMNER, and LOGI, was a personification of fire.

Source: Norroena Society, *Asatrii Edda*, 336; Taunton, *Northern Traditions*, 31

Eleazar the Giant (el-EE-ay-zuhr)

According to Josephus, Romano-Jewish scholar, historian and hagiographer from the first century, the king of Persia sent hostages to Rome to insure peace. Among them was a Jewish individual named Eleazar ("God helped") the GIANT; it was said he stood over ten feet tall. He was a part of the entourage of Darius, son of Artabanes.

Source: DeLoach, *Giants*, 88; Mandel, *Ultimate Who's Who in the Bible*, 152; Wood, *Giants and Dwarfs*, 25

Eleionomae

Variations: Eleionomai

The Eleionomae are a sub-species of the LIMNIAD or NAIADS in Greek mythology; they are the NYMPHS of fresh water marshes.

Source: Bell, *Women of Classical Mythology*, 179; Day, *God's Conflict with the Dragon and the Sea*, 394; Littleton, *Gods, Goddesses, and Mythology*, Volume 11, 999; Maberry, *Cryptopedia*, 112

Elf, plural elves

Variations: Elb, Elfin, Ellyll (plural ellyllon), Erl, Fary, Fay, Fée, Huldrafolk, Mannikin, Ouph, Wight

Elf is a generic word used world-wide to describe a wide array of FAIRY-folk, including DWARFS, GNOMES and TROLLS; it is used interchangeably with the word *fairy*. They answer to their own royalty having their own kings and queens and greatly enjoy celebrating and feasting banquets and weddings. Descriptions of these creatures, from their appearance to their dress, vary widely, as do their disposition and personalities.

In England the elves are divided into two distinct classes: domestic and rural. Domestic elves are a type of household spirit and live symbiotically with mankind on their farms and in their homes, such as the brownies (a species of domestic fairy or HOUSE-SPIRIT from Scottish fairy folklore) and hobgoblins do. Rural elves live in caverns, fields, mountains and wilderness. TROOPING FAIRIES are small, benevolent, and kind, freely helping humans, whereas solitary fairies have a tendency to be injurious and if they choose to assist a person will set a price on their services. Generally speaking, each is skilled at spinning cloth and thread as well as making shoes.

Like British folklore, elves are divided into two classes in Scandinavian folklore, the light elves of the Seelie Court and the DARK ELVES of the Unseelie Court. The voice of the elves in this part of the world is said to be soft and sweet, like the air. Children who are born on a Sunday have the natural ability to see elves and similar such beings.

In Scotland fairies are human size and are often called elves; their Fairyland was known as Elfame.

Common folklore in Wales claims the ellyllon should be respected, as they are the souls of the ancient druids who are too good to be condemned to Hell but not good enough to be allowed to enter Heaven. The ellyllon are assigned the punishment of wandering upon the earth among mankind until Judgment Day when they will be allowed to rise into a higher state of being.

In Africa elves are seasonal fairies and more akin to nature spirits.

Teutonic and Norse folklore claims fairies (huldrafolk) were once the spirits of the dead bringing fertility to the land. Later, they evolved into small, humanoid beings; the beautiful ones were considered to be elves of light while ugly ones were called black or DARK ELVES. Dutch elves (ellefolk) are beautiful creatures with hollow backs.

Source: Ashliman, *Fairy Lore*, 199; Bord, *Fairies*, 2; Illes, *Encyclopedia of Spirits*, 383; Keightley, *World Guide to Gnomes, Fairies, Elves, and Other Little People*, 57, 81; McCoy, *Witch's Guide to Faery*, 171; Stepanich, *Faery Wicca*, Book One, 270

Elle-maid

Variations: Elve-Woman, Wood-Woman

The elle-maids of German and Scandinavian folklore are a nocturnal species of FAIRY. Similar to the cruel and lovely KORRIGAN of Brittany, France, they dance in the grass with such grace, when they offer themselves to a young man resistance is seldom met. These elves are known to also sit by the roadside with food and wine, offering a cup to men as they pass; should any accept and drink the wine, they will go insane. Hauntingly beautiful when seen from the front, the elle-maid is revealed to be hollow when seen from behind. To drive an elle-maid away, make the sign of the Cross in her presence and she will disappear.

Source: Chambers, *Chambers's Journal*, Volumes 19–20, 256; Colburn, *New Monthly Magazine*, 78; Keightley, *World Guide to Gnomes, Fairies, Elves, and Other Little People*, 81, 323

Ellu

The ellu ("the shining ones") from ancient Akkadian and Babylonian mythology was a race of beings and a line of Mesopotamian kings who were, according to legend, the descendants of the Anunnaki Sinhars and the gods.

Source: De Lafayette, *Akkadian-English Dictionary*, 255; Hines, *Gateway of the Gods*, 72

The Emim

Variations: REPHAIM

Before Israel's invasion of Canaan, the Emin ("dreadful ones"), a tribe of GIANTS from Hebrew folklore described as "great, many, and tall," lived in Shaveh Kiriathaim (modern Kureyat), the region eventually taken over by the descendants of Moab.

Source: DeLoach, *Giants*, 8, 89; Hastings, *Encyclopædia of Religion and Ethics: Fiction-Hyksos*, Volume 6, 192

Encelados

Variations: Asterios, Asterius, Enceladus, Enkelados

A GIGANTE from ancient Greek mythology, Encelados ("buzzer") was born of the great goddess Gaea and the god Uranus. He and his siblings were extremely large, immensely strong, and absolutely fearsome to behold as they had dense beards, a thick head of hair, and feet covered with DRAKON scales; they threw flaming oak trees and rocks at the heavens.

Encelados was slain by the virgin goddess Athena (Minerva) during the ten year war against the Olympian gods, the Gigantomachy, who ripped off a section of Sicily, Mount Etna, and threw it down upon him. The volcanic fires of the mountain are to this day said to be Encelados's fiery breath; earthquakes and tremors are said to be his thrashing about in pain.

Source: Apollodorus, *Library of Greek Mythology*, 34–5; Coulter, *Encyclopedia of Ancient Deities*, 167; Daniels, *Encyclopædia of Superstitions, Folklore, and the Occult Sciences of the World*, 1376

Enim

One of the races of GIANTS said to live in Palestine, the Enim ("terrors") were the descendants of the WATCHERs and the women of Canaan; they were described as being gigantic in stature and having great strength.

Source: Aichele, *Violence, Utopia and the Kingdom of God*, 52; Garnier, *Worship of the Dead*, 93–4

Enkidu

In the *Epic of Gilgamesh*, the epic poem from ancient Mesopotamia dating back to 1800 BC, there is a character, a WEREWOLF and WILD MAN, by the name of Enkidu who was created by the god of the sky, Anu, to be an adversary to the hero Gilgamesh. Initially, the two are enemies, but after Gilgamesh defeats Enkidu they become friends and have many adventures together. Enkidu learns culture and refinement from Gilgamesh and in turn teaches his friend humility and respect. The goddess Ishtar wanted to marry Gilgamesh who flatly and violently rejected her; hurt, she begged her father to release the Bull of Heaven to kill the hero; side by side the friends fought and eventually killed the creature. The goddess Ishtar leapt to the wall of Uruk and began to utter a curse upon Gilgamesh, but Enkidu ripped the right hind leg off of the Bull of Heaven and waved it in her face, exclaiming how he wished he could do worse to her than he did to the Bull. For his hubris, Enkidu was haunted by horrific dreams and after twelve sleepless nights, died.

Source: Maberry, *They Bite*, 180; Sanders, *Epic of Gilgamesh*, 88

Eos

Variations: Aurora

A TITAN from ancient Greek mythology, Eos ("dawn") was born one of the three children of the first generation TITAN HYPERION; she was described as being rosy-armed and fingered and would light the earth each day.

Source: Daly, *Greek and Roman Mythology, A to Z*, 141; Westmoreland, *Ancient Greek Beliefs*, 26–7

Ephialtes

Variations: Epihialtes

A GIGANTE from ancient Greek mythology, Ephialtes was born of the great goddess Gaea and the god Uranus ("heaven"). He and his siblings were extremely large, immensely strong, and absolutely fearsome to behold as they had dense beards, a thick head of hair, and feet covered with DRAKON scales; they threw flaming oak trees and rocks at the heavens.

During the ten year war against the gods, the Gigantomachy, he was slain when the god Apollo shot him in the left eye with an arrow and the demigod Hercules (Heracles) shot him in the right.

Source: Apollodorus, *Library of Greek Mythology*, 34–5; Daniels, *Encyclopædia of Superstitions, Folklore, and the Occult Sciences of the World*, 1376

Epimeliad

The Epimeliad were a sub-species of the HAMADRYAD; they were the NYMPHS of apple trees in Greek mythology.

Source: Parada, *Genealogical Guide to Greek Mythology*, 70, 128;

Epimeliades

Variations: Boukolai, Epimelides

In the mythology of the ancient Greeks the epimeliades ("those who care for flocks") were the NYMPHS of tending sheep.

Sources: Antoninus Liberalis, *Metamorphoses of Antoninus Liberalis*, 197; Avant, *Mythological Reference*, 251; Rigoglioso, *Cult of Divine Birth in Ancient Greece*, 87

Epimetheus

A second generation TITAN from ancient Greek mythology, Epimetheus ("hindsight," literally "hind-thought") was the brother of PROMETHEUS ("foresight" literally "fore-thought"). The two sons of the TITAN IAPETUS and the second generation TITAN and OCEANID CLYMENE sided with the Olympian gods in the war against the gods, the Titanomachy; the brothers fought against not only their father but also their two other brothers, ATLAS and MENOETIUS.

Epimetheus and PROMETHEUS were charged

with the responsibility of making man and the animals of the earth and giving each one the necessary facilities to ensure their preservation. Epimetheus had been so generous with his division of abilities when he finally came to man he had nothing left to bestow upon them. PROMETHEUS intervened and ascended into the heavens; with the assistance of the goddess Athena (Minerva) he procured fire and returned to his brother with it as the boon to mankind. Having fire made man more than a match for any of the creatures; this did not please Zeus (Jupiter), the leader of the Olympian gods.

Zeus (Jupiter) had Hephaistos (Vulcan) craft a beautiful but inquisitive woman they named Pandora and gave her as a gift to Epimetheus. PROMETHEUS warned his brother about accepting gifts from Zeus (Jupiter), as he was aware the god was displeased with him for giving the gift of fire to mankind and was looking for a way to bring long-term grief, misery, and long-term illness to humanity. Epimetheus was overcome with the beauty and graces of Pandora and eagerly accepted her as his bride. Next, Zeus (Jupiter) had the god Hermes (Mercury) deliver a beautiful and divine vat to Pandora; he was instructed to inform her she needed to safeguard it and never open it to examine its contents. She agrees and accepts the responsibility and for a time is able to curb her desire to see its contents. One day the strain becomes too great and she opens the lid releasing all sorts of illnesses and plagues upon mankind. Quickly realizing her mistake, she is able to close the lid before Hope was able to escape.

Source: Bulfinch, *Bulfinch's Greek and Roman Mythology*, 18–9; Westmoreland, *Ancient Greek Beliefs*, 91–2

Erix

According to the French Renaissance doctor, Greek scholar, monk, Renaissance humanist, satirist, writer of fantasy, and author of bawdy jokes and songs François Rabelais, Erix was the son of the GIANT GOLIATH and grandson of the TITAN ATLAS; Erix was supposed to have been the inventor of legerdemain and the father of a GIANT named Titius.

Source: Brewer, *Character Sketches of Romance, Fiction and the Drama*, Volume 3, 81; Daniels, *Encyclopædia of Superstitions, Folklore, and the Occult Sciences of the World*, 1376; Ozeli, *Works of Francis Rabelais*, 11

Etin (EHT-in)

Variations: Ettin

In Norse mythology, Etin ("eater") was a JOTUN about whom, beyond a name, there is little to nothing else known.

Source: Grimes, *Norse Myths*, 264; Norroena Society, *Asatrii Edda*, 336

Etis

An OCEANID and TITAN from ancient Greek mythology, Etis was born one of the daughters of the first generation TITAN OCEANIDS and his sister wife TETHYS.

Source: Daly, *Greek and Roman Mythology, A to Z*, 141

Eurybia

A TITAN from ancient Greek mythology, Eurybia was born one of the children of Gaea (earth) and the ancient god of the sea, Pontus; she was said to have a heart of stone yet was bright or shining to behold. By Crius she was the mother of ASTRAEUS, PALLUS, and PERSES.

Source: Daly, *Greek and Roman Mythology, A to Z*, 141; Westmoreland, *Ancient Greek Beliefs*, 22, 788

Eurymedon

The king of the GIGANTES, Eurymedon ("wide ruling") of classical Greek mythology was the first lover of the goddess Hera (Juno) before Zeus (Jupiter) came into power and married her. Hera, a good friend to Gain, the mother of Eurymedon, bore the GIGANTE a son, PROMETHEUS. After his ascension to the throne, the god learned of his wife's old romance and cast Eurymedon into Tartarus and using the excuse of PROMETHEUS' having given fire to mankind, chained him to a rock to have his liver ripped out and eaten daily by an eagle. Hera (Juno), knowing of the Gigantomachy and the role Hercules (Heracles) would play in it, arranged to have the demi-god engaged in a quest when the war began at Phlegra, Eurymedon leading the way. Hermes was able to deliver Hercules to the battle in time to save the gods and Eurymedon and all of his kind were destroyed.

Source: Fontenrose, *Python*, 242; Yasumura, *Challenges to the Power of Zeus in Early Greek Poetry*, 54, 56

Eurynome

An OCEANID and TITAN from ancient Greek mythology, Eurynome was born one of the daughters of the first generation TITAN OCEANIDS and his sister wife TETHYS. She and her husband OPHION were at one time the rulers of Olympus but they were dethroned by TITANS CRONUS and RHEA. She is said to have created the TITAN Eurynmrdon to exist with THEMIS.

Source: Daly, *Greek and Roman Mythology, A to Z*, 141; Westmoreland, *Ancient Greek Beliefs*, 728

Eurytos

A GIGANTE from ancient Greek mythology,

Eurytos was born of the great goddess Gaea and the TITAN Uranus ("heaven"). He and his siblings were extremely large, immensely strong, and absolutely fearsome to behold as they had dense beards, a thick head of hair, and feet covered with DRAKON scales; they threw flaming oak trees and rocks at the heavens. During the ten year war against the Olympian gods, the Gigantomachy, he was slain when CLYTIOS struck with her torches, MIMAS struck with his red-hot missiles, and the god Dionysos (Bacchus) struck with his thyrsus.

In ancient Greek mythology Eurytos ("flowing and expanse") was the name of one of the Centaurs (a creature from Greek mythology, half equine and half human, entangled with issues of sexual boundaries and promiscuity).

Source: Apollodorus, *Library of Greek Mythology*, 34–5; Colvin, *Cornhill Magazine*, Volume XXXVIII, 296; Daniels, *Encyclopædia of Superstitions, Folklore, and the Occult Sciences of the World*, 1376

Ewaipanoma

Sir Walter Raleigh, in his account of Guiana, describes a race of people who have no head; rather their eyes are set in their shoulders and their mouth is located in the middle of their chest. Raleigh claims although he did not actually see any of the Ewaipanoma himself, he strongly believed the eye-witness testimony he heard from all the children in the area. The Ewaipanoma, according to the story, live along the Caoro River which runs through the provinces of Arromaia and Canuri in the empire of Guiana.

Source: Raleigh, *Sir Walter Ralegh's Discoverie of Guiana*, lxii, 158, 199; Wilson, *Caliban*, 45

Eyrgjafa

In Norse mythology Eyrgjafa ("she who gives sandbanks") was one of the ASYNJR and one of the WAVE MAIDENs who gave birth to the god Heimdall.

Source: Anderson, *History and Romance of Northern Europe*, Volume 5, 1018; Norroena Society, *Asatrii Edda*, 336; Rydberg, *Teutonic Mythology*, 407

Fachan

Variations: Direach Ghlinn Eitidh, Fachen, Fachin, Peg Leg Jack

An ATHACH or GIANT from the West Highlands of Scotland, the fachan are described as being ugly; a hand protrudes from their chest, thick fur covers their body, and they have only one leg and eye. They dress in a girdle of deer skins with a mantle of blue feathers as they are jealous of fairies capable of flight. Some folklore claims the fachan are so physically repulsive that seeing one may induce a heart attack. Expert leapers, the fachan are not nearly as agile as a person. Known for their malevolent disposition and hating all living things, they carry a spiked club they use liberally when chasing people out of their territory. They will also use their club or wickedly spiked chain to destroy an entire orchard in a single night. A popular Highland tale tells of a fachan named Nesnas Mhiccallain.

Source: Avant, *Mythological Reference*, 187; Briggs, *Encyclopedia of Fairies*, 129; Campbell, *Popular Tales of the West Highlands*, 298; Maberry, *Vampire Universe*, 116

Fairymaid

In the mythology of the Republic of Trinidad and Tobago the fairymaid is a beautiful creature, having long and lush hair and one small foot shaped like a deer's hoof. Using her magical ability she can seduce a man as well as steal his shadow, leaving him quite insane. Fairymaids are said to live beneath bridges and in the caves behind waterfalls. The males of the species are said to live in the deep ocean and they only meet with the females in deep water pools to breed.

Source: Besson, *Folklore and Legends of Trinidad and Tobago*, 16–7; Prahlad, *Encyclopedia of African American Folklore*, 1295

Fangbodi

A JOTUN from Norse mythology, Fangbodi ("challenger") is mentioned in the skaldic poem *Ragnarsdrápa*, written by Bragi Boddason and composed for Swedish king Björn.

Source: Halpin, *Manlike Monsters on Trial*, 52; Olsen, *Monsters and the Monstrous in Medieval Northwest Europe*, 129

Farbanti (FAHR-bout-i)

Variations: Farbauti ("cruel striker"), Farbuti

In Norse mythology Farbanti ("anger striker" or "the one inflicting harm") was a JOTUN whose job was to ferry the dead across the water and into the underworld; he was also the father of the gods Loki and HELBLINDI by his first wife, the ASYNJR or Aesir LAUFEY (Nal, "needle"), who is described as being slender and weak. Laufey conceived her son Loki when Farbanti struck her with a lightning bolt.

Source: Coulter, *Encyclopedia of Ancient Deities*, 177; Daly, *Norse Mythology A to Z*, 63–4; Lindow, *Norse Mythology*, 111

Faribroth

François Rabelais (AD 1494–1553) compiled the lineage of the GIANTS; according to his works, born the son of SARABROTH, Faribroth "*begot* HURTALI, *a brave eater of pottage (soup) who lived in the time of the Flood.*"

Source: Brewer, *Character Sketches of Romance, Fiction and the Drama*, Volume 3, 80; Daniels, *Encyclopædia of Supersti-*

tions, Folklore, and the Occult Sciences of the World, 1376; Rabelais, *Hours with Rabelais*, 80

The Fates

Variations: Destines, Fata, Fatal Sisters, Moirai ("allotter" or "cutter-off"), Parcae ("those who bring forth the child"), Parcæ

Depicted as three sisters who guide the fate of man rather than control or determine it, many of the classical Greek authors saw them as beings more powerful than the gods. In mythology, they do not play an active part.

In the Late Greek tradition, Clotho's name with its reference to spinning contributed to the Fates being depicted as three elderly women spinning out the thread of a man's life, measuring it, and then cutting it at a specific length.

Homer, the greatest ancient Greek epic poet and author of the *Iliad* and the *Odyssey*, says there was only one god who presided over fate, Moipa, and even the gods were subject to her plans. However, according to Hesiod, the Greek oral poet (ca. 750–650 BC), and all poets after him, there were three such beings born the daughters of Nyx ("night"); their names were Atropos ("inevitable"), Clotho ("the spinner"), and Lachesis ("drawer of lots").

In Upper Brittany, the Fates are referred to as the fetes.

Source: Dixon-Kennedy, *Encyclopedia of Greco-Roman Mythology*, 133; Grant, *Who's Who in Classical Mythology*, 136–7; Huffington, *Gods of Greece*, 22; Roman, *Encyclopedia of Greek and Roman Mythology*, 171; Society for the Diffusion of Useful Knowledge, *Penny Cyclopædia*, Volume 17, 242

Fenja (FEHN-ya)

An ASYNJR from Norse mythology, Fenja ("swampy" or "water-maiden") along with MENJA ("necklace") was a slave purchased by King Frodi Fridleifsson. He kept them chained to a magical mill called Grotti where they were made to grind gold, happiness, and peace without ever being allowed to rest as they were the only ones strong enough to operate the mill. Eventually the two ASYNJR ground out an army led by the sea king Mysing who attacked Fridleifsson, killing him. Mysing then took possession of the mill and bade the two ASYNJR to grind salt, and he too never allowed them rest. The ship upon which the mill had been placed sank causing the ocean to become salty and, presumably, drowning Fenja and MENJA.

Source: Grimm, *Teutonic Mythology*, Volume 2, 864; Lindow, *Norse Myths*, 152; Sturluson, *Prose Edda*, 125

Ferracute

Variations: Ferragus

A GIANT with the strength of forty men, Ferracute

from Turpin's *Chronicle of Charlemagne* was said to have been sent to Nager by Admiraldus with twenty-thousand Turks to confront King Charles. Fearing neither dart nor spear, Ferracute was described as being "*twelve cubits tall, his face a cubit long, his nose a palm, his arms and thighs four cubits, and his fingers three palms in length.*" (A *cubit* is the distance from a man's elbow to the tip of his middle finger.)

Ferracute challenged the king to send out his best warriors to one-on-one combat, and having little choice, the king sent one warrior after another to confront the GIANT. More than twenty of the king's best men were easily defeated in combat by Ferracute, taken captive, and held prisoner. Finally Orlando convinced the king to allow him to fight the Muslim GIANT. The two faced off and after many hours battled one another to a stalemate. They agreed to a temporary truce and returned again the next day to resume battle but this time without horse or spear. When they confronted one another a second time, again they fought, but as before neither was able to gain the advantage, as Ferracute was nearly invulnerable and Orlando could not deliver a shot in his point of vulnerability. Again they called a truce and each lay down in the field to rest. When they awoke before they battled, Orlando and Ferracute talked with one another, mostly about the differences of their religions; Orlando answered all of Ferracute's questions. It was decided between the combatants whoever won this, their final battle, would be the champion of the true faith; Orlando fighting for Christians and Ferracute fighting for the Muslims. The battle resumed and fiercer than ever; Orlando cried out to God for Divine Intervention and was then able to deliver a death blow to the only vulnerable point on the GIANT's body, his navel. Ferracute cried out to Allah but his call went unanswered and his people had to drag him from the field. Orlando was then able to mount an assault against the Turks and rescue the captive warriors of King Charles.

Source: Daniels, *Encyclopædia of Superstitions, Folklore, and the Occult Sciences of the World*, 1376; Rodd, *History of Charles the Great and Orlando*, Volume 1, 25–31

Fierabras

Variations: Fierabras of Alexandria, Fierbras

In medieval French folklore Fierabras the GIANT was the son of the GIANT BALAN. A Saracen (Muslim), he sacked the city of Rome with his father and stole the last two jars of fluid which was alleged to have been used on Christ. The fluid was said to have magical properties and could cure any illness and close any wound. Fierabras was defeated by Oliveros who gave the balm to King Charlemagne so it could be returned to Rome.

Source: Daniels, *Encyclopædia of Superstitions, Folklore, and the Occult Sciences of the World*, 1376; Mancing, *Cervantes Encyclopedia: A-K*, 57, 294; Rose, *Giants, Monsters, and Dragons*, 37–8

Finnr

A DVERG (DWARF) from Norse mythology created by DURINN, Finnr is listed as being one of DURINN'S KIN. He, like the others created, paid particular attention to DURINN's leadership.

Source: Grimes, *Norse Myths*, 260; Wackerbarth, *Beowulf*, xxxii

Fion

According to Gaelic legend, Fion ("wine"), born the son of Comnal, was an enormous GIANT who could place his feet on two mountains and then stoop down to drink from a stream running through the valley.

Source: Daniels, *Encyclopædia of Superstitions, Folklore, and the Occult Sciences of the World*, 1376; Macleod, *Dictionary of the Gaelic Language, in two Parts*, 293

Fiorgwyn

A JOTUN from Norse mythology, Fiorgwyn was the father of the goddess Frigga.

Source: Brewer, *Character Sketches of Romance, Fiction and the Drama*, Volumes 5–6, 81; Daniels, *Encyclopædia of Superstitions, Folklore, and the Occult Sciences of the World*, 1376

Fir Bolg

Variations: Fir Bholg, Fir Bold, Fir Domnann, Firblog, Gailioin

A mythological race, the Fir Bolg ("children of the god/ess Bolg"), according to Irish mythology, were the descendants of the NEMEDIANS, another mythological race led by an individual named Nemed. Run off by the FORMORIANS, Nemed's people found themselves enslaved in Greece for 230 years. They finally escaped their bondage and returned to their homeland on the eve of Lughnasadh; there, led by the five sons of Dela, they claimed land, established five provinces, enthroned kings, and began to live the life they had dreamed of for generations. Thirty-seven years into the Fir Bolg rule the TUATHA DE DANANN, another mythological race, arrived in Ireland. When peace could not be negotiated between them, they fought on the summer solstice near Loch Corrib, the now famous Battle of Magh tureadh. The Fir Bolg lost 1,100 warriors and were driven to the furthest reaches of the Celtic world: Arran, the Hebrides, Islay, Isle of Man, and Rathlind.

Source: Monaghan, *Encyclopedia of Celtic Mythology and Folklore*, 193–4; Mountain, *Celtic Encyclopedia*, Volume 1, 63–4

Fire Giants

Variations: ELDJÖTNAR, Muspels Lydir ("men of Muspel"), Sons of Muspel

Living in the realm of fire, Muspelheim, the FIRE GIANTS of Norse mythology are under the command of SURTR; these Jotnar will eventually cause the destruction of the world after the final battle of Ragnarok on the Plain of Vigdir.

Source: Grimes, *Norse Myths*, 289; Maberry, *They Bite*, 344; Mabie, *Norse Mythology*, 88

Fjolvarr (FYUHL-var)

A JOTUN from Norse mythology, Fjolvarr ("glutton"), the father of seven JOTUN daughters, lived with his family on Algroen Island ("all green island"). For five winters Harbardr, the assumed form and name taken by the god Odin, battled against Fjolvarr; in the end he defeated the JOTUN and won the love and sexual favor of the seven unnamed daughters.

Source: Grimes, *Norse Myths*, 129, 254, 274; Lindow, *Norse Mythology*, 117; Norroena Society, *Asatrii Edda*, 25

Fjolverkr (FYUHL-verk-r)

In Norse mythology Fjolverkr ("pain filled" or "worker") was one of the many named Jotnar (see JOTUN); beyond a name, there is nothing else known.

Source: Norroena Society, *Asatrii Edda*, 346

Fjosnir (FYOHS-nir)

One of the hrymthursars (FROST GIANTS) from Norse mythology, Fjosnir ("stable boy") was born one of the sons of THRAEL and THIR. Fjosnir, his parents, and siblings all lived a hard life of labor performing thankless tasks, such as cleaning, herding goats and swine, placing dung in the fields, and other varied unskilled labor. He and his family became the progenitors of the serving folk and thrall.

Source: Grimes, *Norse Myths*, 27, 301; Norroena Society, *Asatrii Edda*, 346

Fleggr (FLEHG-r)

In Norse mythology Fleggr ("cliff dweller" or "troll") was one of the many named Jotnar (see JOTUN) about whom, beyond a name, there is little or nothing else known.

Source: Norroena Society, *Asatrii Edda*, 336

Foawr

The foawr ("giant") are hideous, humorless, stone throwing GIANTs on the Isle of Man; they are similar to the FORMORIANS. Foawr hunt and devour cattle. Like many of the fay, they are unable to cross running water.

Source: Briggs, *Encyclopedia of Fairies*, 178, Briggs, *Fairies in Tradition and Literature*, 77; Rhys, *Celtic Folklore*, 347

Formorian, plural Formori or Formorians

Variations: Fomhoraiah, Fomóiri, Fomóraig, Fomori, Fomorian, Fomorii, Fomors, Fo-Muir, Formor

At one point in time the Formorians were the fairy race ruling over the country of Ireland long before the Great Flood and were skilled in the magical arts; they were a warlike people and ruled the land with brutality. The Formorians were literally driven off the land and into the sea by the invading TUATHA DE DANANN. Over time these fairies began to de-evolve, and their physical appearance changed into misshapen bodies with an animal-like appearance; no two were alike, some having one leg while another had three, some had the head of a man while another had the head of a goat. These monstrous Formorians became foul tempered, uncultured, and unintelligent.

Historically, the Formorians, tall and strong, were likely an African sea-going people who had joined with some of the NEMEDIANS, now called FIRBOLGS, as they escaped slavery in Thrace seeking to return to Ireland. The Formorians' reach extended far up into the Atlantic, including Ireland, with their strongest beachhead established on Torrey Island. Most authorities place their arrival in Ireland around 1448 BC (though 1000 BC is an early date cited); these Formorians may be the origin of the pejorative phrase, "the black Irish." From their launching point on Torrey Island the Formorians both traded and raided with the FIRBOLGS until they encountered the TUATHA DE DANANN in 710 BC.

Source: Bynum, *African Unconscious*, 53; Bonwick, *Our Nationalities*, 23–4; McCoy, *Witch's Guide to Faery Folk*, 223–4

Fornjotr (FAWRN-yoht-r)

Variations: Fornjotr

A JOTUN of Norse mythology Fornjotr ("destroyer") and his wife Ran-Gullveig were the parents of AEGIR, lord of the sea, KAARE, lord of the wind, and LOGE, lord of fire. One of the oldest figures in all of Norse mythology, Fornjotr may be the progenitor of the HRIMTHURSSAR (FROST GIANTS).

Source: Daly, *Norse Mythology A to Z*, 30; Norroena Society, *Asatrii Edda*, 25; Sturluson, *Prose Edda*, 125

Fracassus

François Rabelais (AD 1494–1553), in his lineage of the GIANTS, listed CHALBROTH as the progenitor of the race. Born the son of MORGANTE, Fracassus was the father of Ferrgas the GIANT.

Source: Brewer, *Character Sketches of Romance, Fiction and the Drama*, Volume 3, 81; Daniels, *Encyclopædia of Superstitions, Folklore, and the Occult Sciences of the World*, 1376; Ozeli, *Works of Francis Rabelais*, 293

Fragr (FRAIG-r)

Variations: Fraeg, Fraegr, Fraegur, Frag

A DVERG (DWARF) from Norse mythology created by Durinn, Fragr ("famous") is listed as being one of DURINN's KIN. He, like the others created, paid particular attention to DURINN's leadership.

Source: Daly, *Norse Mythology A to Z*, 22; Grimes, *Norse Myths*, 7

Frar (FRAHR)

A DVERG (DWARF) from Norse mythology created by Durinn, Frar ("the quick") is listed as being one of DURINN's KIN. He, like the others created, paid particular attention to DURINN's leadership.

Source: Daly, *Norse Mythology A to Z*, 22; Grimes, *Norse Myths*, 7, 267

Fravashis

In Persian mythology the fravashis were winged female beings, similar to the VALKYRIES (NYMPHS of battle) of Norse mythology and the Guardian Angel of Christian folklore; these beings would fly through the air, invisibly, and if satisfied with the offerings made to them, quickly come to the aid of men in need. Each year they would do all they could to see that families under their protection had children and enough rainfall. In times of war, they would fight invisibly alongside their descendants.

Source: Boyce, *Zoroastrians*, 10

Friagabi

Variations: Fimmilena, Friagabis

A VALKYRIE from Norse mythology, Friagabi ("giver of Freedom") was one of the two ALAISIAGAE; she and her companion, BAUDIHILLIE ("ruler of battle"), had their names carved on Hadrian's Wall and were likely worshiped by the soldiers stationed there as goddesses of Fate.

Source: Coulter, *Encyclopedia of Ancient Deities*, 34, 490; Monaghan, *Encyclopedia of Goddesses and Heroines*, 282

Frost Giant

Variations: HRIMGRIMNIR, Hrimporsar, HRIMPURSAR, Hrimpurses, Hrimthorsar, Hrim-Thurar, Hrim-Thurg, Hrimthurren, Hrim-Thurs, HRIMTHURSAR, Hrim-Thursar, Hrimthursen, Hrimthurses, Hrymthursar, Hrymthusar, Reimthursen, Rhimthurs, Rhimthursar, Rhimthursar, Rime Giant, Rime-Giants

According to Norse mythology YMIR was the progenitor of the frost giants; as he slept, the primordial JOTUN begun to sweat and from the sweat of one of his feet they were formed. The frost giants called YMIR AURGELMER. Frost giants, enemies of the Aesir, were said to cause avalanches and make glaciers. This race of Jotnar (see JOTUN) were said to live beneath the roots of the World Tree, Ygdrasil. All the CLIFF GIANTS along with the FROST GIANTS swore to protect Fenriswulf (Fenrir), Hela (Hel), and Jormungandr (the Midgard Serpent).

Source: Anderson, *Norse Mythology*, 173, Grimes, *Norse Myths*, 70, 280; Oehlenschläger, *Gods of the North*, l; Sturluson, *Prose Edda*, 25

Frosti (FRAWST-i)

A DVERG (DWARF) from Norse mythology created by DURINN, Frosti ("frosty") is listed as being one of DURINN's KIN. He, like the others created, paid particular attention to DURINN's leadership.

Source: Grimes, *Norse Myths*, 260; Norroena Society, *Asatrii Edda*, 25

Fulnir

One of the hrymthursars (FROST GIANTS) from Norse mythology, Fulnir ("stinker") was born one of the sons of THRAEL and THIR. Fulnir, his parents, and siblings all lived a hard life of labor performing thankless tasks, such as cleaning, herding goats and swine, placing dung in the fields, and other varied unskilled labor. He and his family became the progenitors of the serving folk and thrall.

Source: Bellows, *Poetic Edda*, 206; Grimes, *Norse Myths*, 27, 267

Fundinn (FUN-din)

Variations: Fundin

In Norse mythology Fundinn ("founder") was one of the earth DVERG (DWARF) created by DURINN.

Source: Grimes, *Norse Myths*, 260; Sturluson, *Prose Edda*, 29, 126

Gabbara

According to François Rabelais (AD 1494–1553), who compiled the lineage of the GIANTS, Gabbara, born the son of the GIANT ARANTHAS, was credited as having invented drinking to one's health; his descendants begot GRANGOUSIER.

Source: Brewer, *Character Sketches of Romance, Fiction and the Drama*, Volume 3, 80; Daniels, *Encyclopædia of Superstitions, Folklore, and the Occult Sciences of the World*, 1376; Rabelais, *Hours with Rabelais*, 80

Gabbaras

Variations: Gabbaras, the Arabian GIANT

According to Pliny the Elder, the Roman author and natural philosopher, during the reign of Claudius (AD 41–54) the GIANT Gabbaras (reports place his height between nine foot three and nine foot nine inches) was placed at the head of the *Legio prima Adiutrix* ("First Auxiliary legion"). Gabbaras so awed his troops, they worshiped him as a god.

Source: Ashton, *Curious Creatures in Zoology*, 37; DeLoach, *Giants*, 95, 139

Gahonga

In the mythology of the Iroquois people of North America, the gahongas are a species of JOGAH said to inhabit rocks and stones; they are described in legend as having great strength and being competent stone throwers. Responsible for making the earth fertile, the gahonga must receive an offering of tobacco before crops are planted.

Source: Aldington, *Larousse Encyclopedia of Mythology*, 438; Converse, *Myths and Legends of the New York State Iroquois*, Issues 125–129, 101; Leddon, *Child's Eye View of Fair Folk*, 44

Galaas

Variations: "The Mighty," "The Moor"

A fearsome GIANT of Arthurian lore, Galaas and his foster father, the GIANT Assiles, terrorize the countries surrounding their land, Eigrun, especially the land under the protection of King Flois of the Green Island. The king had enlisted the assistance of Sir Gawain to act as his champion and resolve the problem of the raiding giants. En route to fulfil his duties, Gawain defeated Galaas at his castle in Eigun, freeing its prisoners and securing an oath of fealty from the GIANT. Gawain slew ASSILES. Galaas may be a relation of the GIANT GALAPAS.

Source: Brewer, *Character Sketches of Romance, Fiction and the Drama*, Volume 3, 58; Bruce, *Arthurian Name Dictionary*, 197

Galapas

A GIANT from Arthurian lore, Galapas fought Arthur in the final battle of the Roman War, the Battle of Soissons. In the conflict, Galapas confronted Arthur wielding the sword Excalibur; Arthur, in a single blow, cut Galapas off at the knees, reducing him to a height more suitable for beheading which soon followed. He may be related to the GIANT GALAAS.

Source: Bruce, *Arthurian Name Dictionary*, 199–200; Green, *Arthuriana*, 189

Galarr (GAL-ar)

Variations: Galar, Galor

Along with fellow rock DVERG (DWARF) and DURINN's KIN-man FJALARR, Galarr ("screamer") slew the hill TROLL or JOTUN GILLINGR and his wife, unnamed in the story, as a means of practice before attempting to slay the god Thor. They also killed Kvaser, the man created during the peace offering between the Aesir and the Vanirand at the end of their war; his blood was drained, mixed with honey and spices, and made into mead.

Source: Grimes, *Norse Myths*, 268; Sturluson, *Prose Edda*, 93

Galligantus

A folkloric GIANT, Galligantus lived with an evil magician named Hocus-Pocus in an enchanted castle atop a high mountain. The pair is able to trick many knights and their ladies into visiting the castle and then transforms them into animals. One of the victims of this trickery was a local duke's daughter who had been transformed into a roe. Galligantus kept two fire-breathing griffins at the castle's gate; just beyond was a sign reading "Whoever can this trumpet blow, will cause the giant's overthrow." According to the fairy tale, Jack the Giant-Slayer was able to pass the guardians as he was wearing his coat of invisibility; he took up the trumpet and blew it hard, causing the gates to fly open and break the enchantment on the castle. Soon thereafter he found and slew Galligantus, as his evil companion rode a whirlwind away, abandoning him to his fate. Jack then returned home with all the newly restored knights and ladies, marrying the Duke's daughter. The head of Galligantus was sent as a gift to King Arthur.

Source: Daniels, *Encyclopædia of Superstitions, Folklore, and the Occult Sciences of the World*, 1376; Doyle, *Story of Jack and the Giants*, 50–5

Gamphasantes

Described by Pliny the Elder in his work, *"Natural History,"* (V,vii) the Gamphasantes were a race of people who did not wear clothes, engage in any sort of combat, or interact with foreigners.

Source: Pliny the Elder, *Natural History of Pliny*, Volume 6, 405; Sprague de Camp, *Lands Beyond*, 221–22

Gana

Variations: Gana-Devatas ("troops of deities")

The dwarflike attendants of the god Shiva, the gana ("multitude" or "people"), according to Hindu mythology, are depicted in both art and literature as plump and rambunctious as they perform whatever duties are required to entertain the god and his wife. On rare occasion they are shown having animal heads. The elephant-headed god Ganesa is regarded specifically as the leader of the gana and there are nine different classes: Abhaswaras, Adityas, Anilas, Maharajikas, Rudras, Sadhyas, Tushitas, Vasus, and Viswas or Viswe-devas. All the gana dwell on Gana-Parvata (Kailasa).

Source: Dowson, *Classical Dictionary of Hindu Mythology and Religion, Geography, History, and Literature*, 106; Pal, *Indian Sculpture*, 31, 252

Gandalue

A GIANT from Spanish folklore, Gandalue was, unlike the rest of this kind, gentle in demeanor and generous in disposition; a native of Lyonesse, he was the master of two castles on an island off in the sea which he had populated with good Christians.

Source: Spence, *Legends and Romances of Spain*, 100

Gandayaks

A DWARF or nature spirit from the mythology of the Iroquois people of North America, the gandayaks have power over and are the guardian spirits of plants, making them fruitful; they also have some control over fish.

Source: Aldington, *Larousse Encyclopedia of Mythology*, 438; Coulter, *Encyclopedia of Ancient Deities*, 185

Ganglati (GANG-lat-i)

Variations: Ganglat

In Norse mythology the JOTUN Ganglati ("lazy," "lazy-goer," "slow moving," "walk slacker," "tardy") was the man-servant of the goddess Hel; he worked for her in the Hall of the Dead, Eljudnir ("wet with sleet"), located in Neflheim.

Source: Grimes, *Norse Mythology*, 268; Lindow, *Norse Mythology*, 172

Ganglot (GANG-luht)

In Norse mythology the JOTUN Ganglot ("slow") was the maid-servant of the goddess Hel; she worked in the Hall of the Dead, Eljudnir ("wet with sleet"), located in Neflheim.

Source: Grimes, *Norse Mythology*, 268; Lindow, *Norse Mythology*, 172

Gangr

Variations: Aurner, Gang, Urner (the Grottesong)

In Norse mythology Gangr ("the faring" or "traveler"), a storm JOTUN, was one of the three sons of OLVALDI; his brothers were IDI and THJASSI and his niece was SKADI. He lived with his family on the south coast of Elivagar and although Jotnar, they were friends of the god Thor.

Source: Daly, *Norse Mythology A to Z*, 35; Grimes, *Norse Mythology*, 268; Rydberg, *Teutonic Mythology*, 639, 648

Garagantua

Variations: Gargantua

A folkloric GIANT, Garagantua once swallowed five pilgrims with their staves while eating a salad;

he used an elephant's tusk as a toothpick and 17,913 cows were needed to give him his daily milk. Gargantua was so large it required 900 ells of linen for the body of his shirt, 200 additional ells for the gussets, 406 ells of velvet for his shoes, and 1,100 cow hides for their soles.

Source: Brewer, *Reader's Handbook of Allusions, References, Plots and Stories*, 378; Daniels, *Encyclopædia of Superstitions, Folklore, and the Occult Sciences of the World*, 1376

Garamantes

Described by Pliny the Elder in his work, *Natural History* (AD 77), the Garamantes were a race of people who did not practice marriage but rather lived in promiscuity with their women.

Source: Pliny the Elder, *Pliny's Natural History*, 52; Sprague de Camp, *Lands Beyond*, 221–22

Gargantuan

According to François Rabelais (AD 1494–1553), who compiled the lineage of the GIANTS, Gargantuan was listed as the father of PANTAGRUEL, the last of the GIANTS named in his given lineage.

Source: Brewer, *Character Sketches of Romance, Fiction and the Drama*, Volume 3, 80; Daniels, *Encyclopædia of Superstitions, Folklore, and the Occult Sciences of the World*, 1376; Rabelais, *Hours with Rabelais*, 80

The Gegenees

In classical Greek mythology, the Gegenees ("earthborn") were a tribe of six-armed GIGANTE who lived on the mountains in Mysia; they had attacked Hercules (Heracles), Jason, and the Argonauts when they had stopped there on route to Colchis, Caucasus. The heroes were able to defeat the tribe of GIGANTE and continue on their journey.

Source: Coulter, *Encyclopedia of Ancient Deities*, 189; Tripp, *Meridian Handbook of Classical Mythology*, 251

Geirahodr (GAYR-a-huhth-r)

Variations: Geirahod, Geirahöd

In Norse mythology Geirahodr ("spear-fighter," "spear of battle") was one of the many named VALKYRIE (a NYMPH of battle), who, beyond a name, there is little if nothing else known.

Source: Grimes, *Norse Myths*, 306; Norroena Society, *Asatrii Edda*, 349

Geiravor (GAYR-a-vuhr)

In Norse mythology Geiravor ("spear-goddess") was one of the many named VALKYRIE (a NYMPH of battle) who, beyond a name, there is little if nothing else known.

Source: Conway, *Falcon Feather and Valkyrie Sword*, 211; Norroena Society, *Asatrii Edda*, 349

Geirdriful (GAYR-driv-ul)

In Norse mythology Geirdriful ("spear-thrower") was one of the many named VALKYRIEs (NYMPHs of battle) about whom, beyond a name, there is little or nothing else known.

Source: Conway, *Falcon Feather and Valkyrie Sword*, 211; Norroena Society, *Asatrii Edda*, 349

Geirolul

Variations: Geirolu

In Norse mythology Geirolul ("spear waver") was one of the many named VALKYRIEs (NYMPHs of battle) about whom, beyond a name, there is little or nothing else known.

Source: Conway, *Falcon Feather and Valkyrie Sword*, 211; Larrington, *Poetic Edda*, 330

Geironul (GAYR-uhn-ul)

One of the many named VALKYRIEs (NYMPHs of battle) in Norse mythology, Geironul ("spear-thrower") is listed with GOLL, HERFJOTUR, HILDR, HLOKK, PRUDR, RADGRIOR, RANDGRIDR, REGINLEIF, SKEGGJOLD, and SKOGUL as one of the eleven VALKYRIES who carry mead to the EINHERJAR in Valhalla.

Source: Anderson, Norse Mythology, 269; Ellis, *Road to Hel*, 69; Norroena Society, *Asatrii Edda*, 349; Puryear, *Nature of Asatru*, 197

Geirröd

Variations: Geirraudr, Geirrøð, Geirrodr, Geirroðr, Geirróðr, Geirröðr, Geirrøðr, Geirrøðr, Geirrodur, Geirrœd, Geirrœth, Geirrøth, Gerrad, Gerriöd, Geyruth

A JOTUN from Norse mythology, Geirröd ("spear reddener") was a FROST GIANT who hated the god Thor. In the skaldic poem by Eilífr Goðrúnarson *Þórsdrápa* ("Thorsdrapa, Lay of Thor") Loki, while in hawk form, was captured by Geirröd; in exchange for his freedom Geirröd demanded the god lure Thor to his castle without his magical belt of strength or his hammer. Loki agreed and managed to meet Geirröd's conditions. En route to the castle they stopped off at the abode of the ASYNJR GRID who when opportunity presented itself informed Thor of Loki's plan. She equipped the god with her iron gloves, magical belt, and her staff, Grídarvöl. When they arrived at the castle Thor was able to slay Geirröd and then began killing all of the FROST GIANTS he could find including Geirröd's two daughters, GJALP and GREIP.

Source: Grimes, *Norse Myths*, 269; Lindow, *Handbook of Norse Mythology*, 137–8

Geirrondul

In Norse mythology Geirrondul was one of the many named VALKYRIES (NYMPHs of battle) about whom, beyond a name, there is little or nothing else known.

Source: Conway, *Falcon Feather and Valkyrie Sword*, 211; Norroena Society, *Asatrii Edda*, 386

Geirskogul (GAYR-skuhg-ul)

One of the many named VALKYRIEs (NYMPHs of battle) in Norse mythology, Geirskogul ("spear-battle") along with her fellow VALKYRIES, GONDULL, GUNNR, HILDR, HJOR, HJORTHRIMUL, SANGRIDE, SKOGUL, SVIPUL, and THRIMUL, would work a great loom together. Raised on spears, the warp was made from the guts of men and was weighed down with human heads; the shuttle was made from an arrow and the spools from swords. The entire weft wept with blood.

Source: Grimes, *Norse Myths*, 21; Norroena Society, *Asatrii Edda*, 349; Puryear, *Nature of Asatru*, 197

Geitir

Variations: Gotharus

A JOTUN from Norse mythology, Geitir ("goat") once tried to gain possession of the goddess Freyja; according to the *Fornmanna* saga Geitir lived in Jothunheim with his kinsmen and descendants, such as JOKULL, LOGI, and KARI.

Source: Rydberg, *Teutonic Mythology*, 64; Sturluson, *Prose Edda*, Volume 5, 191

Gemmagog

Born the son of the GIANT OROMEDON, Gemmagog invented the Poulan shoe (shoes with a spur behind and turned up toes fastened to the knees) which was forbidden by Charles V of France in 1365.

Source: Brewer, *Wordsworth Dictionary of Phrase and Fable*, 469; Daniels, *Encyclopædia of Superstitions, Folklore, and the Occult Sciences of the World*, 1376

Gentle Annis

Variations: Gentle Annie

On the Firth of Cromarty in the Highlands of Scotland, Gentle Annis is the nature spirit and HAG controlling the southwesterly gales and winds in the region. The firth is guarded against wind on the north and east by tall hills but a gap allows sporadic and violent wind bursts to rush through, earning the fay a reputation for treachery. It has been speculated by some folklorists that Gentle Annis is an aspect of Cailleac Bhuer (personification of winter and likely a diminished goddess who was reduced to fairy status), as her name implies an association to the Celtic goddess Anu whose own origins lay in BLACK ANNIS of the Dane Hills.

Source: Briggs, *Encyclopedia of Fairies*, 185; Monaghan, *Encyclopedia of Celtic Mythology and Folklore*, 210; Rose, *Spirits, Fairies, Gnomes, and Goblins*, 126

Gerdr

Variations: Gerd ("earth"), Gerda, Gerth, Gerthr

In Norse mythology Gerdr was the beautiful daughter of the JOTUN GYMER and his wife, the ASYNJR AURBODA ("gravel-offerer"). Gerdr, an ASYNJR, was the beloved wife of the god of rain and sun, Frey. She was courted on Frey's behalf by his faithful servant Skymir who offered her golden apples and a golden ring, but only when Skymir resorted to threats did she relent to be wed after a nine month waiting period.

Source: Anderson, *Norse Mythology*, 446; Andrews, *Dictionary of Nature Myths*, 74; Sturluson, *Prose Edda*, 126

Geryon

Variations: Gêruonês, Geryones, Geryoneus, Geyron

Born the son of Chrysaor (Khrysaor "Golden Sword") and Callirhoe (Calirrhoë), the fearsome three-headed, three-bodied, four-winged, six-handed TITAN Geryon from ancient Greek mythology was said to have lived upon the island of Erytheia ("the reddish") of the mythic Hesperides where he raised a herd of magnificent oxen which fed alongside the herd belonging to the god of the underworld, Hades. The herd was protected by the two-headed dog, Orthrus. In an epic adventure first described by the Greek poet Hesiod (750 and 650 BC) the demi-god and hero Hercules (Heracles) was ordered by Eurystheus for his Tenth Labor to capture and return with the oxen causing him to travel virtually across the known world. After a great many adventures on Hercules's part he eventually arrived upon Erytheia, slew Geryon, his son Erytheia, and the dog Orthrus, and taking the herd of oxen, returned victorious.

Source: Daly, *Greek and Roman Mythology, A to Z*, 60; Daniels, *Encyclopædia of Superstitions, Folklore, and the Occult Sciences of the World*, 1376; Hard, *Routledge Handbook of Greek Mythology*, 60–2; Smith, *Dictionary of Greek and Roman Biography and Mythology*, 94, 108

Gestur

A blind JOTUN from Norse mythology, Gestur poses riddles to Skirnir on his journey to the world below when he intends to visit Gerda.

Source: Oehlenschläger, *Gods of the North*, xliv

Gialp

An ASYNJR from Norse mythology, Gialp ("howler") was one of the WAVE MAIDENS who were mother to the god Heimdall; she was the daughter of the god of the sea, Aegir. She, like her sisters, was said to have snow-white skin, blue eyes, and billowing blond hair; in one hand they carried a golden goblet filled with mead and in the other seashells filled with the finest foods. They wore long transparent robes of green or blue trimmed in white. When not serving food in the hall, they played on the shore in groups of three.

Source: Daly, *Norse Mythology A to Z*, 47; Grimes, *Norse Myths*, 255

Giant

Variations: GIGANTES, Ispolini, Iöunn, Jättar (Swedish), Jättiläiset (Finnish), Jotnar (see JOTUN), OGRES

Giants are a species of fairy animal common to most of the world's mythologies. Universally described as being larger and taller than humans, be it by a few or several hundred feet, they otherwise vary greatly. Depending on the culture, religion, and reason for having a giant in a tale, these beings come in a wide variety of characteristics, descriptions, and personalities. Giants have been wizened war chiefs capable of leading armies while others of their species are barely intelligent enough to talk and walk at the same time, easily outwitted by the Simple Jacks of folklore. Some have said to be gods and the creators of the universe and the progenitors of the great noble families, while others yet are more animal-like, living in caves, barely clothed in furs, wielding a misshapen club, and robbing the countryside of its goats and sheep.

Having great strength is common among giants as well, but this is typically in proportion to their size and not otherwise remarkable. Traditionally, they represent an obstacle a cultural hero must overcome and defeat on a quest. Many tales have characters in them who are described as being a half-giant, where one of its parents was a human.

Giants are good or evil depending on their motivation; for instance, Paul Bunyan from American folklore is a giant who is helpful to humans, assisting in taming the west and bringing civilization to mankind. Many natural landmarks are named after them, for giants are often accredited with having created islands, mountains, rivers, and standing stones.

It appears whenever a giant is particularly bloodthirsty, cruel, and preys on humans to consume for their flesh it is called an OGRE; this would be incorrect, for although an OGRE can be gigantic in size, most are in fact of human size but monstrous in appearance due to their physical deformities.

Giants play a particularly important role in Greek and Norse mythology, representing the forces of nature and violent natural phenomena.

Source: Briggs, Encyclopedia of Fairies, 186–90; Daniels, *Encyclopædia of Superstitions, Folklore, and the Occult Sciences of the World*, 1375–8; Keightley, *World Guide to Gnomes, Fairies, Elves, and Other Little People*, 321; Leeming, *Oxford Companion to World Mythology*, 149; Rose, *Giants, Monsters, and Dragons*, 136–9

Gigante

Variations: GIANT

In Greek mythology the gigante were a race of beings born from Gaea, the earth, when the blood of Uranus ("heaven") fell upon her. They were enormous humanoids, sometimes described as having serpents for feet. Wanting revenge for the death of Uranus, Gaea made the gigante invincible by the use of a special herb to protect them from the Olympian gods, and then she sent her children to battle against them in Gigantomachy. The only way the gigantes could be destroyed was if the Olympians gained the assistance of a mortal; in most renditions of this myth, the individual was the demi-god and hero Hercules (Heracles).

Source: Hansen, *Handbook of Classical Mythology*, 177; Lurker, *Routledge Dictionary of Gods and Goddesses, Devils and Demons*, 69; Smith, *Complete Idiot's Guide to World Mythology*, 238

Gillingr (GIL-ing-r)

Variations: Gilling

A JOTUN from Norse mythology, Gillingr ("loud" or "yeller") was the father of Suttung; not particularly smart or clever, Gillingr and his wife were murdered by the two DWARFS FJALARR and GALARR as practice for the day they would kill the god Thor. The two dwarfs took Gillingr out in a boat to the middle of a lake where they sank it. The dwarfs held fast to flotsam and were able to make their way to the shore but Gillingr was not so clever and drowned. Next the dwarfs waited atop the home of Gillingr with a millstone. When the JOTUN's wife heard the news of the death of her husband she fled her home in grief only to have the two murderous dwarfs roll the millstone on top of her head, crushing her skull and killing her instantly.

Source: Grimes, *Norse Myths*, 49–50; Norroena Society, *Asatrii Edda*, 25

Ginnarr

Variations: Ginnar

A DVERG (DWARF) from Norse mythology created by DURINN, Ginnarr ("seducer") is listed as one of DURINN's KIN. He, like the others created, paid particular attention to DURINN's leadership.

Source: Thorpe, *Elder Edda of Saemund Sigfusson*, 338; Grimes, *Norse Myths*, 260; Sturluson, *Prose Edda*, Volume 5, 27

Giralda

Variations: La Giralda

In Seville, Spain, atop a Moslem minaret which had been converted over into a Christian bell tower stands the giantess (female GIANT) Giralda. Balanced on top of a ball, this living statue is brave and strong and made of brass; whenever the wind blows, so too does her facing, making her also a weathervane. Although she never moves from her location Giralda is said to be the most changeable and inconstant woman in the world.

Source: Brewer, *Reader's Handbook of Allusions, References, Plots and Stories*, 378; Daniels, *Encyclopædia of Superstitions, Folklore, and the Occult Sciences of the World*, 1376; McCloskey, *Signs of Power in Habsburg Spain and the New World*, 62, 69

Gisurab

Variations: Guisorab (Apayao), Guisurab (Isneg)

In Filipino mythology the anthropophagous (man-eating) humanoid GIANT Gisurab is said to live in a cave in the forest near the outskirts of town with his wives, Gungay, Sibbarayungan, and Surab. Using his massive axe and setting snares throughout the forest, the cannibal Gisurab hunts for human men and deer to feed his family.

Source: Paraiso, *Balete Book*, 55; Ramos, *Creatures of Philippine Lower Mythology*, 81

Gjalp (GYALP)

Variations: GIALP, Gjálp, Gjalph, Gjolp, Gjolp

In Norse mythology Gjalp ("yeller") was an ASYNJR, one of the WAVE MAIDENS who gave birth to the god Heimdall. Born the daughter of the FROST GIANT GEIRRÖD, Gjalp, according to Snorri Sturluson's (1179–1241) *Skaldskaparmal*, stood astride the river Vimur while the god Thor was trying to cross it; she was causing the river to swell and overflow with her menstrual fluids and urine. Thor, declaring a river must be damned at its source, used a river stone and throwing it at the ASYNJR, wounded her greatly, causing her to retreat back to her father's castle.

Source: Anderson, *History and Romance of Northern Europe*, Volume 5, 1014; Lindow, *Handbook of Norse Mythology*, 144; Norroena Society, *Asatrii Edda*, 25

Gloi (GLOH-i)

Variations: Gloinn

A DVERG (DWARF) from Norse mythology created by DURINN, Gloi ("the glowing" or "the shining") is listed as being one of DURINN's KIN. He, like the others created, paid particular attention to DURINN's leadership.

Source: Daly, *Norse Mythology A to Z*, 22; Grimes, *Norse Myths*, 260

Godmer

A GIANT from British folklore, Godmer, born the son of ALBION, was a companion of Brute, the mythological first king of England; he was slain by Canutus.

Source: Brewer, *Dictionary of Phrase and Fable*, 531; Daniels, *Encyclopædia of Superstitions, Folklore, and the Occult Sciences of the World*, 1377

Goemagot

A GIANT from Cornish folklore, Goemagot was described as being twelve cubits tall and strong enough to pull an oak tree up from the ground as if it were a hazel wand (a *cubit* is the distance from a man's elbow to the tip of his middle finger). Goemagot wrestled with Corineus and was able to break three of his opponent's ribs before being picked up and hurled off a cliff and into the sea below.

Source: Daniels, *Encyclopædia of Superstitions, Folklore, and the Occult Sciences of the World*, 1377; Worth, *History of Plymouth*, 2

Gog and Magog

In British folklore the good-hearted GIANTS Magog and his twin, Gog, are celebrated heroes. Although the legend of their exploits is older their tale first appeared in print in *The History of Gog and Magog* (1819) by Robin Goodfellow (pseudonym). According to the tale, the twins were born to a miller; they grew into fine young men, much admired. Among their many virtues they were described as being courageous, dexterous, frank of heart, generous of disposition, leaders of an army, masculine in stature, military geniuses, noble, strong, valiant, virtuous, and least of all, mortal.

An evil GIANT by the name of Humbug kidnaps the lively Princess Ladona but the twins come to her rescue and save her. Ladona has a son she names Cockney; Gog and Magog swear to serve him so long as they should live.

Source: Goodfellow, *History of Gog and Magog*, 11–84; Lake, *Weird England*, 15

Gogol

A NURSERY BOGIE from Albanian mythology, the GIANT Gogol is utilized by mothers to frighten their children into not crying, warning them the noise attracts him; presumably he abducts and consumes them.

Source: Elsie, *Dictionary of Albanian Religion, Mythology, and Folk Culture*, 103

Goliah

François Rabelais (AD 1494–1553), who compiled the lineage of the GIANTS, wrote that Goliah's descendants "begot BRIAREOS who had a hundred hands." He was said to have been the son of ATLAS, "who with his shoulders keeps the sky from falling."

Source: Brewer, *Character Sketches of Romance, Fiction and the Drama*, Volume 3, 80; Daniels, *Encyclopædia of Superstitions, Folklore, and the Occult Sciences of the World*, 1376; Rabelais, *Hours with Rabelais*, 80

Goliath of Gath

Variations: Goliath the Gittite, Golyat, Jalut

A GIANT whose story is told both in the Hebrew Bible (Christian Old Testament) and in the *Koran* who was described as standing well over nine feet tall (six cubits; a *cubit* is the distance from a man's elbow to the tip of his middle finger), Goliath of Gath was most likely slain by a young King David, as the bible is contradictory as Elhanan the son of Jaare-oregim, the Bethlehemite, is also accredited with the kill (1 Samuel 17: 49–51 versus 2 Samuel 21:19). When the Philistine army arrived to confront Saul they bragged if anyone could defeat their champion they would retreat. No one volunteered except for David who insisted he could defeat the GIANT as his god YHVH was superior to Dagon, the god emblazoned on the front of Goliath's armor. David selected five stones to bring with him for use in his sling; when he held them together in his hand, they combined to make a perfect sling stone. Using this combined stone, David struck the GIANT in the forehead, killing him instantly and causing him to fall forward.

Ostensibly a Philistine, Goliath is identified as one of the Refaim, a member of the race of GIANTS who were the descendants of the fallen angels. According to Biblical genealogy, David and Goliath were related, as Goliath was the child of Orpah the sister of Ruth, who was David's great-grandmother. Goliath had three brothers, one of which, ISH-BIBENOB, was slain by one of David's warriors.

Source: Dennis, *Encyclopedia of Jewish Myth, Magic and Mysticism*, 111; Smith, *Complete Idiot's Guide to World Mythology*, 134

Goll (GUHL)

Variations: Göl, Gol, Göll, Goli

One of the many named VALKYRIES (NYMPHs of battle) in Norse mythology, Goll ("battle cry," "loud cry," "noisy") is listed with GEIRONUL, HERFJOTUR, HILDR, HLOKK, PRUDR, RADGRIOR, RANDGRIDR, REGINLEIF, SKEGGJOLD, and SKOGUL as one of the VALKYRIES who carry mead to the EINHERJAR in Valhalla.

Source: Conway, *Falcon Feather and Valkyrie Sword*, 211; Ellis, *Road to Hel*, 69; Norroena Society, *Asatrii Edda*, 386; Puryear, *Nature of Asatru*, 199

Golnir

Variations: Gölnir

Golnir ("screamer") was a GIANT mentioned in the *Völsungasaga* (*Volsunga Saga*, a late thirteenth century Icelandic prose work); all said of Golnir was he owned a goat-herd.

Source: Anderson, *Volsunga Saga*, 73; Finch, *Saga of the Volsungs*, 16

Gondull (GUHND-ul)

Variations: Gandul, Gondul, Göndul

A VALKYRIE (a NYMPH of battle) from Norse mythology, Gondull ("enchanted stave," "magic wand," "she-WEREWOLF") along with her fellow VALKYRIES GEIRSKOGUL, GUNNR, HILDR, HJOR, HJORTHRIMUL, SANGRIDE, SKOGUL, SVIPUL, and THRIMUL, would work a great loom together. Raised on spears, the warp was made from the guts of men and was weighed down with human heads; the shuttle was made from an arrow and the spools from swords. The entire weft wept with blood. Gondull was named by Nialssage in her acclaimed battle-weaving song.

Source: Conway, *Falcon Feather and Valkyrie Sword*, 211; Grimes, *Norse Myths*, 21; Grimm, *Teutonic Mythology*, 421; Norroena Society, *Asatrii Edda*, 352; Puryear, *Nature of Asatru*, 195

Gor (GAWR)

In Norse mythology, Gor ("slaughterer") was one of the many named Jotnar (see JOTUN) about whom, beyond a name, there is little or nothing else known.

Source: Norroena Society, *Asatrii Edda*, 336

Gorm

A GIANT from Welsh folklore, Gorm was said to be responsible for the creation of Maes Knoll, Somerset, England. Not particularly clever or smart, the story claims he was walking the English countryside with a spade full of dirt because he had forgotten why he had dug it up and was looking for a place to deposit it. While searching, he stumbled and the mound of dirt fell into Avon Valley and created Maes Knoll; his spade landed and created the area now known as Wansdyke. Fearful of reprisal, Gorm ran, but due to his clumsiness, tripped and fell into the Bristol Channel where he drowned; his body created Flatholm and Steepholm islands.

Source: Briggs, *Fairies in Tradition and Literature*, 74; Rose, *Giants, Monsters, and Dragons*, 149

Grangousia

Variations: Grangousier

According to François Rabelais (AD 1494–1553), the GIANT Grangousia was the king of Utopia in his genealogy of novels entitled *The Life of Gargantua and of Pantagruel*. In his compiled lineage of the GIANTS, he lists Grangousier as having married Gargamelle, daughter of the king of the Parpaillons, in his old age and by her become the father of Gargantuan "who begot PANTAGRUEL."

Source: Brewer, *Character Sketches of Romance, Fiction and the Drama*, Volume 3, 80; Daniels, *Encyclopædia of Superstitions, Folklore, and the Occult Sciences of the World*, 1377; Rabelais, *Hours with Rabelais*, 80

Grantorto

The thundering and tyrannical GIANT Grantorto from Spenser's *Faerie Queene* is confronted in book five by the hero Artegall in order for Irena, symbolic of a peaceful Ireland, to rest easy like the rose, the chief symbol of Tudor heraldry. Grantorto embodied oppression and Roman Catholic aggression. The rescue of Irena from Grantorto is a parallel of the country loyalty to the monarchy and resistance against the Spanish threat.

Source: Daniels, *Encyclopædia of Superstitions, Folklore, and the Occult Sciences of the World*, 1377; Herron, *Spenser's Irish Work*, 95, 100

Gration

Variations: Gratium

A GIGANTE from ancient Greek mythology, Gration ("grater") was born of the great goddess Gaea and the TITAN Uranus ("heaven"). He and his siblings were extremely large, immensely strong, and absolutely fearsome to behold as they had dense beards, a thick head of hair, and feet covered with DRAKON scales; they threw flaming oak trees and rocks at the heavens. Gration was slain by the goddess Artemis (Diana) in personal battle with a silver arrow during the ten year Gigantomachy against the Olympian gods.

Source: Apollodorus, *Library of Greek Mythology*, 34–5; Coulter, *Encyclopedia of Ancient Deities*, 219; Westmoreland, *Ancient Greek Beliefs*, 33

Greip (Grape)

An ASYNJR from Norse mythology, Greip ("gripper") was one of the WAVE MAIDENS who were mother to the god Heimdall; she was the daughter of the god of the sea, Aegir, and the ASYNJR Geirridr. She, like her sisters, was said to have snow-white skin, blue eyes, and billowing blond hair; in one hand they carried a golden goblet filled with mead and in the other seashells filled with the finest foods. They wore long transparent robes of green or blue trimmed in white. When not serving food in the hall, they played on the shore in groups of three.

Greip was the mother of THJAZI the JOTUN who lived in Thrymheim with his daughter Skade.

Source: Anderson, *History and Romance of Northern Europe*, Volume 5, 928, 1023; Daly, *Norse Mythology A to Z*, 47; Grimes, *Norse Myths*, 255; Norroena Society, *Asatrii Edda*, 25

Grendel

Grendel, the monster from the legendary epic saga *Beowulf*, is often overlooked in vampiric folklore, but in truth it is a vampiric creature. In the saga, Grendel is said to be a descendant of Cain; a gigantic monster, half man and half water TROLL. At night he would leave his watery cave, located in Dark Lake, and attack the men of King Hrot's court and all who served him. Grendel would rip them apart with his bare hands, drinking their blood and eating their flesh. A vicious warrior already, he was rendered impervious to swords by a spell cast upon him by his mother, a witch. His only pleasure was killing. Beowulf was asked by the king to slay the beast, which the hero does by ripping off one of his arms in a wrestling match.

The story of Beowulf and his encounter with Grendel is similar to many ancient Norse stories regarding the vampiric revenants known as *drauge* and *draugr* (types of vampiric revenants). Both of these creatures are described as large and exceptionally strong, as Grendel was. Both were said to be able to kill a man in a single swipe, as Grendel did. The draugr was created by magic, and Grendel was protected by the witchcraft his mother placed on him. The draugr was re-imagined when Christianity was introduced; the story of Beowulf was written during the time when the old religion was giving way to the new. Draugr wanted what they had in life—warmth, food, and family—and since they couldn't have it, they gleaned what pleasure they could through death and destruction. Grendel, who also had none of those things, only found pleasure in killing as well. Neither a draugr nor Grendel could be harmed by mere weapons. A draugr could only be defeated by a hero in a wrestling match, which was exactly how Grendel was defeated.

Source: Hoops, *Kommentar zum Beowulf*, 163; Olsen, *Monsters and the Monstrous*, 79; Perkowski, *Vampires of the Slavs*, n.pag.; Robinson, *Tomb of Beowulf*, 185–218; Tolkien, *Beowulf*, 278

Grer

A DVERG (DWARF) from Norse mythology created by DURINN, Grer is listed as being one of DURINN's KIN. He, like the others created, paid particular attention to DURINN's leadership. Grer was a skillful smith who, with ALFRIG, BERLING, and DVALIN, collectively known as the Brisingamen DWARFS, constructed the golden necklace of Freyia.

Source: Grimes, *Norse Myths*, 260; Thorpe, *Northern Mythology*, Volume 1, 32

Grid (Greed)

Variations: Griða, Gridr, Griðr, Grith, Gríth, Grydur

An ASYNJR from Norse mythology, Grid ("green," "violence"), the mother of Vidar (Vidarr) the Silent by Odin, assisted Thor in thwarting the murderous plot of GEIRRÖD to kill Thor. When Loki left the room, she informed Thor of the scheme and lent him her belt of strength, her iron gloves, and her staff Grídarvöl so he would not fall victim to GEIRRÖD. Grid lived in Jarnvidr Forest.

Source: Grimes, *Norse Myths*, 272; Lindow, *Handbook of Norse Mythology*, 137–8; Puryear, *Nature of Asatru*, 200

Grigori (GRE-gorie)

Variations: fallen angels, Irin, The Old Ones, Sentinels, Sons of God ("Bene-Ha-Elohim"), WATCHERS

In Judeo-Christian demonology and mentioned in the Books of Daniel, Enoch, and Jubilees, the Grigori are a collection of fallen angels who were once in servitude to God. These were the ANGELS who banded together, swore a collective oath, and under the direction of Samyaza went directly against God's will by choosing to marry human women and father a race of children known as the NEPHILIM, who by nature were destructive and murderous. The Grigori went on to teach humans the secrets of Heaven, such as astrology, cosmology, gemology, and weaponsmithing. For these sins they were exiled from Heaven, hunted down, and punished. Some sources say the Grigori are bound to wander the earth until Judgment Day when they will be banished to Hell.

Most sources say there are two hundred Grigori but typically only name the leader, the Chief of Tens. They are described as looking like large humans who never slept and usually remained silent.

Source: Davidson, *Dictionary of Angels*, 126–7; Ford, *Bible of the Adversary*, 76; Guiley, *Encyclopedia of Angels*, 365–7; Voltaire, *Essays and Criticisms*, 106; Webster, *Encyclopedia of Angels*, 100

Grim

Variations: Bloody Man, Church Grim, Kirk Grim, Kirkegrim, Kirkigrim

In classical English literature, there is GIANT by the name of Grim (also called Bloody Man) who had the terrible reputation of attacking and consuming pilgrims on their way to the holy land. According to John Bunyon's work *Pilgrim's Progress* (1682), the allegorical Grim was the first of three GIANTS to be confronted (see MAUL and SLAYGOOD) in the company of a pride of lions approached by a group of pilgrims; their guide, Greatheart, stepped forward to protect his charges and savagely slew the cannibalistic GIANT. As it happened, the lions were chained and unable to attck, allowing the pilgrims to pass by safely.

In the folklore of Yorkshire, England, the grim is a tutelary or guardian spirit usually described as having the appearance of a large black dog. It would patrol the building and the property but on stormy nights would go "maraud about." In some stories it would let loose with a mournful BANSHEE-like death-knell when someone in the parish passed away; it may also be seen in the window of the church watching the funeral procession with the expression on its face telling if the person was saved or damned to Hell.

Source: Daniels, *Encyclopædia of Superstitions, Folklore, and the Occult Sciences of the World*, 1377; Rose, *Giants, Monsters, and Dragons*, 154; Simpson, *Dictionary of English Folklore*, n.pag.

Grimliongr (GREEM-ling-r)

In Norse mythology, Grimliongr ("mask-wearer") was one of the many named Jotnar (see JOTUN) about whom, beyond a name, there is little or nothing else known.

Source: Norroena Society, *Asatrii Edda*, 25

Groa

Variations: Gróa, Grôa, Olgefn

In Norse mythology the ASYNJR seer Groa ("green making") was the mother of Orvandel; it was she the god Thor went to after his battle with the JOTUN HRUNGR as he had a piece of flint lodged in his forehead. Groa was successful in loosening the stone but as soon as she heard the joyful news her husband AURVANDILL, whom she had just recently married, was returning home she forgot the rest of the spell.

Source: Grimes, *Norse Myths*, 272; Guerber, *Hammer of Thor*, 52

Grýla

A female GIANT (ASYNJR) or TROLL from Icelandic folklore, the NURSERY BOGIE Grýla and her husband LEPPA LUDI were cannibals who would abduct naughty children and occasionally adult men and stockpile them to consume on Christmas Eve. There are many rhymes, songs, and stories of Grýla dating back as far as the medieval era; her name also appears on lists of female TROLLS compiled by the Icelandic historian, poet, and politician Snorri Sturluson (1179–1241) in his *Prose Edda*. There she is described as having hooves, long tufts of hair and fifteen tails, each of which holds a hundred bags, each containing twenty naughty children. Longer poems about Grýla describe her as being even more hideous, having a beard akin to tangled yarn, deformed nails on every finger, ears which hang so low they brush her shoulders and can touch her nose, eyes black as Hell, goat horns growing from the back of her neck, matted hair, one hundred heads with three eyes on each head, and teeth like blackened stones.

Grýla and her husband LEPPA LUDI were said to have twenty children of their own but she has thirteen boys, collectively known as the CHRISTMAS LADS (*Jolasveinar*), with her first husband.

Source: Raedisch, *Old Magic of Christmas*, 91; Simpson, *Icelandic Folktales and Legends*, 89–90; Watts, *Encyclopedia of American Folklore*, 212

Gryllus, plural: Grylli

Variations: Grillus, plural grilli; Stomach Faces

A humanoid hybrid creature appearing in the margins of medieval manuscripts such as the *Book of Hours*, the gryllus ("cricket," "grunting pig," or "pig") is depicted as having a head where its genitalia should be. It was symbolic for the folly and vice of man.

In eastern Mediterranean countries it was said to have another head in place of a stomach; images of these beings were popular on jewelry in the Greco-Roman period. Although the meaning is now lost, the image of the gryllus made for a powerful amulet.

Plutarch the Greek historian and philosopher mentions them in a version of Odysseus' encounter with the sorceress Circe. When his men were being restored to their original form, one gave an eloquent speech as to why he should retain his form.

Source: Minissale, *Framing Consciousness in Art*, 81; Rose, *Giants, Monsters, and Dragons*, 156–7; Zell-Ravenheart, *Wizard's Bestiary*, 45

Gucup Cakix

In Mayan mythology Gucup Cakix ("seven guacas") was an evil GIANT who pretended to be both the moon and the sun.

Source: Milbrath, *Star Gods of the Maya*, 274

Gudr

Variations: Gud

One of the many named VALKYRIE (a NYMPH of battle) in Norse mythology; Gudr, along with fellow maidens ROTA and SKULD, are always sent by the god Odin to the battlefield to decide which men will die and which will be victorious. Although many and varied VALKYRIES are sent at various times, these three are dispatched on every occasion.

Source: Conway, *Falcon Feather and Valkyrie Sword*, 211; Ellis, *Road to Hel*, 69; Norroena Society, *Asatrii Edda*, 386

Gudrun

One of the many named VALKYRIES (NYMPHs of battle) in Norse mythology; Gudrun ("battle rune") fell in love with a mortal hero named Helgi; when he died she wept so much he rose from the grave and begged her to stop her mourning, as each tear she shed caused him to bleed from his wounds. After she grieved, she married Sigurd, Helgi's half-brother.

Source: Fontenrose, *Python*, 357; Guerber, *Hammer of Thor*, 183

Gullveig

Variations: Gulveig, Heid, Hyrrokkin ("fire-smoked")

One of the ASYNJR in Norse mythology, Gullveig ("gold thirst") was the personification of gold, as she was burned and stabbed three times and still lived; she is associated with the war between the Aesir and the Vanir. When Gullveig begins to practice *seid* she changes her name to Heid and becomes a prophet, a seer, and an observer of magical staffs.

Source: Anderson, *Norræna*, 1023; Lindow, *Norse Mythology*, 154–5

Gunlad (GUN-luhth)

Variations: Gunlöde, Gunnlad, Gunnlaug, Gunnlod ("battle-inviting"), Gunnlöð, Gunnlödd, Gunnlödh, Gunnlödhe, Gunnloth

In Norse mythology, Gunlad ("inviting struggle"), the daughter of SUTTUNGR, was the ASYNJR in charge of the protection of the mead symbolic of poetry which is kept in the cup, Odroerer. Gunlad lives in a well-fortified abode surrounded by stone walls. The god Odin was determined to drink the mead; assuming an alias he set out and by use of therianthropy to shape-shift into a worm, crawled through a small hole and into the home of Gunlad. Once inside he assumes his true form and seduces her. After a three day tryst, she concedes to let him have a sip from each of the three vessels holding the mead, but Odin drinks too deeply and empties each vessel.

Source: Anderson, *Norse Mythology*, 249–52; Grimes, *Norse Myths*, 273; Norroena Society, *Asatrii Edda*, 25; Puryear, *Nature of Asatru*, 201

Gunnr (GUN-r)

Variations: Gunn

A VALKYRIE (a NYMPH of battle) from Norse mythology, Gunnr ("battle," "warrior-maiden"), along with her fellow VALKYRIES GEIRSKOGUL, GONDULL, HILDR, HJOR, HJORTHRIMUL, SANGRIDE, SKOGUL,

SVIPUL, and THRIMUL, would work a great loom together. Raised on spears, the warp was made from the guts of men and was weighed down with human heads; the shuttle was made from an arrow and the spools from swords. The entire weft wept with blood. Gunnr was named by Nialssage in her acclaimed battle-weaving song.

Source: Grimes, *Norse Myths*, 21; Grimm, *Teutonic Mythology*, 4212; Norroena Society, *Asatrii Edda*, 3254

Gurumapa

A NURSERY BOGIE from the folklore of the Newar people of Nepal, the fanged cannibal GIANT Gurumapa preyed upon disobedient children. According to the story, in exchange for assisting a man named Kesh Chandra in carrying home a large quantity of gold to his house in Itum Bahal, Gurumapa would live in his attic and would be able to capture and consume any naughty child; however, over time, Gurumapa gradually altered the arrangement and began taking children whose parents only warned them to behave or Gurumapa may come to get them. The people of the town decided to approach the GIANT and proposed to him that if he left to go and live in the fields of Tinkhya in Kathmandu they would give him an annual feast of boiled rice and buffalo meat; Gurumapa agreed.

Source: Finlay, *Nepal*, 154; Goodman, *Guide to Enjoying Nepalese Festivals*, 21; Slusser, *Nepal Mandala*, 364

Gusir (GUS-ir)

In Norse mythology Gusir ("gusty" or "outpouring") was one of the many named Jotnar (see JOTUN) about whom, beyond a name, there is little or nothing else known.

Source: Norroena Society, *Asatrii Edda*, 342

Guth

Guth was one of the many named VALKYRIES (NYMPHs of battle) in Norse mythology; other than her name appearing in lists with others of her kind, there is nothing else known of her.

Source: Bellows, *Poetic Edda*, 14; Monaghan, *Encyclopedia of Goddesses and Heroines*, 294

Gyges (GUY-yus)

Variations: Gyas, Gyes, Gyes the Big-Limbed

A GIGANTE in ancient Greek mythology, Gyges ("he is land") was born one of the three sons of the TITAN Uranus ("heaven") and the Earth, Gaea. He, along with his brothers BRIAREOS and COTTOS, was said to have fifty heads and one hundred arms, and collectively they would eventually become known as the HECATONCHEIRES ("hundred handers"). The brothers with their unimaginable strength were important allies to the god Zeus (Jupiter) in the

Titanomachy; after winning the war the brothers were sent to Tartarus to be the guards of the defeated TITANS.

Source: Daly, *Greek and Roman Mythology, A to Z*, 64; Daniels, *Encyclopædia of Superstitions, Folklore, and the Occult Sciences of the World*, 1377; Hard, *Routledge Handbook of Greek Mythology*, 66

Gygur (GEEG-ur)

In Norse mythology, Gygur was one of the named ASYNJR; beyond a name, there is nothing else known.

Source: Norroena Society, *Asatrii Edda*, 356

Gymer (GEM-er)

Variations: Gýmer, Gýmir, Gymir

A FROST GIANT from Norse mythology, Gymer ("engulfer" or "transmitting light") was the father of the beautiful ASYNJR GERDR. Gymer lived in Jotunheim and kept a pack of vicious dogs tied to his front gate.

Source: Anderson, *Norse Mythology*, 354; Grimes, *Norse Myths*, 273; Oehlenschläger, *Gods of the North*, xlvi; Vigfússonn *Court Poetry: Volume 2*, 425

Hag

The idea of a hag, an elderly, immortal, ugly, witch-like woman, dates back to ancient Egypt and Greece as well as ancient Celtic folklore. The term is used both in fairy folklore and as a reference to witches, although the latter is considered to be a derogatory term.

In the British Isles hags are fairy beings; likely at one time they were ancient goddesses. In the winter months the hag is depicted as being old and ugly but as the seasons change it becomes younger and more attractive as spring nears. Sometimes the hag is said to be cannibalistic. There are many individual beings considered to be a hag throughout Celtic mythology.

Norse hags may have originally been sacrificial priestesses to the death-goddess, Hel.

In Irish and Scottish folklore the hag is also an ugly being, blind or one-eyed, hairy chinned, hunchbacked, and decrepitly old, but if it is kissed the hag then transforms into a beautiful young woman, a common theme. A good hag will oftentimes assist with spinning while malevolent hags are aligned with dark fay and spirits of the dead seeking to do harm to mankind and livestock.

Source: Guiley, *Encyclopedia of Witches*, 152; Monaghan, *Encyclopedia of Celtic Mythology and Folklore*, 237–8

Hai Ho Shang

A species of MERMAN from Chinese mythology, the highly aggressive hai ho shang ("sea Buddhist priest") haunts the south sea; it is described as having the body of a large fish but the shaved head of a Buddhist monk. The hai ho shang is an exceptionally strong creature, powerful enough to take hold of a fishing vessel and pull it beneath the waves, drowning the entire crew. The hai ho shang may be repelled, in a pinch, by burning feathers, but a more effective method is for someone on the crew to perform a set ritual dance which will drive the creature off. At one time it was common for someone on board to know this dance and be responsible for its execution in addition to their other duties.

Source: Conway, *Magickal Mermaids and Water Creatures*, 61; Rose, *Giants, Monsters, and Dragons*, 166; Zell-Ravenheart, *Wizard's Bestiary*, 46

Hai-Uri

Variations: Adroa, Hai-Uru, TIKDOSHE

Folktales of the Khoikhoi people of South Africa tell of the hai-uri ("dimensional being"), a dangerous male creature; it is described as having only one half of a human body—one arm and leg and one half of a head with one eye and half a nose and mouth. The hai-uri is a cannibal and hunts for its prey by jumping and leaping with its extremely powerful leg, moving as fast as a gazelle. It uses a club to subdue its prey but it will also throw punches, as it is strong enough to break bones with a single blow. This monster consumes nearly every bit of its prey, leaving almost nothing behind. The female version of this creature is called the BI-BLOUK.

Source: Cotterell, *Dictionary of World Mythology*, 241–2; Knudsen, *Fantastical Creatures and Magical Beasts*, 28; Maberry, *Vampire Universe*, 147–48

Haliai

In ancient Greek mythology the haliai ("salt" and "sea") were the NYMPHS of the sea, specifically the rocky and sandy shores.

Sources: Larson, *Ancient Greek Cults*, 139; Nardo, *Gods and Goddesses of Greek Mythology*, 45; Rigoglioso, *Cult of Divine Birth in Ancient Greece*, 87

Hallmundr

A TROLL from Norse mythology, Hallmundr ("stone protection") lived in a large cave behind a glacier with his burly daughter; he was a noted battler of monsters in his youth and wore a large hat which concealed his face. Hallmundr was named in the *Grettis saga Ásmundarsonar* as being stronger than the hero Grettis, an argumentative outlaw.

Source: Miller, *Epic Hero*, 315; Orchard, *Pride and Prodigies*, 159

Hamadryad (ham-a-dry-ad)

Variations: DRYAD, Hamadryádes, Hamadryas, Wood-Women

The hamadryads of Greek mythology were one of twelve species of NYMPHS; they were the NYMPHS of oak trees. It was believed each tree had its own NYMPH and if either one died, so did the other. Because their life was tied to their tree these nature spirits would punish or reward those who abridged or lengthened their existence. *The Deipnosophistae*, written by Athenaeus, an ancient Greek grammarian and rhetorician, named eight different species of hamadryad born of their mother, HAMADRYAS: Aigeiros (black poplar), Ampelos (vines, especially vitis), Balanos (oak), Karya (walnut or hazelnut), Kraneia (dogwood), Morea (mulberry), Ptelea (elm), and Syke (fig).

Source: Berens, *Myths and Legends of Ancient Greece and Rome*, 168; Littleton, *Gods, Goddesses, and Mythology*, Volume 11, 999; Keightley, *World Guide to Gnomes, Fairies, Elves, and Other Little People*, 446

Hanar

In Norse mythology Hanar was one of the rock Dvergar (DWARF; see DVERG) created by DURINN.

Source: Auden, *Norse Poems*, 247; Grimes, *Norse Myths*, 260

Hanau Epe

Variations: Hanau Eepe

A quasi-legendary race of people, the hanau epe are said to have once lived upon Easter Island. According to the legend, upon their arrival the indigenous people, the Hanau momoko ("short-ears"), who are, presumably, the surviving Polynesian population, attempted to enslave them (or lived together in harmony until a conflict arose; sources conflict). A great battle took place and the hanau epe were greatly overwhelmed; all but two were herded together and pushed into a great fire-pit where they were consumed by the flames; this site is known as Ko Te Umu O Te Hanau Eepe ("the Hanau Eepe's Oven"). The two who had escaped being burned alive were soon found and also slain.

Source: Murrill, *Cranial and Postcranial Skeletal Remains from Easter Island*, 67; Routledge, *Mystery of Easter Island*, 280–81

Hapmouche

According to the works of French Renaissance doctor, Greek scholar, humanist, monk, and writer François Rabelais (AD 1494–1553), Hapmouche ("fly nabber") was the son of the GIANT FERRACUTE. Hapmouche was said to have invented the art of drying and smoking beef tongues in chimneys; prior to this, people simply salted the meat as they did for gammons of bacon.

Source: Brewer, *Character Sketches of Romance, Fiction and the Drama*, Volume 3, 82; Daniels, *Encyclopædia of Supersti-*

tions, *Folklore, and the Occult Sciences of the World*, 1377; Ozeli, *Works of Francis Rabelais*, 13

Hardgreipr (HARTH-grehp-a)

Variations: Hardgrepa ("hard-grasping"), Harthgreip

In Norse mythology, Hardgreipr ("hard grip") was an ASYNJR and daughter of the JOTUN warrior VANGNHOFDI, the foster father to the human hero Haddingr.

Source: Norroena Society, *Asatrii Edda*, 357; Saxo, *History of the Danes*, Books 1–9, 29; Sturluson, *Prose Edda*, 196

Hardverkr (HARTH-verk-r)

A JOTUN king from Norse mythology, Hardverkr ("hard worker") and thirty of his kind were slain by Bardr to avenge the death of his father.

Source: Fiske Icelandic Collection. *Mediaeval Scandinavia*, Volume 15, 9; Norroena Society, *Asatrii Edda*, 357

Harpy, plural Harpies ("swift robbers")

Variations: Harpyia, Harpyiai, Hounds of Zeus

Originally the harpies of ancient Greek mythology were born the daughters of the sea NYMPH Electra and an ancient god of the sea and TITAN called Thaumus. Some authors said they were the daughters of OCEANUS and Terra while Gaius Valerius Flaccus, a Roman poet of the Silver Age, believed them to be the daughters of TYPHOEUS.

Stories of harpies described them as beautiful winged women who would appear suddenly, snatch up an object or person and vanish without being seen; any sudden disappearances were credited to them. The harpies of this era were under the dominion of the god Zeus (Jupiter); he would send them out in thunderstorms to do his bidding; for this they became the personifications of storm winds and whirlwinds.

The Greek poet Hesiod (ca. 750–650 BC) named two harpies in his writings, AELLO and OCYPETE. Homer, the greatest of ancient Greek epic poets, added a third harpy to the list, PORDAGE ("fleet-foot"); this creature, he wrote, was married to the western wind Zephyrus and by her husband gave birth to the two great horses of Achilles, Balios and Xanthos. In the stories of Jason and the Argonauts harpies were now being described as vicious, rank smelling bird-like creatures with bodies like vultures, ears like bears, faces like women, and feet and hands hooked like talons carrying off food and treasure in their razor-sharp claws.

In Roman mythology harpies were, according to Virgil's *Aeneid*, said to have attacked Aeneas and his Trojan crew; here the name of another harpy appears, CELAENO.

Source: Daly, *Greek and Roman Mythology, A to Z*, 63; *London Encyclopaedia*, Volume 11, 53

Harr (Hahr)

A DVERG (DWARF) from Norse mythology created by DURINN, Harr ("the high") is listed as being one of DURINN's KIN. He, like the others created, paid particular attention to DURINN's leadership.

Source: Grimes, *Norse Myths*, 260; Norroena Society, *Asatrii Edda*, 357

Hashi Hime (HAH-she HEE-may)

A YŌKAI (a creature of Japanese folklore), the hashi hime ("bridge princess") appears as a topless human woman with her long black hair parted and rolled into seven loops; atop her head is a crown with lit candles. In very rare occasions, the hashi hime may manifest as a male. A powerful nature spirit, this singular being was created by the sheer force of the power of her jealousy and desire for revenge against her philandering husband. After seven days of prayers for divine justice a priest sent a message in a dread as to how she could enact her revenge: first she was to don all red clothing and cover her face and body with poisonous cinnabar. Then she was to do up her hair in seven loops, place a brazier alit with candles atop her head, and carry a rod of pure iron to the Uji River where she was to remain for twenty-one days. If she was still there she would be transformed into a being which would enable her to have the vengeance she sought. Since her vengeance was carried out the hashi hime now attacks travelers as they attempt to cross bridges, in particular happy couples.

Source: Ashkenazi, *Handbook of Japanese Mythology*, 257; Yoda, *Yokai Attack*, 162–6

Haugspori (HOUG-spawr-i)

A DVERG (DWARF) from Norse mythology created by DURINN, Haugspori ("mound raven") is listed as being one of DURINN's KIN. He, like the others created, paid particular attention to DURINN's leadership.

Source: Grimes, *Norse Myths*, 260; Norroena Society, *Asatrii Edda*, 346

Haur (HOUR)

Variations: Haurr

A DVERG (DWARF) from Norse mythology created by DURINN, Haur ("the high") is listed as being one of DURINN's KIN. He, like the others created, paid particular attention to DURINN's leadership.

Source: Grimes, *Norse Myths*, 260; Norroena Society, *Asatrii Edda*, 357

Haustigi (HOUST-ig-i)

In Norse mythology, Haustigi ("autumn") was one of the many named Jotnar (see JOTUN) about whom, beyond a name, there is little or nothing else known.

Source: Norroena Society, *Asatrii Edda*, 357

Havfine (hahv-FEE-nuh)

Variations: HAVMAND, Havstrambe

A species of MERMAID from Norwegian folklore, the havfine, or havfrue if male, were half fish- and half human-looking creatures said to have highly unpredictable tempers. It was considered an ill omen to see one while at sea but it was an even worse portent if they were seen grazing their white cattle upon the shore, as this meant a violent storm was imminent.

Source: Rose, *Giants, Monsters, and Dragons*, 169

Havmand

Variations: Havman

The havmand ("half-man") of Denmark is a species of MERMAN, the male counterpart to the MERMAID; they live at the bottom of the sea or in the cliffs near the shoreline. Considered benign, the havmand are described as being handsome and although bald, have either a green or black beard.

Source: Keightley, *World Guide to Gnomes, Fairies, Elves, and Other Little People*, 152; Lysaght, *Islanders and Water-Dwellers*, 94; Rose, *Giants, Monsters, and Dragons*, 169

Hecatoncheires (hec-a-ton-ki-reez)

Variations: Centimani ("hundred-handed ones"), Hecatonchires, Hekatoncheires, Hekatonkheires, Hekatoncheiro, Hundred-Handed Ones

Three GIGANTES from ancient Greek mythology, these brothers collectively known as the Hecatoncheires ("hundred handed") were BRIAREOS, COTTOS and GYGES. Born of the TITAN Uranus ("heaven") and the Earth, Gaea, each of the brothers had fifty heads and one hundred arms; they possessed unimaginable strength. Their father imprisoned them as well as the CYCLOPS in Tartarus and set the monstrous DRAKAINA Campe to guard them but when Gaea rebelled, she freed them all. The Hecatoncheires allied themselves to the god Zeus (Jupiter) during the Titanomachy; they were able to utilize their size and strength and hurl three hundred boulders at a time against their enemies. After the war was won, the Hecatoncheires were assigned to dwell in Tartarus where they were given the position of being the guardians of the defeated and imprisoned TITANS. BRIAREOS served as Zeus's bodyguard.

Source: Daly, *Greek and Roman Mythology, A to Z*, 64; Daniels, *Encyclopædia of Superstitions, Folklore, and the Occult Sciences of the World*, 1377; Hard, *Routledge Handbook of Greek Mythology*, 66

Hefring (HEHV-ring)

An ASYNJR from Norse mythology, Hefring ("swelling") was one of the WAVE MAIDENS who were mother to the god Heimdall; she was the daughter of the god of the sea, Aegir. She, like her sisters, was said to have snow-white skin, blue eyes, and billowing blond hair; in one hand they carried a golden goblet filled with mead and in the other seashells filled with the finest foods. They wore long transparent robes of green or blue trimmed in white. When not serving food in the hall, they played on the shore in groups of three.

Source: Grimes, *Norse Myths*, 122, 274; Puryear, *Nature of Asatru*, 204

Hefti

In Norse mythology Hefti was one of the rock DVERG (DWARF) created by DURINN.

Source: Auden, *Norse Poems*, 247; Grimes, *Norse Myths*, 260

Heimo

Variations: Heime

In Icelandic folklore Heimo was a GIANT who lived in the same valley as the savage GIANT THURSE. Unbeknownst to Heimo, THURSE hated him and would seize every chance he could to destroy any building Heimo constructed in the valley, as the people who lived there gave tribute to him. Eventually, Heimo discovered THURSE was the cause of his destroyed stronghold and in a rage, donned a suit of light armor, armed himself with a gigantic sword, and began rampaging to THURSE's home atop Solstein. A great battle ensued when the two met, so powerful it shook the earth violently; however in the end, the better armored Heimo defeated THURSE, slaying him.

Source: Grimm, *Teutonic Mythology*, Volume 2, 527; Günther, *Tales and Legends of the Tyrol*, 11–13

Helblindi (HEHL-blind-i)

Variations: Helbindi

The lesser known brother of the trickster god Loki from Norse mythology, Helblindi ("blind" or "he who blinds with death"), his parents FARBANTI and LAUFEY, and other brother BYLEISTR are Jotnar (see JOTUN) and not divine entities. Other than his name, there is no other surviving information of this being.

Source: Daly, *Norse Mythology A to Z*, 48; Rooth, *Loki in Scandinavian Mythology*, 170

Helreginn (HEHL-rehg-in)

A JOTUN of Norse mythology, Helreginn ("death-reginn," "death-smith" or "Ruler over Hel") is named in the *Prose Edda* book, *Skaldskaparmal*; however, other than a name, no other information is ever given.

Source: Norroena Society, *Asatrii Edda*, 357; Simek, *Dictionary of Northern Mythology*, 138–9

Hengjankjoptr (HEHNG-yan-kyuhpt-r)

In Norse mythology, Hengjankjoptr ("hanging-chin") was one of the many named Jotnar (see JOTUN) about whom, beyond a name, there is little or nothing else known.

Source: Norroena Society, *Asatrii Edda*, 357

Henkies

On the Orkney and Shetland Islands the henkies are a species of TROLL or TROW that *henks* ("limps") as they dance. *Henkie knows* are the knolls these creatures would gambol and play around at night.

Source: Briggs, *Abbey Lubbers, Banshees, and Boggarts*, 99; Rose, *Giants, Monsters, and Dragons*, 170; Wright, *Rustic Speech and Folk-Lore*, 170

Herfjoturr (HER-vyuht-ur)

Variations: Harfjoter, Herfjoter, Herfjotur, Herfjötur

In Norse mythology Herfjoturr ("army fetter," "host fetter" or "war-fetter") was listed as one of the eleven VALKYRIES (NYMPHs of battle) who carry mead to the EINHERJAR in Valhalla. She was said to cause warriors to freeze with terror, leading to their death on the battlefield, and thereby deny them entrance to Valhalla.

Source: Ellis, *Road to Hel*, 69; Norroena Society, *Asatrii Edda*, 359; Skyes, *Who's Who in Non-Classical Mythology*, n.pag.

Herja (HER-ya)

In Norse mythology Herja ("devastator") was one of the many named VALKYRIEs (NYMPHs of battle) about whom, beyond a name, there is little or nothing else known.

Source: Conway, *Falcon Feather and Valkyrie Sword*, 211; Grimes, *Norse Myths*, 21; Norroena Society, *Asatrii Edda*, 359

Herkir (HERK-r)

In Norse mythology Herkir ("boorish") was one of the many Jotnar (see JOTUN) about whom, beyond a name, there is little or nothing else known.

Source: Grimm, *Teutonic Mythology*, 1443; Norroena Society, *Asatrii Edda*, 359; Vigfússonn *Court Poetry*: Volume 2, 425

Herring People

In the folklore of the Haida people of the Pacific Northwest Coast of North America, the herring people were one of the many races of supernatural ocean people who lived in underwater villages scattered up and down the shore. Since the ocean people were in control of a large part of the food supply, they not only were held in the highest of regard but were also appealed to for assistance with offerings of rare flicker feathers, grease, and tobacco.

Source: American Museum of Natural History, *Memoirs of the American Museum of Natural History*, Volume 8, Issue 1, 16, 17, 244; Goldenweiser, *Early Civilization*, 63

Hildr

Variations: Gollveig, Hild ("battler"), Hulda, Hilde, Huldr, Huldra, Huldre, Hildur, Hulla, SKEGGJOLD

One of the many named VALKYRIE (a NYMPH of battle) in Norse mythology; Hildr ("battle") was the one who had given the god Odin his two ravens, HUGINN and MUNNIN. Hildr, along with her fellow VALKYRIES GEIRSKOGUL, GONDULL, GUNNR, HJOR, HJORTHRIMUL, SANGRIDE, SKOGUL, SVIPUL, and THRIMUL, would work a great loom together. Raised on spears, the warp was made from the guts of men and was weighed down with human heads; the shuttle was made from an arrow and the spools from swords. The entire weft wept with blood. She is also listed with GEIRONUL, GOLL, HERFJOTUR, HLOKK, PRUDR, RADGRIOR, RANDGRIDR, REGINLEIF, SKEGGJOLD, and SKOGUL as one of the eleven VALKYRIES who carry mead to the EINHERJAR in Valhalla. Hildr was also named by Nialssage in her acclaimed battle-weaving song. Vingskornir was the name of her white horse.

Source: Anderson, *Norse Mythology*, 269; Ellis, *Road to Hel*, 69; Grimes, *Norse Myths*, 21, 23; McClintock, *Cyclopaedia of Biblical, Theological, and Ecclesiastical Literature*, Volume 9, 342; Norroena Society, *Asatrii Edda*, 355

Himantopodes

First described by the Roman author, natural philosopher, and naturalist, Pliny the Elder, in his work *Natural History* (AD 77) the Himantopodes ("strap-foots") were a race of people with feet like leather thongs; it was their nature to crawl rather than walk.

Source: Friedman, *Monstrous Races in Medieval Art and Thought*, 16; Sprague de Camp, *Lands Beyond*, 222

Himerope

Variations: Himeropa

A SIREN from ancient Greek mythology, Himerope ("arousing face" or "longing face") was one of her kind named in the *Odyssey*; she and her sister recognized Odysseus on sight and promised to sing to him an appealing, elaborate, and truthful song of Troy. Homer, the greatest of the ancient Greek epic poets, mentions in his work there are two SIRENS, but only names Himerope.

Source: Monaghan, *New Book of Goddesses and Heroines*, 273; Sardi, *Psychological Activity in the Homeric Circe Episode*, 28

Himinglaeva

Variations: Himinglæva

An ASYNJR from Norse mythology, Himinglaeva ("that through which one can see heaven") was one of the WAVE MAIDENS who were mother to the god Heimdall; she was the daughter of the god of the sea, Aegir. She, like her sisters, was said to have snow-white skin, blue eyes, and billowing blond hair; in one hand they carried a golden goblet filled with mead and in the other seashells filled with the finest foods. They wore long transparent robes of green or blue trimmed in white. When not serving food in the hall, they played on the shore in groups of three.

Source: Grimes, *Norse Myths*, 122, 312; Sturluson, *Prose Edda*, Volume 5, 219

Hiorprimu

In Norse mythology Hiorprimu was one of the many named VALKYRIES (NYMPHs of battle) mentioned by Nialssage in her acclaimed battle-weaving song. Beyond her name, there is little or nothing else known.

Source: Grimm, *Teutonic Mythology*, 421

Hippolytos

Variations: Hippolytus ("stampede")

A GIGANTE from ancient Greek mythology, Hippolytos was born of the great goddess Gaea and the TITAN Uranus ("heaven"). He and his siblings—AGRIUS, ALCYONES, GRATION, MIMAS, POLYBOTES, PORPHYRION, and THOON—were extremely large, immensely strong, and absolutely fearsome to behold as they had dense beards, a thick head of hair, and feet covered with DRAKON scales. During the Gigantomachy, they threw flaming oak trees and rocks at the heavens. Hippolytos was attacked and killed during the battle by the messenger god Hermes (Mercury), who was able to get the advantage as he was wearing the helmet of Hades.

Another version of his birth says he and his many siblings were born fully grown and wearing armor when the blood of a newly castrated Uranus fell to the earth. In this version he was defeated when knocked into a deep chasm in the earth and covered up with many mountains and volcanoes.

Source: Apollodorus, *Library of Greek Mythology*, 34–5; Coulter, *Encyclopedia of Ancient Deities*, 219; Daniels, *Encyclopædia of Superstitions, Folklore, and the Occult Sciences of the World*, 1377; Source: Rose, *Giants, Monsters, and Dragons*, 142, 174

Hippopodes

Variations: Hippopodia

Described by Pliny the Elder in his work *Natural History*, the Hippopodes were a race of people who lived in the Baltic area and have horse hooves rather than feet. As a people, they were said to be "light of foot" and swift runners.

Source: Friedman, *Monstrous Races in Medieval Art and Thought*, 16; Lemprière, *Classical Dictionary*, 331; *London Encyclopaedia*, Volume 11, 261

Hjalmbrimul (HYAHLM-thrim-ul)

In Norse mythology Hjalmbrimul ("battle helm") was one of the many named VALKYRIES (NYMPHs of battle) about whom, beyond a name, there is little or nothing else known.

Source: Norroena Society, *Asatrii Edda*, 359

Hjor

One of the many named VALKYRIES (NYMPHs of battle) in Norse mythology, Hjor, along with her fellow VALKYRIES GEIRSKOGUL, GONDULL, GUNNR, HILDR, HJORTHRIMUL, SANGRIDE, SKOGUL, SVIPUL, and THRIMUL, would work a great loom together. Raised on spears, the warp was made from the guts of men and was weighed down with human heads; the shuttle was made from an arrow and the spools from swords. The entire weft wept with blood.

Source: Grimes, *Norse Myths*, 21;

Hjordrimul (HYUHRTH-rim-ul)

In Norse mythology Hjordrimul ("battle-sword") was one of the many named VALKYRIES (NYMPHs of battle) about whom, beyond a name, there is little or nothing else known.

Source: Norroena Society, *Asatrii Edda*, 359

Hjorthrimul

One of the many named VALKYRIES (NYMPHs of battle) in Norse mythology, Hjorthrimul, along with her fellow VALKYRIES GEIRSKOGUL, GONDULL, GUNNR, HILDR, HJOR, SANGRIDE, SKOGUL, SVIPUL, and THRIMUL, would work a great loom together. Raised on spears, the warp was made from the guts of men and was weighed down with human heads; the shuttle was made from an arrow and the spools from swords. The entire weft wept with blood.

Source: Conway, *Falcon Feather and Valkyrie Sword*, 211; Grimes, *Norse Myths*, 21;

Hlaevangr (LAI-vang-r)

A rock DVERG (DWARF) from Norse mythology created by Durinn, Hlaevangr ("warm-cheeked") is listed as being one of DURINN's KIN. He, like the others created, paid particular attention to DURINN's leadership.

Source: Grimes, *Norse Myths*, 260; Norroena Society, *Asatrii Edda*, 359

Hlathguth (LATH-guth)

Variations: Hlathguth the Swanwhite, Hladgud Svanhvit

One of the many named VALKYRIES (NYMPHs of battle) in Norse mythology, Hlathguth ("necklace-adorned warrior-maiden") was married to Slagfith but after only seven years of marriage left him to become a VALKYRIE.

Source: Bellows, *Poetic Edda*, 2; Monaghan, *Encyclopedia of Goddesses and Heroines*, 294; Norroena Society, *Asatrii Edda*, 360

Hlebardr

A JOTUN from Norse mythology, Hlebardr ("protecting beard") is the individual from whom the god Odin received his *gambanteinn* ("magical wand") and magical arts training; the god then tricked the JOTUN and drove him mad.

Source: Tolley, *Shamanism in Norse Myth and Magic*, Issue 296, 235, 540

Hlevangur

A DVERG (DWARF) from Norse mythology created by DURINN, Hlevangur is listed as being one of DURINN's KIN. He, like the others created, paid particular attention to DURINN's leadership.

Source: Grimes, *Norse Myths*, 260

Hloi (LOH-i)

In Norse mythology Hloi ("the bellowing") was one of the many named Jotnar (see JOTUN) about whom, beyond a name, there is little or nothing else known.

Source: Norroena Society, *Asatrii Edda*, 362

Hlokk (LUHK)

Variations: Hlok, Hlökk, Hlök

One of the many named VALKYRIES (NYMPHs of battle) in Norse mythology, Hlokk ("battle," "din of battle," "lock," "noise") is listed with GEIRONUL, GOLL, HERFJOTUR, HILDR, PRUDR, RADGRIOR, RANDGRIDR, REGINLEIF, SKEGGJOLD, and SKOGUL as one of the VALKYRIES who carry mead to the EINHERJAR in Valhalla.

Source: Conway, *Falcon Feather and Valkyrie Sword*, 211; Ellis, *Road to Hel*, 69; Norroena Society, *Asatrii Edda*, 361

El Hombre Caiman

Variations: Hombre Caimán

A hybrid creature living in the Magdalena River, Colombia, el hombre caiman ("alligator man") is described as being a humanoid alligator; it appears each year on Saint Sebastian's Day, December 18, to hunt for human prey. According to the folklore of Colombia, Magdalena, and Plato el hombre caiman was once a lecherous fisherman who had been tricked and punished by a river spirit.

Source: Budd, *Weiser Field Guide to Cryptozoology*, 75; Cooper, *Social Work Man*, 10

Hoplodamus

A GIGANTE from Arcadian and Greek mythology, Hoplodamus was a leader among his people. When pregnant with Zeus (Jupiter), RHEA went to Hoplodamus at Mount Thaumasion and secured the assistance of him and his people should her husband, CRONUS, come looking to attack her. Although Zeus (Jupiter) was born on Mount Lycaeus, the story of RHEA substituting a stone for her newborn child to feed her husband occurred in Hoplodamus' domain, Mount Thaumasion.

Source: Ogden, *Companion to Greek Religion*, 273; Pausanias, *Pausanias' Description of Greece*, Volume 2, 119

Hosvir (HUHS-vir)

One of the hrymthursars (FROST GIANTS) from Norse mythology, Hosvir ("grey") was born one of the sons of THRAEL and THIR. Hosvir, his parents, and siblings all lived a hard life of labor performing thankless tasks, such as cleaning, herding goats and swine, placing dung in the fields, and other varied unskilled labor. He and his family became the progenitors of the serving folk and thrall.

Source: Grimes, *Norse Myths*, 27, 279; Norroena Society, *Asatrii Edda*, 362

Hraesvelgr (RAIS-vehlg-r)

Variations: Hræsvelgr, Hrosvelger ("windmaker")

A JOTUN from Norse mythology, Hraesvelgr ("corpse swallower") lives in the northern-most regions; wearing regalia of eagle feathers, when he spreads his arms like wings to take flight, he creates the wind which blows. Some versions of the legend say he is a gigantic eagle or a FROST GIANT (HRIMTHURSAR).

Source: Anderson, *Norse Mythology*, 181, 197; Daniels, *Encyclopædia of Superstitions, Folklore, and the Occult Sciences of the World*, 1377; Norroena Society, *Asatrii Edda*, 362; Oehlenschläger, *Gods of the North*, 1-li

Hraudnir (ROUTH-nir)

In Norse mythology Hraudnir ("destroyer") was

a JOTUN; beyond a name, there is nothing else known.

Source: Norroena Society, *Asatrii Edda*, 363

Hraudungr (ROUTH-ung-r)

Variations: Hradung, Hrauding, Hraudung, Hrauðungr, Hrauthung, Hrodung, Raudung

A JOTUN from Norse mythology, Hraudungr ("the hasty") was the father of Agnarr and Geirridr.

Source: Grimes, *Norse Myths*, 279; Norroena Society, *Asatrii Edda*, 362; Rydberg, *Norroena, the History and Romance of Northern Europe*, volume 3, 1026

Hrimgrimnir (REEM-greem-nir)

Variations: Ari, Hrim-Grimnir, Hrímgrímnir, Hrímnir

A JOTUN of Norse mythology, Hrimgrimnir ("frost shoulders" or "rime-grimnir"), a FROST GIANT, was promised Gerd in a curse offered by Skirnir unless she willingly gives into Frey's request to marry him. Hrimgrimnir lived in the coldest and northern-most regions, near where HRAESVELGR in the guise of an eagle takes flight. Some descriptions of Hrimgrimnir describe him as having three heads. He is the brother of Egther and the father of Angrboda.

Source: Crossley-Holland, *Norse Myths*, 57; Grimes, *Norse Mythology*, 279; Lindow, *Norse Mythology*, 183; Norroena Society, *Asatrii Edda*, 362

Hrimnir (REEM-nir)

Variations: BERGELMIR

A JOTUN from Norse mythology, Hrimnir ("frost being" or "frosty") had a daughter named Frigg who once went to earth with an apple she dropped onto the lap of the wife of King Rerir so she may conceive a child.

Source: Norroena Society, *Asatrii Edda*, 362; Skyes, *Who's Who in Non-Classical Mythology*, 90

Hrimpursar (REEM-thurs-ar)

In Norse mythology there are several species of JOTUN; the BERGRISAR are the mountain Jotnar (see JOTUN), whereas the FROST GIANTS were called the hrimpursar and the FIRE GIANTS were the ELDJOTNAR. At the time of Ragnarok they will gather with the others of their kind and wage war against the gods on the Plain of Vigdir.

Source: Maberry, *They Bite*, 344; Norroena Society, *Asatrii Edda*, 362

Hrimr (REEM-r)

Variations: Hreimr, Hreim

One of the hrymthursars (FROST GIANTS) from Norse mythology, Hrimr ("frost" and "shouter") was born one of the sons of THRAEL and THIR. Hrimr,

his parents, and siblings all lived a hard life of labor performing thankless tasks, such as cleaning, herding goats and swine, placing dung in the fields, and other varied unskilled labor. He and his family became the progenitors of the serving folk and thrall.

Source: Grimes, *Norse Myths*, 27, 280; Norroena Society, *Asatrii Edda*, 363

Hrimthursar

Variations: HRIMGRIMNIR, Hrimporsar, HRIMPURSAR, Hrimpurses, Hrimthorsar, Hrim-Thurar, Hrim-Thurg, Hrimthurren, Hrim-Thurs, Hrim-Thursar, Hrimthursen, Hrimthurses, Hrym-thursar, Hrymthusar, Reimthursen, Rhimthurs, Rhimthursar, Rhimthursar, Rime Giant, Rime-Giants

In Norse mythology, the Hrimthursar, a race of Jotnar (see JOTUN), were said to live beneath the roots of the World Tree, Ygdrasil; they were the first FROST GIANTS.

All the CLIFF GIANTS along with the FROST GIANTS (Hrimthursar) swore to protect Fenriswulf (Fenrir), Hela (Hel), and Jormungandr, the Midgard Serpent.

Source: Grimes, *Norse Myths*, 70, 280; Oehlenschläger, *Gods of the North*, 1

Hringvolnir (RING-vuhl-nir)

In Norse mythology, Hringvolnir ("round-pole bearer") was one of the many named Jotnar (see JOTUN) about whom, beyond a name, there is little or nothing else known.

Source: Norroena Society, *Asatrii Edda*, 361

Hripstodi (RIP-stuhth-i)

Variations: Hripstodr ("leaky")

In Norse mythology, Hripstodi ("spotted") was one of the many named Jotnar (see JOTUN) about whom, beyond a name, there is little or nothing else known.

Source: Norroena Society, *Asatrii Edda*, 364

Hrist (RIST)

One of the many named VALKYRIEs (NYMPHs of battle) in Norse mythology, Hrist ("shaker") is listed as one of the two maidens who carry the drinking horn to Odin; the other is MIST.

Source: Conway, *Falcon Feather and Valkyrie Sword*, 211; Ellis, *Road to Hel*, 69; Norroena Society, *Asatrii Edda*, 362; Young, *Prose Edda*, 61

Hroarr (ROH-ar)

In Norse mythology, Hroarr ("spear famous") was one of the many named Jotnar (see JOTUN) about whom, beyond a name, there is little or nothing else known.

Source: Norroena Society, *Asatrii Edda*, 364

Hrodr (ROHTH-r)

An ASYNJR from Norse mythology, Hrodr ("famous" or "glory"), the wife of HYMIR, was a JOTUN friendly to the Aesir.

Source: Norroena Society *Asatrii Edda*, 364

Hrokkvir (RUHK-vir)

In Norse mythology, Hrokkvir ("the stooping" or "whipper") was one of the many named Jotnar (see JOTUN) about whom, beyond a name, there is little or nothing else known.

Source: Norroena Society, *Asatrii Edda*, 364

Hronn

Variations: Hrönn

An ASYNJR from Norse mythology, Hronn ("welling cave") was one of the WAVE MAIDENS who were mother to the god Heimdall; she was the daughter of the god of the sea, Aegir. She, like her sisters, was said to have snow-white skin, blue eyes, and billowing blond hair; in one hand they carried a golden goblet filled with mead and in the other seashells filled with the finest foods. They wore long transparent robes of green or blue trimmed in white. When not serving food in the hall, they played on the shore in groups of three.

Source: Grimes, *Norse Myths*, 122, 253; Sturluson, *Prose Edda*, Volume 5, 219

Hrosspjofr (RAWS-thyohv-r)

Variations: Hrosthjof

In Norse mythology, Hrosspjofr ("horse thief") was one of the many named Jotnar (see JOTUN) about whom, beyond a name, there is little or nothing else known.

Source: Norroena Society, *Asatrii Edda*, 363

Hrund (RUND)

One of the many named VALKYRIEs (NYMPHs of battle) in Norse mythology, Hrund ("striker") was one of the many named VALKYRIE about whom, beyond a name, there is little or nothing else known.

Source: Conway, *Falcon Feather and Valkyrie Sword*, 211; Grimes, Norse mythology, 21; Norroena Society, *Asatrii Edda*, 363

Hrungnir

Variations: Grungner, Hrunger, Hrungni, Hrungr, Runger, Rungir, Rungnir

The largest rock JOTUN in all of Jotunheimr as well as the chief of the FROST GIANTS, Hrungnir ("noisy") lived in a mountainous region known as Grjotangardr; he was also the owner of the horse Goldfax and a shield named Randarr; the shield, like his own head and heart, was made of stone, sharp

edged, and three cornered. Hrungnir had raped Thor's daughter Thurd, so the god had challenged the JOTUN to a duel at the Place of Stones. It was a violent and long battle, but Thor eventually slew his opponent, even with a stone lodged deep in his head. It is said this is the point where the JOTUN lost faith in the idea of slaying Thor and storming Asgard. Hrungnir's horse was given to Thor's youngest son, Mangi, for the role he played in the battle. After the clash with Hrungnir, Thor visited the ASYNJR GROA to remove the flint from his forehead.

Source: Daly, Norse Mythology A to Z, 97–8l; Grimes, *Norse Myths*, 280; Selbie, *Encyclopædia of Religion and Ethics*, Volume 12, 253; Vigfússonn *Court Poetry*: Volume 2, 425

Hrymr (REM-r)

Variations: Hrym, Rym, Ryme, Rymer

A JOTUN from Norse mythology, Hrymr ("decrepit") was one of the leaders of Ragnarok; he steers the vessel *Naglfar*, a ship constructed from the finger- and toenails of dead men, from the east.

Source: Jones, *Medieval Literature in Translation*, 427; Norroena Society, *Asatrii Edda*, 365

Hsiao

A chimerical creature from Chinese folklore, the hsiao is described as an owl-like humanoid, having an ape's body, a dog's tail, and a man's face. Its presence foretells of an upcoming prolonged drought.

Source: Borges, *El Libro de los Seres Imaginarios*, 103

Human Snakes

In the mythology of the Seminole people of Florida and Oklahoma, human snakes are a species of powerful humanoid monsters known for spreading evil about the community. One story related how a medicine man was able to rid his village of their influence. Once it had been discovered they were the cause of a young man growing more ill each day, he placed the ashes of menstrual blood inside a medicine bag made of deerskin and took it, along with a menstruating woman, to the cave where the human snakes were living. Upon arrival the woman, under the direction of the medicine man, lowered the medicine bag into the cave; this caused the creatures to transform into their true forms, horrific looking half-human and half-snake creatures. The human snakes writhed in agony until they all died.

Source: Rose, *Giants, Monsters, and Dragons*, 180

Humbaba

Variations: Humwawa, Humbaba the Terrible, Huwawa, Kumbaba

A monstrous GIANT from Assyrian, Babylonian, and Sumerian mythology, Humbaba had been appointed by Enlil to be the keeper of the cedar trees in the Land of the Living. Humbaba was a terror to any mortal who entered into the forest; he was described as having breath like death, the face of a lion, a mouth like fire, the roar of a storm flood, and the teeth of a dragon; no one ever escaped his wrath. The cultural hero Gilgamesh was determined to fight Humbaba and entered into the forest with his companion ENKIDU. The different versions of the story vary to some degree but ultimately the hero instigates a fight with his opposition by intentionally cutting down one of the sacred cedar trees. A battle ensues; in the end Gilgamesh beheads Humbaba, earning him the unwanted attention of the goddess Ishtar, which segues into the legend of the BULL OF HEAVEN.

Source: Fontenrose, *Python*, 168–69; van der Toorn, *Dictionary of Deities and Demons in the Bible*, 432; Zell-Ravenheart, *Wizard's Bestiary*, 50

Hundolfr (HUND-ohlv-r)

In Norse mythology, Hundolfr ("hound ELF" or "wolf hound") was one of the many named Jotnar (see JOTUN) about whom, beyond a name, there is little or nothing else known.

Source: Norroena Society, *Asatrii Edda*, 365

Hurtali

François Rabelais (AD 1494–1553), who compiled the lineage of the GIANTS, listed Hurtali as "a brave eater of pottage (soup) who lived in the time of the Flood." Hurtali was born the son of the GIANT FARIBROTH and was the father of the GIANT NEMBROTH.

Source: Brewer, *Character Sketches of Romance, Fiction and the Drama*, Volume 3, 80; Daniels, *Encyclopædia of Superstitions, Folklore, and the Occult Sciences of the World*, 1376; Rabelais, *Hours with Rabelais*, 80

Hvalr (VAL-r)

In Norse mythology Hvalr ("whale") was one of the many named Jotnar (see JOTUN) about whom, beyond a name, there is little or nothing else known.

Source: Norroena Society, *Asatrii Edda*, 365

Hyades

Variations: The PLEIADES

In ancient Greek mythology the Hyades was the collective name for the daughters of Oceanos and Aethra (or ATLAS and PLEIONE; sources conflict) who served as the nurses for the infant god Zeus (Jupiter) upon Mount Nysa. These rain NYMPHS, numbering widely between two and seven, died of grief when their brother died after being gored by a wild boar.

In another version of the story the sisters were responsible for the care of the infant god of wine Dionysos (Bacchus). When their task was complete they were rewarded by having their youth restored to them and transformed into a constellation.

Source: Dixon-Kennedy, *Encyclopedia of Greco-Roman Mythology*, 167; Monaghan, *Encyclopedia of Goddesses and Heroines*, 256, 260

Hymir (HEM-ir)

Variations: Hrymer, Hyme, Hymer, Hýmer

In Norse mythology, Hymir ("creeper" or "the miserly") was a JOTUN; he was the husband to the ASYNJR HRODR, the mother of the god Tyr, to whom he was a foster-father. Hymir's mother, an ASYNJR named Gmir, had 900 heads. Hymir once owned a cauldron large enough to brew all the ale for the Aesir at one time; when he would not give it to them Thor and Tyr stole it from him. He was also the owner of a prize, large black oxen named Himinbrjoter; Thor was in the area and needed bait to go fishing and being impatient and quick to anger, ripped the animal's head free of its body to use for bait. Hymir was angry with but also fearful of Thor; nevertheless he went fishing with the god; the head of Himinbrjoter worked too well, as it hooked the Midgard serpent, Jormungandr. Thor struggled to pull it in so he could slay the creature but Hymir became frightened and cut the line before the god could drag the monster ashore. Hymir was later slain by Thor.

Source: Grimes, *Norse Myths*, 281; Oehlenschläger, *Gods of the North*, li; Norroena Society, *Asatrii Edda*, 366

Hyperenor

In classical Greek mythology, Hyperenor ("super man") was one of the five SPARTI who went on to become the progenitors of the five leading families of the city of Thebes who formed the military caste.

Source: Apollodorus, *Apollodorus' Library and Hyginus' Fabulae*, 22, 47; Dixon-Kennedy, *Encyclopedia of Greco-Roman Mythology*, 86; Hard, *Routledge Handbook of Greek Mythology*, 296

Hyperion (hi-pee-re-on)

A TITAN from classical Greek mythology, Hyperion ("the one above") was born one of the many children of Gaea and Uranus ("heaven"); his siblings are CRIUS, COEUS, CRONUS, IAPETUS, MNEMOSYNE, OCEANUS, PHOEBE, RHEA, TETHYS, THEIA, and THEMIS. Collectively the siblings were known as the Titanides. Hyperion was associated with astronomy, brightness, light, and like his son, the second generation TITAN HELIOS (Sol), was representative of the sun. Married to his sister THEIA, they had three children, EOS ("dawn"), HELIOS ("sun"), and Selene ("moon"). According to Bulfinch, HYPERION was one of the elder gods whose dominion was later transferred; his went to Apollo.

Source: Bulfinch, *Bulfinch's Greek and Roman Mythology*, 4; Daly, *Greek and Roman Mythology, A to Z*, 71; Roman, *Encyclopedia of Greek and Roman Mythology*, 246

Hyrrokin

Variations: Hirrokin, Hyrrockin, Hyrroken, Hyrrokkin, Hyrrokkinn

An ASYNJR from Norse mythology, Hyrrokin ("one who was burned") appears in the story of the funeral of the god Baldr. According to the legend, the gods were unable to set fire to Baldr's ship, *Hringhorn*. Hyrrokin appeared astride a wolf bridled with a snake. She dismounted and no sooner had she placed her foot upon the vessel than fire erupted from the beams so powerfully, the land itself quaked.

Source: Grimes, *Norse Mythology*, 281; Grimm, *Teutonic Mythology*, 525

I–Mu Kuo Yan

In Chinese folklore and legend the I–Mu Kuo Yan were a race of anthropomorphic GIANTS described in the *Great Imperial Encyclopedia* (1726) as having only one eye in the middle of their forehead, similar to the CYCLOPS of ancient Greek and Roman mythology, a body covered in feathers, and bird wings rather than arms.

Source: Rose, *Giants, Monsters, and Dragons*, 189; Zell-Ravenheart, *Wizard's Bestiary*, 52

Iapetus (i-ap-e-tus)

Variations: Iapetos, Japetus

A TITAN from classical Greek mythology, Iapetus was born the child of the TITANS Uranus ("heaven") and the Earth, Gaea; siblings were COEUS, CRIUS, CRONUS, HYPERION, MNEMOSYNE, OCEANUS, PHOEBE, RHEA, TETHYS, THEIA, and THEMIS. Collectively the siblings were known as the Titanides. His wife CLYMENE is usually listed as being the daughter of his brother and sister, OCEANUS and TETHYS; together they had four sons, a second generation of TITANS—ATLAS, EPIMETHEUS, MENOETIUS, and PROMETHEUS.

Source: Bulfinch, *Bulfinch's Greek and Roman Mythology*, 18–9; Daniels, *Encyclopædia of Superstitions, Folklore, and the Occult Sciences of the World*, 1375–8

Iara (Ee-yara)

Variations: Mboiacu, Yara

An iara is a vampiric spirit or witch from Brazil, depending on the way it died. If a person dies vio-

lently or before their time, dies outside the Catholic Church, is not given a proper Catholic burial, or is buried in the jungle, the person will become the vampiric spirit type of iara. However, if a living person sells their soul to the devil for power, they will become the vampiric witch type of iara.

The iara, no matter how it came to be, can, in its human guise, sing a beautiful, SIREN-like song which will lure men into the jungle. There is a protective chant which can be uttered as soon as a man hears the iara's song, but he must be quick, otherwise he is doomed. Once the iara has secured a victim, it uses therianthropy to shape-shift into a snake with red eyes and, using a form of mesmerism, hypnotizes its prey, after which it will drain off his blood and semen. It leaves the bodies of those it has killed near waterways.

Source: Bryant, *Handbook of Death*, 99; de Magalhães, *Folk-lore in Brazil*, 75, 81; Prahlad, *Greenwood Encyclopedia of African American Folklore: A-F*, 160

Iarnhaus

In Norse mythology, Iarnhaus ("iron skull") was one of the many named Jotnar (see JOTUN) about whom, beyond a name, there is nothing else known.

Source: Grimm, *Teutonic Mythology*, Volume 2, 533

Iberius

The earliest Roman geographer, Pomponius Mela, who wrote around AD 43, claimed the TITAN Iberius, son of the god Poseidon (Neptune), was the tutelary god of Ireland and his brother ALBION was the tutelary god of Britain. A third sibling, ATLAS, was the protector or tutelary divinity of some western land associated with the ocean.

Source: Spence, *History of Atlantis*, 104

Idi (ITH-i)

Variations: Ide, Ide-Slagfin, Slagfmnr

In Norse mythology, Idi ("eager" or "lively"), AURNIR and THJAZI are the sons of the storm JOTUN Olvalde; their mother was the ASYNJR GREIP. Idi was the uncle of the ASYNJR SKADI and his hall was known as Elivagarwhich ("Ide's chalet").

Source: Anderson, *Norrœna*, 974; Grimes, *Norse Myths*, 268; Rydberg, *Teutonic Mythology*, 645

Ifrikish ibn Kais

In Hebrew folklore the GIANTS who managed to escape the massacre of the city of Jericho fled under the leadership of Ifrikish ibn Kais to Africa. Upon arrival, they killed the king of the country; they decided to settle in and became its new occupants. Their descendants are the Berbers.

Source: DeLoach, *Giants*, 147; Singer, *Jewish Encyclopedia*, Volume 5, 659

Igpupiara

Variations: Hipupiara, Iara, Oyara, Uiara

A species of MERMAN and woman from Brazilin folklore, the igpupiara ("dweller in water") is described as having a humanoid torso, a seal-like head, and a body resembling the tail of a fish; its gigantic arms end in webbed fingers. The igpupiara lures people into the water and then attacks, killing them, and consumes breasts, eyes, fingers, genitalia, noses, and toes of the victim.

Source: Meurger, *Lake Monster Traditions*, 200; Rose, *Giants, Monsters, and Dragons*, 188; Zell-Ravenheart, *Wizard's Bestiary*, 51

Ijiraq, plural: ijirait

Among the Inuit people of northern Canada the ijirait ("one that hides" or "those who have something about the eyes") are a species of invisible nature spirits who are particularly powerful; normally these creatures are invisible to humans but shamans and some individuals under the right circumstances can see them. They are described as humanoid with caribou-like features such as a muzzle nose; they wear caribou skin clothes. The eyes and mouths of the ijirait are set lengthwise causing them to blink sideways. Although anthropomorphic they have the ability of therianthropy and can shape-shift into the form of a caribou. They have excellent eyesight, are fast runners, and strong as wolves. Their presence is indicated by the sound of a person whistling. They are known to retaliate if one of their own kind is killed.

Living in the hills and mountains in great stone houses, ijirait live their lives similarly and parallel to humans. When the natives were using dog sleds so were the ijirait; when the motorized snow sleds became popular and the norm, the ijirait upgraded as well. When an ijiraq shops in a store, no matter how much merchandise they purchase, the store's stock does not deplete. Ijirait can interfere with a person's memory causing them to forget what they have seen; the person will one day recall the experience, but only after some time has passed.

Ijirait only attack those who are cowardly and timid; the only people who are safe from them are those who have a *kigjugaq* (tattoos between their eyes). When they capture a person they remove the flesh from their shinbones or have it eaten away by worms. Although it is painful, survivors will then be transformed into fast runners. Ijirait are said to own an object much like a mirror which shows them what is happening among the human beings.

Ijirait dislike everything from the sea as well as anything connected to childbirth. If a woman has ever seen one of the Ijirait and one day later visits a woman while she is in labor, the visitor will go insane.

Source: Laugrand, *Inuit Shamanism and Christianity*, 173–7; Van Deusen, *Kiviuq*, 277, 355

Ikalu Nappa

A species of MERMAID from the Inuit people of the Artic regions, the ocean dwelling ikalu nappa has the upper body and face of a woman and the lower body of a fish.

Source: Rose, *Giants, Monsters, and Dragons*, 188; Zell-Ravenheart, *Wizard's Bestiary*, 51

Imd

In Norse mythology Imd was an ASYNJR, one of the WAVE MAIDENS who gave birth to the god Heimdall.

Source: Anderson, *History and Romance of Northern Europe*, Volume 5, 1027; Norroena Society, *Asatrii Edda*, 25

Imr (EEM-r)

Variations: Im

Born the son of the JOTUN VAFTHRUDNER, Imr ("doubt") of Norse mythology was the brother to the ASYNJR MODGUDR.

Source: Grimes, *Norse Mythology*, 281; Rydberg, *Norroena*, Volume 3, 1027

Indracittran

In Indian mythology, Indracittran was a named GIANT about whom, beyond a name, there is nothing else known.

Source: Brewer, *Character Sketches of Romance, Fiction and the Drama*, Volume 3, 82; Daniels, *Encyclopædia of Superstitions, Folklore, and the Occult Sciences of the World*, 1377

Intulo (in-TOOL-oh)

In the rural South African province of Kwalulu Nata, the native Zulu people believe in a creature they call Intulo. Described as walking upright in a human fashion, it appears to be a hybrid of a man and a lizard or alligator. Intulo is said to be a psychopomp (death omen), a messenger of death sent by the Great One to claim those whose time it is to die.

Source: Maberry, *Vampire Universe*, 161–62; Teachers' Curriculum Institute, *Ancient World History Activity Sampler*, 26; Zell-Ravenheart, *Wizard's Bestiary*, 52

Inuaruvligasugssuk

A GIANT from the folklore of the Inuit people of Canada, Inuaruvligasugssuk was even larger than the GIANT INUGPASUGSSUK; he was described as having a horrible appearance and only two teeth in his mouth. Selfish, quick to anger, and easily fooled, he was slain by INUGPASUGSSUK. Huuququliqpuq, his wife, was also slain by him as she attempted to avenge the death of her husband.

Source: Bennett, *Uqalurait*, 174

Inugpasugssuk

A GIANT from the folklore of the Inuit people of Canada, Inugpasugssuk was gargantuan; he ate whales as men eat fish and his lice were as long as a man's forearm. Fortunately, he was of a pleasant disposition and inclined to assist fishermen with their catch whenever possible. In one story when his wading through the ocean created waves large enough to engulf a village, he picked up the entire settlement and moved it to a safe location. Inugpasugssuk and his wife once tried to swap spouses with a human couple but the results were fatal for the humans; feeling so much remorse over their act, ,they adopted a human child to raise, but soon it began to grow to gigantic proportions. One day, while still a child it returned to its native village to visit its birth family. Unfortunately the child was so large no one recognized him and he was unable to fit into even the largest home. The child returned to Inugpasugssuk and his wife.

Source: Bennett, *Uqalurait*, 174; Brower, *Earth and the Great Weather*, 93; Rose, *Giants, Monsters, and Dragons*, 190

Inuragullit

A type of monster from Inuit folklore, the inuragullit ("DWARF") are recognized for having humanoid behavior and motivations and therefore were not considered to be animals such as one would hunt, but a type of "other," or creature.

Source: Halpin, *Manlike Monsters on Trial*, 205

Invunche (Een-iwn-che)

Variations: Incunche

Of all the vampiric beings, creations, and creatures, the invunche ("master of the hide") is perhaps the most pitiable. It is said in Chile a witch will kidnap a firstborn male child while it is an infant and take it back to her cave, a place accessible only through an underground lake entrance. Once the baby is in her lair, the witch first breaks one of its legs and twists it over the baby's back. The other leg, arms, hands, and feet are broken and disjointed and twisted into unnatural positions. A hole is cut under the right shoulder blade and then the right arm is inserted through it so the arm will look as if it's growing off the child's back. The baby's head is gradually bent and shaped over time as well so it will be misshapen. After the procedure is completed, the witch then rubs a magical ointment over the mangled infant, causing it to grow thick hair all over its body. Finally, its tongue is cut down the center so it resembles a snake's forked tongue. A baby no longer, the invunche is from then on fed a diet of human flesh, completing the transformation.

The creature is never able to leave the witch's cave lair, as it does not have the physical capability of swimming due to the imposed deformities of its body, unless the witch chooses to use her magic to fly it out. Otherwise its primary duty is to act as a guardian of her cave, killing anyone who enters it, unless they know the secret to entering the cave without violence—kissing it on its posterior. The creature can emit a blood-curdling scream that may freeze a man with fear, permanently.

The invunche has control over a lesser being, a TRELQUEHUECUVE. The invunche uses it to lure young girls to the water, abduct them, and bring them back to him so it can then drain them dry of their blood. It is believed only a hero can kill a TRELQUEHUECUVE and an invunche.

Source: Beech, *Chile and Easter Island*, 324; Roraff, *Chile*, 98; Rose, *Giants, Monsters, and Dragons*, 190

Iqalu-Nappa

Variations: Qilalugak-Nappa

A type of sea creature from Inuit folklore, the iqalu-nappa ("half-fish") is basically a species of MERMAN, larger than a human, whose humanoid body transforms below the waist into that of a fish.

Source: Halpin, *Manlike Monsters on Trial*, 199, 205

Ishbi-benob

Variations: Ishbibenob

A GIANT in the Philistine army, Ishbi-benob is one of the Refaim, a race of GIANTS who were the descendants of the GRIGORI; he was also the brother of the GIANT GOLIATH who was slain by a young David. Ishbi-benob was engaged in battle with David, holding him aloft and placing his new sword beneath the king so as he fell, his body would be cut in two. Just as David was about to be dropped onto the blade, youth Abishai, the brother of Joab, intervened by saying a word of power which caused David to hover in the air. Taking advantage of the moment, Abishai then killed a confused Ishbi-benob.

Source: DeLoach, *Giants*, 148; Dennis, *Encyclopedia of Jewish Myth, Magic and Mysticism*, 111; Mandel, *Ultimate Who's Who in the Bible*, 250

Isungr (EES-ung-r)

A JOTUN from Norse mythology, Isungr ("child of the ice" or "iceling") was kin to the WAVE MAIDEN GREIP and Ivaldi's sons, the Elves.

Source: Norroena Society, *Asatrii Edda*, 366

Jack-in-Irons

Jack-in-Irons was a nocturnal GIANT from the folklore of Yorkshire, England. Covered in chains and the heads of his past victims, Jack-in-Irons patrolled lonely roads with his large spiked club.

Source: Avant, *Mythological Reference*, 473; Froud, *Faeries*, 102; Monaghan, *Encyclopedia of Celtic Mythology and Folklore*, 266; Wright, *Rustic Speech and Folk-Lore*, 194

Jalpan

A species of NYMPH from Punjab folklore, the jalpan are said to be both very dangerous and highly seductive.

Source: Barber, *Dictionary of Fabulous Beasts*, 90

Jari

A rock DVERG (DWARF) from Norse mythology created by Durinn, Jari ("fighter") is listed as being one of DURINN's KIN. He, like the others created, paid particular attention to DURINN's leadership.

Source: Daly, *Norse Mythology A to Z*, 22; Grimes, *Norse Myths*, 260

Jarnsaxa (YAHRN-saks-a)

Variation: Jārnsaxa

An ASYNJR from Norse mythology, Jarnsaxa ("ironstone," "iron knife," or "she who crushes iron") was one of the WAVE MAIDENS who was mother to the god Heimdal; she was the daughter of the god of the sea, Aegir. She, like her sisters, was said to have snow-white skin, blue eyes, and billowing blond hair; in one hand they carried a golden goblet filled with mead and in the other seashells filled with the finest foods. They wore long transparent robes of green or blue trimmed in white. When not serving food in the hall, they played on the shore in groups of three.

Source: Anderson, *Norse Mythology*, 440; Daly, *Norse Mythology A to Z*, 47; Grimes, *Norse Myths*, 255

Jarnvids

Variations: Jarnvid, Jarnvidiur

An ASYNJR of Norse mythology, Jarnvids lived in the forest known as Jarnvidr ("Iron wood") east of Midgard. She and the JOTUN HRODVITNER were the parents of the Vars, the two wolves HATI and SKOLL who chased the moon and sun across the sky.

Source: Anderson, *Norse Mythology*, 451; Thorp, *Northern Mythology*, Volume 2, 451

Jelim

A race of GIANT from Albanian mythology, the Jelim are believed to be the progenitors of the Cams of the Saranda region.

Source: Elsie, *Dictionary of Albanian Religion, Mythology, and Folk Culture*, 131

Jengu, plural Miengu

MERMAID-like nature spirits from the mythology of Cameroon, miengu are similar to MAMI WATA of Africa and the Caribbean. Miengu live in rivers as well as the sea and are described as having a gap-toothed smile and long, woolly hair. In addition to carrying messages from the people to the world of spirits the benevolent miengu will also cure their devotees of illness, grant them fair weather and good luck, protect them from epidemics, and gift them victory in competitions.

Source: Austen, *Middlemen of the Cameroons Rivers*, 21; Leddon, *Child's Eye View of Fair Folk*, 53; Rosen, *Mythical Creatures Bible*, 134

Jentil, plural jentilak

According to Basque mythology, during the Neolithic Age a race of humans were living side-by-side with a race of GIANTS known as the Jentil ("gentle"); these beings taught them how to grow corn as well as metallurgy.

Source: Pavitt, *Ancient Symbolism Within the Heart*, 22

Jenu

One of the GIANTS of the four winds from Migmaq myth and legend, Jenu is said to be a cannibal who prefers to consume the flesh of children.

Source: Metallic, *Metallic Migmaq-English Reference Dictionary*, 217

Jogah

In the Iroquois mythology the jogah are a species of nature spirit similar to NYMPHS, resembling humans, but standing only a foot or so tall; usually they are invisible and are said to perform important tasks. The jogah wear pants and vests made of squirrel pelts they decorate with feathers. Male jogah usually shave their head or cut their hair into a Mohawk while the women simply braid their hair.

There are three different types of jogah, the GAHONGO, GAHONGAS, and the OHDOWAS.

Source: Chopra, *Academic Dictionary of Mythology*, 155; Leddon, *Child's Eye View of Fair Folk*, 44; Savill, *Pears Encyclopaedia of Myths and Legends*, 202

Jokao

Variations: Stonecoats

In the mythology of the Iroquois and Seneca people of the United States of America, the Jokao was a race of cannibalistic GIANTS whose entire bodies were covered with stone platelets. According to legend they were engendered during an especially severe winter. Famine was everywhere and people would have to first consume their neighbors before turning on their own family members; many people escaped the winter, crossing the river and into the warm south, but those who remained became the Jokao.

Source: Rose, *Giants, Monsters, and Dragons*, 196; Roth, *American Elves*, 76

Jokull (YUHK-ul)

In Norse mythology, Jokull ("glacier") was one of the many named Jotnar (see JOTUN) about whom, beyond a name, there is nothing else known.

Source: Norroena Society, *Asatrii Edda*, 367

Jotun (Yoo-tun), plural: Jotnar

Variations: Eoten, Etin, Hrym, Jetunn, Jöttin, Jotnar, Jötunn, Jute, Iotunn, Thurse

Powerful and wise, on par with the gods, the Jotnar of Norse mythology were mostly pictured as gigantic beings, but some were the size of humans. Living in Jotunheimr, the Jotnar came in many forms, some having multiple limbs; there were the BERGRISAR, the ELDJOTNAR, and the HRIMPURSAR. The first Jotnar were created while YMIR was exploring Ginnungagap; as he slept near Muspelheimr its heat caused him to sweat; the moisture from his left arm formed a male and a female Jotun. His left foot sweated a son with six heads who was named Thrudgelmir. Not all Jotnar were the enemy of the Aesir; in some stories they are devoted friends. There are also instances of the Aesir having relationships with Jotnar, such as the union of Frey and his wife GERDR, which produced children. Many Aesir have some Jotun blood in their veins. There are many Jotnar about whom nothing is known but a name.

Source: Anderson, *Norse Mythology*, 38–40; Daniels, *Encyclopædia of Superstitions, Folklore, and the Occult Sciences of the World*, 1377; Grimes, *Norse Myths*, 286; Norroena Society, *Asatrii Edda*, 336–401

Joukahainen (joukahainen)

Variations: Youkahainen

A GIANT described as a "lean Lapp boy" and a knowledgeable sage from Finnish mythology in the epic poem *Kalevals*, Joukahainen was the arch-rival of the main character, a powerful old shaman named Väinämöinen. The young and garrulous giant met the hero on a road; neither would move aside to let the other pass and so began a verbal battle of wits and words. At first Joukahainen had the upper hand, but Väinämöinen spun a web and nearly killed the GIANT. To save his life Joukahainen promised the hand of his sister, Aino, in marriage to the hero; she drowned herself instead. Angered, Joukahainen stalked Väinämöinen and shot his riding stag out from underneath him. Väinämöinen fell into the primordial sea, Pohjola. Joukahainen was thereafter demonized as a character.

Source: Pentikäinen, *Kalevala Mythology*, 190, 239; Rose, *Giants, Monsters, and Dragons*, 198

Jud

Variations: Xhudhi, Xhulli

Both a GIANT and a ghost from Albanian mythology, the Jud is the personification of evil; it has the ability to assume the form of animals, such as a dog, donkey, goose, ox, or snake. In the form of a horse it will throw its rider off and then trample him to death; the only escape is to roll directly beneath the horse's belly. The jud will also wander about town looking for drunk people to frighten; when it finds one it will appear suddenly and beat them up.

Source: Elsie, *Dictionary of Albanian Religion, Mythology, and Folk Culture*, 140

Juliance

A GIANT from Arthurian folklore, Juliance slew, in battle, Sir Gherhard of Wales.

Source: Daniels, *Encyclopædia of Superstitions, Folklore, and the Occult Sciences of the World*, 1377; Malory, *History of the Renowned Prince Arthur*, Volume 1, 176

Jurua

Variations: Jarawa, Juruwin ("sea spirit")

In the folklore of the people of the Andaman Islands the jurua ("other people") are a race of supernatural beings believed to live under the sea. Devouring anything which falls in the water, the jurua will throw their invisible spears at the legs of fishermen and swimmers. A successful hit means the victim will suffer a cramp and enables the jurua to better drag them beneath the waves, drowning them before consuming their body. The jurus live in underwater cities with their wives and children. They utilize underwater boats to travel great distances and are said to supplement their daily diet with the consumption of fish.

Source: Radcliffe-Brown, *Andaman Islanders*, 140–1; Rose, *Spirits, Fairies, Leprechauns, and Goblins*, 171

Juterna-Jesta

An ASYNJR from Norse folklore, Juterna-Jesta was a beautiful maiden in love with the JOTUN TORGE; she had caught the attention of another JOTUN by the name of SENJEMAND who lived on Senjen Island. Juterna-Jesta rejected SENJEMAND's proposal, telling him he was too old and ugly for her; enraged he shot a flint arrow at her but her lover TORGE saw the incoming missile and threw his hat up into the air to foul the shot and in doing so, saved her life.

Source: Guerber, *Hammer of Thor*, 163–4; Rose, *Giants, Monsters, and Dragons*, 327

Kaare

Variations: Kari, Kâri

A JOTUN of Norse mythology, Kaare was born one of the three sons of FORNJOTR the personification of the storm; his wife was named Ran-Gullveig. Kaare was the lord of the wind; his brother Æger was the lord of the ocean and LOGE was the lord of the fire.

Source: Anderson, *Norse Mythology*, 445; Coulter, *Encyclopedia of Ancient Deities*, 254; Grimes, *Norse Myths*, 283

Kabandha

Variations: Visvavasu

An evil and monstrous gigantic creature slain by Rama, Kabandha ("headless torso") was born a son of the goddess Sriand. According to the Rama myth cycle, unaware of his boon of immortality for having performed a *tapas* (penance) given to him by Brahma, Visvavasu as Kabandha, as he was originally called, attacked Indra who, using his divine discus, compressed Visvavasu's body into a new form during the battle. After the battle, he was now called Kabandha ("headless torso") as his head and neck were pushed into his chest, a mouth with oversized teeth was located in the middle of his chest, and a single eye appeared in his breast. Indra then gave the GIANT two long hands saying only when Rama cut off his hands would he gain back his original form. Eventually Kabandha happened upon Rama and his companion Lakshmana as they were in the forest looking for Sita. Kabandha grabbed up each one in a hand and began to squeeze; the men pulled their weapons and each cut off one of the GIANT's hands. Pleased, Kabandha told them his story before passing away; he also advised they visit the monkey king, Surgiva, to learn more of Sita's abduction. Rama burned Kabandha's body in a pyre and he was reborn once again as Visvavasu.

Source: Parmeshwaranand, *Encyclopaedic Dictionary of Puranas*, Volume 1, 711; Williams, *Handbook of Hindu Mythology*, 166–7

Kakamora

In the province of the Solomon Islands, upon the island of Makira, there is said to be living in the inaccessible inland caves or within the fruit and nut trees a tiny race of people or NATURE-SPIRITS known as the Kakamora. Although generally benign toward humans they will attack with their long, sharp nails and tiny teeth if provoked. Described as having a dark complexion, although some have been said to be fair skinned, their long straight hair comes down to their knees and they wear no clothes. The kakamora are exceedingly strong, stand about three feet tall, and stoop over as they run.

Sources: Barber, *Dictionary of Fabulous Beasts*, 91; Forth, *Images of the Wildman in Southeast Asia*, 243; Stanley, *South Pacific Handbook*, 920

Kaldgrani (KALD-gran-i)

In Norse mythology, Kaldgrani ("cold moustache" or "cold mouth") was one of the many named Jotnar (see JOTUN) about whom, beyond a name, there is little else to nothing known.

Source: Norroena Society, *Asatrii Edda*, 369

Kaleva

Elias Lönnrot (1802–1884), a Finnish collector of traditional Finnish oral poetry, wrote in his dictionary of Finnish mythology that Kaleva was a primordial JOTUN and the progenitor of the species; they lived in Kalevala. Kaleva is also said to be the father of the Kaleva people, the Kalevaines.

Source: Pentikäinen, *Kalevala Mythology, Revised Edition*, 155, 261

Kalevipoeg

Variations: Kalevide, Kullervo

A GIANT and hero from Estonian folklore, Kalevipoeg ("Kalev's son") was the youngest son of Kalev and Kinda, born after his father's death. The entire story of his life and death is told in the Estonian national epic *Kalevipoes* (1857).

The story begins with Kalevipoeg traveling to Finland in search of his kidnapped mother; he purchases a sword but while drunk accidentally kills the blacksmith's son and is cursed by the enraged father. The sword is then thrown into the river. Upon his return to Estonia Kalevipoeg defeats his brothers in a stone throwing contest and becomes king. He makes many improvements to the land, constructing forts and towns. Traveling to the end of the world, he defeats Satan in a battle of strength and rescues three maidens from Hell. When war breaks out and his faithful companions are slain Kalevipoeg turns rule over to his brother and retreats into the forest, depressed. While crossing a river, his legs are cut off by the sword the blacksmith threw into it years ago, miles upstream. He dies and in Heaven Taara restores his legs and sends him to the gates of Hell where he is to stand guard.

Source: Hajdú, *Ancient Culture of the Uralian Peoples*, 275–8; Oinas, *Studies in Finnic Folklore*, 69

Kalonoro

WILD MEN from Malagasy folklore, the kalonoro are said to be a race of small humanoids living in the forest surrounding the Marojejy Mountains, described as being *hafahafa* ("bizarre, frightening"), having backward turned feet and eyes glowing like red-hot coals.

Source: Martinez, *Mysterious Origins of Hybrid Man*, n.pag.

Kara

One of the many named VALKYRIES (NYMPHs of battle) in Norse mythology; Kara's story is largely lost and fragmented at best. According to what is known, she was the daughter of Halfdan, the man who raised Helgi as a foster-son. She becomes visible one day and confesses to Helgi she has been watching him—and here the poem breaks off with the story picking back up in the midst of battle, Helgi having slain the man who killed his father. A complication occurs involving Kara's two brothers, and because of it, both Helgi and Kara are slain.

Source: Bellows, *Poetic Edda* 79; Vigfússon, *Eddic Poetry*, 130

Kari (KAHR-i)

A JOTUN from Norse mythology, Kari ("wind"), one of the leaders of the FROST GIANTS (HRIMPUR-SAR), was the brother of Jifir Gymir and LOGI, father of JOKULL, and the son of FORNJOT. In some folklore Kari is a storm GIANT, the father of Bel, SKADI, Thaiassi, and THRYM.

Source: Norroena Society, *Asatrii Edda*, 368; Rose, *Giants, Monsters, and Dragons*, 204

Katallan, plural: Katallani

Variations: Ciklop ("Cyclopes," plural: Ciklopi), SYQENHENJERI ("dog-eyed man eater")

A species of CYCLOPES from Albanian and Balkan mythology, the katallan ("assassin," "henchman," or "murderer") are an anthropophagous race of GIANTS who lived in a cave, having one eye in their forehead and no knees.

Source: Elsie, *Dictionary of Albanian Religion, Mythology, and Folk Culture*, 150–1

Kataw

In the Visayan islands of the Philippines, the kataw is believed to be a species of water fairy similar to the MERMAID or SIREN. Described as looking like a beautiful, light skinned woman from the waist up, the lower body of the kataw is a fish, covered in shiny scales; they are said to have a notable fishy smell. In addition to having control over fish the kataw had the ability to haunt a person's dreams.

Source: Dumont, *Visayan Vignettes*, 200; Ramos, *Creatures of Midnight*, 67

Katyn Tayuuq

Variations: Katyutayuuq

In Inuit folklore from the people of the eastern region of the Hudson Bay, Katyn Tayuuq is a horrific GIANT, the bulk of which is her enormous head; the only other parts of her body easily seen are her descended vulva, pendulous breasts, and her feet. She is said to be able to enter a person's home at will.

Source: Rose, *Giants, Monsters, and Dragons*, 204

Katytayuuq

A type of monster from Inuit folklore, the katytayuuq of the Hudson Bay region in Canada are said to be humanoid in appearance but have small, tattooed heads; their breasts are located above their mouths on their cheeks and their genitalia are located beneath their mouth. They and their male counterparts known as the TUNNITUAQRUK scavenge behind humans on the trail searching out scraps.

Source: Rose, *Giants, Monsters, and Dragons*, 204

Keen Keengs

A race of flying GIANTS from the mythology of the native Australian people, the Keen Keengs are the descendants of the primordial GIANTS who first inhabited the land; they are said to live in the caves of the Dreamtime and are described as being exceptionally tall humanoids with only two fingers and a thumb on each hand with a set of ribbed bat-like wings. The Keen Keengs were the guardians of the flame of their fire god which was kept in the center of the cavern complex they dwelt in.

Source: Eliot, *Universal Myths*, 163; Rose, *Giants, Monsters, and Dragons*, 204–5

Kefsir (KEHV-sir)

One of the hrymthursars (FROST GIANTS) from Norse mythology, Kefsir ("bastard" or "whore-master") was one of the sons of THRAEL and THIR. His family lived a hard life performing thankless tasks, such as cleaning, herding goats and swine, and placing dung in the fields. They became the progenitors of the serving folk and thrall.

Source: Grimes, *Norse Myths*, 27, 283; Norroena Society, *Asatrii Edda*, 368

Kerkopes

In ancient Greek mythology Kerkopes was the collective name of two brothers, small and simian in their appearance; they were well known not only for their thievery but also for being cheaters and liars who deceived men as they traveled all over the world. During the time the demi-god and hero Hercules (Heracles) was married to Xenodike he encountered them while they had slipped into his camp and attempted to steal his weapons as he slept. Hercules captured the Kerkopes and tied them upside down to either end of a pole in the fashion a hunter would do to his recently slain prey. It was only then the brothers remembered a warning their mother had given them, to beware the black-bottomed man; and from their unique view they were able to clearly see Hercules' buttocks were dark and rather hairy where not covered by his lion skin. Realizing the warning had come to pass the brothers joked about it, amusing even Hercules. Because of their good humor, the demi-god released them. Unfortunately the Kerkopes attempted to cheat the god Zeus (Jupiter); for this crime, he had them turned into stone.

Source: Hard, *Routledge Handbook of Greek Mythology*, 274–5; March, *Penguin Book of Classical Myths*, 214

Kibaan

Minuscule humanoids from Filipino folklore, the Kibaan are described as being only a few feet tall, with backward facing feet, fair skin, long hair nearly touching the ground, and a mouth filled with golden teeth. Said to live in the Bangar tree and bushes frequented by fireflies, their favorite creature, the Kibaan will gather together at night and, playing on tiny guitar-like instruments, sing. Usually these little beings are harmless in their mischief, stealing loose change, shiny keys, and yams out of the fire pit, but if one of their children were to be injured by a human, the Kibaan are quite vengeful.

Source: Ramos, *Creatures of Philippine Lower Mythology*, 61; Redfern, *Most Mysterious Places on Earth*, 113

Kifri

The powerful GIANT who was the personification of atheism, blasphemy, and infidelity, Kifri was an enchanter with a voice like thunder from Persian folklore. Described as having vermillion colored eyes and long tangled hair, when he was enraged, smoke and fire escaped from his nostrils. In a fit of depression and rage, after giving a long and blasphemous speech to Heaven, Kifri committed suicide by hurling a huge boulder up into the air and allowing it to crash down on his head.

Source: Brewer, *Reader's Handbook of Allusions, References, Plots and Stories*, 510; Daniels, *Encyclopædia of Superstitions, Folklore, and the Occult Sciences of the World*, 1377; Morell, *Tales of the Genii*, 11–14

Kijimuna

Variations: Akakanaza, Bungaya, Ki No Mono ("monster of trees"), Kijimun, Kiji-mun, Kijimunaa

Specific to the island of Okinawa, Japan, the kijimuna are a type of DRYAD or NYMPH living in the trees and guiding and protecting humans. Described as having red fur or hair, these nature spirits will try to assist fishermen in their task; it is believed any fish caught with one eye was through the assistance of the kijimuna, as it is prone to take a bite of the catch. The temperament of the kijimuna ranges from delightfully playful to slightly annoying. Walking in the shallow water at night, they carry a lantern; the kijimuna are afraid of octopuses.

Source: Hendry, *Interpreting Japanese Society*, 172; Sered, *Women of the Sacred Groves*, 52; Sakihara, *Okinawan-English Wordbook*, 93

Kijo

Female OGRES from Japanese folklore, the kijo were said to live deep within the forest; their bodies were covered with white hair and they were prone to cannibalistic tendencies. Kijo were said to be able to fly like a moth and could navigate the narrow mountain passes with great ease. A cannibal kijo is born once every sixty years.

Source: Brinklye, *Japan, Its History, Arts and Literature*, Volume 5, 215; Davis, *Myths and Legends of Japan*, 355; Rose, *Giants, Monsters, and Dragons*, 208

Killer Whale People

Variations: Ha'lx'aixxtlenox

In the folklore of the Haida people of the Pacific Northwest Coast of North America, the killer whale people were one of the many supernatural ocean people who lived in underwater villages scattered up and down the shore. Since the ocean people were in control of a large part of the food supply, they not only were held in the highest of regard but were also appealed to for assistance with offerings of rare flicker feathers, grease, and tobacco. According to the folklore, when they arrived at their homes they would take off their black and white skins and live like GIANTS beneath the waves. Their homes always had a huge mouth painted on them and the posts were carved killer whales and to either side of the door was a painting of a fish known as the melxani'gun. The killer whale people are the arch-enemy of the shark people.

Source: Boas, *Tsimshian Mythology*, 480–84; Goldenweiser, *Early Civilization*, 63

Kilyakai

Described as being a hybrid of demons, nature spirits, and Neanderthals, the Kilyakai of Papu New Guinea are a tribe of small and incredibly evil humanoids living in the dense jungle. These malignant beings are said to sneak into a town and steal children and pigs when not hiding in bushes and shooting people with darts infected with malaria. The Kilyakai kidnap children in order to imbue their own demonic nature into them in order to populate their race.

Source: Lawrence, *Gods, Ghosts and Men in Melanesia*, 153; Maberry, *Vampire Universe*, 175

Kirata

A race of hybrid beings said to live in the central

Himalayas, the Kirata were described in the *Ramayana* as literally being half human and half tiger; their upper body is of a tiger and their lower half human. The Kirata were foresters and mountaineers who ate a diet of raw fish and were said to live in the water. The females of the species were described as being "gold-colored and pleasant to behold" even with the sharply pointed hair knots they wore.

Source: Dowson, *Classical Dictionary of Hindu Mythology and Religion, Geography, History, and Literature*, 158; Vālmīki, *Ramayana of Valmiki*, 142, 300; Zell-Ravenheart, *Wizard's Bestiary*, 57

Kleggi (KLEHG-i)

Variations: Kreggi

One of the hrymthursars (FROST GIANTS) from Norse mythology, Kleggi ("hay giver" and "horsefly") was born one of the sons of THRAEL and THIR. Kleggi, his parents, and siblings all lived a hard life of labor performing thankless tasks, such as cleaning, herding goats and swine, placing dung in the fields, and other varied unskilled labor. He and his family became the progenitors of the serving folk and thrall.

Source: Grimes, *Norse Myths*, 27, 283; Norroena Society, *Asatrii Edda*, 368

Knockers

Variations: Black DWARFS, BUCCA, Bwca, COBLYN, Cobylnaus, Garthornes, Gommes, Koblernigh, Knackers, SPRIGGANS, Tommyknockers, Wichlein Paras

In Cornwall, England, knockers were DWARFS or a species of kobold living in caves and mines; they earned their name by the knocking noises they made to direct miners where to dig. When danger was near they would knock rapidly. Knockers did not like the sound of whistling and would throw handfuls of gravel, harmlessly, at the offender. To keep on their good side, miners would leave a portion of their food for them.

Generally the knockers were described as standing about two feet tall and dressed like a miner carrying a lunch pail and pick. There was also the belief knockers were the souls of the Jewish individuals who were responsible for the crucifixion and death of Jesus Christ; as punishment they had been condemned to work in tin-mines until the Resurrection.

Source: Courtney, *Cornish Feasts and Folk-Lore*, 61, 128; Evans-Wentz, *Fairy Faith in Celtic Countries*, 165; Illes, *Encyclopedia of Spirits*, 576; McCoy, *Witch's Guide to Faery Folk*, 147, 255–6

Kolga

Variations: Kólga

An ASYNJR from Norse mythology, Kolga ("coal black," "raging sea" or the poetical term for a wave, "the cool one") was one of the WAVE MAIDENS who were mother to the god Heimdall; she was the daughter of the god of the sea, Aegir. She, like her sisters, was said to have snow-white skin, blue eyes, and billowing blond hair; in one hand they carried a golden goblet filled with mead and in the other seashells filled with the finest foods. They wore long transparent robes of green or blue trimmed in white. When not serving food in the hall, they played on the shore in groups of three.

Source: Grimes, *Norse Myths*, 122, 284; Sturluson, *Prose Edda*, Volume 5, 219

Köll (KUHL)

Variations: Koll

In Norse mythology the JOTUN KÖLL ("cold") and his sister, the ASYNJR SELA, were slain by Egill; beyond his name, there is little or nothing else known.

Source: Norroena Society, *Asatrii Edda*, 368; Rydberg, *Our Fathers' Godsaga*, 196

Kollimalaikanniyarka

Variations: Seven Maidens

A type of NYMPH from the mythology of India, the Kollimalaikanniyarka ("seven maidens from the kolli mountains") were charged with the task of educating Kattavarayan, the son of Parvati and Siva. They assisted him in learning magic. There were at least two sets of the Kollimalaikanniyarka, some names include: Annamuttu, Cavutayi, Karuppalaki, Karuppayi, Nallatankaj, Nallatankal, Nalli, Ontayi, Puvayi, Ukantalaki, and Valli.

Sources: Hiltebeitel, *Criminal Gods and Demon Devotees*, 86, 440; Rose, *Spirits, Fairies, Leprechauns, and Goblins*, 183

Kopuwai

Maori of New Zealand have in their mythology a scaly GIANT, or OGRE, named Kopuwai ("belly of water" or "a wet place"). One of many GIANTS who settled in the south, he is the only one who has any number of tales attributed to him. In his best known tale he swallowed the entirety of the Molyneux River in order to capture a Rapuwai woman named Kaiamio; for this he was transformed into the Old Man of the Range and sent to live in the mountains of central Otago. Kopuwai was the master of a pack of ten two-headed dogs. When Kopuwai was finally transformed into a pillar of stone, his pack dispersed. Six of them took refuge in a cave on a riverbank; they too were transformed into stone and their heads are said to still remain sticking out of the water of the *Ka-waikoukou* to this day.

Source: Polynesian Society (N.Z.), *Journal of the Polynesian Society*, Volume 27, 152–53

Koro-pok-guru

Variations: Koropok-guru, Korobokkuru, Koropokkur, Koropokkuru

The koro-pok-guru ("people of the hollows") were a race of diminutive, highly civilized people which once lived in the archipelago of Japan but were, according to Ainu folklore, driven to extinction by the Ainu.

The name koro-pok-guru has been translated by different scholars with an array of meanings, such as "dwellers in holes," "the people having depressions" as well as "people below the leaves of the butterbur plant."

Source: Yamashita, *Making of Anthropology in East and Southeast Asia*, 57, 62–63

Korrigan

Variations: Cornik, Corrigan, Koril, Kornikaned, Ozeganned, Poulpikan, Teuz

Believed to have originated in ancient Gaul on the Isles des Saints in the British sea, the korrigaan stand no more than two feet tall but have perfectly proportioned bodies and a head full of flowing, long hair which they take great care of. Sometimes they are said to have vespid (wasplike) wings. The only clothing they wear is a long white veil they wrap and wind around their body. Typically the korrigan are seen at night when they are at their most beautiful; by day their eyes are red, their hair white, and their faces deeply wrinkled. Fond of music and with a voice suitable for singing, the korrigan are one of the few species of fairy not fond of dancing.

Although the korrigan will steal children they do not leave a CHANGELING in the child's place; rather they take children they consider need to be protected. Only those children who wear a scapular or rosary about their neck are safe from abduction as they have a great abhorrence to the holy Virgin Mary of Christian folklore. The sound of pealing church bells will drive them away.

There is the general belief the korrigan were created when the princesses of Armorica refused to convert to Christianity; they were cursed by God, transformed into FAIRY-beings. Although their breath is said to be deadly, the all-female race of the korrigan must take mortal men as their lovers in order to perpetuate their race. These fairies have the ability of therianthropy and can shape-shift into any form they desire, predict the future, travel from one location to another with the speed of thought, and cure most illnesses by means of charms they create.

Source: Keightley, *World Guide to Gnomes, Fairies, Elves, and Other Little People*, 420, 431–2; Monaghan, *Encyclopedia of Celtic Mythology and Folklore*, 275; Spence, *Legends and Romances of Brittany*, 35–8

Kukudh, plural Kukudhi

There are three beings in the southern Albanian mythology by the name of kukudh—one is a ghost; one is a humanoid creature; and one is a demon.

The ghost kukudh is the returned spirit of a person who found no peace or rest in the grave and consequently will take up residence in the home of a miser and haunt it. It is a popular folkloric belief if an exceptionally brave hero spends a night in such a house and survives the kukudh the hero would then become the heir to the owner of the property, also inheriting the unspent fortune.

The humanoid creature known as a kukudh is described as looking like a heavyset, short man with one to seven goats' tails. Invulnerable to nearly all types of physical damage, this humanoid commits random acts of evil and can only be slain by use of a noose made of grapevines.

The third and most prevalent conception of the kukudh is of it being a female demon carrying cholera and spreading it wherever it travels.

Source: Elsie, *Dictionary of Albanian Religion, Mythology, and Folk Culture*, 153

Kumba (KUM-ba)

One of the hrymthursars (FROST GIANTS) from Norse mythology, Kumba ("stumpy" and "stupid") was born one of the daughters of THRAEL and THIR. Kumba, her parents, and siblings all lived a hard life of labor performing thankless tasks, such as cleaning, herding goats and swine, placing dung in the fields, and other varied unskilled labor. She and her family became the progenitors of the serving folk and thrall.

Source: Grimes, Norse Myths, 27, 284; Norroena Society, *Asatrii Edda*, 369

Kung-Lu

Variations: Dsu-The, Ggin-Sung, Tok

A monstrous humanoid from the folklore of the Himalayas, the large and fur-covered kung-lu ("mouth man") is a species consisting entirely of males; they need to abduct and rape human women in order to continue their kind. When the child is born it is about the size of a six-month-old human infant; sadly the mother never survives the ordeal. These simian (ape-like) creatures are said to live high up in the mountains; when they crave meat or are in need of a mate they blaze a trail of broken trees to a village where they will consume men and abduct women.

Source: Maberry, *Vampire Universe*, 187; Sanderson, *Abominable Snowmen, Legend Come to Life*, 242

Kuniya (Coo-nee-ah)

In the Australian Dreamtime the Kuniya were a race of snake people or an individual female (the story varies), similar to the naga, as they were part human and part python. According to the folklore Kuniya traveled to a place known as Uluru to lay her eggs; while there she came upon the place where the LIRU, a race of snake people (or an individual brown snake as the story varies) had killed her nephew. The LIRU mocked Kuniya for her sadness, enticing her anger and vengeance; she performed a powerful dance and spat poison into the sand, sending it deep into the ground. Now in a full rage, Kuniya hefted up her ax and hit the first LIRU warrior she saw "at first gently, then fatally." Today, the terrain is said to bear the battle scars, as there are fig and gum trees growing which are poisonous and deep grooves from the ax and snake tracks carved into the stones.

Source: Farfor, *Northern Territory*, 272; Kng, *Tracing the Way*, 11–2

Kuperan

Variations: Kuppiron, Kuprian

Kuperan was a GIANT and an ally of the dragon in the Middle High German epic poem, *Nibelungenlied* ("The Song of the Nibelungs"). Living high up in the mountains with the dragon, Kuperan is the guardian of the only sword by which the dragon can be slain and commands a legion of GIANTs as well. Bearing a shield a foot thick and "hardened with dragon's blood," Kuperan does battle against the hero Seyfrid (Siegfried). He wore gilded armor, a helm which increased his strength, and wielded a four cornered club razor sharp at every angle.

It has been speculated Kuperan and the dragon of the poem are in fact the same character as they never appear in the same place at the same time; although the hero of the poem, Seyfrid, does battle and kills each in turn.

Source: Keightley, *World Guide to Gnomes, Fairies, Elves, and Other Little People*, 208; McConnell, *Companion to the Nibelungenlied*, 56–8; Thoms, *Lays and Legends of Various Nations*, 67–8

Kushtaka

Variations: Land Otter People

In Tlingit mythology the Kushtaka are an extremely terrifying race of beings as they prey upon those who drown or die in the woods, take their soul back to their village, and begin a transformation process which will turn the victim into one of them. This is a frightful concept to the Tlingit as the transformation destroys the person's soul and does not allow for it to reincarnate. There are ceremonies which can be performed to prevent the Kushtaka from claiming the soul of a person who has drowned and their body has not been recovered. Children are particularly susceptible to Kushtaka abductions, as they are prone to wander off from their parents and the Kushtaka have the ability to shape-shift into the form of family members or friends of those they are trying to abduct. As the transformation of the soul takes some time, it is possible for a shaman to rescue it. Dogs are a means by which the Kushtaka can be warded off, as they are afraid of them and the animals' barking will force them to reveal themselves for what they really are. Although the Kushtaka are a danger to humans they have been known to assist their own relatives.

Source: Pelton, *Images of a People*, 20

Kyrmir

In Norse mythology, Kyrmir ("screamer") was one of the many named Jotnar (see JOTUN) about whom, beyond a name, there is little or nothing else known.

Source: Norroena Society, *Asatrii Edda*, 25

Laestrygones (les-trig'-o-neez)

Variations: Laestrygonians, Laistrygones

A tribe of cannibalistic GIGANTE from ancient Greek mythology, the Laestrygones only appear in the story of Odysseus as he attempts to make his way home after the Trojan War ended. The king of the Laestrygones, Lamus, ruled over the island of Telepylos; when Odysseus and his fleet put in there one of his men was taken and eaten. Odysseus and his men ran back to their ship and set sail as quickly as they could but the GIGANTE managed to harpoon all the ships except for the one Odysseus himself was making his escape upon. All hands were captured and consumed by the Laestrygones.

Source: Berens, *Myths and Legends of Ancient Greece and Rome*, 311; Daly, *Greek and Roman Mythology, A to Z*, 84; Dixon-Kennedy, *Encyclopedia of Greco-Roman Mythology*, 186

Lahmi (Lah-Me)

The brother GOLIATH OF GATH, Lahmi ("foodful," "full of bread," or "lustful craving"), also a GIANT, carried a "spear with a shaft like a weaver's rod" and fought for the Philistine army. In the Hebrew Bible (Christian Old Testament) Chronicles 20:5 says Elhanan, son of Jair, killed him in single combat at Gob.

Source: DeLoach, *Giants*, 88, 174; Jernigan, *Giant Killers*, n.pag.; Mandel, *Ultimate Who's Who in the Bible*, 406

Lahmu

Variations: Lahmyu, Lakhmu, Ur-Sag ("hero" and "lion")

According to Akkadian-Babylonian mythology, the first born son and creature of the dragon goddess Tiamat, Lahmu is described as a fierce GIANT with long hair and beard; it is represented in art by three long curly strands, symbolic for massive quantities of hair. He is also depicted as fighting lions, perhaps to control their urge for violence. Lahmu has dominion over the flow of the sea and of the fish and in later times becomes a monstrous guardian for Assyrian kings and then a protective household spirit.

Lahmu has a sister, the primordial goddess and first born daughter of Tiamat, Lahamu. Together they were the parents of the gods Anshar and Kishar; the husband and wife siblings are never mentioned apart.

Source: De Lafayette, *New de Lafayette Mega Encyclopedia of Anunnaki*, Volume 5, 1329; Ford, *Maskim Hul*, 147; Jordan, *Dictionary of Gods and Goddesses*, 170

Lamia, plural: Lamiak

Variations: Lamin, plural: Lamiak, Laminak

In Basque mythology the lamiak were a species of creature with duck-like feet living in rivers and springs; they are easily comparable to the NYMPHS of ancient Greece. Typically female, the lamiak were said to spend much of their time sitting upon the bank and combing out their waist-length hair with golden combs, similar to MERMAIDS. When approached, they would dive into the safety of the water.

The lamiak do not have a fixed appearance; it varies according to the role they are going to play in the moral lesson story being told. They appear as young and rapturously beautiful to hideously ugly. They also do not have a fixed nature. Sometimes they use their magic to punish those who tell lies and other times they act as a mediator between nature and the social order of man. They are quick to punish those who act out of greed and are firm believers of living by mutual assistance and reciprocity. Lamiak also take an interest in assisting industrious women, controlling moral behavior, decreasing or increasing people's wealth, and overseeing male sexuality. Their male counterpart is called MAIDE.

Source: Bullen, *Basque Gender Studies*, 145–6; Gimbutas, *Living Goddesses*, 174–5; Williams, *Essays in Basque Social Anthropology and History*, 109–111

Lampades

The Lampades were a species of torch-bearing infernal NYMPHS of the Underworld, inhabiting the rivers there. Although Greek in origin, their parentage is uncertain; it is possible they were the daughters of the goddess Nyx and any number of river gods of Hades. The lampades were described by Alkman, an ancient Greek lyrical poet from Sparta who worked in the 7th century BC; he described them as being the lamp-bearing entourage of Hekate as well as prophets.

Source: Illes, *Encyclopedia of Spirits*, 619; Rigoglioso, *Cult of Divine Birth in Ancient Greece*, 87

Lampong

A species of DWARF from Filipino folklore, the lampong at first appear to be one-eyed white deer, and as they approached, they seem to become at least two feet taller. The bright eyed and long bearded lampong wear a tall, black two-peaked cap upon their head; they consider themselves to be guardians of the animals of the forests and will tempt a man to shoot at them knowing their magic will cause the hunter's first five shots to always miss. If the hunter is persistent and manages to strike an animal or even the lampong itself, it will transform into a DUENDE and have its revenge.

Source: Ramos, *Creatures of Philippine Lower Mythology*, 9; Wilson, *Ilongot Life and Legends*, 8–8

Laufey (LAU-fee-eh)

Variations: Laufeia, Nal ("needle")

An ASYNJR in Norse mythology, Laufey ("leafy island") was the mother of the god Loki by the JOTUN FARBANTI. Described as being feeble and slender, she was most likely a goddess as otherwise Loki would not have been counted among the gods.

Source: Lindow, *Norse Mythology*, 208, 235; Oehlenschläger, *Gods of the North*, liii

Leanhaum-Shee

Variations: Leanan-Sidhe, Leanhaun-Shee, Leanhaun-Sidhe, Lhiannan Shee

On the Isle of Man, located in the middle of the northern Irish Sea, there is a type of vampiric fay that appears to its victims as a beautiful young woman but to everyone else is invisible; it is called a leanhaum-shee. It will try to seduce a man, and if it is successful, its magic will cause him to fall in love with it. If he does, the leanhaum-shee will take him as a lover; if he does not, it will strangle him to death and then drain his corpse of blood. Little by little it will drain off its lover's life-energy during intercourse. The leanhaum-shee also collects his blood and stores it in a red cauldron, which adds to its magical properties. (It is believed the cauldron is the source of its power, what gives the leanhaum-shee its ability to shape-shift into a white deer and keeps it looking young and beautiful, and not the ability of therianthropy.) The vampire also feeds small amounts of the blood to her lover so he will be inspired to write love poems. Eventually, the man will become nothing more than a used-up husk and die.

Source: Jones, *On the Nightmare*; Moorey, *Fairy Bible*, 162–5; O'Connor, *Book of Ireland*, 50–2; Wilde, *Ancient Legends*, 169, 257–9

Leggjaldi (LEHG-yald-i)

One of the hrymthursars (FROST GIANTS) from Norse mythology, Leggjaldi ("huge legs" or "long shanks") was born one of the sons of THRAEL and THIR. Leggjaldi, his parents, and siblings all lived a hard life of labor performing thankless tasks, such as cleaning, herding goats and swine, placing dung in the fields, and other varied unskilled labor. He and his family became the progenitors of the serving folk and thrall.

Source: Grimes, *Norse Myths*, 27, 285; Norroena Society, *Asatrii Edda*, 370

Leimakid

Variations: Leimonaids

The Leimakids were a sub-species of the LIMONIAD from ancient Greek mythology; they were the NYMPHS of meadows.

Source: Conner, *Everything Classical Mythology Book*, 275

Leppa Ludi

Variations: Leppaludi

The NURSERY BOGIE Leppa Ludi, a GIANT or TROLL from Icelandic folklore, and his wife, GRÝLA, were cannibals who would abduct naughty children and occasionally adult men and stockpile them to consume on Christmas Eve. Leppa Ludi and his wife were said to have twenty children of their own but he had a son named Skjoda out of wedlock with an unnamed female.

Source: Raedisch, *Old Magic of Christmas*, 91; Simpson, *Icelandic Folktales and Legends*, 89–90; Watts, *Encyclopedia of American Folklore*, 212

Lestrigo

The brother of the GIANTs ALBION and BERGION, Lestrigo was the oppressive and tyrannical king of Italy.

Source: Roof, *Popular History of Noble County Capitals and Greater Albion*, 13

Lestrigons

Variations: Leontini

A race of GIGANTES living in Sicily, the Lestrigons were utilized by the god of the sea, Nep-

tune, to punish the hero Ulysses for having destroyed the eye of his CYCLOPES son POLYPHEMUS. On approach to the island, Ulysses sent two of his men ahead to request permission to land but the king of the Lestrigons, ANTIPHATES, captured and consumed one; the other escaped to warn his captain.

Source: Bell, *Bell's New Pantheon*, 70

Leto

Variations: Latona

A TITAN from ancient Greek mythology, Leto was born one of the two children of the first generation TITAN COEUS; she was described as being the most gentle of her kind, beautiful, and having lovely ankles. By the god Zeus (Jupiter), she was the mother of the twin gods Apollo and Artemis (Diana).

Source: Daly, *Greek and Roman Mythology, A to Z*, 141; Westmoreland, *Ancient Greek Beliefs*, 27, 41

Leuce

Variations: Leuka, Leukas

The Leuce ("white") were a sub-species of the HAMADRYAD, the NYMPHS of white poplar trees in Greek mythology.

Leuce was also the name of the individual HAMADRYAD who was raped by the god of the Underworld, Hades (Dis). According to the legend his wife, Persephone (Proserpina), was so angry she turned the NYMPH into a white poplar tree.

Source: Day, *God's Conflict with the Dragon and the Sea*, 410; Larson, *Greek Nymphs*, 160–1; Littleton, *Gods, Goddesses, and Mythology*, Volume 11, 603

Leucosia

Variations: AGLAOPE

Sea NYMPHS from ancient Greek mythology, Leucosia ("the fair" or "white being") and her sisters, LIGEIA and PARTHENOPE, were born the daughters of the MUSE Melpomene and the god Achelous and the companion to Persephone; after her abduction by Hades (Dis) the sisters asked the gods for wings so they might go in search of their friend. The request granted, the three NYMPHS were transformed into bird-women hybrids, the SIRENS. Leucosia sang while PARTHENOPE played the lyre and LIGIA played the flute. Together they would harmonize along the rocky shoreline and lure sailors to turn their ships to hear their melodic songs, wrecking their vessels. Then the sisters would capture and devour the men.

Source: Drury, *Dictionary of the Esoteric*, 297; Hunt, *New Monthly Magazine and Universal Register*, 276

Leyak (Lee-ack)

Variations: Leak

On the Indonesian island of Bali, there is a type of vampiric witch called a leyak. By day, the witch looks and acts like everyone else in its community, but at night, it will search through the local cemeteries for human entrails it'll use to make a magical formula. If there are no suitable corpses in the cemetery to pillage, the leyak will harvest what it needs from a sleeping person. The elixir it brews will give it the ability of therianthropy so it may shape-shift into a tiger as well as being able to rip its head free from its body so it may fly off in search of prey, dragging its entrails behind it, much like the PENANGGLAN and the numerous other vampires who use this method for hunting. Leyak can also cause crops to fail as well as start epidemics and famine. In addition to shape-shifting into a tiger it can also become a bald-headed GIANT, a ball of light (corpse candle), a monkey with golden teeth, a gigantic rat, a riderless motorcycle, or a bird as large as a horse. Should a leyak possess a person, the victim is called *pengeleyakan*. No matter what form the leyak is in, it should always be considered a highly dangerous and unpredictable monster.

Leyak drink the blood of both animals and humans, but they are particularly fond of the blood of women who just gave birth and newborn babies. One is often seen wandering along back roads, crossroads, cemeteries, forests, ravines, and the seashore. If on a moonless night dogs begin to whimper, it is said a leyak is near. Gourmet food left outside your house is usually offering enough to appease one.

The leyak can be restored to harmony with nature through an elaborate, high-level ceremony called *mecaru*. The ceremony requires blood sacrifice. However, according to Balinese folklore, the leyak's magic only works on the isle of Bali. Java and the other small islands are safe from its attack and if the witch can be moved there, it would be rendered impotent.

There is a temple built in the town of Pura Dalem Penataran Ped, Bali, in honor of Ratu Gede Mecaling, the patron saint of all leyak witches.

Source: Howe, *Gods, People, Spirits and Witches*, 23, 90, 168, 195; Jennaway, *Sisters and Lovers*, 204; Mack, *Field Guide to Demons*, 240

Ligeia

Variations: Ligea, THELXIOPE

Sea NYMPHS from ancient Greek mythology, Ligeia ("maiden face" or "shrill") and her sisters, LEUCOSIA and PARTHENOPE, were born the daughters of the MUSE Melpomene and the god Achelous and the companion to Persephone; after her abduc-

tion by Hades (Dis) the sisters asked the gods for wings so they might go in search of their friend. The request granted, the three NYMPHS were transformed into bird-women hybrids, the SIRENS. Ligia played the flute while PARTHENOPE played the lyre and LEUCOSIA sang. Together they would harmonize along the rocky shoreline and lure sailors to turn their ships to hear their melodic songs, wrecking their vessels. Then the sisters would capture and devour the men.

Source: Drury, *Dictionary of the Esoteric*, 297; Hunt, *New Monthly Magazine and Universal Register*, 276

Liitr (LOOT-r)

Variations: Litr

In Norse mythology, Liitr ("the disgraceful") was one of the many named Jotnar (see JOTUN) about whom, beyond a name, there is little to nothing else known. It is possible through a mistranslation Liitr was Litr, slain by the god Thor.

Source: Norroena Society, *Asatrii Edda*, 372

Limnades

Variations: Leimenides, Limnatides

The Limnades were a sub-species of the NAIADS. NYMPHS of freshwater lakes, they were born the children of Bolbe, one of the named OCEANIDS, according to classical Greek mythology.

Source: Avant, *Mythological Reference*, 291; Bell, *Bell's New Pantheon*, 47; Chopra, *Academic Dictionary of Mythology*, 198; Maberry, *Cryptopedia*, 112

Limoniad

Variations: Limniad

The Limoniad were one of twelve species of NYMPHS in Greek mythology; they were the NYMPHS of flowers and meadows.

Source: Bell, *Bell's New Pantheon*, 47; Chopra, *Academic Dictionary of Mythology*, 176; Littleton, *Gods, Goddesses, and Mythology*, Volume 11, 999

Liru

In the Australian Dreamtime the Liru were a race of poisonous snake-people warriors (or an individual brown snake as the story varies) who had killed the nephew of KUNIYA and then mocked her grief. The ensuing battle which took place between KUNIYA and Liru altered the landscape of southwest Uluru, Australia, where evidence, it is said, is still apparent in the deeply scarred rocks.

Source: Farfor, *Northern Territory*, 272; Kng, *Tracing the Way*, 11–2

Lofa

A cannibalistic humanoid from the mythology of the Chickasaw Indians from Mississippi and

Oklahoma, United States of America, the lofa attacks camps to kill the men and abduct the women as it needs them to propagate their species. If one of their own is ever killed the rest of the pack will go to great lengths to retrieve the body. The lofa are very intelligent, extremely hostile, malicious, vile creatures who smell so terrible that their stench can kill a person. They are tall, nearly ten feet, and have overly long arms and undersized heads.

Source: Brown, *Southern Indian Myths and Legends*, 83–4; Maberry, *Vampire Universe*, 202

Lofar

A rock DVERG (DWARF) from Norse mythology created by DURINN, Lofar is listed as being one of DURINN's KIN. He, like the others created, paid particular attention to DURINN's leadership and is possibly one of the progenitors of Dwarven-kind.

Source: Grimes, *Norse Myths*, 260; Thorpe, *Northern Mythology*, Volume 2, 9

Loge (loo-gee)

Variations: Logi ("log flame"), Haloge

A JOTUN of Norse mythology, Loge was born one of the three sons of FORNJOTR the storm personified and his wife Ran-Gullveig. Loge was the lord of the fire; his brother Æger was the lord of the ocean and KAARE was the lord of the wind. Loge, along with BRANDINGI, EIMNER, and ELDR, was the personification of fire.

Source: Anderson, *Norse Mythology*, 445; Norroena Society, *Asatrii Edda*, 25; Sturluson, *Prose Edda*, 128; Taunton, *Northern Traditions*, 31

Loha-Mukha

A race of monstrous GIANTS from Hindu mythology, the loha-mukha ("iron faced"), one of the KRAVYAD, have faces made of iron and only one leg and foot. In spite of what would seem to be a handicap, these humanoid cannibals are cunning hunters living exclusively off of humans who wander into their territory.

Source: Coulter, *Encyclopedia of Ancient Deities*, 293; Rose, *Giants, Monsters, and Dragons*, 227

Loni (LOHN-i)

A rock DVERG (DWARF) from Norse mythology created by DURINN, Loni ("lazy") is listed as being one of DURINN's KIN. He, like the others created, paid particular attention to DURINN's leadership.

Source: Daly, *Norse Mythology A to Z*, 22; Grimes, *Norse Myths*, 260; Norroena Society, *Asatrii Edda*, 372

Loreley

In exoteric magic and occultism the loreley is essentially an UNDINE. In German folklore Loreley was a golden haired SIREN who sat upon a rock in the Rhine now known as Loreley Rock playing a lyre and luring men to their death.

Source: Blavatsky, *Theosophical Glossary*, 191; Wägner, *Asgard and the Gods*, 240–1

Lund-Folk

Variations: Grove-damsels (Lundjungfrur), Lof jerskor, Lofjerskor

Protectors of sacred groves in Swedish folklore, the invisible lund-folk ("grove-folk") are similar to the HAMADRYADS of ancient Greek mythology and the NATS from Burmese folklore. Within the grove, the tree which is most vigorous is the one in which the lund-folk has taken up residence within its shade. In exchange for a place to live the lund-folk give the tree health and prosperity as well as punishing anyone or anything which would do it harm.

Source: Porteous, *Forest in Folklore and Mythology*, 189; Thorpe, *Northern Mythology*, Volume 2, 71

Machlyes

Hermaphroditic humanoids described in medieval bestiaries, Machlyes were said to live in the deserts of Africa. Pliny the Elder, the Roman author and natural philosopher, described the Machlyes as being androgynous and fully able to perform and fulfil the sexual act of either gender. He further added these beings had upon the right side of their chest a male pectoral while on the left they had a woman's breast so they could nurse their young.

Source: Fritze, *Travel Legend and Lore*, 235; Williams, *Deformed Discourse*, 172

Mairu, plural mairuak ("moors")

Variations: Intxisu, Intxisuak

In Basque mythology the mairuak ("moor") were a species of mountain dwelling GIANTS who built dolmens; after the introduction of Christianity, these creatures died out from the mythology.

Source: Sherman, *Storytelling*, 57

Mandi

According to Agatharchides (Agatharchus) of Cnidus, a Greek historian and geographer (second century BC), Cleitarchus (Clitarchus), a historian of Alexander the Great, (mid to late 3rd century BC), Megasthenes, a Greek ethnographer and explorer of the Hellenistic period, and Pliny the Elder, the Roman author and natural philosopher, the Mandi were a race of short-lived people dwelling in the country of Macrobii. Seldom living past forty years old, the women were able to bear a child at the age of seven, but interestingly, could only give birth once in a lifetime. The primary food source for the Mandi is locusts.

Source: Kalota, *India as Directed by Megasthenes*, 57; Pliny the Elder, *Natural History of Pliny*, Volume 2, 133

Mannegishi

In the folklore of the Algonquian speaking Cree Indians there is a race of humanoids living either in or near the water known as the mannegishi; when seen, they are usually crawling along the rocks and ledges on the banks or tipping over canoes and small boats. Sometimes the mannegishi are spoken of as being tricksters but they intentionally drown the people they capsize, dragging them beneath the surface. Described as being lanky, tall, thin limbed, and having six fingers and an oversized head without a mouth or nose, the mannegishi breathe through their skin and are said to speak telepathically.

Source: Hallenbeck, *Monsters of New York*, 84; Keel, *Eighth Tower*, 124

Margutte

A GIANT from French folklore standing nearly ten feet tall, Margutte died of laughter while watching a monkey pulling on a pair of boots. According to the story Morganete, while on his search for Roland, was being accompanied by the GIANT Margutte. One night, after a particularly large feast, Margutte fell fast asleep; Morganete took the opportunity to play what he suspected to be a harmless prank on his friend by hiding his boots. Upon waking Margutte could not find his boots and after a careful search came upon a monkey who had found them; the little creature was playing with them, putting them on and taking them off over and over again. Margutte was so amused by the sight he fell into a fit of riotous laughter, his body bursting apart.

Source: Daniels, *Encyclopædia of Superstitions, Folklore, and the Occult Sciences of the World*, 1377; Warner, *Library of the World's Best Literature, Ancient and Modern*, Volume 20, 1892

Matuku-tangotango

Variations: Matuku, Matuku-takotako

An OGRE chief from Māori mythology, Matuku-tangotango was the slayer of Wahieroa, the father of the demi-god and hero Rata. Matuku-tangotango lived in an underground cave known as Putawarenuku and kept the bones of his prize there. Rata had learned from one of the OGRE's servants the monster could be killed at the time of the new moon while at a particular fountain where he would wash his face and hair. Following the advice he was given, Rata successfully killed Matuku-tangotango and retrieved his father's bones.

Source: Tregear, *Maori-Polynesian Comparative Dictionary*, 232

Maugys

Variations: Maboun, Malgiers, Mauugeys

A GIANT from British folklore, Maugys was the guardian of a bridge leading to a castle wherein a beautiful maiden called the Maiden of the White Hand (Lady of Sinadoune) was besieged. One of King Arthur's knights, Sir Lybius, battled Maugys in order to free the Lady. After a battle lasting the length of a summer's day, the knight was victorious.

Source: Ackerman, *Index of the Arthurian Names in Middle English*, Volume 10, 153; Bruce, *Arthurian Name Dictionary*, 340; Daniels, *Encyclopædia of Superstitions, Folklore, and the Occult Sciences of the World*, 1377

Maul

Maul, GIANT of Sophistry, appeared in the Christian allegory *Pilgrim's Progress* (1678) by John Bunyan. Maul was the second of three GIANTS confronted on the journey (see GRIM and SLAYGOOD); he was killed by the everyman character, Greatheart, who pierced him under the fifth rib with a sword as the travelers attempted to leave the Valley of the Shadow of Death. Maul had held a grudge against Greatheart for being a good scout and enabling Christian pilgrims to travel from the darkness into the light.

Source: Bunyan, *Works of that Eminent Servant of Christ, John Bunyan*, 146, 158, 164; Daniels, *Encyclopædia of Superstitions, Folklore, and the Occult Sciences of the World*, 1377

Mazikeen

Variations: Shehireem, Shideem

In Jewish mythology the mazikeen were the offspring of Adam after his expulsion from the Garden of Eden; during his 130 years of banishment, and according to the Talmud, all of the children he fathered during this period were born some sort of demon, spirit, or specter of the night. The mazikeen ranked between men and angels and were mortal; they were also very similar to the DJINN of Arabic folklore. From their angelic heritage they inherited the ability to become invisible at will, foretell the future, and fly on their wings; from their human heritage they inherited the ability to consume drink and food, marry and have children, but also became mortal. Using therianthropy they could also shapeshift into any form they pleased and knew a great deal of enchantments and magic.

Source: Keightley, *Fairy Mythology Illustrative of the Romance and Superstition of Various Countries*, 499–500; Urbane, *Gentleman's Magazine*, Volume 103, Part 1, 436

Meliads

Variations: Ash Tree NYMPHS, Melia, Meliade, Meliae, Meliai

In the mythology of the ancient Greeks the Meliads were a sub-species of the HAMADRYAD; they were NYMPHS living in and protecting ash and fruit trees, specifically apple trees. These NYMPHS were born the children of the goddess Gaea from the spilt blood of the god Uranus; they were the guardians to the golden apples belonging to the goddess Hera (Juno).

Source: Antoninus Liberalis, *Metamorphoses of Antoninus Liberalis*, 197; Littleton, *Gods, Goddesses, and Mythology*, Volume 4, 440; Parada, *Genealogical Guide to Greek Mythology*, 128; Westmoreland, *Ancient Greek Beliefs*, 117, 775

Memegwesi, plural: memegwesiwak

In the folklore of the Algonquian Indians of North America, the memegwesiwak are described as being a race of hairy faced DWARF-NYMPH-SIRENS living along the riverbanks and inside of hollow boulders. Said to travel in groups, the memegwesiwak—also comparable to the fay of Celtic folklore—only allow themselves to be seen by the "pure of mind" and children, steal quite often from camps, and speak with a nasal twang.

Source: Chamberlain, *Journal of American Folk-lore*, Volume 13, 243; Hallenbeck, *Monsters of New York*, 84

Meminiteu

In the Inuit mythology of the Innu people the meminiteu is a person who became a cannibal and a threat to their community, as in hunting their own kinsmen; they possess great cunning, shamanistic power, and impressive strength but are always defeated by a hero who is spiritually strong.

Stories about the meminiteu are not considered by the Innu to be the retelling of actual events within contemporary memory (*tipatshimuns*) but rather myth (*atanukans*).

Source: Henriksen, *I Dreamed the Animals*, 27, 318

Menehune

A race of dwarflike humanoids standing about two feet tall from Hawaiian mythology, the menehune were described as being small of stature, having a characteristic distended belly, and living in caves deep in the jungle of a hidden valley called Pu'ukapele. Superb craftsmen noted for their extreme orderliness, they were born the children of Wahieloa and Pele. The menehune sustain themselves with a diet of bananas, koele-palau (sweet-potato pudding), luau (cooked taro leaves), pala-ai (squash), and pudding made from *haupia* (the starch plant). For personal entertainment they enjoy cliff diving, foot races, *ke'a-pua* (shooting arrows), *maika* (quoits), *olo-hu* (top spinning), *puhenehene* (hide the thimble), sled races, and *uma* or *kulakuai* (hand wrestling). The chief of the menehune is

always a kahunas (soothsayer) and he is accompanied by a court of fun-makers, minstrels, musicians, and storytellers, furnishing him with amusement on the nose flute, shark skin drum, ti-leaf trumpet, and the ukeke. The most renowned of their early chiefs was named Ola.

Source: Beckwith, *Hawaiian Mythology*, Volume 1940, Part 1, 259, 327; Wichman, *Kaua i*, 13, 14, 15, 18

Menja (MEHN-ya)

An ASYNJR from Norse mythology, FENJA ("swampy") and Menja ("jewel maiden" or "necklace") were slaves purchased by King Frodi Fridleifsson; he kept them chained to a magical mill called Grotti where they were made to grind gold, happiness, and peace without ever being allowed to rest as they were the only ones strong enough to operate the mill. Menja would sing as the two operated the mill, loudly and with a heavy heart. Eventually the two ASYNJR ground out an army led by the sea king, Mysing, who attacked Fridleifsson, killing him. Mysing then took possession of the mill and bade the two ASYNJR to grind salt; he too never allowed them rest. The ship upon which the mill had been placed sank, causing the ocean to become salty and, presumably, drowning FENJA and Menja.

Source: Grimm, *Teutonic Mythology*, Volume 2, 864; Lindow, *Norse Myths*, 152; Sturluson, *Prose Edda*, 130

Menoetius

Variations: Menoitio, Menoitios

A TITAN born one of the many children of Iapetos and his wife, and the second generation TITAN and OCEANID CLYMENE, Menoetius ("doomed might") was exceedingly proud and presumptuous; during the Titanomachy the god Zeus (Jupiter) struck him with a thunderbolt, sending him instantly to Tartarus.

Source: Cotterell, *Dictionary of World Mythology*, 180; Room, *Who's Who in Classical Mythology*, 342

Mermaid

Variations: BEN-VARREY, Gorgone, Haffrii, Halfway People, Ocean Men, Maighdean-Mara, Mary MORGAN, Morgens, Morrough, Moruach ("sea maid"), Moruadh, Muir-Gheilt, Murdhuch'a, Nereis, Samhghubh'a, SIREN, Sirena, Suire

Mermaids ("sea maidens"), beings half fish and half women, have permeated the folklore of the ocean since ancient times. Described as beautiful enchantresses, destructive and seductive as the ocean itself, the mermaid also personifies the dangers of rocky coastlines and treacherous waters.

The physical appearance of the mermaid likely dates back to the ancient Babylonian god of the sea,

Oannes, and his companions, the Atargatis (Derketo). These companions were in their earliest times depicted as wearing cloaks but over time the cloaks evolved into fish tails. Oannes, an early adaptation of the Sumerian fish-god, Ea, was worshiped as the beneficial aspects of the ocean and a sun god; conversely the Atargatis came to be worshiped as moon-goddesses and represented the ocean's more destructive aspects.

The physical description of the mermaid has not changed much since its inception. Typically described as having flowing and long hair either sea-green or sun-ray yellow, they hold mirrors in their hands, symbolic of the moon, as they sit upon the rocks grooming. There are some folklores where the mermaid is not attractive, said to have green teeth, a porcine (piglike) nose, and red eyes. The domain of the mermaid is said to be on the bottom of the sea, made of priceless pearls and coral.

These fairy creatures possess a natural fear of man and will quickly flee as soon as they realize they have been seen by mortal eyes. Both mermaids and mermen (see MERMAN) long to have a mortal's soul and according to the legend any one of the merfolk can acquire one if a human falls in love with it. In tales involving the romance of a mermaid and a mortal, the creature will use its singing to lure the sailor in. In the tragic versions of the tales the ship is dashed along the rocky coast or the mermaid takes her would-be love down to the depths and inadvertently drowns him. In the less romanticized tales, mermaids are vicious and cause the ships to wreck, drowning the survivors at will.

The mermaid of ancient Greece did not have any piscean attributes but rather looked exactly like a human. Greek mermaids can, however, change their form at will. Usually benevolent, merfolk in Grecian folklore can become malevolent and unpredictable.

In European folklore the mermaids wore a cap upon their heads called a *cohuleen druith*; this magical garment granted them some degree of protection. Should a mermaid be taken as a wife this cap needed to be stolen and kept by the husband, as it would prevent her from returning to the ocean; this is similar to the folklore of the SEAL WOMEN's coat and SWAN MAIDEN's cloak.

Source: Andrews, *Dictionary of Nature Myths*, 118–19; Briggs, *Encyclopedia of Fairies*, 287–89; Dixon-Kennedy, *Encyclopedia of Greco-Roman Mythology*, 205; Matson, *Celtic Mythology A to Z*, 82–3; Monaghan, *Encyclopedia of Celtic Mythology and Folklore*, 325–7

Merman, plural mermen

Variations: Blue Men, DINNY-MARA, Dooinney Marrey, Dunya Mara, HAVMAND, Ocean Men

Mermen are the male counterpart of the MERMAID. In the folklore of ancient Greece, mermen were traditionally offspring of a sea god, such as Poseidon (Neptune), but could also be identified with the conch shell-dwelling TRITONS.

In Irish and Scottish folklore the merman is rarely attractive, described as having piggy eyes, breath stinking of rotting fish, and a nose blushed red from having consumed too much brandy from the ships it wrecked.

As the Scandinavian HAVMAND, the merman is rather handsome and has a black or green beard and hair. Living on the bottom of the sea or in the caves in the cliffs along the shore, this version of the merman is considered to be a benign creature.

Source: Briggs, *Encyclopedia of Fairies*, 290; Dixon-Kennedy, *Encyclopedia of Greco-Roman Mythology*, 205; Keightley, *Fairy Mythology*, 152; Monaghan, *Encyclopedia of Celtic Mythology and Folklore*, 327

Merrow

Variations: Moruach, Moruadh, Murdhuacha

The merrow is a species of merfolk (see MERMAID and MERMAN) from British folklore. The females, very similar to many of the MERMAID myths, are known to wear a magical cap called a *cohuleen druith*; it provides protection as they swim in the ocean. Should this cap ever become lost or stolen this water fairy cannot return to its subterranean home. Merrows have clear or white webbing between their fingers and although they have been known to form unions with mortal men would rather lure one to the ocean's depths. If ever a female merrow is taken as a wife, its *cohuleen druith* must be kept from it. So long as it never gains possession of its cap the merrow will be able to resist the call of the sea, but the instant it is returned the creature will abandon its family and return to the ocean as quickly as possible.

The male merrows are as hideously ugly as they are aggressive; they have been described as having green hair, long green teeth, a porcine (piglike) nose, and red eyes. On the bottom of the ocean they are said to keep the souls of all the sailors they have drowned locked up in cages. Male merrows also wear a *cohuleen druith* and although there are tales of them loaning an extra cap to a mortal there are virtually no stories of them taking a human bride.

Source: Eason, *Fabulous Creatures, Mythical Monsters, and Animal Power Symbols*, 151; Froud, *Faeries*, 121; Keightley, *Fairy Mythology*, 152; Spence, *Minor Traditions of British Mythology*, 50–2; Wallace, *Folk-lore of Ireland*, 90

Methone

Born the daughter of the GIGANTE ALCYONEUS, Methone was, according to the ancient Greek historian Hegesander, one of the ALCYONII; she and her sisters, ALKIPPA, ANTHE, ASTERIA, DRIMO, PAL-LENE, and PHOSTHONIA, are named in his six-volume work *Commentaries* (*Hypomnemata*).

Source: Blunck, *Solar System Moons*, 83; Smith, *Dictionary of Greek and Roman Biography and Mythology*, 108

Mgn (THUHG-n)

In Norse mythology Mgn ("host receiver") was one of the many named VALKYRIES (NYMPHs of battle) about whom, beyond a name, there is little or nothing else known.

Source: Norroena Society, *Asatrii Edda*, 391

Mialucka

In the mythology of the Kana Indian tribe in the American mid-west, the mialucka was a race of beings with oversized heads and long hair; they were subaquatic and subterranean dwellers who would attempt to lure lone travelers into remote places; after an encounter with one of the mialucka, the person became insane and would thereafter live as a *catamite* or a *mi quga*. In ancient times it was believed the mialucka were the benefactors of the Indians, as they created the first buffalo calf and three buffalos from wet clay; then they constructed the bow and arrow and taught the Indians how to use them to hunt the buffalo.

Source: Powell, *Congressional Serial Set*, 386

Midi (MITH-i)

In Norse mythology Midi ("the average" or "middleman") was one of the many named Jotnar (see JOTUN) about whom, beyond a name, there is nothing else known.

Source: Norroena Society, *Asatrii Edda*, 374

Midvitnir (MITH-vit-nir)

Variations: Fjalarr, MJODVITNIR, SUTTUNGR

A JOTUN from Norse mythology, Midvitnir ("mead wolf," "mid wolf" or "sea wolf") lived in Okolnir, a region of Muspellheimr, in a mead-hall named Brimir. He stole the Precious Mead out of Asgard and returned to his hall with it, storing it in the skull of Heidraupnir and horn of Hoddrofnir guarded by his son, SOKMIMIR. Odin, under the guise of Svidrir, recaptured the Precious Mead, beheading SOK-MIMIR with SURTR's fiery sword, med sviga laeva.

Source: Grimes, *Norse Myths*, 58; Rydberg, *Teutonic Mythology*, 659

Migamamesus

Variations: Mikamwes

A DWARF or ELF from the folklore of the Micmac, a tribe of Native Canadians living in Quebec; these nature spirits were described as resembling the Puck from British folklore and lived in the Gaspe Mountains, Quebec, where on moonlit nights they would dance in the glades and play tricks on anyone who happened upon them.

Source: Porteous, *Forest in Folklore and Mythology*, 145; Rose, *Spirits, Fairies, Leprechauns, and Goblins*, 220

Mimas, the Giant

A GIGANTE from ancient Greek mythology, Mimas was born the son of the TITAN Uranus ("heaven") and the Earth, Gaea. He and his siblings were extremely large, immensely strong, and absolutely fearsome to behold as they had dense beards, a thick head of hair, and feet covered with DRAKON scales; they threw flaming oak trees and rocks at the heavens.

Mimas was slain during the ten year war against the Olympian gods, the Gigantomachy, when Hephaistos hit him in the head with molten metal.

Source: Apollodorus, *Library of Greek Mythology*, 34–5; Daniels, *Encyclopædia of Superstitions, Folklore, and the Occult Sciences of the World*, 1376

Mimir (MEEM-ir)

Variations: Asvinr ("asa-friend"), Baugreginn ("artisan of gold rings"), Brimir ("sea being"), Fimbulbulr ("great teacher"), Glaevaldr ("shining ruler"), Gudmundr ("gift of the gods") Heiddraupnir ("reward dropping"), Hoddmimir ("treasure Mimir"), Lofarr ("the praised"), Mím, Mime, Mimer, Mími, Mímir, Mîmir, Mímr, Modsognir ("mead drinker"), Mogbrasir ("son of YMIR"), Neri ("one that binds"), Nidi ("Underworld being"), NORI ("sailor"), Norr ("one that binds"), Norvi ("one that binds")

The JOTUN from Norse mythology who kept guard over Mimirsbrunnr Well at the Jotunheimr root of Ygdrasil, Mimir ("memory" and "wise") was described as being old and having a long, silver beard. He and his sister BESTLA were born of the arm sweat of YMIR. He was the uncle to the gods Odin, Ve, and Vilie and all of the Aesir went to him when seeking wisdom, each paying dearly for a drink from his well. For instance, Odin sacrificed one of his eyes for foresight and wisdom.

Glasisvellir ("glasir-fields") was the name of Mimir's Underworld domain located directly beneath the root; located there was the treasure hoard known as Hoddgoda, filled with many divine artifacts. Each day Mimir took a drink from the well using Gjallarhorn as his drinking horn.

Source: Daly, *Norse Mythology A to Z*, 69; Grimes, *Norse Myths*, 287; Norroena Society, *Asatrii Edda*, 335, 336, 351, 354, 357, 361, 371, 374, 375, 376, 377

Minata-Karaia

A race of people living deep in the wilderness of the Brazilian rainforests, the Minata-Karaia of Kamaiura folklore are described as basically humanoid except for two very distinctive features. The first is that the men of the species have a hole in the top of their head which produces a whistling sound; the second is from beneath their armpits grow clusters of *minatas* (coconuts) which they are perpetually plucking, knocking against their head, and consuming.

Source: Covey, *Beasts*, 65; Updike, *Picked-Up Pieces*, 454–5

Mist

One of the many named VALKYRIEs (NYMPHs of battle) in Norse mythology, Mist ("mist") is listed as one of the two maidens who carry the drinking horn to Odin; the other is HRIST.

Source: Conway, *Falcon Feather and Valkyrie Sword*, 211; Ellis, *Road to Hel*, 69; Sturluson, *Prose Edda*, 61

Mjodvitnir

A DVERG (DWARF) from Norse mythology, Mjodvitnir ("mead wolf") is named in the *Voluspa* part of the *Poetic Edda*. It has been speculated the JOTUN MIDVITNIR and Mjodvitnir may be the same individual.

Source: Daly, *Norse Mythology A to Z*, 22; Rydberg, *Teutonic Mythology*, Volume 2, 654

Mjoll (Myuhl)

A JOTUN from Norse mythology, Mjoll ("fresh powdery snow") was a son of Snær (Snaar) ("snow"). Mjoll was also the name of one of the three daughters of Kare ("wind"); her sisters were called Drifta ("snow drift") and Fonn ("packed snow").

Source: Norroena Society, *Asatrii Edda*, 370; Ross, *Old Norse Myths, Literature and Society*, 286, Sturluson, *Prose Edda*, 106

Mnemosyne

A female TITAN from classical Greek mythology, Mnemosyne ("mindful") was born the daughter of the TITAN Uranus ("heaven") and the Earth, Gaea; siblings were COEUS, CRIUS, CRONUS, HYPERION, IAPETUS, OCEANUS, PHOEBE, RHEA, TETHYS, THEIA, and THEMIS. Collectively the siblings were known as the Titanides. As the personification of memory Mnemosyne was often confused with the MUSE of memory, Mneme. Mnemosyne was the mother of the nine MUSES by the god Zeus (Jupiter).

Source: Casey, *Remembering*, 318; Daly, *Greek and Roman Mythology A to Z*, ix, 1, 19, 222

Modsogner (MOHTH-sawg-nir)

Variations: Modsognir, Motsognir

According to Norse mythology, the Aesir created the DVERG (DWARF) Modsogner ("mead-drinker") from the squirming maggots eating the flesh of the fallen JOTUN; he was then given the title and honor of Chief of the DVERG as he possessed a promethean power of creating. He is described as being short in stature with arms long enough to reach the ground when standing. With the assistance of the DVERG (DWARF) DURINN, they created the DWARFS, the story of which is told in the *Voluspa* part of the *Poetic Edda*. After the creation of the race, Modsogner disappears altogether from the mythology; because of this some scholars suspect he is an aspect of MIMIR.

Source: Coulter, *Encyclopedia of Ancient Deities*, 29, 359; Norroena Society, *Asatrii Edda*, 374; Rydberg, *Teutonic Mythology*, 241–2

Mogthrasir

A little-known JOTUN from Norse mythology, Mogthrasir ("desiring sons" or "strive for sons") is the father of the three benevolent ASYNJR living on Mogthrasir Hill who assist and protect the humans surviving Ragnarok; he is mentioned nowhere else in the Eddic poems. Mogthrasir is associated with the idea of human continuity after the battle of Ragnarok.

Source: Bellows, *Poetic Edda*, 82, 264; Crossley-Holland, *Norse Myths*, 288

Mokkerkalfe (MUHK-ur-kahlv-i)

Variations: Mokkurkalf, Mokkurkalfi

A JOTUN made of clay in Norse mythology, Mokkerkalfe ("cloud-calf") was created by HRUNGNIR to assist him in his battle against the god Thor. Although he was created with the heart of a mare, when Mokkerkalfe accompanied his creator he sweated with nervousness before the battle and upon arrival, upon seeing Thor, urinated on himself in fear. Mokkerkalfe was destroyed by Thjalfe, shattered into many pieces.

Source: Anderson, *Norse Mythology: Or, The Religion of Our Forefathers*, 55, 309; Norroena Society, *Asatrii Edda*, 375; Oehlenschläger, *Gods of the North*, lv

Molpe

Variations: Molpa, Molpea, Molpee, Molpey, Molpi, Molpie, Molpy

According to the ancient Greek poet Cherilus of Samos, AGLAOPHONOS, Molpe ("music") and THELXIOPE were three SIRENS of Greek mythology, a species of injurious NYMPH born the offspring of the ancient god of the sea, PHORCYS. Described as being half bird and half woman, she and her sisters would perch on the rocky Sicilian coastline and lure sailors in with their melodious song; once caught, their prey were eaten alive. Although they hunted along the coastline Molpe and her sisters lived inland in a meadow.

Source: Leland, *Unpublished Legends of Virgil*, 37; Roman, *Encyclopedia of Greek and Roman Mythology*, 443; Smith, *Dictionary of Greek and Roman Biography and Mythology*, 817

Morgan, plural Morganes

Variations: Morgen, mari-morgans, Maries Morgan, Morganes, Sea Morgan

In Breton, the MERMAID is called a morgan ("sea-women") or morverc'h ("sea-daughters"); fond of combing out their long hair these fair beings are known to lure in sailors with their beautiful singing voice, let their ship dash on the rocks, snatch up the sailors, and take them down to the bottom of the sea or a deep pond where their palace of crystal and gold resides.

Source: Archibald, *Sixpence for the Wind*, 38–9; Keightley, *World Guide to Gnomes, Fairies, Elves, and Other Little People*, 433

Morgante

A ferocious, Islamic Turkish GIANT of French folklore who was converted over to Christianity by Orlando and thereafter attempted to live his life by the chivalric code, although he did not ever earn the right to compete in chivalric combat, he participates in civilized society in spite of his size and monstrous appearance. Morgante cannot ever be a true knight, as he cannot meet the basic requirements such as the ability to ride a horse, wear armor, or wield a sword; his armor is the metal tongue of a large church bell. Morgante also cannot properly participate in courtly love, although he does care for one knight's neglected and pregnant mistress. It appears he marries the Princess Florinetta, whom he rescued from a hoard of evil GIANTS, but before his happiness can settle in, he dies from a crab bite upon his exposed heel.

Source: Daniels, *Encyclopædia of Superstitions, Folklore, and the Occult Sciences of the World*, 1377; Triplette, *Pagans, Monsters, and Women in the "Amadis" Cycle*, 57–60

Moroaica

In the Romanian folklore, there are people who are considered to be living vampires, the MOROI (males) and the moroaica (females). Indicators of this condition are present at birth, such as being born with a caul or a tail, and when these conditions are present, it is usually in the female, as male living vampires are very rare. The moroaica is described as having blue eyes, red hair, red patches of skin on

her face, and twin hearts. They have the same array of abilities as the MOROI.

Source: Ashley, *Complete Book of Vampires*, 344; Broster, *Amagqirha*, 60; Day, *Vampires*, 14, 70–73, 109, 116

Moroi

Variation: Moroancă, Moroaica, Moroii, Muroaïcă, Strigoii Viu ("live vampire"), Strigoi

In the Romanian folklore, there are people who are considered to be living vampires, the moroi (males) and the MOROAICA (females). Indicators of this condition are present at birth, such as being born with a caul or a tail, and when these conditions are present, it is usually in the female, as male living vampires are very rare.

A moroi ("living male vampire") can easily be detected by his male pattern baldness; it occurs even at a very young age. Although there is no doubt they are living people and fully human, they display vampiric tendencies as well as supernatural abilities, such as draining the life-energy from animals, crops, and people. It is also believed they gather with others of their kind, both living and undead, to teach each other the black magic they have learned. They can drink honey from a hive, which will cause all of the bees living there to die. Although moroi rarely drink blood, they still have the ability of therianthropy and at night shape-shift into a cat, dog, a glowing ball of light like a corpse candle (a glowing, spectral ball of glowing light), hen, raven, and wolf. When one dies, it will rise up as a type of vampiric revenant called a *strigoica* unless a stake has been driven through its heart or the body has been decapitated and burned to ash.

Source: Ashley, *Complete Book of Vampires*, 344; Broster, *Amagqirha*, 60; Day, *Vampires*, 14, 70–73, 109, 116

Morsognir

A DVERG (DWARF) from Norse mythology, Morsognir ("the mightiest") is named in the *Voluspa* part of the *Poetic Edda*; beyond a name, there is nothing else known.

Source: Daly, *Norse Mythology A to Z*, 22

Moss People

Variations: Greenies, Wild, Wood, Timber

The moss people of southern Germany are described as DWARF-life beings standing about as tall as a three-year-old child and living in a communal environment. Overall, these beings appear to be aged, grey-skinned, hairy, and clad in moss. The females of the species wear cocked hats and green clothes faced with red; they will approach wood cutters to ask for or trade for food by cooking, giving advice, or washing clothes. The female moss people are of a nicer disposition than the males who live deep in the woods. Sometimes the moss people are described as being very small and having wings attached to their back; when this is the case, these FAIRY-like beings are oftentimes mistaken for butterflies.

These fairies are relentlessly hunted by their flying, invisible natural enemy, the Wild Huntsman.

Source: Keightley, *World Guide to Gnomes, Fairies, Elves, and Other Little People*, 230–31; McCoy, *Witch's Guide to Faery Folk*, 276–7; Telesco, *Kitchen Witch Companion*, 21

Mugello

Variations: Mugillo

A GIANT from French folklore, Mugello plundered the countryside north of Florence; he wielded a six-balled mace in combat against the knight Averardo de Medici, while he was serving as a commander under Charlemagne. After Mugello was defeated Averardo removed three of the balls from the much-feared mace and after having them emblazoned upon the family crest used their image over the entranceway of the many pawnshops he and his family owned.

Source: Daniels, *Encyclopædia of Superstitions, Folklore, and the Occult Sciences of the World*, 1377; Smith, *Ever Wonder Why*, 3

Muldjewangk

In Aboriginal Australian mythology Muldjewangk was said to be a gigantic and malicious MERMAN–like creature from the Dreamtime living in the Murray River in South Australia; the folklore has never been clear if this is an individual entity or a species. According to one tale it once wrapped its oversized arms around a riverboat and threatened to pull it down into the murky depths. As the captain of the ship was about to open fire some Aboriginal elders who were on board warned him against harming the creature but the captain opened up fire. Although Muldjewangk was driven off the captain soon fell ill and his body was covered in blisters; he died in agony six months later. In more modern times the Muldjewangk is considered to be a NURSERY BOGIE, a monster which will pull in children who walk too near the river's edge.

Source: Cox, *Wicked Waters*, 15; le Roux, *Myth of 'Roo*, 102

Muma Pădurii

A forest-dwelling HAG of Romanian folklore, Muma Pădurii ("forest mother") is a type of NURSERY BOGIE said to kidnap children who become lost in the woods and turn them into trees; she is also known to deprive children of their sleep. Similar to BABA YAGA, Muma Pădurii lives in a hut perched on rooster feet.

Source: Johns, *Baba Yaga*, 75

Mundilfare

Variations: Mundilfari

A JOTUN of Norse mythology, Mundilfare was the father of two children, a son named Maane ("moon") and a daughter named Sol ("sun"), whom he believed to be the most beautiful things in all the world. Unfortunately Mundilfare's boldness for naming his children after Dagr and NOTT did not go unnoticed by the gods so they took his children up into the heavens. Maane was given the horse Alsvider to ride, guiding Nott on her path to Midgard, *manvergr* ("moonway" or "Milky Way"). Sol was given two horses, Alsvin and Arvakr, and she was made to ride before Dagr, guiding him on his course around Midgard and stabilizing his path as it was erratic.

Source: Daly, *Norse Mythology A to Z*, 71; Grimes, *Norse Myths*, 11–12

Muse

Variations: Aganippides, Castalides, Libethrides, Nymphae Libethrides

In Greek and Roman mythology a muse was a beautiful NYMPH known for its dancing and singing; it recited poetry as the gods ate their meals. Over time the role of the muse changed and they evolved to beings akin to lesser gods inspiring human artists. There is no unified mythology explaining the parentage of the muses; a wide array of gods and goddesses have been credited with it.

Throughout Greek mythology the muses have been associated with many events; they gave the Sphinx her riddle, taught Echo how to play music, and taught healing and prophecy. However, they were malicious and vindictive when contradicted.

According to Pausanias, a second century Greek geographer and traveler, there were originally three muses, Aoide ("song" or "voice"), Melete ("occasion" or "practice"), and Mneme ("memory"). Collectively, they formed the ideals of the poetic arts. Later, a fourth muse was introduced, Arche. In the Hellenistic period, the muses were assigned divisions of poetry which they were said to oversee and inspire.

Source: Littleton, *Gods, Goddesses, and Mythology*, Volume 11, 921–26; Peterson, *Mythology in Our Midst*, 121–23; Parker, *Mythology*, 44

Musilindi

A species of dragon or a race of naga from the Indian mythology, the Musilindi are described as having serpentine bodies, humanoid heads, two arms, and wings. These beings have the gift of therianthropy and can shape-shift into a human or a snake.

Source: Dekirk, *Dragonlore*, 36

Mycalesides

In ancient Greek mythology the mycalesides were the species of mountain NYMPHS living on Mycale, located in what is now modern Turkey.

Source: Smith, *Dictionary of Greek and Roman Biography and Mythology*, 1128

Nahgane

A race of terrifying GIANT from the folklore of the Slavey Indians of Canada, the nahgane will abduct children who wander out into the woods without being accompanied by a parent. This NURSERY BOGIE is utilized by parents to keep their children from wandering off into the woods.

Source: Rose, *Giants, Monsters, and Dragons*, 262; Roth, *American Elves*, 115

Naiad

Variations: The Heleionomai, Naiade, Naide, Nais

The naiad ("to flow" or "running water") of Greek mythology were one of twelve species of NYMPHS; they were associated with freshwater lakes, rivers, and springs whereas the NEREIS were specifically associated with the Mediterranean Sea and the OCEANIDS with saltwater sources in general.

It was believed by the ancient Greeks that all the water of the world was connected by one underground system, and therefore naiads were not restricted to remaining locked to their water source; they could travel through the subterranean waterways from one water source to another. However, if their body of water ever dried up or was somehow destroyed, the associated water fairy would die. Naiads were said to have the ability to foretell mortals' destiny and generally predict the future. These nature spirits were typically said to have been born the daughters of the god Poseidon (Neptune), Zeus (Jupiter), the goddess Gaea, or one of the many OCEANIDS or river gods, but individual origin stories are not uncommon. Because naiads are not mortal women they have the privilege of being sexually aggressive and active without shame.

Although generally benign, naiads could prove to be very dangerous as they were well known to act on their jealous tendencies. Punishments from a naiad ranged from being drowned to being struck blind.

According to the Greek oral poet, Hesiod, in one of his fragmented poems a naiad declares "a crow lives for nine human generations, a stag lives four times as long as a crow, a raven three times as long as a stag, a PHOENIX nine times as long as a raven, and a NYMPH 10 times as long as a PHOENIX." Assuming a human generation is 20 years, a NYMPH can reasonably expect to live 194,000 years. A DRYAD lives only as long as its tree and a naiad similarly coexists with her spring.

Many times in Greek mythology when the name of a character was introduced it was given as, for instance, "daughter of Asopos." Ancient Greeks would have known Asopos was a lesser known river god and therefore his daughter was a naiad. Very often naiads' names had the suffex –nais ("naiad") or –rhoe, but not always. Some of the historical known and named naiads are Aba, Abarbarea, Abarbaree, Aegina, Aegle, Aia, Alcinoe, Alexirhoe, Anchirhoe, Anippe, Annaed, Anthedon, Arethusa, Argyra, Bateia, Bistonis, Byzia, Caliadne, Callirrhoe, Castalia, Charybdis, Chlidanope, Cleochareia, Corycia, Creusa, Daphne, Diogeneia, Diopatre, Drosera, Echenais, Harpina, Ismenis, Kalybe, Kleodora (Cleodora), Langia, Lara, Lethe, Lilaea, Liriope (Leiriope), Melaina, Melite, Memphis, Metope, Minthe, Moria, Nana, Neaera, Nicaea, Nomia, Orseis, Pegasis, Periboea, Pitane, Polyxo, Praxithea, Salmacis, Sparta, Strymo, STYX, Telphousa, Thronia, Tiasa, and Zeuxippe.

Source: Day, *God's Conflict with the Dragon and the Sea*, 391–95; Hansen, *Classical Mythology*, 41, 242; Keightley, *World Guide to Gnomes, Fairies, Elves, and Other Little People*, 444; Larson, *Greek Nymphs*, 2–4; Littleton, *Gods, Goddesses, and Mythology, Volume 11*, 999

Nain (NAH-in)

Variations: Nainn

A DVERG (DWARF) from Norse mythology, Nain ("corpse") is named in the *Voluspa* part of the *Poetic Edda*. He along with BAFURR, BIFURR, BOMBOR, DAIN, NAR, NIPING, NORI, and "hundreds of others" worked together to create the fetter Gleipnir to bind Fenrir.

Source: Crossley-Holland, *Norse Myths*, 35; Daly, *Norse Mythology A to Z*, 22; Norroena Society, *Asatrii Edda*, 376

Najade

The najade are a species of water NYMPH from Slavic folklore.

Source: Coulter, *Encyclopedia of Ancient Deities*, 333

Nali (NAHL-i)

A DVERG (DWARF) from Norse mythology, Nali ("corpse" or "death") is named in the *Voluspa* part of the *Poetic Edda*. He was created by DURINN making him one of DVALIN'S HOST who lived in Juravale's Marsh.

Source: Daly, *Norse Mythology A to Z*, 22; Norroena Society, *Asatrii Edda*, 376

Nalusa Falaya

Variations: Bohpoli ("thrower" or "woman cry"), Hattak Chito ("big man"), Kowi Anakasha ("forest dweller"), Kwanokasha

In the folklore of the Choctaw people of the southeastern United States, the nalusa falaya are anthropomorphic beings about the height of a man, speaking with a human voice and having very small eyes, long pointed ears, long brown or grey hair, a long nose, and a deeply shriveled face. Nalusa falaya live in woods near swampland and are occasionally mistaken for the KASHEHOTAPOLO.

At dusk the nalusa falaya hunt by walking the wood line and calling out game sounds, luring hunters to the area; once their prey is in sight they make another call which causes the hunters to fall to the ground and sometimes even lose consciousness. While the hunter is unable to prevent attack the nalusa falaya will insert small thorns into his hands or feet, giving him the power to inflict evil onto others. Typically the hunter is unaware anything has happened to him until the power is unconsciously tapped and he commits malicious acts.

Adolescent nalusa falaya, appearing as small luminous bodies along the marsh edge, have the ability to remove the internal organs from people at night, causing them horrific pain.

Source: Bastian, *Handbook of Native American Mythology*, 135–6; Eberhart, *Mysterious Creatures*, 367; Lynch, *Native American Mythology A to Z*, 63; Sierra, *Gruesome Guide to World Monsters*, 13

Napaea

The Napaea ("she of the valley") are one of the twelve species of NYMPHS; they are the NYMPHS of valleys with grazing herds (see ATLANTID, DRAYAD, HAMADRYAD, HYAD, LIMNIAD, LIMONIAD, NAIAD, NEREID, NYMPH, OCEANID, OREAD).

Source: Littleton, *Gods, Goddesses, and Mythology, Volume 11*, 999; White, *Progressive Latin Reader*, 162

Napaeae

The napaeae ("a wooded dell") of Greek mythology are a beautiful but shy sub-species of the NAPAEA; they are the NYMPHS of glens in mountain valleys. Associated with the goddess Artemis (Diana), they often accompany her.

Source: Avant, *Mythological Reference*, 291; Bell, *Bell's New Pantheon*, 95, 112; Daly, *Greek and Roman Mythology A to Z*, 102

Nar (NAHR)

A DVERG (DWARF) from Norse mythology, Nar ("corpse") is named in the *Voluspa* part of the *Poetic Edda*. He, along with BAFURR, BIFURR, BOMBOR, DAIN, NAIN, NIPING, NORI, and "hundreds of others," worked together to create the fetter Gleipnir to bind Fenrir.

Source: Crossley-Holland, *Norse Myths*, 35; Daly, *Norse Mythology A to Z*, 22; Norroena Society, *Asatrii Edda*, 376

Narve

Variations: Nare, Narfi, Nere, Njorve

A JOTUN of Norse mythology, Narve ("he who binds") was the first of his kind to inhabit Jotunheim; he was a friend of Odin and a kinsman to Urd, the NORN of the Past, and her sisters. Poetry, or at least the source of poetry, was known as *niderfi Narfa* ("the inheritance left by Narve to his descendants"); this indicates Narve, being the first resident of Jotunheim, was also the first to preside over the Fountain of Wisdom and Inspiration and upon his death left it to his descendants as their inheritance.

Source: Rydberg, *Norroena*, Volume 2, 612–17; Rydberg, *Teutonic Mythology*, 416–7

Nati (NAT-i)

In Norse mythology, Nati ("keen" or "nettle") was one of the many named Jotnar (see JOTUN) about whom, beyond a name, there is nothing else known.

Source: Norroena Society, *Asatrii Edda*, 376

Nawao

Variations: Ka Lahui Mu Al Maia o Laau Hakeeke

The Nawao ("wild people") were a race of large and powerful GIANTS from Hawaiian mythology; their progenitor was named Kane Hoa Lani (Lua Nuu). The Nawao were hunters, once numerous but now exterminated to the last, and did not associate with the *kanakas*, the people who lived on the various islands.

Source: Beckwith, *Hawaiian Mythology*, 321; Fornander, *Fornander Collection of Hawaiian Antiquities*, 270–1

Neda

An OCEANID and TITAN from ancient Greek mythology, Neda was born one of the daughters of the first generation TITAN OCEANIDS and his sister wife TETHYS; she is usually listed as one of the nurses of the infant god Zeus (Jupiter).

Source: Coulter, *Encyclopedia of Ancient Deities*, 340; Daly, *Greek and Roman Mythology, A to Z*, 141

Nembroth

François Rabelais (AD 1494–1553), who compiled the lineage of the GIANTS, described Nembroth as the father of ATLAS, who "with his shoulders keeps the sky from falling; who begot GOLIAH."

Source: Brewer, *Character Sketches of Romance, Fiction and the Drama*, Volume 3, 80; Daniels, *Encyclopædia of Superstitions, Folklore, and the Occult Sciences of the World*, 1376; Rabelais, *Hours with Rabelais*, 80

The Nemedians

According to Irish legend the FIR BOLG were the descendants of the children of Nemed ("privileged son"), a son of Noah, or Nemedians ("privileged people") as they were called. Originally consisting of four men and four women, their presence on the island marks the beginning of the Third Age of Irish prehistory; as the small clan grew they added four lakes and numerous crop fields to the island's landscape and introduced sheep to the ecology. The FORMORIANS, envious of the Nemedians' prosperity, began a clan war with them, and although they lost four initial battles, an epidemic killed Nemed and two thousand of his people were slain. After losing control of the island and being forced to pay a devastating tribute, the Nemedians rallied and attacked the FORMORIAN stronghold on Tory island, managing to kill their king. Although triumphant, the Nemedians paid a steep price as only thirty of them remained; the Third Age of Ireland's pre-history comes to a close when the Nemedians leave their island home.

Source: Monaghan, *Encyclopedia of Celtic Mythology and Folklore*, 194; Stookey, *Thematic Guide to World Mythology*, 30

Nephilim (ne-fil-IM)

Variations: Anaki, ANAKIM ("the long-necked ones"), EMIM ("fearful ones"), Fallen Ones, the "giants of Canaan," Gibborim, Ivvim, N'philim, Nefilim, Neflim, Nephel (plural: Nephelim), Nephelim, Nephelin, Nepillim, Nephites (plural: Nephi'im), REPHAIM ("dead ones"), ZAMZUMMIM

In the Book of Genesis, the Book of Numbers, and noncanonical Christian and Jewish writings, we are told the Nephilim ("rejects") are a race of evil GIANTS who were born the offspring of human women and fallen angels, making them semi-divine beings. Their name in Hebrew means "fallen ones" or "those causing others to fall." Most sources describe them as being extraordinarily large when compared to the height of a man and being warlike by nature. There are six different types of Nephilim: Anakim ("long-necked" or "wearers of necklaces"), Awwim ("devastators" or "serpents"), EMIM ("fearful ones" or "terrors"), Gibborim ("GIANT heroes"), Repha'im ("dead ones" or "weakeners"), and the ZAMZUMMIM ("achievers").

The Nephilim were destroyed in the great flood God sent to wipe the world clean of sin; however, He allowed ten percent of the disembodied spirits of the race to remain upon the earth in order to act as demons. They are to attempt to lead mankind astray until the Final Judgment.

Source: Eberhart, *Mysterious Creatures*, 373; Icke, *Biggest Secret*, 41, 43, 46; Mathers, *Kabbalah Unveiled*, 249; Schwartz, *Tree of Souls*, 454–9; Shuker, *Mysteries of Planet Earth*, 126–31; Smith, *Book of Deuteronomy*, 19; Zimmerer, *Chronology of Genesis*, 77

Nereids

Variations: Neriads, Nereides, Nêreïdes, Nêrēïdes, Nereis, Nerine

Nereids are one of the twelve different species of NYMPH in classical Greek mythology; they are the NYMPHS of the Mediterranean Sea in general and the Aegean Sea in particular. Born the daughters of NEREUS and DORIS, an OCEANID, the Nereids ("wet ones") are blue- and golden-haired sea NYMPHS, often found in the company of Poseidon (Neptune), the god of the sea. Always friendly and well known to help sailors who are caught in dangerous storms, the nereids are described as being both beautiful and youthful. Typically they are depicted naked, holding fish in their hands, and surrounded by dolphins, hippocamps, and various sea animals. On occasion they have been portrayed as being half maiden and half fish, like a MERMAID.

Living in the underwater palace of their father, these sea-NYMPHS each have a golden throne of their own within the palace. They pass their time riding dolphins, spinning, and weaving. Thetis, the wife of Peleus and mother of Achilles, is portrayed as their leader.

Typically, the nereids are said to be fifty in number, although some sources claim there are as many as a hundred. Homer names thirty-three of the nereids in his works. In Modern Greek folklore the word *nereid* is used when referring to all fairies and NYMPHS and not strictly the sea-NYMPHS.

The hermetic and neo-Platonic doctrine from which all medieval medicine and science was founded describes four Elemental classes, Air, Earth, Fire, and Water; accordingly the Nereids (see UNDINES) belong to the Water class, GNOMES to Earth, salamanders (the hermetic symbol of fire) to Fire, and sylphs to Air.

Source: Briggs, *Encyclopedia of Fairies*, 192–3; Daly, *Greek and Roman Mythology A to Z*, 90; Dixon-Kennedy, *Encyclopedia of Greco-Roman Mythology*, 217; Evans-Wentz, *Fairy Faith in Celtic Countries*, 290, Littleton, *Gods, Goddesses, and Mythology*, Volume 11, 999

Nereus

A TITAN from ancient Greek mythology, Nereus was the eldest son born to Gaea (earth) and the ancient god of the sea, Pontus. Quite unlike many other gods of the sea, he was kingly, helpful, and wise; he lived in the depths of the ocean with his many daughters collectively known as the NEREIDS. Nereus is only mentioned in a handful of tales; in one the cultural hero and demi-god Hercules (Heracles) wrestles him, attempting to force the god into revealing the path to the Hesperides. Although he shape-shifted into fire, water, and an array of animals, Nereus could not break the hold of Hercules. In another tale he carries a cup to Hercules which HELIOS (Sol) offered to lend to the godling.

Source: Daly, *Greek and Roman Mythology, A to Z*, 141; Hard, *Routledge Handbook of Greek Mythology*, 51

Nesnas (Nes-NAHS)

Variations: Nesnás

Arabic and Judaic traditions refer to the nesnas as both a race of man and apes as well as a species of demonic creature or hybrid. The nesnas was born the offspring of a shikk (a demonic creature from Arabic folklore) and of a human being. The creature appears as a human with half a head, half a body, one arm, and one leg on which it very agilely hops quickly. It eats grass. The nesnas's appearance causes fear. It is said to live in the woods of El-Yemen. A species of winged nesnas is said to inhabit the island of Raij in the sea of Es-Seen. The people of Hadramót eat this creature and claim its meat is sweet.

Source: Burton, *Arabian Nights*, 354; Knowles, *Nineteenth century*, Volume 31, 449; Lane, *Arab Society in the Time of the Thousand and One Nights*, 45; Placzek, *Popular*, 160–1; Poole, *The Thousand and One Nights*, 33; *Popular Science Monthly*, 660–1

Nevinbimbaau

In Melanesian mythology, particularly of the folkloric beliefs of the people of the Malekula Island, Vanuat, Nevinbimbaau is a cannibal ogress (female OGRE) associated with the hero-god Ambat. Nevinbimbaau is said to have created the island her people live on by transporting soil in a gigantic clamshell she carried on her back. Although she has never been seen her voice can be heard in the roar of a bull.

Source: Monaghan, *Encyclopedia of Goddesses and Heroines*, 155; Rose, *Giants, Monsters, and Dragons*, 266

Nickneven

Variations: Queen of Elfame

A HAG from the folklore of the Highlands of Scotland, the Nickneven is a gigantic and malicious OGRE; it was mentioned by the Scottish makar poet William Dunbar's work *Flyting of Dunbar and Kennedy* and referred to as the Queen of Elfame.

Source: Rose, *Giants, Monsters, and Dragons*, 267

Nidi (NITH-i)

Variations: Nide, Nithi

A rock DVERG (DWARF) from Norse mythology, Nidi ("underworld being") is named in the *Voluspa* part of the *Poetic Edda*. He, like the others of his kind, was homely and had a black complexion, an oversized head, short, stout legs, and most notably, strange green eyes set off by crow's feet.

Source: Daly, *Norse Mythology A to Z*, 22; Grimes, *Norse Myths*, 291; Norroena Society, *Asatrii Edda*, 377

Nieh-Erh Kuo Yan

One of the many races of monstrous people described by travelers' tales, the tiger-striped Nieh-Erh Kuo Yan ("people of the whispering ears") people of Chinese folklore had ears that, if not pinned up in some fashion, would reach down to their waist.

Source: Rose, *Giants, Monsters, and Dragons*, 267

Nimerigar

Variations: Ninimbe, Ninimbeb, Ninimpi, Ninumbee, Nu'numbi, Toyanum

In the folklore of the Arapaho, Bannock, Goshute, Shoshone, and Uto-Aztecan Native American people the nimerigar are a type of nature spirit, a race of little people living in mountain caves; they are protectors of the land, using bows and poison-tipped arrows to defend their territory and to hunt deer. Standing between two and three feet tall, they also are said to have oversized heads and stubby legs.

Source: Alexander, *Fairies*, 200; Eberhart, *Mysterious Creatures*, 388

Ningyo

First recorded in AD 619 during the twenty-seventh year of the reign of Empress Suiko, the Ningyo ("human fish") are a species of fairy animal from Japanese folklore; their name is typically translated as MERMAID, but they are in fact not human or MERMAID-like in appearance.

Originally the ningyo were described as having a crest of thick fur atop their head; humanoid, webbed fingers; a simian (ape-like) mouth; small Piscean teeth; and golden scales. Like the SIREN, these beings have a hauntingly beautiful voice, similar to a flute or skylark; their song does not consist of words but is nevertheless still hypnotic.

In their underwater domain, the ningyo lived in a highly intricate society; they were believed to be highly skilled in the art of healing and magic. If a fisherman caught one, it was considered to bring about misfortune and storms so these fairies were usually thrown back. If a ningyo was willing to offer up a bit of itself, anyone who consumed any amount of its flesh would be granted immortality. The blood of the ningyo was said to have the ability to heal any wound. However to take these elements from the fairy without its permission was to be the victim of dire consequences.

In the modern telling of the mythology the ningyo is now described as looking like a traditional MERMAID, having long black hair rather than the golden or green of Celtic folklore. Elusive and avoiding human contact, it is believed to bring good luck when sighted. It is also believed when they cry their tears are precious pearls of considerable value.

Source: Loar, *Goddesses for Every Day*, 72; Rosen, *Mythical Creatures Bible*, 132; Yamaguchi, *We Japanese*, 318; Zell-Ravenheart, *Wizard's Bestiary*, 73

Niping (NIP-ing-r)

Variations: Nipingr

A DVERG (DWARF) from Norse mythology, Niping ("the dark") is named in the *Voluspa* part of the *Poetic Edda*. He along with BAFURR, BIFURR, BOMBOR, DAIN, NAIN, NAR, NORI, and "hundreds of others" worked together to create the fetter Gleipnir to bind Fenrir.

Source: Crossley-Holland, *Norse Myths*, 35; Daly, *Norse Mythology A to Z*, 22; Norroena Society, *Asatrii Edda*, 377

Nor (Nohr)

Variations: Norfi ("narrow"), Norr

An ASYNJR from Norse mythology, Nor ("sailor") was the mother of the ASYNJR NOTT.

Source: Grimes, *Norse Myths*, 291; Norroena Society, *Asatrii Edda*, 377

Nordre

Variations: Nodri, Nordri ("little scrap" or "north")

In Norse mythology Nordre was one of the many DVERGAR (DWARFS) named in the *Voluspa*, the first and best known poem of the *Poetic Edda* (AD 985). He was also one of the four DWARFS appointed by the gods to hold up the sky which they constructed from the skull of YMIR. AUSTRE held up the East, Nordre held the North, SUDRE held the South, and VESTRE held the West; each held up one corner of the earth which is described as a flat, plate-like piece of land.

Source: Anderson, *Norse Mythology*, 183; Crossley-Holland, *Norse Myths*, 183; Grimes, *Norse Myths*, 9; Norroena Society, *Asatrii Edda*, 378; Sturluson, *Prose Edda*, 26; Wägner, *Asgard and the Gods*, 311

Nori (NOHR-i)

In Norse mythology Nori ("lad" or "sailor") was one of the DVERGAR (DWARFS) created by the DWARF DURINN. He, along with BAFURR, BIFURR, BOMBOR, DAIN, NAIN, NAR, NIPING, and "hundreds of others," worked together to create the fetter Gleipnir to bind Fenrir.

Source: Grimes, *Norse Myths*, 260; Norroena Society, *Asatrii Edda*, 376

Norn (Nawrn), plural Nornir ("proclaimers")

Variations: Norni, Nornie, Norny

Variations of Pluralization: Nornas, Nornies, Norns

In Norse mythology the nornir are a type of DJINN or FATE unequally directing and shaping the destiny of mankind. Described as three old women named SKULDR, URDR, and VERDANDI, they spin the threads of destiny into a tapestry, determining the course of human lives and the history of the world—all things Fated to happen. The Nornir live in their hall near the Urdarbrunnr Well which is located under the shade of the tree Ygdrasil in a sanctuary called Gimle or Vingolf. They finished their weaving at Ragnarok.

SKULDR is the youngest of the three and personifies the future; she also has dominion over the VALKYRIEs (NYMPHs of battle). VERDANDI, the middle norn, personifies the present; URDR, the eldest, personifies the past.

There are also lesser nornir, racially descended from the ALFS, Æser (the gods), and the DVERGAR (DWARFS); these were said to assist in the birth of future eminent individuals, bestow gifts upon them, and foretell their future. These nornir are the ones who apply a good life and future to a person; those individuals who seem to fall into one misfortune after another are the victims of a malignant alignment of a specific norn.

Source: Du Chaillu, *Viking Age*, 385, 387, 389; Grimes, *Norse Myths*, 291; Keightley, *World Guide to Gnomes, Fairies, Elves, and Other Little People*, 64–5; Norroena Society, *Asatrii Edda*, 4, 378

Nott

Variations: Natt, Nat, Niol

An ASYNJR from Norse mythology, Nott ("night") was born the daughter of the JOTUN NOR and Narfi in the grassy dales beneath Ygdrasil; she was described as being dusky-haired and of swarthy complexion. Nott was married three times; with her first husband, Naglifar, she had a son named Audr; with the second, Anar, a daughter named Jordr; and with the third, Dellingr, a son named Dagr.

Source: Daly, *Norse Mythology A to Z*, 92; Grimes, *Norse Myths*, 291; Lindow, *Norse Mythology*, 92

Nulayuuiniq

A GIANT and cannibal from the folklore of the Povungnituk people of the eastern Hudson Bay region of Canada, Nulayuuiniq was born during a time of great famine in her people's village; shortly after her birth she grew to gigantic proportions and in her hunger, began to consume all of her villagers. When a neighboring village came to assist with donations of food all they discovered was the gigantic infant wearing her mother's parka. They ran in fear, Nulayuuiniq chasing after them, squalling. Unable to keep up with their dogsleds, she fell to the ground exhausted and transformed into a boulder.

Source: Gilmore, *Monsters*, 100; Rose, *Giants, Monsters, and Dragons*, 271

Nunhyunuwi

In Cherokee mythology the nunhyunuwi is a cannibal and a GIANT; it is completely made of stone.

Source: Dixon-Kennedy, *Native American Myth and Legend*, 176; Savill, *Chapter 7. Oceania and Australia. Chapter 8. The Americas*, Volume 4, 210

Nursery Bogie

Variations: Frightening Figures

A nursery bogie is any fairy animal or being used by parents to frighten children into good behavior; they appear in many cultures. Generally, these beings have a frightening appearance and an extremely harsh or deadly means to deal with mortals. Nursery bogie warnings are used to protect crops and keep children away from dangerous environments and situations.

Source: Briggs, *Encyclopedia of Fairies*, 313; Rose, *Spirits, Fairies, Leprechauns, and Goblins*, 241; Wright, *Rustic Speech and Folk-Lore*, 198

Ny

Ny was one of the many DVERGAR (DWARFS) named in the *Voluspa*, the first and best known poem of the *Poetic Edda* (AD 985). Ny was the son of MODSOG-NER-Mimmer in the sense it was he who created and gave the DWARF life.

Sources: Daly, *Norse Mythology A to Z*, 22, Rydberg, *Teutonic Mythology*, Volume 2, 640

Nyi (NEE-i)

Variations: Nae, Næ, Ny

In Norse mythology Nyi ("new," "renewed") was one of the rock DVERGAR (DWARFS) created by the DWARF DURINN; he was symbolic of the new moon.

Source: Grimes, *Norse Myths*, 260, 291; Norroena Society, *Asatrii Edda*, 377; Sturleson, *Viking Anthology*, n.pag.

Nymph

In ancient Greek folklore, the nymphs were lesser deities or nature spirits whose dominion or realm was over a cave, glade, landform, ocean, river, stream, tree, well, or the like. Depicted nude and having a reputation for being promiscuous, these beings frequently were the companions or lovers to the gods. Small and beautiful, these seductive fairies could also choose to marry and live out a life with a mortal man. They were honored with prayers and sacrifices made to them at cairns and shrines.

There are twelve different species of nymph: the ATLANTID were any and all the offspring of the primordial Titan ATLAS; DRYADs were the nymphs of the forests and trees, the oak in particular; HAMADRYADs were the nymphs of trees in general; the HYADS were the daughters of ATLAS and AETHRA; LIMNIADS were the nymphs of lakes, marshes, and swamps, they were dangerous to travelers; LIMONIADs were the nymphs of the flowers and meadows; NAIADs were nymphs of the freshwater lakes, rivers, and springs; the NAPAEA were the nymphs of valleys with grazing herds; the NEREIDs were the sea-nymphs of the Mediterranean Sea in general and the Aegean sea in particular; OCEANIDs were the nymphs of the fountains, oceans, and streams; the OREADs were the nymphs of grottoes and mountains; and the PLEIADES were any one of the seven daughters born of ATLAS and PLEIONE.

Originally the word *nymph* signified a newly married woman, taken from the Greek word "bride" and "veiled."

Some of the named nymphs are: ABA, BENTHESIKYME, CHALCIS, DROSERA, and ERATO.

Source: Keightley, *World Guide to Gnomes, Fairies, Elves, and Other Little People*, 444; Littleton, *Gods, Goddesses, and Mythology*, Volume 11, 999; McCoy, *A Witch's Guide to Faery Folk*, 286; Rose, *Spirits, Fairies, Leprechauns, and Goblins*, 242

Nyr (Neer)

Variations: Nýr

A DVERGAR (DWARF) from Norse mythology, Nyr ("new") is named in the *Voluspa*, the first and best known poem of the *Poetic Edda* (AD 985).

Source: Crossley-Holland, *Norse Myths*, 183; Daly, *Norse Mythology A to Z*, 22; Norroena Society, *Asatrii Edda*, 378; Wägner, *Asgard and the Gods*, 311

Nyrad (NEER-ahth-r)

Variations: Nýrádr

Nyrad ("cunning" or "new council") was one of the many DVERG (DWARFS) named in the *Voluspa*, the first and best known poem of the *Poetic Edda* (AD 985).

Sources: Crossley-Holland, *Norse Myths*, 183; Daly, *Norse Mythology A to Z*, 22; Norroena Society, *Asatrii Edda*, 378; Skyes, *Who's Who in Non-Classical Mythology*, 53; Wilkinson, *Book of Edda called Völuspá*, 12

Oakmen

Variations: Oak Men

Oakmen are a species of male DWARFS from German fairy folklore; they are the guardians of the sacred oak groves. Although not friendly to mankind there are no stories of oakmen ever having harmed a human. In British folklore oakmen are more akin to the HAMADRYADS of Greek folklore, a type of nature spirit living within oak trees, protecting the forest and wildlife while harassing humans.

Source: Briggs, *Folklore of the Cotswalds*, 121; McCoy, *Witch's Guide to Faery Folk*, 288; Monaghan, *Encyclopedia of Celtic Mythology and Folklore*, 365; Rose, *Spirits, Fairies, Leprechauns, and Goblins*, 243

Oceanid, plural Oceanids or Oceanides

Variations: Nymphae Artemisiae ("NYMPHS of Artemis"), Nymphae Oceanides ("oceanid NYMPHS"), Nymphai Artemisiai, Nymphai Okeaninai, Ocean NYMPHS, Oceanide, Okeanides, Okeanids, Okeaninai

The Oceanids of Greek and later Roman mythology are one of twelve species of NYMPHS; they are the NYMPHS of fountains, oceans, and streams. Generally considered to be alluring, gentle, and sweet by nature, the oceanids, unlike the DRYADS, wander the ancient world, visiting glades, plains, and woodlands; there are numerous stories of how their beauty attracted the attention of the gods, satyrs (a type of nature spirit), and various sylvan creatures. According to the ancient Greek oral poet Hesiod, the Oceanids were the NYMPHS which formed the retinue of the goddess Artemis (Diana); they were likely nephelai, nymphs of the clouds.

The TITANS OCEANUS and TETHYS were the parents to some 6,000 children, 3,000 of which were their daughters who were known collectively as the Oceanids and were counted among the second generation TITANS, their names being CLYMENE, DIONE, DORIS, ELECTRA, ETIS, EURYNOME, NEDA, PLEIONE, and STYX. All of the Oceanids were the patronesses of a particular cloud, flower, lake, pasture, pond, river, sea, or spring; they were described as being beautiful even compared to the Greek goddesses. Although most sources will say the Oceanids were strictly females, others include their brothers among them; traditionally the sons of OCEANUS and TETHYS are considered to be river gods, collectively known as the Potamoi ("rivers"). The Oceanids were closely related to the NEREIDS, the NYMPHS of the Mediterranean Sea.

There are many ancient sources naming the individual Oceanids. Some of them include: Callianassa, Eidyia, Hesione, Iakhe, Khryseis, and Lyris.

Source: Daly, *Greek and Roman Mythology A to Z*, 92; Hesiod, *Works of Hesiod, Callimachus, and Theognis*, 20; Roman, *Encyclopedia of Greek and Roman Mythology*, 341

Oceanus

Variations: Okeanos

A TITAN from classical Greek mythology, Oceanus was born the child of the TITAN Uranus ("heaven") and the Earth, Gaea; siblings were COEUS, CRIUS, CRONUS, HYPERION, IAPETUS, MNEMOSYNE, PHOEBE, RHEA, TETHYS, THEIA, and THEMIS. Collectively the siblings were known as the Titanides. He married his sister TETHYS and together they were the parents of twenty-five rivers and 6,000 children, 3,000 of which were their daughters, known collectively as the OCEANIDS. One of the most important rivers he fathered was the River Styx, the barrier between Earth and Hades. Oceanus was the personification of the freshwater river encircling the earth. Although Oceanus appears in many genealogies he is not apparent in cult practices or elsewhere in mythology.

Sources: Bulfinch, *Bulfinch's Greek and Roman Mythology*, 4, 26, 138; Roman, *Encyclopedia of Greek and Roman Mythology*, 341

Ocypete

Variations: Ocypode, Ocythoe, Okypete

One of the four named harpies from ancient Greek mythology, Ocypete ("swift flier" or "swift wing") was originally a storm or nature spirit associated with the weather and was accordingly blamed for storms and undesirable winds (see HARPY). According to the ancient Greek poet Hesiod in his work *Theogony* ("Theogonia," circa 700 BC) where he describes the genealogy of the gods, there were only two harpies, AELLO and Ocypete, the winged daughters of ELECTRA and Thaumas; therein he commented only on how swiftly the sisters could fly.

The Roman poet Valerius Flaccus said there were three harpies, adding CELAENO to the list. Homer, the greatest of ancient Greek epic poets, rounded off the list of named harpies with PODARGE.

Legend tells us the gods plagued Phineus, a seer who had lost his sight, with two harpies, AELLO and Ocypete, who would without fail swoop down from the sky and steal his every meal leaving just enough food for him to survive. Two of the Argonauts, Calais and Zetes, were the sons of the god Boreas and, having wings, volunteered to pursue and slay the creatures in exchange for Phineus' assistance. In the chase AELLO grew exhausted and fell, crashing into the Tigres River; Ocypete managed to fly as far as the Strophades Island where she swore to never return nor bother Phineus again in exchange for her life.

Source: Apollodorus, *Gods and Heroes of the Greeks*, 56; Littleton, *Gods, Goddesses, and Mythology*, Volume 10, 611, 614; *London Encyclopaedia*, Volume 11, 53

Odmience

In Polish folklore an odmience ("changed one") was a species of malicious CHANGELING. When a type of vampiric NYMPH-like demon known as the BOGINKI ("little princess") attacked a newborn child, it left the odmience in its place so it could consume the infant.

Source: Deck-Partyka, *Poland, a Unique Country and Its People*, 278; Maberry, *Crytopedia*, 232

Offerus

Variations: Adokimus, Offro, Reprehus, Reprobus

According to Christian folklore, the GIANT Offerus was born the son of a heathen king and his wife, the queen, who had prayed in secret to the Virgin Mary for a child. The king had his son dedicated to the god Apollo and Machmet. After growing to gigantic proportions and having incredible strength he swore to only serve the bravest and strongest; he found kings and Satan were each cowards and weak. In search of a new master he happened upon a holy hermit who converted him to Christianity and baptized him, renaming Offerus Christopher. Not devout in his new faith, declaring he would neither fast nor pray, he did agree to carry pilgrims across a raging river and did so diligently for a year. One stormy night he carried a small child across the river who grew heavier and heavier with each step until Christopher almost did not make it across with his charge. The child revealed himself as The Redeemer of the World and bade Christopher to plant his walking stick in the ground; the next day a miracle occurred as the cane became a fruit-bearing palm tree. The miracle converted many but the king of the region imprisoned Christopher and after many long months of cruel torture, he was beheaded.

Source: Cohen, *Of Giants*, 120; Daniels, *Encyclopædia of Superstitions, Folklore, and the Occult Sciences of the World*, 1377; Herbermann, *Catholic Encyclopedia*, Volume 3, 728–9

Offoti (OHV-voht-i)

In Norse mythology, Offoti ("big-foot") was one of the many named Jotnar (see JOTUN) about whom, beyond a name, there is little or nothing else known.

Source: Norroena Society, *Asatrii Edda*, 25, 379

Oflugbarda (UHV-lug-barth-a)

Variations: Oflugbardi

In Norse mythology, Oflugbarda ("strong beard") was one of the many named Jotnar (see JOTUN) about

whom, beyond a name, there is little or nothing else known.

Source: Norroena Society, *Asatrii Edda*, 25, 380

Og (Ahg)

A GIANT from Hebrew Scriptures, Og ("round") was the king of Bashan, a land east of the Jordan River, twenty-two miles long and containing over sixty cities; he lived in his capital, Ashtaron. Og and his people were the remnants of the REPHAIM ("GIANTS"). Og, a mighty king who demanded respect, was so tall he required a bed more than thirteen feet long. Rabbinical literature claims him to be SIHON's brother and likely the grandson of Shamhazai, a fallen angel.

Source: Cohen, *Of Giants*, 21; DeLoach, *Giants*, 2, 16, 54, 263; de Rothschild, *History and Literature of the Israelites*, 143; Mandel, *Ultimate Who's Who in the Bible*, 510

Ogias

Variations: Ohia

A GIANT first mentioned in the Babylonian Talmud (Nidah, chapter 9), Ogias was said to be the son of the fallen angel Samhazai and the father of the Giants OG and SIHON. One of the apocryphal Hebrew texts, *Ogias the Giant*, also known as *The Book of Giants*, tells the tale of how Ogias fought a dragon in the time before the Biblical Deluge.

Source: Daniels, *Encyclopædia of Superstitions, Folklore, and the Occult Sciences of the World*, 1377; Jensen, *Manipulating The Last Pure Godly DNA*, 165–6

Ogladnir (OH-glath-nir)

In Norse mythology, Ogladnir ("the unhappy" or "ungladdner") was one of the many named Jotnar (see JOTUN) about whom, beyond a name, there is little or nothing else known.

Source: Norroena Society, *Asatrii Edda*, 25, 380

Ogre

Variations: Ogro, Orculli, Norrgens

All throughout fairy folklore exists the ogre, a cannibalistic humanoid with an extremely malicious temperament. Described as larger and more broad than a man but not quite the size and strength of a GIANT, the ogre is variously defined as being hairy, carrying a club, and having an overly large head. The female of the species is called an ogress.

It has been suggested the word *ogre* originated in the pre–Christian folklore of the Scandinavian Vikings. The Norse term *yggr* ("lord of death") was a title of the god Odin to whom human sacrifices were made. As the stories of Odin spread to the British Isles and were retold over the years the god eventually evolved into a GIANT living in the clouds and consuming human flesh; the word *yggr* transformed into the word *ogre*. Some sources claim *ogre* was a French word originally created by author Charles Perrault (1628–1703) for his book *Histoires ou Contes du temps Passé* (1697) while other sources say it was first used by his contemporary, Marie-Catherine Jumelle de Berneville, Comtesse d' Aulnoy (1650–1705).

The fairy mythology of Yorkshire, England, has more GIANT and ogre folklore than any other location in the world. In Scandinavian folklore the words ogre and TROLL are oftentimes used interchangeably.

Some famous ogres from folklore, literature and mythology are Allewyn, Babau, Babou, Balardeu, Croque-mitaine (Croquemitaine), Dents Rouge, Fine Oreille, Galaffre, Grand Colin, Huorco, L'Homme Rouge, Orch, Orlo, Pacolet, Pere Fouettard, Pere Lustucru, Pier Jan Claes, Raminagrobis, Saalah, and Tartaro.

Source: Hamilton, *Ogres and Giants*, 16–18; McCoy, *Witch's Guide to Faery Folk*, 29, 230–31; Perrault, *Histoires ou Contes du temps Passé*, 60–2, 112–18

Ohdowas

Variations: Odhows

In the mythology of the Iroquois People of North America, the *ohdowas* ("underground people") are a species of JOGAH ("DWARF") living in the dim and sunless Underworld, a realm of forests and plains populated with many species of animals. Ohdowas are described as being small in stature but very brave and diligent in their work, as it is their task to see to it the creatures of the Underworld do not escape to the world above; this is a great responsibility as many of the creatures of the Underworld are noxious and venomous beasts. Ohdowas must receive an offering of weapons, usually broken or burned, in order for the spirits to receive them, and food in order to continue their work.

Source: Alexander, *Mythology of All Races*, Volume X North America, 28, Coulter, *Encyclopedia of Ancient Deities*, 252, 360; Leddon, *Child's Eye View of Fair Folk*, 44

Oinn (OH-in)

Variations: Óinn, Óin, Oin

In Norse mythology Oinn ("the shy") was one of the rock DVERGAR (DWARFS) created by the DWARF DURINN; he was named in the *Voluspa*, the first and best known poem of the *Poetic Edda* (AD 985).

Source: Daly, *Norse Mythology A to Z*, 22; Grimes, *Norse Myths*, 7, 293; Norroena Society, *Asatrii Edda*, 379

Okkvainkalfa (UHK-vin-kalv-a)

Variations: Okkvinkalfa, Ökkvinkalfa, Økkvinkalfa

One of the hrymthursars (FROST GIANTS) from Norse mythology, Okkvainkalfa ("fat legs" or "spindleshanks") was born one of the daughters of THRAEL and THIR. Okkvainkalfa, her parents and siblings all lived a hard life of labor performing thankless tasks, such as cleaning, herding goats and swine, placing dung in the fields, and other varied unskilled labor. She and her family became the progenitors of the serving folk and thrall.

Source: Grimes, *Norse Myths*, 27, 293; Norroena Society, *Asatrii Edda*, 379

Ole-Higue

Variations: Fire Ross, Ole Higue

A vampiric witch-like creature in the folklore of the people of Guyana and Jamaica, the ole-higue ("old HAG") is said to be a nocturnal, female blood-drinking being similar to BABA YAGA of Russian folklore. During the daylight hours the ole-higue can pass for a normal person but at night the creature will shed its skin and take flight, seeking out its prey, a baby asleep in its cradle. When it finds its meal the ole-higue will slip into the home, unseen, and drain the child of its blood.

To rid a village of this creature, a baby dressed in blue sleeping clothes is laid in its crib; nearby a bowl of rice and uncooked asafetida are placed and a magical spell is said over these items. When the ole-higue arrives it will then be compelled by the magic to count each grain of rice; if it becomes distracted it will have the need to begin all over. When the dawn breaks the villagers will enter the room with the sleeping child and be able to beat the ole-higue to death.

Source: Durrant, *Historical Dictionary of Witchcraft*, 150; Gulmahamad, *Stories and Poems by a Guyanese Village Boy*, 201–2

Olentzero

According to Basque legend Olentzero is the last of his kind, a JENTIL, a race of GIANTS said to have lived in the Pyrenees Mountains; his story is remarkably similar to Santa Claus and Saint Nicholas. He was found by a family who were living in the woods, taken in, and raised as one of their own; Olentzero grew up to become an excellent wood-carver and enjoyed using his extraordinary talent to create toys he would gift to the children in the nearby village. When Olentzero died saving a child from a house fire, a fairy returned him to life and health and gifted him with immortality in order to continue making and giving away toys. He is said to do this once a year, during the midnight hour on December twenty-fourth, each year.

Source: Pemberton, *Myths and Legends*, n.pag.; Sherman, *Storytelling*, 57

Olrun

Variations: Sigrun ("she who knows the victory runes")

One of the many named VALKYRIEs (NYMPHs of battle) in Norse mythology, there is little else known about Olrun ("one knowing ale rune") beyond his name.

Source: Monaghan, *Encyclopedia of Goddesses and Heroines*, 294; Puryear, *Nature of Asatru*, 233–4

Olvaldi

Variations: Allvaldi, Alvaldi, Ivaldi, Ölvaldi

One of the Jotnar (see JOTUN) of Norse mythology, Olvaldi ("high ruler") was the father of GANGR, IDI and THJAZI by his wife, GREIP; his granddaughter was SKADI. When Olvaldi died, rich in gold from his many years of plunder, his three sons divided up his hoard by each taking a mouthful of it at a time. Each of his descendants was, even after the division of property, extremely wealthy, "the greatest scales in all the Worlds could not begin to measure the smallest portion of it."

Source: Daly, *Norse Mythology A to Z*, 78; Grimes, *Norse Myths*, 104, 293; Norroena Society, *Asatrii Edda*, 333

Onditachiae

Variations: THUNDERBIRDS, Thunderers

In the folklore of the Huron Native American tribe of the northeastern United States of America, the Onditachiae are a race of beings having the body of a human but the head of a cock turkey; these beings are only ever seen during storms as they were the personification of lightning, rain, and thunder.

Source: King, *Thunderbird and Lightning*, 55; Rose, *Giants, Monsters, and Dragons*, 278

Ondudr (UHND-uth-r)

In Norse mythology Ondudr ("opponent") was one of the many named Jotnar (see JOTUN) about whom, beyond a name, there is little or nothing else known.

Source: Norroena Society, *Asatrii Edda*, 379

Oni (OH-nee)

Variations: Tengu, Yama-Biko (male), Yama-Bito ("mountaineer"), Yama-Chichi, Yama-Otoko, Yama-Uba (female)

In Japanese demonology the oni ("to hide or conceal") were originally a species of invisible spirits which later evolved into gigantic, demonic humanoid beings with horns, sharp nails, and wild hair. Occasionally these creatures were depicted in art with a number of eyes, fingers, and toes. Their skin is commonly red or blue but can be any color; they wear tiger-skin loincloths and carry a kanabō, a heavy oak wood club with iron spikes or studs on one end.

Oni have the ability to cause earthquakes and eclipses, and allow enemy invasions. Seasonal ceremonies and festivals are held to drive the oni away. Monkey statues ward against oni approaching. These demons prey upon the souls of evil people; only by performing a ceremony called *oni-yarabi* can a tainted soul be saved. The sage Nichiren ("sun-lotus") created a special school of Buddhism to combat the oni and reform his people.

Source: Bush, *Asian Horror Encyclopedia*, 141; Hackin, *Asiatic Mythology*, 443–4; Mack, *Field Guide to Demons*, 116–8; Sosnoski, *Introduction to Japanese Culture*, 9; Turner, *Dictionary of Ancient Deities*, 363

Ophion

Variations: Ophioneus

A GIGANTE or TITAN from ancient Greek mythology, serpentine Ophion ("snake") and his wife EURYNOME were at one time the rulers of Olympus but they were dethroned by CRONUS and RHEA, cast into the ocean. Zeus (Jupiter) eventually cast Ophion into Tartarus; this was likely the serpentine monster the god had to wrestle to obtain his position as king of the gods.

Source: Bartlett, *Mythology Bible*, 216; Ogden, *Dragons, Serpents, and Slayers in the Classical and Early Christian Worlds*, 36

Ordulph

A GIANT from British folklore, Ordulph was noted for his remarkable strength; in one story he ripped the gates of the city of Exeter off their hinges because he was not granted admission quickly enough. Rocks and bolts went flying in every direction; portions of the wall were flung across the city, frightening the citizens. The king believed Ordulph came to his great strength by having made a pact with the Devil. In Tavistock, Ordulph would stand with one foot on either side of the road, which according to folklore was twenty feet across, and as animals were driven down the road he would, using only a small knife, sever their heads from their bodies. His bones are said to be preserved in a church in Cornwall.

Source: Bray, *Borders of the Tamar and the Tavy*, 438; Hunt, *Popular Romances of the West of England*, 76–7

Oread

Variations: Orends, Orestiad

The oreads ("mountain") of ancient Greek mythology were one of the twelve species of NYMPHS; they were the NYMPHS of grottoes, mountains, ravines, and valleys. Living lives virtually identical to human females, the oreads were associated with the goddess Artemis (Diana) because when she hunted she preferred mountains and rocky precipices.

An oread was usually known by the name of the mountain or hill on which she lived, for example, the Claea were the oreads of Mount Calathion, the Daphnis were the oreads of Mount Parnassus, the Idae were the oreads of Mount Ida, the Nomia were the Oreads of Mount Nomia in Arcadia, the Othreis were the oreads of Mount Othrys, Malis, and the Peliades were the oreads of Mount Pelia.

Some of the names of the more commonly known oreads are Alcyone, Britomartis, CELAENO, Cynosura, Echo, ELECTRA, Kola, Kyllene, Kouratni, Maia, Merope, Nomia, Oenone, Pitys, PLEIADES, Sterope (Asterope), and Taygete.

Source: Antoninus Liberalis, *Metamorphoses of Antoninus Liberalis*, 60; Keightley, *World Guide to Gnomes, Fairies, Elves, and Other Little People*, 444; Littleton, *Gods, Goddesses, and Mythology*, Volume 11, 999; Pausanias, *Pausanias' Description of Greece*, Volume 2, 279

Oreus, Giant

Variations: Oreios, Oureios

An anthropophagous (man-eating) GIGANTE from the mythology of the ancient Greeks, Oreus and his twin brother AGRIUS were Thracian by birth and the children of the NYMPH Polyphonte and a bear. Described as being half-bear and half-human, the cannibal brothers had a ferocious temper and would not only insult but attack and consume travelers. The twins were an affront to Zeus (Jupiter) who ordered Mercury to destroy them; however Ares (Mars) intervened on their behalf as their mother was the daughter of Thrassa, one of his own daughters. Rather than be utterly destroyed, the twins were transformed into birds of prey as punishment for their crimes.

Oreios (Orobios) was also the name of a Centaur (a creature from Greek mythology, half equine and half human, entangled with issues of sexual boundaries and promiscuity) who attended the wedding of Pirithous, became drunk on wine, and following the lead of EURYTUS who assaulted Hippodame, began to assault and rape any women they could grab. A great Centauromachy then followed.

Source: Colvin, *Cornhill Magazine*, Volume XXXVIII, 296; Lemprière, *Classical Dictionary*, 36

Orgoglio

A hideous GIANT from Italian folklore, Orgoglio ("arrogant pride," or "man of sin") was said to stand as tall as three men. As a character in Spenser's *Faerie Queene*, club-wielding Orgoglio is nearly an undefeatable opponent who is only defeated by Arthur. According to the story, his father was Aeolus, the god of the wind, who impregnated the "womb of the earth" with air; he was birthed during an earthquake covered in slime, making him the embodiment of three of the four elements. Morally corrupt, physically revolting, and amazingly strong, Orgoglio is portrayed more as a monster, a subhuman creature, than as an intelligent humanoid.

Source: Daniels, *Encyclopædia of Superstitions, Folklore, and the Occult Sciences of the World*, 1377; Rudolf, *Clerks, Wives and Historians*, 157–60

Ori (OHR-i)

A rock DVERG (DWARF) from Norse mythology created by DURINN, Ori ("raging") is listed as being one of DURINN's KIN. He, like the others created, paid particular attention to DURINN's leadership.

Source: Daly, *Norse Mythology A to Z*, 22; Grimes, *Norse Myths*, 260; Norroena Society, *Asatrii Edda*, 380

Orion

Variations: Urion

A GIGANTE from ancient Greek mythology, Orion has obscure origins. Some tales claim he was the son of the Boiotian hero Hyrieus from an ox hide which had been urinated on by the gods Hermes, Poseidon (Neptune), and Zeus (Jupiter) and then buried for ten months. Other tales say he was a son of the god of the sea Poseidon (Neptune) and Euryale. Handsome and tall, Orion had the natural ability to walk on water. His first wife, Side, was so attractive she was cast into Hades because her beauty rivaled Hera's (Juno). He then courted Merope, daughter of King Oinopion, but was tricked into drinking a sleeping potion and while under its effect had his eyes removed. Eventually his sight was restored and he was gifted with a house created by Hephaistos. Just as with his birth, the death of Orion is also uncertain. Some stories say he was slain because he challenged Artemis (Diana) to a discus throwing contest while other tales say while he was attempting to rape the Hyperborean handmaiden Opis, he was shot with an arrow by Artemis (Diana).

Source: Daniels, *Encyclopædia of Superstitions, Folklore, and the Occult Sciences of the World*, 1377; Daly, *Greek and Roman Mythology, A to Z*, 107; Rose, *Handbook of Greek Mythology*, 93–4

Ork

Variations: HYMIR, Il Orco, Lorge, Norge, Norglein, Norkele, Orco, Orge

In South Tyrolean folklore, Ork is a good natured DWARF or house-spirit but in very old tales he was described as being an anthropophagous (man-eating) devil; it is possible Ork may have at one time been the Roman god of the underworld, Orcus.

Source: Wagenwoorf, *Studies in Roman Literature, Culture and Religion*, 103

Oromedon

The Latin elegiac poet Sextus Propertius records in his work the GIANT Oromedon as being one of his kind who fought in the Gigantomachy against the gods; there is a mountain on the island of Cos named after him, as he was said to be buried there. Oromedon is also the name of the GIANT who was the father of GENNAGOG.

Source: Brewer, *Wordsworth Dictionary of Phrase and Fable*, 469; Daniels, *Encyclopædia of Superstitions, Folklore, and the Occult Sciences of the World*, 1376

Oskrudr (UHS-kruth-r)

In Norse mythology Oskrudr ("bellower," "screamer," or "unshrouded") was one of the many named Jotnar (see JOTUN) about whom, beyond a name, there is little or nothing else known.

Source: Norroena Society, *Asatrii Edda*, 380

Otos

Variations: Otus

A GIGANTE from ancient Greek mythology, Otos was born of the great goddess Gaea and the TITAN Uranus ("heaven"); he was a brother of EPHIALTES; collectively they were known as the ALOADAE, the sons of ALOEUS, but their parents were alleged to be his wife Iphimedia and the god of the sea, Poseidon (Neptune). According to Pliny the Elder, the Roman author and natural philosopher, Otos grew nine inches per month, reaching a final height of forty-six cubits (sixty-six feet; a *cubit* is the distance from a man's elbow to the tip of his middle finger) tall. Sources vary as to whether or not the brothers were GIGANTE or merely extremely tall as well as their parentage and if they took part in the Gigantomachy.

Source: Daniels, *Encyclopædia of Superstitions, Folklore, and the Occult Sciences of the World*, 1377; Hansen, *Handbook of Classical Mythology*, 100

P-Skig-Demo-Os

Variations: M-ska-gwe-demo-os

In the folklore of the Abenaki Indians P-Skig-Demo-Os was once considered to be an anthropophagous (man-eating) predator, hunting her male victims from the shadows by using a mournful cry to draw them into her cannibalistic clutches. A being of complete and utter evil, P-Skig-Demo-Os is also exceptionally spiteful; so much so that anyone who even thinks piteous thoughts of her will suffer with bad luck and likely never fall in love. In more modern times, however, P-Skig-Demo-Os has become a NURSERY BOGIE utilized to frighten children into good behavior.

Source: Maberry, *Vampire Universe*, 252

Pallas

A TITAN from ancient Greek mythology, Pallas ("handsome") was born of the great goddess Gaea and the TITAN Uranus ("heaven"). He and his siblings ASTRAEUS and PERSES were extremely large, immensely strong, and absolutely fearsome to behold as they had dense beards, a thick head of hair, and feet covered with DRAKON scales; they threw flaming oak trees and rocks at the heavens.

Pallas, like the GIGANTE ENCELADOS, was slain by the virgin goddess Athena (Minerva); she peeled his flesh from his body and donned it as armor while she continued to fight against other GIGANTE during the Gigantomachy.

There is also a NAID named Pallas, born the daughter of the river god, Triton; she was the childhood playmate of the virgin goddess Athena (Minerva) as they shared a passion for combat.

Source: Apollodorus, *Library of Greek Mythology*, 34–5; Daniels, *Encyclopædia of Superstitions, Folklore, and the Occult Sciences of the World*, 1377

Pallene (pal-LEEN)

Born the daughter of the GIGANTE ALCYONEUS, Pallene ("brandishing" or "wielding powerful weapons") was, according to the ancient Greek historian Hegesander, one of the ALCYONII; she and her sisters are named in his six-volume work *Commentaries (Hypomnemata)*. In most stories her father, ALCYONEUS, died during the Gigantomachy but in one tale it was told her father had "an unnatural passion" for his daughter and ruined her chances of ever being wed by murdering all of her suitors in a wrestling match. So many men had died in this fashion the arena floor was stained red with their blood. One day a champion of Justice named Bacchos sought the hand of Pallene and accepted her father's challenge. It was difficult, but ultimately Bacchos was victorious; immediately upon being declared the winner he took up a sharp thyrsus and killed ALCYONEUS; the bloodied weapon was then presented to Pallene as a token of his devotion and love.

Source: Bell, *Bell's New Pantheon*, 110; Blunck, *Solar System*

Moons, 83; Groves, *Baby Names That Go Together*, 168; Smith, *Dictionary of Greek and Roman Biography and Mythology*, 108

Pan

Variations: FAUN, Paniskoi ("little Pans"), Satyr

A species of goat and human hybrids, the panes of ancient Greek mythology were said to be the descendants of the god Pan (Faunus); their ancient Roman counterparts would have been Fauns (or Fauni), descendants of the nature spirit and god Faunus and his wife, Fauna. Panes would assist Pan (Faunus) in tending his flocks of cattle and swine; generally, when left to amuse themselves, they were mischievous, at their worst, leading travelers astray.

Source: Hard, *Routledge Handbook of Greek Mythology*, 215; Society for the Diffusion of Useful Knowledge, *Penny Cyclopaedia*, Volume 10, 208

Pangu

Variations: P'an Ku

A GIANT in Chinese mythology, Pangu is also worshiped as a creator god; his first appearance was in *Wuyun Linianji* and was described as having the head of a dragon and the body of a serpent. In some versions of the tales he has the head of a cat, the body of a serpent, and tiger paws. In sculpture Pangu is shown as manlike but having a horn in the middle of his forehead, as it was believed in ancient times all people had a horn they used for hunting; as they neared death, the horn grew soft and fell off.

In one myth originating in Henan Province Pangu was said to be the creator of the world as well as its manager. After he created humans he convinced the beautiful and radiant sisters, Moon and Sun, to take turns standing atop a very tall mountain, illuminating the day and the night. In a myth from Gansu Province Pangu, after he separated the earth from Heaven, created an ox out of clay and his own saliva and breathed life into it so it would be the beast to bear the burden of the weight of the world. He also created a rooster to ensure the ox would never fall asleep. Each time there is an earthquake it is the rooster rousing the sleepy ox.

Source: An, *Handbook of Chinese Mythology*, 188–9; Roberts, *Chinese Mythology, A to Z*, 92

Panotti

Variations: Panotii, Panotioi

Described by Pliny the Elder, a Roman author, naturalist, natural philosopher, and army and naval commander, the Panotti ("all ears") were a race of people with fan-shaped ears so large they covered their whole body; at night they used one ear as a pillow and the other as a blanket. When frightened the people of Panotti would take an ear in each hand and, flapping like a bird, take flight into the air. The island these people live upon was said to be located off of Scythia and named Panotti after its inhabitants.

Source: Bovey, *Monsters and Grotesques in Medieval Manuscripts*, 10; Pliny the Elder, *Natural History of Pliny*, Volume 1, 343

Pantagruel

François Rabelais (AD 1494–1553) compiled the lineage of the GIANTS. He lists Pantagruel ("all thirsty") as the son of GARGANTUAN; his mother, Badebec, died while giving birth to him during a drought. The height of Pantagruel is never given; although a GIANT, he was short enough to sit in a classroom and to travel by ship yet tales claim he once used his tongue to protect an army from a violent storm, and had an entire society living in his mouth of which he was unaware. Additionally, it was said when he passed gas, the earth shook for twenty-nines miles all around and produced fifty-three thousand men and women each, creating a race of pygmies.

Source: Brewer, *Character Sketches of Romance, Fiction and the Drama*, Volume 3, 82; Daniels, *Encyclopædia of Superstitions, Folklore, and the Occult Sciences of the World*, 1377; Weinstock, *Ashgate Encyclopedia of Literary and Cinematic Monsters*, 246

Parthenope

Variations: Pisinoe

Sea NYMPHS from ancient Greek mythology, Parthenope ("the tuneful") and her sisters, LEUCOSIA and LIGEIA, were born the daughters of the MUSE Melpomene and the god Achelous; they were the companions to Persephone. After her abduction by Hades (Dis) the sisters asked the gods for wings so they might go in search of their friend. The request was granted; the three NYMPHS were transformed into bird-women hybrids, the SIRENS. Parthenope played the lyre while LEUCOSIA sang and LIGIA played the flute. Together they would harmonize along the rocky shoreline and lure sailors to turn their ships to hear their melodic songs, wrecking their vessels. Then the sisters would capture and devour them.

Source: Drury, *Dictionary of the Esoteric*, 297; Hunt, *New Monthly Magazine and Universal Register*, 276

Patagon

Variations: Pata-gonians

A race of GIANTS from medieval folklore, the Patagon ("big feet") were said to live in Patagonia, a region now shared by Argentina and Chile in South America. According to his logs, Ferdinand

Magellan, the Portuguese explorer, captured two of the Patagon with the intent of sending them back to the court of Charles the Fifth for his Cabinet of Curiosities but they escaped. One of the GIANTS was never recovered but the other was recaptured, baptized Pau and shipped back to Spain; it died of scurvy before the ship's arrival.

Source: DeLoach, *Giants*, 227; Reif-Hülser, *Borderlands*, 97

Pegaeae

Variations: The Pegaiai

The pegaeae were a sub-species of the NAIADS; they are the NYMPHS of fresh water springs and fountains in classical Greek mythology.

Source: Avant, *Mythological Reference*, 295; Conner, *Everything Classical Mythology Book*, 17, 276; Maberry, *Cryptopedia*, 112

Peisinoë

One of the SIRENS from ancient Greek mythology, Peisinoë ("persuading mind"), although ancient writers do not agree on their names or numbers, is typically one of a trio of sisters, grouped with AGLAOPE and THELXEPEIA, born the daughters of Achelous and Thelxiepia.

Source: Apollodorus, *Library*, Volume 2, 290; Smith, *Dictionary of Greek and Roman Biography and Mythology*, Volume 3, 840

Pelorus

In classical Greek mythology, Pelorus ("giant") was one of the five SPARTI who went on to become the progenitors of the five leading families of the city of Thebes who formed the military caste.

Source: Apollodorus, *Apollodorus' Library and Hyginus' Fabulae*, 22, 47; Dixon-Kennedy, *Encyclopedia of Greco-Roman Mythology*, 86; Hard, *Routledge Handbook of Greek Mythology*, 296

Perses

Variations: The God Who Laid Waste

A second generation TITAN from ancient Greek mythology, Perses was born of the first generation TITAN CRIUS, a god of leadership. He and his siblings ASTRAEUS and PALLAS were extremely large, immensely strong, and absolutely fearsome to behold as they had dense beards, a thick head of hair, and feet covered with *drakon* (a species of Greek dragon) scales; they threw flaming oak trees and rocks at the heavens. With ASTERIA Perses had a single child, the powerful and mysterious goddess Hecate.

Source: Daly, *Greek and Roman Mythology, A to Z*, 141; Hard, *Routledge Handbook of Greek Mythology*, 48–9; Westmoreland, *Ancient Greek Beliefs*, 27, 71, 788

Phoebe (FEE-bee)

A TITAN from classical Greek mythology, Phoebe ("bright") was born the child of the TITANS Uranus ("heaven") and the Earth, Gaea; her siblings were COEUS, CRIUS, CRONUS, HYPERION, IAPETUS, MNEMOSYNE, OCEANUS, RHEA, TETHYS, THEIA, and THEMIS. Collectively the siblings were known as the Titanides.

Traditionally associated with the moon, the golden-crowned Phoebe and her brother COEUS were the parents to three daughters, ASTERIA, Hekate, and LETO; although according to the Greek poet Hesiod in his work *Theogony*, Hekate was the only offspring of their union.

Source: Roman, *Encyclopedia of Greek and Roman Mythology*, 408–9; Westmoreland, *Ancient Greek Beliefs*, 27, 42, 71

Phorcys

A TITAN and sea god from ancient Greek mythology, Phorcys was born one of the children of Gaea (earth) and the ancient god of the sea, Pontus; he was the father of the GORGONS by his sister, CETO. In art he was depicted as an anthropoid with crab claws for legs, a fish tail, and spiky red skin.

Source: Conner, *Everything Classical Mythology Book*, 43; Daly, *Greek and Roman Mythology, A to Z*, 141

Phosthonia

Variations: Phthonia

Born the daughter of the GIGANTE ALCYONEUS, Phosthonia ("light") was, according to the ancient Greek historian Hegesander, one of the ALCYONII; she and her sisters, ALKIPPA, ANTHE, ASTERIA, DRIMO, METHONE, and PALLENE, are named in his six-volume work *Commentaries* (Hypomnemata).

Source: Blunck, *Solar System Moons*, 83; Smith, *Dictionary of Greek and Roman Biography and Mythology*, 108

Pleiades

Variations: Pleiad, Seven Sisters

The pleiades ("flock of doves" or "sailing ones") are one of the twelve species of NYMPHS according to the ancient Greek mythology; they were any one of the seven daughters born of the primordial TITAN ATLAS and of the OCEANID PLEIONE ("sailing queen"). The pleiades, with their half-sisters the HYADES, were the attendants of the goddess Artemis (Diana). The pleiades were romantically pursued by ORION for seven years and were only able to escape his advances when the god Zeus (Jupiter) answered their prayers for help and transformed them all into doves.

The names of the seven pleiades are Alcyone ("Queen who wards off evil [storms]"); Asterope (also known as Sterope) ("lightning," "sun-face," and "twinkling"); CELAENO (also known as Celaino) ("swarthy"); Dryope (also known as Merope) ("bee-eater," "eloquent," and "mortal"); ELECTRA ("amber," "bright," or "shining"); Maia ("mother" or "Nurse"); and Taygete (also known as Taygeta) ("long-necked"). Maia was the eldest of her sisters.

Source: Larson, *Greek Nymphs*, 7; Littleton, *Gods, Goddesses, and Mythology*, Volume 11, 999; Rigoglioso, *Cult of Divine Birth in Ancient Greece*, 163; Rose, *Spirits, Fairies, Leprechauns, and Goblins*, 263

Pleione

An OCEANID and TITAN from ancient Greek mythology, Pleione ("sailing queen") was born one of the daughters of the first generation TITAN OCEANIDS and his sister wife TETHYS. Pleione was the wife of the TITAN ATLAS; she was the mother of the PLEIADES, one of the twelve species of NYMPHS.

Source: Daly, *Greek and Roman Mythology, A to Z*, 141; March, *Penguin Book of Classical Myths*, 297

Podarge

Variations: Podarce ("fleet-footed")

One of the four named harpies from ancient Greek mythology, Podarge ("swift foot") was originally a storm or nature spirit associated with the weather and was accordingly blamed for storms and undesirable winds (see HARPY).

According to the ancient Greek poet Hesiod, in his work *Theogony* (*Theogonia*, circa 700 BC) where he describes the genealogy of the gods, there were only two harpies, AELLO and OCYPETE, the winged daughters of ELECTRA and Thaumas; therein he commented only on how swiftly the sisters could fly. The Roman poet Valerius Flaccus said there were three harpies, adding CELAENO to the list. Homer, the greatest of ancient Greek epic poets, rounded off the list of named harpies with Podarge.

In very early Greek writings it was said as the HARPY Podarge grazed in a meadow by the stream of OCEANUS she caught the attention of Aquilo (Zephyrus), the West Wind; this union gave birth to the marvelous and swift horses of Achilles, Balios and Xanthos, who pulled his chariot.

Source: Howey, *Horse in Magic and Myth*, 129; Littleton, *Gods, Goddesses, and Mythology*, Volume 10, 611, 614; *London Encyclopaedia*, Volume 11, 53

Polybotes

Variations: Polubutes, Polyboles

A GIGANTE from ancient Greek mythology, Polybotes ("cattle lord") was born of the great goddess Gaea and the TITAN Uranus ("heaven"). He and his siblings were extremely large, immensely strong, and absolutely fearsome to behold as they had dense beards, a thick head of hair, and feet covered with DRAKON scales; they threw flaming oak trees and rocks at the heavens. In art it was common for Polybotes to be depicted as having huge serpents for arms.

During the war against the gods, he was slain when the god Poseidon (Neptune) chased him across the sea to the island of Coss, then known as Nisyron. The god tore off a piece of the island and threw it at Polybotes with fatal accuracy.

Source: Apollodorus, *Library of Greek Mythology*, 34–5; Daniels, *Encyclopædia of Superstitions, Folklore, and the Occult Sciences of the World*, 1376

Polyphemus

Variations: Polyphem, Polyphemos

From Greek mythology, ACAMAS, along with Polyphemus ("mush fame") and PYRACMON, were, according to Homer's *The Iliad*, a new breed of CYCLOPS born from the union of the original CYCLOPES and the women who lived upon Mount Etna.

Polyphemus lived in a cave on the side of Mount Etna herding sheep and was in love with the NYMPH Galatea. When Polyphemus discovered Galatea with her beloved, Acis, he crushed the man's skull with a rock. The gods transformed the weeping Galatea into a stream which emptied out into the ocean, taking her far away from the murdering CYCLOPS. Polyphemus became so enraged he swore to kill all humans who came to his land.

As a CYCLOPS named in Homer's epic poem *Odyssey* (circa 750 BC), Polyphemus was born the son of the god of the sea, Poseidon (Neptune), and the NYMPH Thoosa; no matter his lineage, his story appears in book nine.

Polyphemus, a goat and sheep herder, captured the Greek hero Odysseus and twelve of his men when they landed upon his island seeking to resupply their ship. Sealing the group inside his cave home with a gigantic rock too large for them to move collectively, Polyphemus snatched up two of the men, dashed out their brains, consumed their bodies, and then took a restful sleep. In the morning when he awoke, Polyphemus repeated the act with two more of Odysseus's men. Upon his return at dinner-time, Polyphemus consumed another two men, but now the hero, who gave his name as being Outis ("nobody"), had developed a plan of escape. First Odysseus prepared a goatskin of wine for the CYCLOPS which caused Polyphemus to fall into a deep sleep; then Odysseus and his remaining men rammed a sharpened post into the being's eye, blinding him. Polyphemus cried out "Nobody has blinded me" in his anger which caused his fellow CYCLOPES to believe it was a means of punishment sent by the gods, so they did not interfere. Odysseus and his men then tied themselves to undersides of the sheep of Polyphemus and waited for him to remove the boulder blocking their escape. Once safely aboard their ship Odysseus could not help but brag and called out it was he who defeated the mighty Polyphemus; by listening carefully to the boast the CYCLOPS was able to hurl a boulder nearly to the point of origin of the call and almost destroyed the departing vessel.

Source: Daniels, *Encyclopædia of Superstitions, Folklore, and the Occult Sciences of the World*, 1377; Graves, *Greek Myths*, n.pag.; Rose, *Giants, Monsters, and Dragons* 91, 294

Porphyria

According to François Rabelais (AD 1494–1553), who compiled the lineage of the GIANTS, Porphyria was born the son of the HECATONCHEIRE Briareus (BRIAREOS) and was himself the father of the GIANT ADAMASTOR.

Source: Brewer, *Character Sketches of Romance, Fiction and the Drama*, Volume 3, 80; Daniels, *Encyclopædia of Superstitions, Folklore, and the Occult Sciences of the World*, 1376; Rabelais, *Hours with Rabelais*, 80

Porphyron

Variations: Porphyrion

A GIGANTE from ancient Greek mythology, Porphyron ("growing crimson," "swelling") was born of the great goddess Gaea and the TITAN Uranus ("heaven"). He and his siblings were extremely large, immensely strong, and absolutely fearsome to behold as they had dense beards, a thick head of hair, and feet covered with DRAKON scales; they threw flaming oak trees and rocks at the heavens. Of all the GIGANTE, he was considered to be their leader and his brother ALCYONEUS was considered to be the mightiest. As long as Porphyron fought on the land, he was immortal.

During the ten year war against the gods, the Gigantomachy, Porphyron stood in the ocean, grabbed up the island of Delos and threw it at the god Zeus (Jupiter); he was soon thereafter slain when Zeus retaliated, hurled and landed a thunderbolt upon him at the same time the hero Hercules (Heracles) managed a fatal shot with an arrow.

Source: Apollodorus, *Library of Greek Mythology*, 34–5; Daniels, *Encyclopædia of Superstitions, Folklore, and the Occult Sciences of the World*, 1377; Smith, *Dictionary of Greek and Roman Biography and Mythology*, 498

Porpoise People

In the folklore of the Haida people of the Pacific Northwest Coast of North America, the porpoise people were one of the many supernatural ocean people who lived in underwater villages scattered up and down the shore. Since the ocean people were in control of a large part of the food supply, they not only were held in the highest of regard but were also appealed to for assistance with offerings of rare flicker feathers, grease, and tobacco.

Source: Goldenweiser, *Early Civilization*, 63

Porus

François Rabelais (AD 1494–1553) compiled the lineage of the GIANTS. He lists Porus as the son of AGATHO and as the GIANT who fought against Alexander the Great. Porus is also listed as the father of ARANTHAS.

Source: Brewer, *Character Sketches of Romance, Fiction and the Drama*, Volume 3, 80; Daniels, *Encyclopædia of Superstitions, Folklore, and the Occult Sciences of the World*, 1376; Rabelais, *Hours with Rabelais*, 80

Posio

According to Pliny the Elder, the Roman author and natural philosopher, during the reign of Caesar Augustus, Posio the GIANT was the husband of SECUNDILLA; they were reported as being six inches taller than the GIANT GABBARAS. The bodies of Posio and SECUNDILLA were said to have been preserved as objects of curiosity in the Museum of the Sallustian family as they stood ten feet and three inches tall.

Source: Ashton, *Curious Creatures in Zoology*, 37; Wood, *Giants and Dwarfs*, 22

Potameides

The potameides of ancient Greek mythology were a sub-species of the NAIADS, the NYMPHS of fresh water rivers.

Source: Avant, *Mythological Reference*, 295; Day, *God's Conflict with the Dragon and the Sea*, 394; Maberry, *Cryptopedia*, 112

Pricolic

In Romania, in addition to the vampiric revenant called a pricolic, there is a vampiric creature by the same name, but it is born of an incestuous relationship and has a tail. This person has the ability to shape-shift into a dog, although whether this is a given talent or something gifted to the pricolic by the Devil remains to be answered. While in his dog form, the pricolic mingles in the company of wolves. The person will find it begins to spend more and more time in its other form, until eventually, one day, it shape-shifts into a wolf and, giving in to its wanderlust, joins a pack. To prevent it from attacking family and livestock, the pricolic can be kept at bay by leaving offerings of food for it to eat.

Source: Melton, *Vampire Book*

Prometheus

A benevolent second generation TITAN, Prometheus ("having forethought") was the only character in all of ancient Greek mythology to defy the god Zeus (Jupiter) in a heroic fashion. In one version of the myth he created the first humans; when Zeus called to him to assist in deciding how best humanity should make sacrificial offerings to him, the TITAN tricked the god into accepting animal bones and fat, allowing mankind to retain the flesh and edible organs. Upon discovering the deception Zeus withheld the use of fire from man but Prometheus, realizing their survival depended on its use, stole it from the heavens and delivered it to earth. Enraged, Zeus plotted revenge against Prometheus and commissioned Hephaistos (Vulcan) to create a companion species to Prometheus' all-male race, a beautiful but treacherous female they named Pandora ("all gifts"). The first woman married Prometheus' simple-minded brother Epimetheus ("afterthought"); she later became responsible for releasing all of the evil into the world. For the trickster TITAN, Zeus had Prometheus chained to a mountain crag where every day an eagle would come, rip his liver from his body and devour it; during the night the organ would grow back and the wound would heal. This punishment was delivered daily for untold years until the hero Hercules (Heracles) rescued Prometheus.

Source: Daly, *Greek and Roman Mythology, A to Z*, 121–3; Dowden, *Companion to Greek Mythology*, 52, 54, 130; Hard, *Routledge Handbook of Greek Mythology*, 96

Prudr

Variations: Hlok, Prúðr, Thurd

One of the many named VALKYRIE (a NYMPH of battle) in Norse mythology, Prudr ("power") is listed with GEIRONUL, GOLL, HERFJOTUR, HILDR, HLOKK, RADGRIOR, RANDGRIDR, REGINLEIF, SKEGGJOLD, and SKOGUL as one of the VALKYRIES who carry mead to the EINHERJAR in Valhalla.

Source: Conway, *Falcon Feather and Valkyrie Sword*, 211; Ellis, *Road to Hel*, 69

Pugot

Variations: Cafre, Child-Snatcher, Kafar, Mánguang Anak, Numputol, Pugut

A headless, and occasionally armless, black-skinned humanoid from Filipino folklore, the pugot ("dark" or "headless") has a strong smell about it, and can be found living in abandoned buildings, deserted places, and inside trees. Terrifying in appearance, with blood gushing from its severed stumps, the pugot may snatch up a person and carry them off some distance, but is otherwise harmless; however, encounters with these creatures have been known to cause insanity in some individuals. Consuming centipedes and snakes and enjoying smoking oversized cigars, these creatures also have the ability to shape-shift into various animal forms, all of which have the ability to breathe fire out of their mouth. Some descriptions of the pugot say they are as large as a bull and have tusks protruding from their mouth; moving very quickly through the jungle, they are said to hunt and consume humans.

Source: Eugenio, *Philippine Folk Literature*, 434; Maberry, *Vampire Universe*, 60; Ramos, *Creatures of Midnight*, 13; Rose, *Giants, Monsters, and Dragons*, 300

Puntan

A primordial GIANT from Micronesian legend, Puntan was said to be a vastly large and omnipotent being which came into being of his own accord. After eons of life when he felt he was going to die he gave his sister, Fu'una, precise directions as to how to handle his remains: his back was to become the earth, his chest the sky, his eyes the sun and the moon, and his eyebrow the rainbow.

Source: Flood, *Micronesian Legends*, 1–2; Rose, *Giants, Monsters, and Dragons*, 300

Qilaluga-Nappa

A type of monster from Inuit folklore, the qilaluga-nappa ("half white whale") is basically a species of MERMAN, much larger in size than a human, whose humanoid body transforms at the waist into the lower body of a white whale.

Source: Manlin, *Manlike Monsters on Trial*, 199, 205

Rachaders

Variations: Rach'aders

The Rachaders were the second tribe of GIANTS or evil DJINN in Hindu mythology which made the earth subject to their rule; ultimately they were punished by the gods Shiva and Vishnu.

Source: Brewer, *Dictionary of Phrase and Fable*, 1033; Ruoff, *Standard Dictionary of Facts*, 340; Southey, *Southey's Commonplace Book*, Volume 4, 253

Radgrior (RAHTH-greeth)

Variations: Radgrid, Ráðgri'ðr ("counsel of peace," "Gods' peace")

In Norse mythology Radgrior ("counsel truce" or "violent counsel") was a VALKYRIE (a species of battle NYMPH) who, along with GEIRONUL, GOLL, HERFJOTUR, HILDR, Hlokk, PRUDR, RANDGRIDR, REGINLEIF, SKEGGJOLD, and SKOGUL, served the EINHERJAR ale in Valhalla.

Source: Anderson, Norse Mythology, 269; Ellis, *Road to Hel*, 69; Norroena Society, *Asatrii Edda*, 380

Radsvidr (RAHTHS-vith-r)

Variations: Radsvid

An earth DVERG (DWARF) from Norse mythology, Radsvidr ("council wise" or "swift council") is named in the *Voluspa* part of the *Poetic Edda*.

Source: Daly, *Norse Mythology A to Z*, 22; Norroena Society, *Asatrii Edda*, 381; Sturluson, *Prose Edda*, 26

Raidne

In classical Greek mythology, Raidne ("improvement") was one of the named SIRENS, a type of malicious NYMPH born the offspring of the ancient god of the sea, PHORCYS. Half bird and half woman, she and her sisters would perch on the rocky Sicilian coastline and lure in sailors with their melodious song; once caught, their prey were eaten alive. Although the SIRENS hunted the coastline they lived in an inland meadow.

Source: Roman, *Encyclopedia of Greek and Roman Mythology*, 443; Sherman, *Storytelling*, 416; Smith, *Dictionary of Greek and Roman Biography and Mythology*, 817

Ran (Rahn)

Variations: GULLVEIG, Rana, Ran-Gullveig

An ASYNJR from Norse mythology, Ran ("rapacity" or "robber") was the wife of Aegir, god of the sea. The personification of the dangerous and destructive forces of the ocean, Ran is said to have an extremely malicious disposition and take great delight in drowning sailors and dashing ships upon the rocks.

Source: Norroena Society, *Asatrii Edda*, 381; Oehlenschläger, *Gods of the North*, lix

Randgridr (RAND-greeth)

Variations: Rádgrídr, RADGRIOR, Ragridr, Randgrid, Randgrith ("shield bearer"), Randgríðr ("shield of peace"), Rathgrith, Rostgridr

One of the many named VALKYRIES (a species of battle NYMPH) in Norse mythology, Randgridr ("shield destroyer") is listed with GEIRONUL, GOLL, HERFJOTUR, HILDR, HLOKK, PRUDR, RADGRIOR, REGINLEIF, SKEGGJOLD, and SKOGUL as one of the eleven VALKYRIES who carry mead to the EINHERJAR in Valhalla.

Source: Anderson, Norse Mythology, 269; Conway, *Falcon Feather and Valkyrie Sword*, 211; Ellis, *Road to Hel*, 69; Norroena Society, *Asatrii Edda*, 381

Rangbein (RANG-bayn)

Variations: Rangbeinn

In Norse mythology Rangbein ("bent bone" or "bowlegged") was one of the many named Jotnar (see JOTUN) about whom, beyond a name, there is little or nothing else known.

Source: Norroena Society, *Asatrii Edda*, 381;

Rangda

In Balinese mythology Rangda ("widow") is a female demonic witch, queen of the leyaks (a type of vampiric witch) and the enemy of the benevolent spirit king, BARONG. In dance dramas she is depicted as being a frightful old woman with pendulous breasts, wearing hardly any clothing; her eyes bulge from her head, boar-like tusks protrude from her mouth, her hair is long and white, her long tongue lolls from her mouth, and she has claw-like finger- and toenails; her voice is loud and shrill and she is prone to releasing terrifying BANSHEE-like shrieks.

Legend says Rangda was an eleventh century Balinese queen banished from court for practicing black magic against the king's second wife. After the death of the king, Rangda brings about a plague, killing half the population.

BARONG, an eternal force of good and narcissistic on a cosmic scale, is the enemy of Rangda and childeater, prostitute, and the personification of black magic, death, and evil. In the stories he is always able to thwart her plans but never truly defeats or destroys her.

Source: Beers, *Women and Sacrifice*, 51–3; Rosen, *Mythical Creatures Bible*, 353

Rapha

Variations: Ha Rapha (The Rapha), Rapha of Gath

According to some biblical scholars, Rapha ("Giant") of Gath was the father of five sons, all GIANTS, the most noteworthy of which was GOLIATH OF GATH, the GIANT slain by a young King David; other scholars believe Rapha was not in fact a GIANT but an ancient ancestor to which many GIANTS traced their lineage. The example most cited appears in 2 Samuel 21:18 which reads "In the course of time, there was another battle with the Philistines, at Gob. At that time Sibbekai the Hushathite killed Saph, one of the descendants of Rapha." It has been suggested by some Rapha was in fact not a GIANT but rather a demigod or god of the Underworld.

Source: Mandel, *Who's Who in the Jewish Bible*, 331; Ward, *Homiletic Review*, Volume 26, 509

Rarog (RAH-rook)

Variations: Jarog, Rarach, Rarch, Rarich, Swarog

In Polish folklore Rarog was a DWARF who had the ability to shape-shift into a falcon, hawk, and whirlwind. It was an old custom to throw a knife into a whirlwind in order to attempt to kill the supernatural being within; some believed Rarog was a demon or spirit. While averting their eyes, they would say "a belt around your neck" in hopes it would strangle itself and die.

Source: Dvornik, *The Slavs*, 49; Jakobson, *Selected Writings*, 7

Reginleifr (REHG-in-lay v-r)

Variations: Reginleif

One of the many named VALKYRIES (a species of battle NYMPH) in Norse mythology; Reginleifr ("heritage of the gods," "the mighty," "power trace") is listed with GEIRONUL, GOLL, HERFJOTUR, HILDR, HLOKK, PRUDR, RADGRIOR, RANDGRIDR, SKEGGJOLD, and SKOGUL as one of the VALKYRIES who carry mead to the EINHERJAR in Valhalla.

Source: Conway, *Falcon Feather and Valkyrie Sword*, 211; Ellis, *Road to Hel*, 69; Norroena Society, *Asatrii Edda*, 381

Rephaim

Variations: Refa'im

One of the races of GIANTS said to live in Palestine, the Rephaim ("dispensers of fertility" or "weakeners") were the descendants of the WATCHERS and the women of Canaan; they were described as being gigantic of stature and having great strength. In the War of the Four Kings the Rephaim were listed among those defeated along with the EMIM and the ZUZIM. The Raphaite civilization were said to be cave dwellers.

Source: Aichele, *Violence, Utopia and the Kingdom of God*, 52; Garnier, *Worship of the Dead*, 93–4; Singer, *Jewish Encyclopedia*, Volume 5, 657

Rhea

Variations: Magna Mater deorum Idaea ("great mother of gods idaean"), Thea

A TITAN from classical Greek mythology, Rhea was born the daughter of the TITANS Uranus and the Earth, Gaea; her siblings were COEUS, CRIUS, CRONUS, HYPERION, IAPETUS, MNEMOSYNE, OCEANUS, PHOEBE, TETHYS, THEIA, and THEMIS. Collectively the siblings were known as the Titanides. In both Greek and Roman mythology Rhea is symbolic of the moon and in symbology she utilized the swan, a beautiful and gentle creature but also a formidable opponent.

Rhea married her brother CRONUS and together they had six godling children, three boys (Hades [Dis], Poseidon [Neptune], and Zeus [Jupiter]) and three girls (Demeter [Ceres], Hestia [Vesta], and Hera [Juno]). Because there had been a prophecy his children would one day remove him from power, CRONUS consumed each of his children shortly after their birth. Overcome with grief after the consumption of her children, Rhea sought out the advice of her mother, Gaea, who suggested she replace the next child born with a stone and hide the infant. When her son Zeus (Jupiter) was born Rhea did as her mother said.

Source: Lemprière, *Classical Dictionary*, 785; Littleton, *Gods, Goddesses, and Mythology*, Volume 2, 414

Rindr (RIND-r)

Variations: Rind, Rinda, Rinde, Rindur, Rindus, Wrindr

An ASYNJR from Norse mythology, Rindr ("the wise") is also sometimes said to be a goddess or a human princess, but no matter her species or how the story is told, she was impregnated by the god Odin and gave birth to the last of the Aesir, a son named Váli (Bous).

Source: Grimes, *Norse Myths*, 295; Norroena Society, *Asatrii Edda*, 381

Risir (Rye-seer)

Variations: Hrisi, Rísi

A species of JOTUN in Norse folklore, the risir are described as being not only handsome but more beautiful than the ELVES; they were also easy to get along with, as intelligent as the average person, and the advisors of the TROLLS. One of the legendary leaders of the risir was named Gudmundr ("gift of the gods") and he ruled the land of Risaland, a frozen mountain chain separated them from Greenland.

Source: Fossum, *Norse Discovery of America*, 51; Waggoner, *Sagas of Giants and Heroes*, vx-i

Ritho

Variations: Rion, Rions

A GIANT from medieval Arthurian folklore, Ritho was noted for being fierce and strong; he lived upon Mount Aravius (Mount Snowdon). Ritho was in the custom of removing the beards from all the kings he had slain and making them into furs for himself. According to the story he had already collected the beards of twenty kings and was seeking out a total of thirty in all. He had, in his estimation, generously offered his victims the opportunity to donate their beards rather than having to fight, die, and lose them nevertheless; in the medieval era, this would have been taken as a deeply profound insult, as the beard was symbolic of a king's manhood. Ultimately, Arthur defeats the GIANT, killing him but admitting Ritho was the second most powerful and fierce GIANT he ever confronted.

Source: Daniels, *Encyclopædia of Superstitions, Folklore, and the Occult Sciences of the World*, 1378; Bruce, *Arthurian Name Dictionary*, 425; Wheatley, *Merlin*, ccxxiii-iv

Rota (ROHT-a)

Variations: Róta

One of the many named VALKYRIEs in Norse mythology, Rota ("creator of confusion," "she who causes turmoil"), along with fellow maidens GUDR and SKULD, is always sent by the god Odin to the battlefield to decide which men will die and which will be victorious.

Source: Ellis, *Road to Hel*, 69; Norroena Society, *Asatrii Edda*, 349

Rusalka, plural: Rusalki

Variations: Chertovka ("demoness"), Khitka ("abductor"), Loskotukha ("tickler"), Shutovka ("joker")

A rusalka is a species of succubus-like water NYMPH from Slavic folklore. Its name loosely translates to mean "MERMAID." Rusalki are seen as the demons of the dualistic quality of nature, created when a woman dies an unnatural death, such as in a drowning, dying unbaptized, dying a virgin, or having committed suicide. They are described as looking like pale, lithe, startlingly beautiful women with loose and wild-looking green hair or as ugly large-breasted creatures. Most commonly seen in the summer and winter, rusalki prey upon men, using their charms to lure men into the water where they will tickle them to death. Controlling the cycles of the moon, these creatures are said to direct the clouds across the sky as well as control the weather and rainfall. The rusalki are the symbol of life and death and live in the forest near rivers or lakes during spring and summer months; they live in the water in the winter months. Each individual rusalka has a unique persona with her own tale.

Source: Andrews, *Dictionary of Nature Myths*, 165; Mack, *Field Guide to Demons*, 19–21; Phillips, *Forests of the Vampire*, 67; Riasanovsky, *California Slavic Studies*, Vol.11, 65–6; *Slavic and East European Folklore Association Journal*, Volume 3, Issue 2, 59, 62

Saci

Variations: Saci-Perere

In Afro-Brazilian folklore the saci is a one-legged primordial DWARF; described as wearing a red hood and smoking a pipe made of a seashell, he also had holes in his hands in some stories. The saci have magical powers and travel by means of whirlwinds. Less of a prankster and more of a minor annoyance, saci cause eggs to not hatch, release animals from their pens, and spill salt. Saci cannot cross running water and are compelled to untie knots.

Source: Maberry, *They Bite*, 320–21; Peek, *African Folklore*, 179

Saekarlsmuli (SAI-karls-mool-i)

In Norse mythology, Saekarlsmuli ("sea-man's mouth" or "seaman's nose") was one of the many named Jotnar (see JOTUN) about whom, beyond a name, there is nothing else known.

Source: Norroena Society, *Asatrii Edda*, 382

Salbanelli

Born of the union between the SALVANELLI and a *strega* ("witch"), the salbanelli are quarter-fairy beings from the folklore of northern Italy; they are considered to be fairy hybrids.

Source: Arrowsmith, *Field Guide to the Little People*, 105; Grimassi, *Hereditary Witchcraft: Secrets of the Old Religion*, 83

Salfangr (SAL-vang)

Variations: Salfang

In Norse mythology Salfangr ("bargain grasper" or "hall robber") was one of the many named Jotnar (see JOTUN) about whom, beyond a name, there is little to nothing else known.

Source: Norroena Society, *Asatrii Edda*, 382

Salmon People

In the folklore of the Haida people of the Pacific Northwest Coast of North America, the salmon people were one of the many supernatural ocean people who lived in underwater villages scattered up and down the shore. Since the ocean people were in control of a large part of the food supply, they not only were held in the highest of regard but were also appealed to for assistance with offerings of rare flicker feathers, grease, and tobacco.

Source: Goldenweiser, *Early Civilization*, 63

Salvanelli

Variations: Sanguanello

Born of the union between the AGUANE and the SILVANI, the Salvanelli were half-fay beings from the folklore of northern Italy. The name of these hybrids refers to the glint of light from the surface of a mirror or the sparkling surface of water. It was not unusual for a salvanelli to take a *strega* ("witch") as its mate, as Italian fay and witches were said to share a common bloodline. Children produced from this coupling are known as SALBANELLI.

Source: Arrowsmith, *Field Guide to the Little People*, 107; Grimassi, *Hereditary Witchcraft: Secrets of the Old Religion*, 83; Rose, *Spirits, Fairies, Leprechauns, and Goblins*, 282

Samendill (SAM-ehn-dil)

In Norse mythology Samendill ("familiar foe") was one of many Jotnar (see JOTUN) about whom, beyond a name, little to nothing else is known.

Source: Norroena Society, *Asatrii Edda*, 383

Samodiva (Sah-mo-de-va)

Variations: Divi-Te Zeni ("demon women"), Samodivi, Samovili

A type of vampiric wood NYMPH or nature spirit from Bulgaria, the samodivi (as they are collectively called) look like young women, wearing their hair down and loose, and occasionally sighted with wings. They live in old trees or in natural caves and are said to dress in simple clothes tied with a green belt decorated with feathers, a bow and quiver slung across their back. With little to fear, as they not only have the natural ability to fly but also have control over all the elements, samodivi patrol the woods riding upon the backs of stags whose bridle tack is reined with live snakes. Should a samodiva ("divinity" or "devil") happen across a hunter, it will kill him, taking the unfortunate person's head as a trophy and draining the body dry of its blood. Should he escape, it will cause a drought in his village.

Anyone who comes across a samodiva dancing at night in the woods will not be able to resist joining it, and will enjoy its merrymaking all night long. When the sun rises, only the samodiva remains, as its dance partner is never seen again.

There is a Serbian myth in which a samodiva named Villa raised Prince Marko, nursing him at her own breast. The prince developed supernatural powers. He rode upon a winged horse named Dapple and had a samodiva stepsister named Gyura.

Source: Georgieva, *Bulgarian Mythology*, 75, 81; MacDermott, *Bulgarian Folk Customs*, 68, 69; McClelland, *Slayers and Their Vampires*, 103; Perkowski, *Vampires of the Slavs*, 42

San-Shen Kuo Yan

A race of monstrous people from Chinese folklore, the San-Shen Kuo Yan are described as having a single head conjoined to three bodies.

Source: Rose, *Giants, Monsters, and Dragons*, 319

Sangride (SAN-greeth)

Variations: Sangrid, Sangridr, Sanngrid, Sanngridr

A VALKYRIE (NYMPH of battle) in Norse mythology, Sangride ("true destroyer") along with her fellow VALKYRIES GEIRSKOGUL, GONDULL, GUNNR, HILDR, HJOR, HJORTHRIMUL, SKOGUL, SVIPUL, and THRIMUL would work a great loom together. Raised on spears, the warp was made from the guts of men and was weighed down with human heads; the shuttle was made from an arrow and the spools from swords. The entire weft wept with blood.

Source: Conway, *Falcon Feather and Valkyrie Sword*, 211; Grimes, *Norse Myths*, 21; Grimm, *Teutonic Mythology*, 421; Norroena Society, *Asatrii Edda*, 383

Saos

A race of GIANTS who originated from Kheiber, the Saos had a well-defined culture and religion; numerous, they founded many settlements and lived peacefully until Moslems entered into their region and through violence and war attempted to convert them to their faith. Those Saos who eventually converted were allowed to live as the slaves of the Moslems, but the ones who remained steadfast in their faith were slaughtered to the last.

Source: DeLoach, *Giants*, 60

Sarabroth

According to François Rabelais (AD 1494–1553), who compiled the lineage of the GIANTS, Sarabroth was listed as the son of CHALBROTH, "the progenitor of the race," and was the father of FARIBROTH.

Source: Ozeli, *Works of Francis Rabelais*, 11; Rabelais, *Hours with Rabelais*, 80

Satyr

In Greek mythology, satyrs are a type of nature spirit living in the mountains and woods; described as having the upper half of a man and the lower half of a goat, curly hair, flat noses, full beards, pointed ears, a long thick tail, and short goat horns atop their head, in art they were often depicted wearing a wreath of ivy and carrying a *thyrsus* (the rod of Dionysus [Bacchus] tipped with a pine cone).

There are many creation stories for the satyrs; according to the Greek poet, Hesiod, they were born of the five OREAD granddaughters of Phoroneus and were described as being "worthless and unsuitable for work." The satyrs' fondness for wanton carousing made them perfect companions for the gods Dionysus (Bacchus) and Pan (Faunus). Lovers of boys, women, and wine, they play bagpipes, cymbals, castanets, and pipes and love to dance with NYMPHS. Older satyrs were referred to as *sileni* and younger ones were called *satyrisci*.

Source: Conner, *Everything Classical Mythology Book*, 191–92; Hansen, *Classical Mythology: A Guide to the Mythical World of the Greeks and Romans*, 279–80; Littleton, *Gods, Goddesses, and Mythology*, Volume 11, 1256

Sceadugenga

A creature mentioned in the Old English epic poem *Beowulf*, sceadugenga ("shadow-goer" or "wanderer in the darkness") may have been a reference to the story's antagonist, GRENDEL; it has come to reference nature spirits who, with the ability to shape-shift, are neither wholly alive nor deceased.

Source: Amodio, *Anglo Saxon Literature Handbook*, 304; Sedgefield, *Beowulf*, 23, 223

Sciapod

Variations: Monoscelans, plural Monocoli; Sciapod ("shadow foot"), Sciapods, Sciopod, Skiapod, Skiapode

A race of men first described by Pliny the Elder

(AD 23–79) in his work *Historia Naturalis* (AD 77), they were later mentioned in many fourteenth century traveler journals. The sciapods had one foot so large they could lie on their back and use it as a sunscreen. Fast runners, they lived on the fragrance of fruit alone; if ever they should breathe in corrupted air, they would die. There was also mention of a four-legged species of sciapod who would use one of its legs for shade while walking on the other three.

Source: Barber, *Dictionary of Fabulous Beasts*, 128; Rose, *Giants, Monsters, and Dragons*, 253, 323

Sea-Grizzly Bear People

In the folklore of the Haida people of the Pacific Northwest Coast of North America, the sea-grizzly bear people were one of the many supernatural ocean people who lived in underwater villages along the shore. Since the ocean people were in control of a large part of the food supply, they not only were held in the highest regard but were appealed to for assistance with offerings of rare flicker feathers, grease, and tobacco. They have been described as having fins attached to their arms.

Source: Goldenweiser, *Early Civilization*, 63

Sea-Satyr

A species of MERMAN, the sea-satyr is depicted as having arms which end in pincers, the head of a horned animal, and short webbed feet.

Source: White, *Book of Beasts*, 266; Zell-Ravenheart, *Wizard's Bestiary*, 86

Seatco

In the folklore of the Indians living in the Pacific northwest the Seatco, neither animal nor man, are said to live around and in the beautiful lake located at the base of Loo-wit Mountain (Mount Saint Helens), United States of America. These beings were the spirits of people from many different tribes who had been cast out for their evil tendencies; having banded together, they called themselves the Seatco, after their leader, and did little but commit acts of evil and wrongdoing.

The Seatco caused storms to ravish the coast, throwing dead fish upon the beach, and tipping over canoes, drowning their occupants. They were also great impersonators, mimicking the sound of animals, birds, and the wind passing through the trees; furthermore they could make these sounds seem either near or far off. Whenever an Indian killed one of the Seatco, the tribe would retaliate and kill twelve people from the offender's tribe.

The leader of these spirits, Seatco, was a GIANT terrible to behold as his face was animalistic; he was taller than the tallest fir tree and had a voice which roared louder than the ocean. Seatco was also immensely strong, able to destroy an entire forest, pulling it up by the roots, create a mountain range by stacking boulders, cause earthquakes, and change the course of a river by blowing hard.

Source: Clark, *Indian Legends of the Pacific Northwest*, 46, 63, 125; Washington State, *Report of the Governor of Washington Territory*, 59

Secundilla

According to Pliny the Elder, the Roman author and natural philosopher, during the reign of Caesar Augustus POSIO and Secundilla, the husband and wife GIGANTES, were six inches taller than the GIGANTE GABBARAS. The bodies of POSIO and Secundilla were said to have been preserved in the Museum of the Sallustian family.

Source: Ashton, *Curious Creatures in Zoology*, 37; Wood, *Giants and Dwarfs*, 22

Seilenoi

Variations: Seilenos

Lustful nature spirits of Greek mythology who were a part of the retinue of the god Bacchus (Dionysos), the seilenoi were relentless in their music, pursuit of NYMPHS, and wine-drinking. Seilenoi are easily mistaken for SATYRS in art, as they are depicted as anthropoids with bestial features who are male and visibly aroused; in early art, SATYRS were shown with horse ears, legs, and tails but in the Hellenistic period they took on more of the semblance of a goat having horn-stubs and cloven hooves.

Seilenoi first appear in text as the lovers of the mountain NYMPHS in Homeric Hymn to Aphrodite (Venus). Devoted to their merry-making, drinking, and carousing, seilenoi are utter cowards and will flee confrontation except on the occasion when they are in a Dionysiac frenzy.

The leader of the species is named Seilenos and was said to have been a philosopher, preacher, scholar, and tutor to a young Bacchus (Dionysos).

Source: Coulter, *Encyclopedia of Ancient Deities*, 431; Hard, *Routledge Handbook of Greek Mythology*, 212–13; Rose, *Handbook of Greek Mythology*, 128

Sela (SEHL-a)

In Norse mythology Sela ("woman") was an ASYNJR slain by Egill; she was the sister of the JOTUN KÖLL. Beyond her name, there is little or nothing else known.

Source: Norroena Society, *Asatrii Edda*, 383; Rydberg, *Our Fathers' Godsaga*, 196

Senjemand

A JOTUN from Norse folklore, Senjemand lived on Senjen Island and was in a constant state of anger as a nun on nearby Grypto Island would sing her morning hymn which he could not help but hear. Senjemand was in love with a beautiful maiden ASYNJR named JUTERNA-JESTA but when he proposed to her, she scornfully rejected him as being both too old and ugly to marry. Enraged, he shot a flint arrow at her while she was at home, some eighty miles away. TORGE, also a GIANT, saw the arrow approaching JUTERNA-JESTA, whom he also was in love with, and threw his hat up in the air to intercept the missile and foul the shot. Fearful of TORGE's wrath, Senjemand prepared to escape but the sun rose and turned him, the hat, and arrow into stone, today called Torghatten Mountain.

Senjemand is also the name of the species of mountain-dwelling Jotnar (see JOTUN) associated with the Island of Senjen.

Source: Guerber, *Hammer of Thor*, 163–4; Rose, *Giants, Monsters, and Dragons*, 327

Sheshai

A GIANT from Hebrew Scriptures, Sheshai, along with his brother TALMAI, ruled over their people, the ANAKIM, from the country of Hebron (Kirjath-Arba). Their eldest brother, AHIMAN, was the most feared of the three sons of ANAK. Sheshai was described as being six cubits tall (approximately nine feet; a *cubit* is the distance from a man's elbow to the tip of his middle finger).

Sheshai and his brothers were, according to the Book of Judges, slain by Judah.

Source: DeLoach, *Giants*, 260; Taylor, *Calmets Great Dictionary of the Holy Bible*, n.pag.

Shtriga (Stree-ga)

Variation: Stringla

Albanian folklore tells of a female VAMPIRIC WITCH known as a shtriga, which preys on children. By day the being lives as a normal member of the community, even attending church; but at night it hunts for children in its animal form of a bee, fly, or moth. It approaches the child while it is asleep and steals their life-energy, leaving the body completely undisturbed in the bed. Parents oftentimes leave a piece of garlic-flavored bread near their sleeping child as a repellent to the shtriga.

To determine who in the community may be a shtriga, it is said to wait until everyone has gone into the church to celebrate mass. Then, while everyone is inside, using some pig bones make a cross and hang it over the church doors. Everyone who is not a shtriga will be able to pass through the door, leaving the shtriga trapped within.

Shtriga periodically spit up blood—some say it is the blood of their victims. It is believed if you

take some of the blood and place it on a silver coin and then wrap it in a cloth, it can be used as a charm to keep the shtriga away.

Source: American Folklore Society. *Journal of American Folklore*, Volume 64, 309; Kane, *The Dreamer Awakes*, 56, 59; Lockyer, *Nature*, Volume 113, 25; Royal Anthropological Institute of Great Britain and Ireland. *Man*, Volume, 23–25, 190–91

Si-Te-Cah

A race of red-haired GIANTS from Paiutes folklore, the Si-te-cah ("tule eaters"; *tule* is a fibrous reed used to construct their assault rafts; it was not a plant native to the region) were so hostile the region's tribes of Indians banded together and waged war against them. After many months of fighting, the Indians were able to force the Si-te-cah into what is now called Lovelock Cave, Nevada, United States of America. Refusing to come out, the Indians threw kindling, covered the opening with brush, and set it all ablaze, killing the GIANTS to the last.

Source: Joseph, *Unlocking the Prehistory of America*, 235; Olsen, *Sacred Places North America*, 59

Siats

In the folklore and legends of the Ute people in the Great Basin region of the United States of America there was a race of cannibalistic, monstrous humanoids known as the siats; the females of the species were known as BAPETS.

Source: Rose, *Giants, Monsters, and Dragons*, 39

Sídhe

Variations: Aes Sídhe, Aos Sí, Si, Sidhe, Sith

Sídhe ("people of the [FAIRY] hills" or "something which controls the elements") is the word used in Ireland and the highlands of Scotland to name the very tall, shining race of fairy people who are believed to belong to both the earthly and heavenly realms. The word *sidhe* and TUATHA DE DANANN are used interchangeably. Their name is derived from the ancient barrows or fairy forts where they are believed to reside.

The sídhe are said to be extremely beautiful and although youthful in appearance give the impression of being aristocratic, mature, and powerful, not just in body but in ability and mind as well. Sídhe were generally skillful artisans but were considered experts and excelled in baking, crafts, dancing, hunting, metalwork, music, rades, spinning, and weaving. Many of their tales will show they held beauty, fertility, generosity, love, loyalty, order, and truth in very high regard; they would repay in kind any generosity or hospitality afforded to them. They would offer their assistance to their favorite humans and would on occasion take one as a lover or spouse.

Some families still claim their bloodline caries sídhe blood, such as the MacLeodse of Scotland.

Many animals, both domestic and wild, are associated with sídhe and there are numerous stories of their great love of horses. Although as a general rule fairy horses were beautiful they were also too dangerous and wild for a mortal to ride; fairy cattle were generally benign and helpful to mankind.

Source: Evans-Wentz, *Fairy Faith in Celtic Countries*, 59; McCoy, *Witch's Guide to Faery Folk*, 20; Rose, *Spirits, Fairies, Leprechauns, and Goblins*, 4

Sigrdrifa (SIG-r-dreev-ah)

Variations: Driva, Idun,

One of the many named VALKYRIEs (NYMPHs of battle) in Norse mythology; Sigrdrifa ("giver of glory," "victory blizzard") was the lover of Volund in the legendary saga *Ynglingasaga* written by the Icelandic historian and poet Snorri Sturluson around 1225.

Source: Puryear, *Nature of Asatru*, 233; Sturleson, *Viking Anthology*, n.pag.

Sigurdrifta

One of the many named VALKYRIEs (NYMPHs of battle) in Norse mythology; Sigurdrifta was the wisest of her kind but once denied victory to a hero to whom Odin had already promised victory. For her punishment, Odin stung her with sleeping thorns causing her to fall into a sleep so deep she would not awaken until a man completely without fear came and claimed her for his wife. The hero Sigurd found her high up in the mountains surrounded by a ring of fire. He removed her armor, as it had grown into her flesh, and awakened her asking to be taught wisdom. After speaking at length of magic runes and sorcery she fell back asleep. Sigurdrifta is often mistaken for and associated with BRUNHILDE.

Source: Monaghan, *New Book of Goddesses and Heroines*, 281; Sturleson, *Viking Anthology*, n.pag.

Sihon (si-hahn)

A GIANT from Hebrew Scriptures, Sihon ("tempestuous") was a king and like King OG of Bashan, he and his people were the remnants of the REPHAIM ("GIANTS"). He was said to be very powerful, commanding great respect, and had under his command an army which stood as a threat against the Hebrews. Sihon was said to resemble OG in bravery and stature. Rabbinical literature claims him to be OG's brother and likely the grandson of Shamhazai, a fallen angel.

Source: DeLoach, *Giants*, 263; de Rothschild, *History and Literature of the Israelites*, 143; Mandel, *Ultimate Who's Who in the Bible*, 601, 651

Silvani

The nature spirits of the mountains of northern Italy known as the AGUANE were said to be able to successfully mate with the silvani ("wooded") thereby producing offspring known as SALVANELLI. Described as looking like winged wood-NYMPHS, they had a ghost-like appearance and dressed in animal furs and red clothing.

Source: Euvino, *Complete Idiot's Guide to Italian History and Culture*, 274; Grimassi, *Hereditary Witchcraft: Secrets of the Old Religion*, 83; McCoy, *Witch's Guide to Faery Folk*, 311–12

Sindur

An ASYNJR from Norse mythology, Sindur ("dusk") one of the WAVE MAIDENS who were mother to the god Heimdall; she was the daughter of the god of the sea, Aegir. She, like her sisters, was said to have snow-white skin, blue eyes, and billowing blond hair; in one hand they carried a golden goblet filled with mead and in the other seashells filled with the finest foods. They wore long transparent robes of green or blue trimmed in white. When not serving food in the hall, they played on the shore in groups of three.

Source: Daly, *Norse Mythology A to Z*, 47; Grimes, *Norse Myths*, 255

Sippai (Sip-i)

Variations: Saph

A GIANT of Gath, Sippai ("bason-like") was likely one of Goliath's four brothers; he was described as standing at such an enormous height everyone who saw him could not help but stare. In the battle between Israel and the Philistines at Gob, one of King David's men, Sibecai the Hushathite, is said to have killed him.

Source: DeLoach, *Giants*, 260, 271; Mandel, *Ultimate Who's Who in the Bible*, 601, 651

Siren

Variations: Agloaopheme, Seirenes

In ancient Greek mythology the sirens ("bewitching ones" or "those who bind") were a type of malicious NYMPH born the offspring of the ancient god of the sea, PHORCYS (Phorkys), or from the drops of blood hitting the earth from the broken horn of Acheloos; ancient sources conflict. Half bird and half woman, the sisters would perch on the rocky Sicilian coastline and lure in sailors with their melodious song; once caught, their prey were eaten alive. Although the Sirens hunted the coastline they lived inland in a meadow.

Homer, the greatest ancient Greek epic poet and author of *The Iliad* and *Odyssey*, named only two sirens, but on vases they were usually depicted as three. Occasionally, the sirens were portrayed as being bearded. As time progressed their number increased to five and grew as authors continued to add to their flock.

Over time, ancient writers evolved the sirens into MERMAID-like beings who would sit on the rocky shoreline using their beautiful singing voice to lure sailors into the jetty where their ships would wreck. In these later myths the only way to kill a siren was to resist their song; if this was accomplished, the being would kill itself.

Some ancient writers say the sirens lived on the island Anthemoessa but other authors say they lived on three small rocky islands called Sirenum scopuli.

According to the ancient Greek poet Cherilus of Samos, AGLAOPHONOS ("beautiful voice"), MOLPE, and THELXIOPE were the three sirens of Greek mythology; however, Chearchus listed the three sirens as being LEUCOSIA ("the fair" or "white being"), LIGEIA ("maiden face" or "shrill"), and PARTHENOPE ("the tuneful"). Other named sirens were AGLAOPE, AGLAOPHONOS, HIMEROPE, LEUCOSIA, LIGEIA, MOLPE, PARTHENOPE, PEISINOË, RAIDNE, TELES, THELCHTEREIA, THELXEPEIA, and THELXIOPE.

Source: Daly, *Greek and Roman Mythology A to Z*, 118; Fox, *Greek and Roman*, 262–63; Leland, *Unpublished Legends of Virgil*, 37; Littleton, *Gods, Goddesses, and Mythology*, Volume 11, 1269; Smith, *Dictionary of Greek and Roman Biography and Mythology*, 817

Sirin

Variations: Ptitsa Sirin ("sirin bird")

A creature of Russian folklore which likely originated in Persian folklore, the sirin was described as having the face (and sometimes the breasts) of a beautiful maiden but the body of a bird; unlike the SIREN of Greek folklore using its voice to lure sailors to their death, the sirin used its enchanting voice as a reward gifted upon the virtuous. In art the sirin was depicted as having a long peacock tail with distinctive eyes patterned upon it and wearing a crown upon its head. Flying down from heaven it would sing its song to the fortunate few; but it would be the last thing they ever heard, as anyone who has ever listened to its song would instantly forget everything and then die. The sirin is considered to be a heavenly bird of happiness; her counterpart is the ALKONOST, the bird of sorrow.

Source: Alexander, *Fairies*, 153; Dixon-Kennedy, *Encyclopedia of Russian and Slavic Myth and Legend*, 258

Siyokoy (sho-koy)

A species of MERMEN from Filipino folklore, the siyokoy, counterpart to the female sirena (see MERMAID), has the upper body of a man and the lower body of a fish or, in some stories, is an anthropoid whose body is covered in glistening brown or green fish scales and webbed feet. Some descriptions also give them long, green tentacles and gill slits. Siyokoy drown fishermen and consume them for food.

Source: de Las Casas, *Tales from the 7,000 Isles*, xvi; Newton, *Hidden Animals*, 167

Sjofn (SYUHV-n)

An ASYNJR from Norse mythology, Sjofn ("love"), who is sometimes considered to be a goddess, was only concerned with turning the attention of people's minds toward love and romance.

Source: Daly, *Norse Mythology A to Z*, 7; Norroena Society, *Asatrii Edda*, 346; Rydberg, *Norroena, the History and Romance of Northern Europe*, Volume 3, 1035

Skadegamutc (skuh-da-goo-much)

Variations: Skudakumooch', Skite'kmuj

A species of cannibalistic, vampiric GIANTS from northeastern United States of America and Canadian folklore, the skadegamutc ("ghost witch") are corpses by day but at night become active, roaming spirits seeking out a meal of human blood and flesh. A skadegamutc may also be a living person who has the ability to send their spirit out at night in order to hunt. These spirits have been described as looking like a floating ball of light, similar to a will-o'-the-wisp, or as a vague, wispy humanoid form.

The only known methods of destruction of a skadegamutc are to find the location of its corpse, or reveal the identity of the person, and throw it into a roaring fire, destroying it.

Source: Bonvillain, *Native Nations*, 101; Eberhart, *Mysterious Creatures*, 504

Skadi (SKATH-i)

Variations: Andrdis, Skada, Skade, Skadhi, Skaði, Skathi

One of the ASYNJR from Norse mythology, Skadi ("damage," "scathe" or "shadow"), born the daughter of Thjassi making her one of the Aesir, was a well-known skier and hunter; she was married to Njord but lived with the god Odin as his wife on Mannheimr (Thrymheim) and by him had many children, one of which was a son named Seemingr (Saeming). She was also the lover of the god Loki. Eventually, she officially ended her marriage to her husband and married Ullr. Skadi is also sometimes counted as being a goddess of ski and snow.

Source: Grimes, *Norse Myths*, 297; Lindow, *Norse Mythology*, 96, 219, 268; Norroena Society, *Asatrii Edda*, 385

Skafidr (SKA-vith-r)

Variations: Skafidur

A rock DVERG (DWARF) from Norse mythology created by Durinn, Skafidr ("the scraper") is listed as being one of DURINN'S KIN. He, like the others created, paid particular attention to DURINN'S leadership.

Source: Daly, *Norse Mythology A to Z*, 22; Grimes, *Norse Myths*, 7, 260; Norroena Society, *Asatrii Edda*, 385

Skalli (SKAL-i)

In Norse mythology, Skalli ("bald headed") was one of the many named Jotnar (see JOTUN) about whom, beyond a name, there is nothing else known.

Source: Norroena Society, *Asatrii Edda*, 385

Skalmold (SKAL-muhld)

In Norse mythology Skalmold ("sword age" or "sword time") was one of the many named VALKYRIEs (NYMPHs of battle) about whom, beyond a name, there is little or nothing else known.

Source: Conway, *Falcon Feather and Valkyrie Sword*, 211; Norroena Society, *Asatrii Edda*, 385

Skeggjold (SKEHG-yuhld)

Variations: Skegold, Skeggold, Skeggjöld

One of the many named VALKYRIEs in Norse mythology, Skeggjold ("battle axe") is listed with GEIRONUL, GOLL, HERFJOTUR, HLOKK, PRUDR, RADGRIOR, RANDGRIDR, REGINLEIF, SKEGUL, and SKOGUL as one of the eleven VALKYRIEs who carry mead to the EINHERJAR in Valhalla.

Source: Conway, *Falcon Feather and Valkyrie Sword*, 211; Ellis, *Road to Hel*, 69; Norroena Society, *Asatrii Edda*, 385

Skerkir (SKERK-ir)

In Norse mythology, Skerkir ("the noisy") was one of the many named Jotnar (see JOTUN) about whom, beyond a name, there is little or nothing else known.

Source: Norroena Society, *Asatrii Edda*, 385

Skirfir (SKIR-vir)

A rock DVERG (DWARF) from Norse mythology created by DURINN, Skirfir ("skillful artisan") is listed as being one of DURINN'S KIN. He, like the others created, paid particular attention to DURINN'S leadership.

Source: Daly, *Norse Mythology A to Z*, 22; Grimes, *Norse Myths*, 260; Norroena Society, *Asatrii Edda*, 386

Skogsfru

Variations: Skogsrå, Skogsnufa, Skogsnufvar

A species of woodland NYMPH form Danish and Swedish folklore, the skogsfru ("lady [ruler] of the forest" or "WOOD-WIFE") are dangerous and predatory fairies seeking out foolish young men; their typical victims are lumberjacks and hunters.

Although they have the ability to shape-shift into an owl, a skogsfru will appear in a camp as a small but beautiful woman; it will make merry, drinking and singing songs around the campfire until she is able to lure one man away. If the man goes off with it, he will never be seen again; the best way to avoid an encounter with this fay is to pretend not to see it when it wanders into camp.

Source: Keightley, *World Guide to Gnomes, Fairies, Elves, and Other Little People*, 153; MacCulloch, *Celtic and Scandinavian Religions*, 133; Rose, *Spirits, Fairies, Leprechauns, and Goblins*, 295

Skogul (SKUHG-ul)

Variations: Skögul

One of the many named VALKYRIEs (a species of battle NYMPH) in Norse mythology, Skogul ("battle," "rager") along with her fellow VALKYRIES GEIRSKOGUL, GONDULL, GUNNR, HILDR, HJOR, HJORTHRIMUL, SANGRIDE, SVIPUL, and THRIMUL would work a great loom together. Raised on spears, the warp was made from the guts of men and was weighed down with human heads; the shuttle was made from an arrow and the spools from swords. The entire weft wept with blood. She is also listed with GEIRONUL, GOLL, HERFJOTUR, HLOKK, PRUDR, RADGRIOR, RANDGRIDR, REGINLEIF, SKEGGJOLD, and SKEGUL as one of the VALKYRIES who carry mead to the EINHERJAR in Valhalla.

Source: Conway, *Falcon Feather and Valkyrie Sword*, 211; Ellis, *Road to Hel*, 69; Grimes, *Norse Myths*, 21; Norroena Society, *Asatrii Edda*, 386

Skoll (Skuhl)

Variations: Sköll

A JOTUN in wolf form, Skoll ("mockery") was born the son of the god Loki; according to Thorgrimr's *Rhymes* and Snorri Sturluson's (1179–1241) *Prose Edda* he spends his day chasing Sol across the sky. When the day arrives Skoll is able to finally catch up with the sun, he will consume it and bring about the beginning of Ragnarok.

Source: Jennbert, *Animals and Humans*, 50; Norroena Society, *Asatrii Edda*, 386; Zell-Ravenheart, *Wizard's Bestiary*, 90

Skramr (SKRAHM-r)

In Norse mythology, Skramr ("the frightening") was one of the many named Jotnar (see JOTUN) about whom, beyond a name, there is little or nothing else known.

Source: Norroena Society, *Asatrii Edda*, 386

Skrati (SKRAT-i)

In Norse mythology, Skrati ("TROLL") was one of the many named Jotnar (see JOTUN) about whom, beyond a name, there is little or nothing else known.

Source: Norroena Society, *Asatrii Edda*, 386

Skrymer

Variations: Skrymir ("big fellow" or "the large")

A JOTUN from Norse mythology, Skrymer ("boaster") was said to have met the god of thunder, Thor, as he was traveling to Utgard and caused him to lose his way and become lost. Skrymer may have been the god Loki in disguise who had set out to annoy and enrage his brother by first becoming a traveling companion and then being overly friendly, helpful, and exceedingly annoying; she snored all night long, kept their food in a provison sack Thor was not clever enough to open, and caused them to become lost.

Source: Anderson, *Norse Mythology*, 312–20; Norroena Society, *Asatrii Edda*, 386; Oehlenschläger, *Gods of the North*, lxii

Skserir (SKAIR-ir)

In Norse mythology, Skserir ("cutter," "dusk" "twilight") was one of the many named Jotnar (see JOTUN) about whom, beyond a name, there is little or nothing else known.

Source: Norroena Society, *Asatrii Edda*, 385

Skuld

Variations: Skulda, Skulld, Skuldr

One of the many named VALKYRIE in Norse mythology, Skuld ("debt," "necessity," "spinster," "what shall become"), the youngest of the NORNS, along with GUDR and ROTA are always sent by the god Odin to the battlefield to decide which men will die and which will be victorious. Although many and varied VALKYRIE are sent at various times, these three are dispatched on every occasion and she is considered to be their leader.

As the youngest of the three nornir (see NORN), the ASYNJR and VALKYRIE Skuld ("shall be") personifies the future, VERDANDI personifies the present and URDR the eldest personifies the past; all of them are described as looking like old women spinning the threads of a person's destiny into a gigantic tapestry showing the lives of all gods, people, and the history of world—but only of the events fated to happen. She is described as wearing a veil and carrying a scroll. Skuld and her sisters live near Urdarbrunnr Well and see to the upkeep of Ygdrasil.

Sources: Conway, *Falcon Feather and Valkyrie Sword*, 211; Daly, *Norse Mythology A to Z*, 94; Ellis, *Road to Hel*, 69; Grimes, *Norse Myths*, 307

Slaygood

Variations: Slay-Good, Slay Good

In classical English literature, there is GIANT by the name of Slaygood; he was the third of three giants confronted by the everyman character Greatheart (see GRIM and MAUL). According to John Bunyan's work *Pilgrim's Progress* (1682) the allegorical Slaygood hired thieves to work the King's Highway, abducting and murdering pilgrims en route to Vanity Fair; he would then consume their bodies.

Source: Bunyan, *Works of that Eminent Servant of Christ, John Bunyan*, 154, 158, 164, 169; Greaves, *Glimpses of Glory*, 512

Snotra (SNAWT-ra)

An Asynjr from Norse mythology, Snotra ("the courtly" or "the wise") was noted for being both beautiful and having exquisite manners. It has been suspected by some scholars Snotra was a creation of Snorri Sturluson (1179–1271), the Icelandic historian, poet, and politician.

Source: Daly, *Norse Mythology A to Z*, 94; Norroena Society, *Asatrii Edda*, 387

Soini

Variations: Kalkki ("servant"), Kalki ("rogue" or "schalk"), Kullervo

A GIANT and hero from Estonian folklore, Soini was troublesome from his birth. Beginning when he was only three nights old, he trampled his swaddling clothes apart; when he was sent away then and there a smith took Soini in to look after his own child but the GIANT clawed out its eyes, killed it, and then set its cradle on fire. Next he was sent to construct a fence but did so by weaving together pine trees and tying them fast with snakes. When he was older he was employed as a cow driver. One morning the housewife baked a stone in his bread to play what she perceived to be a harmless prank. Soini was enraged when he cut into the loaf and the stone dulled his knife. Playing his idea of a prank back he summoned all the bears and wolves to him; killed the herd of cows and oxen, used their bones to construct musical horns, and then drove the new herd of bears and wolves back to the farm. Soini is deemed a hero in Estonia because of his youthful rudeness and his personal contempt for man's occupations.

Source: Grimm, *Grimm's Household Tales*, 384–5; Grimm, *Teutonic Mythology*, Volume 2, 552–3

Sokmimer (SUHK-meem-ir)

Variations: Sokkmimir ("sinking MIMIR"), Sokkmi'mir, SURTR

A JOTUN from Norse mythology, Sokmimer ("Mimer of the deep") was the personification of the destructive powers of an ocean maelstrom; he was slain by the god Odin.

Source: Anderson, *Norse Mythology*, 200, 458; Norroena Society, *Asatrii Edda*, 387

Solovey-Razboynik

Variations: Rakhmanovich, Solovey Rakhmatovich, Solovewy Razboynik

In Russian and Siberian folklore Solovey-Razboynik ("Nightingale the robber"), the thief of Vor Rakhmano, was a supernatural thief who lived in the forest and killed people with his whistle. The hero Ilya Muromet had to pass this monster on his way to Kiev, Ukraine. Perched in an oak tree, Ilya Muromet smashes Solovey-Razboynik in his white chest, knocking him out of the branches and to the ground, dead.

Source: Kessler, *Cultural Mythology and Global Leadership*, 327; Mangus, *Heroic Ballads of Russia*, 37–8

Somr (SOHM-r)

Variations: Sumarr

A JOTUN from Norse mythology, Somr ("seemly" or "summer") was the personification of summer.

Source: Norroena Society, *Asatrii Edda*, 388

Sorginak

Variations: Sorgina

In Basque mythology the NYMPH-like sorginak were said to be the assistants of the goddess Mari; they were healers, midwives and said to have constructed the megaliths which dot the countryside. The sorginak would also, on Mari's request, take the possessions of those individuals who cheat, lie, steal, and selfishly conceal their personal wealth.

In modern times the word *sorginak* is used in a negative fashion and is synonymous with *witch*.

Source: Bullen, *Basque Gender Studies*, 145–6; Esteban, *Feminist Challenges in the Social Sciences*, 116

Sparti

Variations: The Sown, Spartae, Spartoi

In classical Greek mythology, the Sparti ("sown men") was the collective name for the individuals who went on to become the progenitors of the five leading families of the city of Thebes who formed the military caste.

The city of Thebes was founded by Cadmos, the son of Agemor and Telepha. While attempting to make a sacrifice to Athena (Minerva), a dragon attacked and killed most of his men; under the advice of the goddess he removed the creature's teeth and planted them. Instantly men sprang up from the ground fully grown, armed, and armored; they began fighting one another until only five remained: CHTHONIUS, ECHION, HYPERENOR, PELORUS, and UDAEUS. These autochthonous beings should not be confused with the sown men created by King Aeetes when attempting to prevent Jason and Medea from stealing the Golden Fleece.

Source: Daly, *Greek and Roman Mythology, A to Z*, 29; Dixon-Kennedy, *Encyclopedia of Greco-Roman Mythology*, 86, 205; Westmoreland, *Ancient Greek Beliefs*, 233, 509, 717

Sprettingr (SPREHT-ing-r)

Variations: Spretting

In Norse mythology, Sprettingr was one of the many named Jotnar (see Jotun) about whom, beyond a name, there is nothing else known.

Source: Norroena Society, *Asatrii Edda*, 388; Vigfússonn *Court Poetry: Volume 2*, 425

Starkath Aludreng

An eight-armed JOTUN from Norse mythology, Starkath Aludreng kidnapped the daughter of the king of Alfheim (southeastern Norway), Alfhild, and raped her. According to the *Vikarsbalk* saga, King Alf appealed to the god of thunder, Thor, for his daughter's return. The god slew Starkath Aludreng, rescued the princess, and returned her to her father.

Source: Chadwick, *Stories and Ballads of the Far Past*, 88; Olrik, *Heroic Legends of Denmark*, 4

Stenwyken

Variations: Stuan-Aw-Wkin

Cannibal GIANTS from Okanagan folklore, the stenwyken are a race of hairy GIANTS who reek of burning hair and raid winter storehouses for their berries, dried meat, fish, and roots; they are also known for stealing women to keep as mates.

Source: Eberhart, *Mysterious Creatures*, 521

Steropes

From classical Greek mythology, Steropes ("lightning") along with ARGES ("flashing" or "thunderbolt") and BRONTES ("thunder") are the three elder CYCLOPS, the sons of Uranus and Gaea. He and his brothers were all born with a single eye in the middle of their forehead and were exceedingly strong. Their siblings were the HECATONCHEIRES and the TITANS. After the rise of the Olympian gods, Steropes ("thunder") and his brothers were slain by the god Apollo because they created the thunderbolt which killed his son, Asclepius.

Source: Daly, *Greek and Roman Mythology A to Z*, 39–40; Daniels, *Encyclopædia of Superstitions, Folklore, and the Occult Sciences of the World*, 1375–8;

Stigandi (STIG-and-i)

In Norse mythology, Stigandi ("leading," "striding") was one of the many named Jotnar (see Jotun) about whom, beyond a name, there is nothing else known.

Source: Norroena Society, *Asatrii Edda*, 388

Storverkr (STOHR-verk-r)

Variations: Storverk

In Norse mythology, Storverkr ("mighty worker," "strong worker") was one of the many named Jotnar (see JOTUN) about whom, beyond a name, there is nothing else known. According to the *Vikarsbalk* saga, he was born the son of the eight-armed JOTUN STARKATH ALUDRENG and Alfhild, the daughter of King Alfheim, whom he had kidnapped and raped.

Source: Norroena Society, *Asatrii Edda*, 388; Olrik, *Heroic Legends of Denmark*, 4

Straw-Drinkers

Variations: Gens Ore

According to Pliny the Elder in his work *Natural History*, the straw-drinkers were a race of beings similar to the ASTOMI of India. Straw-drinkers have ridged faces and neither nose nor mouth but rather a single orifice by which they breathe, eat, and drink through a straw; it is assumed because of their lack of mouth they are incapable of speaking.

Source: Friedman, *Monstrous Races in Medieval Art and Thought*, 19, 29; Kline, *Maps of Medieval Thought*, 143, 151

Struthopodes

The Struthopodes ("sparrow-footed") were a race of people said to live in the southern part of India and were described in medieval bestiaries; the females of the species had extremely tiny feet, as small as a bird's, but the males had gigantic feet, a cubit in length (a *cubit* is the distance from a man's elbow to the tip of his middle finger).

Source: Pliny the Elder, *Natural History of Pliny*, Volume 2, 132; Urban, *Gentleman's Magazine and Historical Review*, Volume 2, 535

Stumi

In Norse mythology, Stumi ("pitch dark") was one of the many named Jotnar (see JOTUN) about whom, beyond a name, there is nothing else known.

Source: Norroena Society, *Asatrii Edda*, 388

Styx

An OCEANID and TITAN from ancient Greek mythology, Styx was born the first and most eminent of the daughters of the first generation TITAN OCEANIDS and his sister wife TETHYS; she and the TITAN PALLAS have four children together: Force, Power, Rivalry, and Victory. As she was the first to side with Zeus (Jupiter) at the outbreak of the Titanomachy, he allowed her and her children to stay in his own home during the war and granted her elevated status on Mount Olympus.

Source: Daly, *Greek and Roman Mythology, A to Z*, 141; Westmoreland, *Ancient Greek Beliefs*, 103

Sudre

Variations: Sudri

In Norse mythology Sudre was one of the four DVERGAR (DWARFS) who were appointed by the gods to hold up the sky which they constructed from the skull of YMIR. AUSTRE held up the East, NORDRE held the North, Sudre held the South, and VESTRE held the West.

Source: Anderson, *Norse Mythology*, 183; Grimes, *Norse Myths*, 9; Norroena Society, *Asatrii Edda*, 388; Sturluson, *Prose Edda*, 26

Surdi

A DVERG (DWARF) from Norse mythology, Surdi is mentioned by name only in the *Voluspa* part of the *Poetic Edda*.

Source: Daly, *Norse Mythology A to Z*, 22

Surtr

Variations: DURNIR, Durinn, Durnin, SOKMIMIR, Sokkmimir, Surt, Surter, Surti, Surtur, Svarthofsi

One of the ELDJÖTNAR (FIRE GIANT) from Norse mythology, Surtr ("black," "blackened by fire," "swarthy") ruled over all of his kind. Living in the furthest reaches of the south in a land called Muspelheim, he was the bearer of a fiery sword known as Med Sviga Laevi. It is said in the final battle of Ragnarok, on the Vigridr Plain, Surtr will kill the god Freyr and then throw his sword, letting it consume the worlds in fire.

Scholars have speculated the characters of Durinn, Drunir, SOKMIMIR, and Surtr are all the same being as they all have a story where their son is slain by the god Odin in nearly the exact same manner.

Source: Grimes, *Norse Myths*, 300; Norroena Society, *Asatrii Edda*, 388; Oehlenschläger, *Gods of the North*, lxiii; Rydberg, *Teutonic Mythology*, 443–4

Susukaikaigeda

Variations: Susukaikai-geda

A race of short anthropoids living in swampy places, the diurnal susukaikaigeda, males and female alike, are described as having only one breast upon their chest. Living lives similar to mankind, these normally peaceful beings avoid contact with humans and are in fact frightened by sightings of them.

Source: Renner, *Primitive Religion in the Tropical Forests*, 84; Seligman, *Melanesians of British New Guinea*, 649

Suttungr (SUT-ung-r)

Variations: Fjalarr, Suttung

In Norse mythology, Suttungr was born the son of the JOTUN GILLINGR and the brother of BAUGI. Suttungr received a portion of Precious Mead as weregild from the DVERGAR (DWARFS) FJALARR and GALARR for having killed his parents. GUNLAD, the daughter of Suttungr, was made to be the guardian of the mead in his mountain stronghold, Hnitb-horg, but it was still stolen by the god Odin. Sut-tungr, who could not swim, had visited his parents often when they were alive; he resented the fact his brother BAUGI did not and was their favorite child.

Source: Daly, *Norse Mythology A to Z*, 96–7; Grimes, *Norse Myths*, 300

Svadi (Svao'i)

The JOTUN Svadi ("slippery") was one of the sons of the god of thunder, Thor; he lived in the north beyond Misty Ocean, upon Mount Blesanerg, and was the owner of a large cache of gold.

Source: O'Connor, *Icelandic Histories and Romances*, 186; Vigfússon, *Icelandic Sagas and Other Historical Documents*, Volume 3, 3, 463

Svarangr (SVAHR-ang-r)

Variations: Svárang, Svårang, Svarang

In Norse mythology Svarangr ("the bad," "the hard," and "the stodgy"), one of the Jotnar (see JOTUN), was the father of the sons who battled the god of thunder, Thor; they threw mountains at the god while he guarded the river Ifing. Thor battled and defeated the sons. Beyond Svarangr's name, there is little else known of this JOTUN.

Source: Grimes, *Norse Myths*, 129, 300; Norroena Society, *Asatrii Edda*, 389

Svartálfar (Svart-alfs)

Variations: Alfar, Dökkálfar ("DARK ELVES")

In Norse mythology, the Svartálfar ("black spir-its") are fairies who live in the underground world of Svartálfaheim; their name likely is derived from their habit of avoiding the light as opposed to their nature. Described as looking like ugly and mis-shapen humans with skin darker than a starless night, the svartálfar are often used interchangeably in stories with the DVERGAR (DWARFS) and DARK ELVES. Greedy and troublesome, the Svartálfar, like the DWARFS, were created from the maggots of the GIANT YMIR's rotting flesh and are reputed as being magnificent smiths, creating magical armor and weapons. The Svartálfar are associated with fertility, giving them a substantial following among the ancient Norse people.

Source: Illes, *Encyclopedia of Spirits*, 17; Keightley, *World Guide to Gnomes, Fairies, Elves, and Other Little People*, 68; Littleton, *Gods, Goddesses, and Mythology*, Volume 11, 58; Rose, *Spirits, Fairies, Leprechauns, and Goblins*, 10

Svartr (SVART-r)

In Norse mythology, Svartr ("the black" or "swarthy") was one of the many named Jotnar (see JOTUN) about whom, beyond a name, there is noth-ing else known.

Source: Norroena Society, *Asatrii Edda*, 389

Svasudr (SVAH-suth-r)

Variations: Svasud

In Norse mythology, Svasudr ("the delightful"), one of the many named Jotnar (see JOTUN), was said to have a pleasant nature and was the father of the summer; beyond this, there is nothing else known of him.

Source: Norroena Society, *Asatrii Edda*, 389; Rydberg, *Norroena, the History and Romance of Northern Europe*, Vol-ume 3, 1036

Svava (SVAHV-a)

Variations: Sváfa

In Norse mythology Svava ("sleeper") was one of the many named VALKYRIES (NYMPHs of battle); she was also a daughter of King Eylimi and likely the aunt of Sigurd the dragon slayer.

Source: Norroena Society, *Asatrii Edda*, 388; Orchard, *Cassell's Dictionary of Norse Myth and Legend*, 157

Sveid (SVAYTH)

In Norse mythology Sveid ("clamor") was one of the many named VALKYRIES (NYMPHs of battle) about whom, beyond a name, there is little or noth-ing else known.

Source: Conway, *Falcon Feather and Valkyrie Sword*, 211; Norroena Society, *Asatrii Edda*, 389

Sviarr (SVEE-ar)

Variations: Sviar

A rock DVERG (DWARF) from Norse mythology created by Durinn, Sviarr ("waner") is listed as being one of DURINN's KIN. He, like the others cre-ated, paid particular attention to DURINN's leader-ship. He was named in the *Voluspa*, the first and best known poem of the *Poetic Edda* (AD 985).

Source: Bellows, *Poetic Edda*, 7; Crossley-Holland, *Norse Myths*, 183; Grimes, *Norse Myths*, 260; Young, *Prose Edda*, 175

Svior

A DVERG (DWARF) from Norse mythology, Svior ("wise") was named in the *Voluspa*, the first and best known poem of the *Poetic Edda* (AD 985).

Source: Acker, *Poetic Edda*, 218; Daly, *Norse Mythology A to Z*, 22; Macdowall, *Asgard and the Gods*, 311

Svipul

Variations: Svipull

One of the many named VALKYRIES in Norse mythology, Svipul ("battle") along with her fellow VALKYRIES GEIRSKOGUL, GONDULL, GUNNR, HILDR, HJOR, HJORTHRIMUL, SANGRIDE, SKOGUL, and THRIMUL would work a great loom together. Raised on spears, the warp was made from the guts of men and was weighed down with human heads; the shuttle was made from an arrow and the spools from swords. The entire weft wept with blood. Svipul was named by Nialssage in her acclaimed battle-weaving song.

Source: Conway, *Falcon Feather and Valkyrie Sword*, 211; Grimes, *Norse Myths*, 21; Grimm, *Teutonic Mythology*, 421; Norroena Society, *Asatrii Edda*, 390

Swan Maiden

Variations: Fairy Brides

The idea of a swan maiden is a very old one and exists in several cultures, such as Celtic, Oriental, Slavic, and Teutonic traditions. The topic of swan maidens was very popular in Victorian England. As the name implies, these beings have the ability to shape-shift between bird and human form in one of two ways: either of their own free will by means of a magical garment or as a secret magical condition, such as a lover promising to never break a specific promise or taboo.

Usually swan maidens appear in groups of three; they are beautiful beyond measure and can be found near a water source spinning or weaving. They love to dance and swim. In Celtic folklore they also always wear a magical golden chain which allows them to leave Midgard.

Swan maidens, unlike other fairy brides, are sexually aggressive, oftentimes approaching the man of their intent and seducing him. In stories, once the marriage of a swan maiden takes place, even if it is against her will, and children have been born and her domestic duties established, a happy ending to the tale is impossible. The supernatural world the fairy left behind will reclaim her; she will either return of her own free will, her spouse will break his promise or taboo, or a tragic event will take her life.

Source: Grimm, *Teutonic Mythology*, Volume 4, 429; Hastings, *Encyclopedia of Religion and Ethics*, Part 23, 125–26; Welch, *Goddess of the North*, 71–2

Syceus

Variations: Sykeas, Sykeus

A GIGANTE from ancient Greek mythology, Syceus ("fig tree") took part in the Gigantomachy; when confronted by the god Zeus (Jupiter), Syceus turned and fled the battle, and his mother, Gaea, took him into her arms and transformed him into the first fig tree in order to save his life.

Source: Cook, *Zeus: A Study in Ancient Religion*, Volume 2, Part 2, 1103; Porteous, *Lore of the Forest*, 178

Syn (Sen)

In Norse mythology Syn ("denial") was originally one of the ASYNJR; she was a guard at the door to Frigg's great hall. Later, she was worshiped as a goddess who would keep people out of dwellings who were not intended to enter; defendants at trials would also call upon her.

Source: Anderson, *Norse Mythology*, 458; Daly, *Norse Mythology A to Z*, 99; Norroena Society, *Asatrii Edda*, 390

Syqenhenjeri

A species of CYCLOPS from southern Albanian mythology, the syqenhenjeri ("dog-eyed man-eater") are said to be flesh eaters, capturing humans, roasting them in ovens, and then eating them as food.

Source: Elsie, *Dictionary of Albanian Religion, Mythology, and Folk Culture*, 248

Syrbotae

Variations: Sorebotes

A species of GIANT mentioned in many medieval bestiaries, the syrbotae were said to live in Africa and stand about eight cubits tall (a *cubit* is the distance from a man's elbow to the tip of his middle finger).

Source: Pliny the Elder, *Pliny's Natural History*, Volumes 1–3, 160; Weber, *Process of the Seuyn Sages*, 327

Syrictae

Variations: Syrictæ

A nation of tribal nomads, the Syrictae are a race of people who were described in medieval bestiaries as not having a nose but rather two small holes in its place. Additionally, it has been written that "after the manner of snakes they have their legs and feet limmer, wherewith they crawl and creep." This description lent itself to the idea the Syrictae were reptilian anthropoids.

Source: Coleridge, *Encyclopædia Metropolitana*, Volume 23, 371

Talamaur (Tall-ah-mor)

Variation: Talamur, Tarunga

On the Banks Islands of Australia as well as on the Polynesian Islands there is a type of living vampire known as a talamaur, which can be a force for good or for evil, depending on the person. Greatly feared by the community he lives in, the possibility of being banished or even being stoned to death is very real. It is believed all talamaur are capable of astral projection and speak to ghosts. Some are said to have a spirit or a ghost as a familiar.

If the talamaur is an evil and predatory vampire, he will attack people who are dying or the newly dead, feeding off the last bits of their life-energy. Should he attack a healthy person, he will do so while they are asleep, ripping their heart out of their chest and consuming it while it is still beating in order to enslave their soul. The souls of those he has consumed surround him and are forced to act as a protective shield. This mass of souls is called a *tarunga*, and its specific powers vary depending on the capability of the souls which compose it.

To test if a person is a talamaur, he is held over a pile of burning leaves and forced to breathe in the smoke. If he is a vampire he will confess, giving a full account of all his crimes and naming all of the spirits he controls.

Source: Codrington, *Melanesians*, 222; Royal Anthropological Institute, *Journal*, Volume 10, 285; Summers, *Vampire: His Kith and Kin*, 227

Talmai

Variations: Talmia, Tanmahu

A GIANT from Hebrew Scriptures, Talmai, along with this brother SHESHAI, ruled over their people, the ANAKIM, from the country of Hebron (Kirjath-Arba). Their eldest brother, AHIMAN, was the most feared of the three sons of ANAK. Talmai was depicted on a wall inside of the tomb of Oimenepthah I as being tall and light skinned.

Talmai and his brothers were, according to the Book of Judges, slain by Judah.

Source: DeLoach, *Giants*, 278; Taylor, *Calmets Great Dictionary of the Holy Bible*, n.pag.

Tanngnidr (TAN-nith-r)

In Norse mythology Tanngnidr ("teeth grinder") was one of the many named VALKYRIES (NYMPHs of battle) about whom, beyond a name, there is little or nothing else known.

Source: Conway, *Falcon Feather and Valkyrie Sword*, 211; Norroena Society, *Asatru Edda*, 390

Tapagoz

A classification of GIANT in Armenian folklore, the tapagoz had either one or three heads but no matter the number, each head had only a single eye in the middle of its forehead, similar to the CYCLOPES of Greek mythology. These giants were particularly large; it was believed a single tooth of theirs weighed one hundred eighty pounds and one of their heads more than eighteen hundred pounds. In one folktale a tapagoz kidnapped Smizar, the daughter of King Zarzand, and kept her imprisoned in his castle until the hero Zurab (later renamed Aslam) slew the GIANT and rescued her.

Source: Berman, *Shamanic Themes in Armenian Folktales*, 71–2; Rose, *Giants, Monsters, and Dragons*, 353

Tapairu

The tapairu ("peerless ones") is the collective name for the four daughters of the female demon Miru, an ugly and deformed creature who cooks and consumes human souls in her underworld home. The tapairu are nature spirits, beautiful beyond imagining, and will often ascend into our world near sunset and upon a mat of banana leaves under a moon-lit sky perform a dance known as the *Tautiti*, named after their brother whom they honor with their performance. Their footfalls are so light and dainty, they do not leave a mark upon the leaves. The names of the four tapairu are Karaia-i-te-ata (Karaia of the Morn), Kumu-tonga-i-te-po (Kumu-Tonga of the night), Te Poro (the Point), and Te Rau-ara (Pandanus leaf).

Source: Anderson, *Myths and Legends of the Polynesians*, n.pag.; Porteous, *Lore of the Forest*, 141

Tarabusan

The second of four deadly monsters in the Moro tradition, Tarabusan was a GIANT who lived upon Mount Bita; he was so large it was said he could crush a man's head beneath his foot and grind it to pieces.

Source: Hurley, *Swish of the Kris*, 264

Tártalo

Variations: Tartaro

In Basque folklore the Tártalo is a one-eyed cave-dwelling GIANT, comparable to the CYCLOPES of Greek mythology.

Source: Daniels, *Encyclopædia of Superstitions, Folklore, and the Occult Sciences of the World*, 1378; Miguel de Barandiarán, *Selected Writings of José Miguel De Barandiarán*, 92

Taudombi

Living in the springs and swamps, the taudombi of Melanesian folklore are believed to be extremely long lived if not immortal anthropoids. As a race of invisible beings the taudombi live lives similar to humans, dressing in like clothing, raising families, and tending to their gardens; only people with second sight are able to see them. The taudombi laugh when they see humans, and although their laughter cannot be heard, they also will then throw rocks at the person; the rocks are real and can do actual damage to their intended target.

Source: Seligman, *Melanesians of British New Guinea*, 649

Telchines

In the mythology of ancient Greece, the telchines ("sea children") were the first inhabitants of the Isle of Rhodes. In the oldest myths the telchines were said to have been nine dog-headed enchantresses who had flippers for hands. They were believed to have founded Iaiysos, Kamros, and Lindos; they created the first statues of the god and the sickle CRONUS used to castrate Uranus. The telchines were the nurses to the god of the sea, Poseidon (Neptune), and created his trident for him; the god fell in love with the telchines' sister, Alia, and by her had six sons and a daughter, the NYMPH Rhodos.

In later versions of the myth, the telchines no longer had dog heads and flippers and were born the sons of Pontos and Thalassa; as artisans and magicians they were also the ministers of the god Zeus (Jupiter). Alia, one of the sisters of the telchines, became the lover of Poseidon (Neptune) and they were the parents of the NYMPH RHODOS. When the male telchines would not let the goddess of love, Aphrodite (Venus), land upon their island she cast an incestuous love spell upon them which caused the brothers to rape their mother, Alia. In their shame the brothers hid in the bowels of the earth and became demons. Poseidon (Neptune), in a rage, flooded the island but the goddess Artemis (Diana) alerted the remaining telchines allowing them to escape.

In all there are nine brothers and a sister; only the names of four of the brothers are known—Antaeus, Lycus, Megalesius, and Ormenos—and the sister, the sea-woman Halia. According to the legend, the brothers, known for their ability to make rain, once mixed water from the River Styx with sulphur, and the result was disastrous, destroying the crops.

There are some scholars who believe the telchines were a race of ancient people, dwarflike in appearance, which were conquered by Greek invaders, similar to how the FORMORIANS were invaded and defeated by the TUATHA DE DANANN.

Source: Coulter, *Encyclopedia of Ancient Deities*, 457; Facaros, *Northern Spain*, 405; Graves, *The Greek Myths*, 54; Rose, *Spirits, Fairies, Leprechauns, and Goblins*, 307

Teles

In classical Greek mythology, Teles ("perfect") was one of the named SIRENS, a type of malicious NYMPH born the offspring of the ancient god of the sea, PHORCYS. Half bird and half woman, she and her sisters would perch on the rocky Sicilian coastline and lure in sailors with their melodious song; once caught, their prey were eaten alive. Although the Sirens hunted the coastline they lived in an inland meadow.

Source: Roman, *Encyclopedia of Greek and Roman Mythology*, 443; Sherman, *Storytelling*, 416; Smith, *Dictionary of Greek and Roman Biography and Mythology*, 817

Tepegoz

Variations: Tepe Goz

A CYCLOPES-like monster from Azerbaijani folklore, Tepegoz ("pinnacle eye"), with his one eye in the middle of his forehead, was a vicious being from his childhood, having chewed the nose off of one playmate and the ear off of another. Born of a PERI, his mother had gifted him with a magical ring which would protect him from the arrows and swords of mankind. Roaming the countryside of Oghuz, Tepegoz, an ugly cannibal, consumed every shepherd and traveler he came across. Many regional heroes tried to put an end to him but Tepegoz was more than a match until the unlikely hero Basat managed to behead him with a magical sword.

Source: Fee, *Mythology in the Middle Ages*, 226–8; Köprülü, *Early Mystics in Turkish Literature*, 264

Tethys

Variations: THEMIS

A beautiful TITAN from classical Greek mythology, Tethys, taller than a mountain, was born the child of the TITAN Uranus and the Earth, Gaea; her siblings were COEUS, CRIUS, CRONUS, HYPERION, IAPETUS, MNEMOSYNE, OCEANUS, PHOEBE, RHEA, THEIA, and THEMIS. Collectively the siblings were known as the Titanides. She and her husband, OCEANUS, were the parents of some 6,000 children, 3,000 of which were their daughters who were known collectively as the OCEANIDS; one of her daughters was Metis, the first wife of the god Zeus (Jupiter). Tethys and her husband also raised Hera (Juno), another wife of Zeus.

Sources: Hard, *Routledge Handbook of Greek Mythology*, 40; Westmoreland, *Ancient Greek Beliefs*, 103

Thaon

A GIGANTE from ancient Greek mythology, Thaon was slain during the ten year war against the Olympian gods, the Gigantomachy, by the FATES.

Source: Brewer, *Wordsworth Dictionary of Phrase and Fable*, 476; Coleman, *Dictionary of Mythology*, 1004; Daniels, *Encyclopædia of Superstitions, Folklore, and the Occult Sciences of the World*, 1378

Thardid Jimbo

In Australian folklore, Thardid Jimbo was said to be a cave-dwelling GIANT over seven feet tall with powerful arms and legs. His primary diet consisted of blue tongued and frilled lizards, goannas, and snakes; he would hunt for these creatures daily but was described as being the enemy of man, having big, cruel, and wicked eyes. Although not overly intelligent Thardid Jimbo was smart enough to know his brute strength and size was not enough to defeat an intelligent man in battle; although aware of this, he fell prey to the flattery of a clever and fair woman who was able to kill him, roasting him alive in a cave as if it were a giant oven.

Source: Coleman, *Dictionary of Mythology*, 1004; Smith, *Myths and Legends of the Australian Aborigines*, 273–6

Thaumas, Titan

An eminent TITAN from ancient Greek mythology, Thaumas was born one of the children of Gaea (earth) and the ancient god of the sea, Pontus; in traditional and ancient Greek mythology he was also a god of the sea as well as the father of the HARPIES by the sea NYMPH ELECTRA. Additionally, Thaumas fathered the fleet-footed goddess of the rainbow, Iris.

Source: Daly, *Greek and Roman Mythology, A to Z*, 141; Westmoreland, *Ancient Greek Beliefs*, 22, 24, 699

Theia (Thi-a)

A TITAN from classical Greek mythology, Theia was born one of the six daughters of the TITAN Uranus and the Earth, Gaea; her siblings were COEUS, CRIUS, CRONUS, HYPERION, IAPETUS, MNEMOSYNE, OCEANUS, PHOEBE, RHEA, TETHYS, and THEMIS. Collectively the siblings were known as the Titanides. In many genealogies Theia is not listed as one of the TITANS; when she is mentioned, she has married her brother, HYPERION, and become the mother of three gods: EOS (the dawn), HELIOS (Sol) (the sun), and SELENE (the moon).

Sources: Brewer, *Reader's Handbook of Allusions, References, Plots and Stories*, 1010; Coulter, *Encyclopedia of Ancient Deities*, 169; Roman, *Encyclopedia of Greek and Roman Mythology*, 484

Thelchtereia

One of the three SIRENS from ancient Greek mythology, Thelchtereia ("enchantress" or "soothing watcher") is typically one of a trio of sisters (although ancient writers do not agree on their names or numbers) grouped with AGLAOPE and PEISINOË, born the daughters of Achelous and Thelxiepia.

Source: Apollodorus, *Library*, Volume 2, 290; Monaghan, *New Book of Goddesses and Heroines*, 273

Thelxepeia

Thelxepeia ("soothing words") was one of the SIRENS from ancient Greek mythology; although ancient writers do not agree on their names or numbers she is typically one of a trio, grouped with AGLAOPE and PEISINOË.

Source: Sardi, *Psychological Activity in the Homeric Circe Episode*, 28; Smith, *Dictionary of Greek and Roman Biography and Mythology*, Volume 3, 840

Thelxiope

In classical Greek mythology, Thelxiope ("beguiling the mind") was one of the named SIRENS, a type of malicious NYMPH born the offspring of the ancient god of the sea, PHORCYS. Half bird and half woman, she and her sisters would perch on the rocky Sicilian coastline and lure in sailors with their melodious song; once caught, their prey were eaten alive. Although they hunted the coastline, Thelxiope and her kind lived inland in a meadow.

According to the ancient Greek poet Cherilus of Samos, AGLAOPHONOS, MOLPE, and Thelxiope were the three SIRENS of Greek mythology.

Source: Austern, *Music of the Sirens*, 40; Leland, *Unpublished Legends of Virgil*, 37; Roman, *Encyclopedia of Greek and Roman Mythology*, 443

Themis

A TITAN from classical Greek mythology, Themis was born the child of the TITAN Uranus and the Earth, Gaea; siblings were COEUS, CRIUS, CRONUS, HYPERION, IAPETUS, MNEMOSYNE, OCEANUS, PHOEBE, RHEA, TETHYS, and THEIA. Collectively the siblings were known as the Titanides. Themis was skilled in foretelling the future and is sometimes called the goddess of Justice.

Source: Lemprière, *Classical Dictionary*, 785; Parker, *Mythology*, 21, 22, 33

Thiassi (THYAZ-i)

Variations: Fjallgylder ("mountain wolf"), Thiasse, Thiazi, Thjasse, Thjasse-Volund, Thjassi, Thjazi ("Giant"), Voland, Volundr

A JOTUN from Norse mythology, Thiassi was the personification of winter; he was born the son of GREIP and Ivalde and was the brother to AURNIR and IDI, and possibly Idun, guardian of the magic apples, as well. His daughter was the ASYNJR SKADI and his hall was called Thrymheim.

Because Idun refused to give the cruel JOTUN one of the magical apples which would transform him into a handsome and youthful version of himself, Thiassi stole Idun away and kept her imprisoned. Loki managed her escape, carrying her off in the form of a falcon, but Thiassi gave chase as he was able to don eagle feathers and have the ability to fly. As they neared the walls of Valhalla, the gods waited for Loki to pass overhead and then set a huge fire they had prepared. When Thiassi came near the heat the smoke choked and weakened him, causing him to fall from the sky and making him easy prey for the gods to finish off. They tossed his body upon the pyre and let it burn to ashes.

Source: Coulter, *Encyclopedia of Ancient Deities*, 462; Guerber, *Hammer of Thor*, 73; Oehlenschläger, *Gods of the North*, xxxviii

Thir (THEE)

Variations: Thi, Thy, Thyr

One of the hrymthursars (FROST GIANTS) from Norse mythology, Thir ("bondswoman," "drudge") was an intensely hideous woman, with a bent back, bowed legs, dark skin, flat nose, receding chin and forehead, and her few remaining teeth were stained brown. The moment THRAEL saw her, he fell deeply in love. The two married and had twelve sons—Dirgraldi, DROTTR, DRUMBER, FJOSNIR, FULNIR, HOSVIR, HRIMR, KEFSIR, KLEGGI, Klurr, LEGGJALDI, and Lutr—and nine daughters—Ambatt, ARINNEFJA, DRUMBA, Eikintjasna, Kulba, OKKVAINKALFA, TOTRUGHYPJA, TRONUBEINA, and YSJA. A family of hard workers, they worked the land and toiled day and night. Thir and her husband were the progenitors of the thrall class.

Source: Crossley-Holland, *Norse Myths*, 19; Grimes, *Norse Myths*, 27, 301; Mortensen, *Handbook of Norse Mythology*, 136; Norroena Society, *Asatrii Edda*, 393

Thjodreyrir (THYOHTH-ray-rir)

Variations: Pjofireynir, Thjothrörir, Thodrœrer

A DVERG (DWARF) from Norse mythology, Thjodreyrir ("waker of the people") sang songs of blessings—"*Power to the Aesir, success to the Elves (Light Elves), and wisdom to the Hroptatyr (Odin)*"—outside the doors of Dellingr's hall each day at dawn.

Source: Grimes, *Norse Myths*, 7, 109, 302; Norroena Society, *Asatrii Edda*, 391; Rydberg, *Norroena, the History and Romance of Northern Europe*, Volume 2, 367

Thoas

A GIGANTE from ancient Greek mythology, Thoas ("fast") was born the son of the TITAN Uranus ("heaven") and the Earth, Gaea. He and his siblings were extremely large, immensely strong, and absolutely fearsome to behold as they had dense beards, a thick head of hair, and feet covered with DRAKON scales; they threw flaming oak trees and rocks at the heavens. Thoas took part in and was slain during the Gigantomachy by the Fates who beat him and AGRIUS to death with bronze clubs.

Source: Coulter, *Encyclopedia of Ancient Deities*, 469; Dixon-Kennedy, *Encyclopedia of Greco-Roman Mythology*, 138; Westmoreland, *Ancient Greek Beliefs*, 819

Thoon

A GIGANTE from ancient Greek mythology, Thoon was born of the great goddess Gaea and the god Uranus. He and his siblings were extremely large, immensely strong, and absolutely fearsome to behold as they had dense beards, a thick head of hair, and feet covered with DRAKON scales; they threw flaming oak trees and rocks at the heavens. Thoon took part in the Gigantomachy and was slain by the FATE Parcæ (Parcae), who beat him to death with a bronze cudgel.

Source: Apollodorus, *Library of Greek Mythology*, 34–5; Coulter, *Encyclopedia of Ancient Deities*, 469

Thorin (THAWR-in)

Variations: Thorinn

An earth DVERG (DWARF) from Norse mythology, Thorin ("bold one," "daring") is named in the *Voluspa* part of the *Poetic Edda*; beyond a name, little else is known.

Source: Daly, *Norse Mythology A to Z*, 22; Grimes, *Norse Myths*, 302; Norroena Society, *Asatrii Edda*, 391

Thrael (THRAIL-ar)

Variations: Thraelm, Tral

One of the hrymthursars (FROST GIANTS) from Norse mythology, Thrael ("thrall") was born a son of AI and Edda. Thrael married THIR and they, along with their children, worked the land; their sons were: DIGRALDI, DROTTR, DRUMBR, FJOSNIR, Fulnor, HOSVIR, HRIMR, KEFSIR, KLEGGI, Klurr, LEGGJALDI, and LUTR; their daughters were Ambatt, ARINNEFJA, DRUMBA, Eikintjasna, KUMBA, OKKVAINKALFA, TOTRUGHYPJA, TRONUBEINA, and YSJA. A family of hard workers, they worked the land and toiled day and night. Thrael and his wife were the progenitors of the slave or thrall class.

Source: Grimes, *Norse Myths*, 302; Norroena Society, *Asatrii Edda*, 392

Thrainn (THRAH-in)

Variations: Thrain, Throin, Throinn

In Norse mythology Thrainn ("craver," "swift," or "threatening") was one of the rock DWARFS created by the DWARF DURINN. He was mentioned in passing in the *Voluspa*, the first and best-known poem of the *Poetic Edda* (AD 985).

Source: Auden, *Norse Poems*, 247; Crossley-Holland, *Norse Myths*, 183; Daly, *Norse Mythology A to Z*, 22; Grimes, *Norse Myths*, 260, 302; Norroena Society, *Asatrii Edda*, 392

Thriae

Variations: Thriai

In ancient Greek mythology the Thriae ("little stones") were a trio of NYMPHs who lived upon Mount Parnassus beneath a ridge, raised the god Apollo, and are credited with having invented the art of prophetic divination by use of throwing stones; although widely accepted to be a trio, the names given for them throughout ancient sources are Corycia, Daphnus, Kleodora, Melaina, and Thiua. Some sources claim the cause of their prophetic gift was a honey-based elixir while others say they dropped little stones into urns filled with water and "read" the results, possibly from the ripples created.

Source: Monaghan, *Goddesses in World Culture*, Volume 1, 147; Rosen, *Mythical Creatures Bible*, 168–9

Thrima

Variations: Þrima

In Norse mythology Thrima ("battle") was one of the many named VALKYRIEs (NYMPHs of battle) about whom, beyond a name, there is little or nothing else known.

Source: Norroena Society, *Asatrii Edda*, 391; Rydberg, *Our Fathers' Godsaga*, 201

Thrimul

Thrimul along with her fellow VALKYRIES GEIRSKOGUL, GONDULL, GUNNR, HILDR, HJOR, HJORTHRIMUL, SANGRIDE, SKOGUL, and SVIPUL, would work a great loom together. Raised on spears, the warp was made from the guts of men and was weighed down with human heads; the shuttle was made from an arrow and the spools from swords. The entire weft wept with blood.

Source: Grimes, *Norse Myths*, 21, 302, 306;

Thrivaldi (THRI-vald-i)

Variations: Þrívaldi, Thrívaldi

In Norse mythology Thrivaldi ("as strong as three") was a nine-headed JOTUN slain by the god Thor.

Source: Grimes, *Norse Myths*, 302; Norroena Society, *Asatrii Edda*, 391; Thorpe, *Northern Mythology*, Volume 1, 134

Thror (Throhr)

In Norse mythology Thror ("inciter of strife") was one of the rock DVERGAR (DWARFS) created by DURINN.

Source: Auden, *Norse Poems*, 247; Daly, *Norse Mythology A to Z*, 22; Grimes, *Norse Myths*, 260

Thrudgelmir

Variations: Þrúðgelmir, Thrudgelmer, Thrúdgelmir

In Norse mythology, Thrudgelmir ("strength yeller") was one of the many named Jotnar (see JOTUN), a FROST GIANT; he was created from the sweat of YMIR's left foot and born with six heads. Thrudgelmir was the father of BERGELMIR.

Source: Anderson, *History and Romance of Northern Europe*, Volume 5, 1037; Coulter, *Encyclopedia of Ancient Deities*, 465

Thrudr (THROOTH-r)

Variations: Thurd ("counsel truce" or "violent counsel"), Thrud, Thrúdr

In Norse mythology Thrudr ("mighty") was born the daughter of the god Thor and his wife, Sif; she was one of the VALKYRIEs (NYMPHs of battle) who served the EINHERJAR ale in Valhalla, however, there is little of her personally in the folklore. Thrudr was wed to the DVERG (DWARF) Alvis while Thor was away and when he returned was not pleased with

the match. The god went to their home and tricked Alvis into staying up all night talking with him; as the first rays of the sun appeared in the sky, Alvis was transformed into stone.

Source: Anderson, Norse Mythology, 269; James, *Devotional*, 43–4; Norroena Society, *Asatrii Edda*, 391

Thrymr (THREM-r)

Variations: Ryme, Thrym, Thrymer, Þrymr ("uproar"), Trym, Thrymur

A JOTUN from Norse mythology, Thrymr ("crash" or "noisy") was a king of the hrymthursar (FROST GIANTS); he had the ability to create powerful snowstorms. During the time the hammer of Thor, Mjölnir, had been stolen and hidden in the bowels of the earth, Thrymr revealed to the god Loki the terms by which the hammer would be returned—the goddess Freya was to marry him. Naturally Freya flatly refused and Loki had to convince Thor to don a dress and pretend to be her long enough to retrieve his hammer. Eventually Thor complied and, veiled in women's garb, assumed Freya's identity and married Thrymr. During the wedding feast, after consuming a whole roasted ox, eight salmon, and three barrels of wine, Thrymr gifted to his new bride Mjölnir; Thor, hammer in hand, revealed his true identity and slew the Jotnar in attendance.

Source: Cotterell, *Dictionary of World Mythology*, 188; Grimes, *Norse Myths*, 303; Norroena Society, *Asatrii Edda*, 391; Oehlenschläger, *Gods of the North*, lxiv

Thurse

In Icelandic folklore Thurse was a savage GIANT living in the bare, jagged, steep peaks of Solstein in the same valley as the GIANT HEIMO. Thurse, taller and stronger than his neighbor, hated him and took every opportunity to destroy any building HEIMO constructed. When it was discovered Thurse was the cause of the destruction of his stronghold, HEIMO donned light armor and wielding an enormous sword scaled the mountain to attack his enemy. Thurse heard his rival approaching and hefted up a huge beam for a weapon. The two fought a savage battle, but in the end the better armored HEIMO won, slaying Thurse.

Source: Günther, *Tales and Legends of the Tyrol*, 13

Tigolopes

An anthropoid-like creature or race depicted in medieval bestiaries, the tailed tigolopes were said to have lived in Asia and had webbed feet; in art they were shown holding a *thyrsus*, a short staff with a pinecone on its top.

Source: Brown, *God and Enchantment of Place*, 193; Jones, *Medieval Naturel World*, xxv, 58

Tikdoshe

An evil DWARF from Zulu folklore, Tikdoshe was described as having only one arm and one leg, similar to the HAI-URI. Violent natured, it fought humans, killing those it defeated but rewarding the victors by sharing with them its magical secrets.

Source: Cotterell, *Dictionary of World Mythology*, 241; Lynch, *African Mythology, A to Z*, 85; Zell-Ravenheart, *Wizard's Bestiary*, 95–6

Ting Ling Kuo Yan

A race of monstrous humanoids from Chinese folklore, the Ting Ling Kuo Yan had anthropoid bodies and heads covered with hair but had the legs and hooves of horses, giving them both great speed and stamina as they could run over one hundred miles a day.

Source: Rose, *Giants, Monsters, and Dragons*, 360

The Titans

Variations: The Titane

In Greek mythology the Titans were the race of beings which preceded and were the progenitors of the Olympian gods; most Greek authors say there were twelve Titans, six male and six female, all born the children of Gaea (earth) and Uranus ("heaven"). The sons were CRIUS, COEUS, CRONUS, HYPERION, IAPETUS, and OCEANUS; the daughters were MNEMOSYNE, PHOEBE, RHEA, TETHYS, THEIA, and THEMIS. Gaea also had a number of children with the ancient god of the sea, Pontus, and many scholars include these children among the Titans; their names are CETO, EURYBIA, NEREUS, PHORCYS, and THAUMAS. The children of Gaea's children, the second generation of Titans, were also all considered to be Titans by ancient Greek scholars: ASTERIA, ASTRAEUS, ATLAS, EOS, EPIMETHEUS, HELIOS (Sol), LETO, MENOETIUS, PALLAS, PERSES, PROMETHEUS, and SELENS. Also included in the list of Titans were the eldest daughters of OCEANIOS and his sister wife, TETHYS; they were collectively known as the OCEANID: CLYMENE, DIONE, DORIS, ELECTRA, ETIS, EURYNOME, NEDA, PLEIONE, and STYX. It was the children of Cronus of Rhea who were considered to be the first of the Olympians.

The Titans were worshiped as gods by the ancient Greeks up to and throughout the Golden Age (circa 500 to 300 BC); when the Hellenes came to the islands, their gods in tow, they supplanted the native people and their religion. The mythology grew and Zeus (Jupiter) led a battle of generations called the Titanomachy which lasted ten years. In the end, most of the Titans were killed; those defeated were imprisoned in the deepest section of the Underworld known as Tartarus; it is surrounded with a bronze fence and has a bronze gate which is guarded by the HECATONCHEIRES.

Source: Daly, *Greek and Roman Mythology, A to Z*, 141; Roman, *Encyclopedia of Greek and Roman Mythology*, 493

Tityos

Variations: Tityus, Tituos

In Greek mythology Tityos ("risker") was counted as one of the GIGANTES; although there are several origin stories of his birth, most claim he was born the son of Gaea and the god Zeus (Jupiter). In one version his mother was the NYMPH Elara whom Zeus kept hidden throughout her pregnancy, burying her in the ground; Tityos was born, erupting from the earth. In another version, he was born of Gaea but nursed by Elara. No matter how he came to be, sources say he was the father of Europa.

Tityos is best known for his attempt to rape Zeus's consort LETO. Unsuccessful, he was slain, shot full of arrows by Apollo and Artemis (Diana) or struck dead by a thunderbolt from Zeus (Jupiter). No matter how he died, Tityos was condemned to Tartarus where his body, stretched painfully over nine acres of land, had its liver ripped out and consumed daily by a pair of snakes (or vultures; ancient sources vary). Because of the nature of his punishment, Tityos is sometimes confused with the TITAN PROMETHEUS.

Source: Coulter, *Encyclopedia of Ancient Deities*, 469; Daniels, *Encyclopædia of Superstitions, Folklore, and the Occult Sciences of the World*, 1378; Fox, *Greek and Roman [mythology]*, 175; Roman, *Encyclopedia of Greek and Roman Mythology*, 493–4

Torge

A JOTUN from Norse folklore, Torge was the lover of a beautiful ASYNJR maiden named JUTERNA-JESTA; unfortunately she had caught the eye of an old and ugly JOTUN by the name of SENJEMAND who lived on Senjen Island. JUTERNA-JESTA rejected his attention and affection and in his rage he shot at her with a flint arrow. Fortunately Torge saw the incoming missile and threw his hat up into the air to foul the shot; his hat was described in the story as being one thousand feet high and proportionally tall and thick.

Source: Guerber, *Hammer of Thor*, 163–4; Rose, *Giants, Monsters, and Dragons*, 327

Tork

Variations: Tork Angegh

A DEV, GIANT, or OGRE from Armenia folklore, Tork was once an angry and raging individual who eventually came to master his temper and become a hero, after a fashion. In most of his stories, it is his reputation for a propensity for violence which enables him to overcome obstacles. He is described as being gigantic and having eyes as blue as heaven, eyebrows as black as pitch, a hooked nose, a veritable hump, teeth like hatchets, fingernails like knives, and being thick chested like a mountain with a waist resembling a rocky vale.

Tork was also immensely strong; as a child he could crumble up boulders into pebbles with his hands. Although a skilled architect and mason, Tork was by trade a shepherd; as lions and tigers feared him, these creatures would protect his flocks. If he should destroy a town by accident or in a fit of anger, he was quick to rebuild it. Meek and modest, he was not vengeful nor was he a glutton, as his favorite foods were honey, milk, and yogurt.

Source: Hacikyan, *Heritage of Armenian Literature*, 388–9

Tornit

Variations: Inlanders

According to the mythology of the Inuit people of Alaska and Canada the tornit were a race of GIANTS, fast, large, and strong, but awkward and bleary-eyed; this allowed the Intuits to drive them from the land. Generally the tornit were good-natured but there are stories of their hostility and of their stealing women who go walking in the fog. The tornit were said to be afraid of dogs and would stay hidden from men.

Source: Alexander, *North American [mythology]*, 3; Boas, *Race, Language, and Culture*, 512

Torto

Variations: Tartalo

A being of the mountains, Torto is a CYCLOPS from Basque mythology in the region of Marquina; it is said to live in a cave and in NURSERY BOGIE fashion kidnaps unruly youths. Torto was said to be gigantic in size and have a pale complexion.

Source: Miguel de Barandiarán, *Selected Writings of José Miguel De Barandiarán*, 92

Totrughypja

Variations: Tötrughypja

One of the hrymthursars (FROST GIANTS) from Norse mythology, Totrughypja ("clothed in rags") was born one of the daughters of THRAEL and THIR; she was described as only ever being clothed in cast-off clothing and rags.

Source: Crossley-Holland, *Norse Myths*, 20; Grimes, Norse Myths, 27, 304

The Tritons

A race of aquatic GIANTES from ancient Greek mythology, the Tritons were part of the entourage of the god of the sea, Poseidon (Neptune); they had the upper body of a human and the lower body of a fish. Sporting with the NEREIDS, the Tritons were seen as nature spirits of low status among the pantheon but were a favorite subject of artists, especially when families of these creatures were the subject.

Triton, an individual being of Greek mythology, was depicted as a MERMAN and was considered by some to be the god of Lake Tritonis in Lybia. In one myth he was wrestled by the cultural hero Hercules (Heracles), forced to give the route to the Hesperides. His descendants, in some accounts, were called the Tritons and were depicted as having scaled bodies, gills beneath their ears, and fingernails which were in fact small seashells.

Source: Andrews, *Dictionary of Nature Myths*, 211; Barber, *Dictionary of Fabulous Beasts*, 144; Hard, *Routledge Handbook of Greek Mythology*, 106; Zell-Ravenheart, *Wizard's Bestiary*, 96

Troglodytes

A race of beings mentioned by Pliny in his *Natural History* (AD 77), the troglodytes were said to live in caves and live on a diet of snake meat. Unable to vocalize human speech, they easily communicated to one another through a series of clicks and squeaking noises.

Source: Pliny the Elder, *Pliny's Natural History. In Thirty-seven Books*, Volumes 1–3, 139; Sprague de Camp, *Lands Beyond*, 221–22

Troll

Variations: Berg People, Foddenskkmaend, Guild Neighbors, Guild-folk, Hill Men, Hill-People, Holder-Folk, Hollow-Men, Jutul, Orcs, Rise, Trolds, Trows, Trulli, Tusse, Underground-People

In Scandinavian myth, trolls are one of the four species of fairies and are generally described as being the enemies of mankind; they also appear as such in the folklore of Finland, Germany, Russia, and Siberia. Larger and stronger than humans, these cannibalistic fairy beings came to be the size of humans over time. Usually trolls have a hunchback and a long, bent nose, and dress in grey coats and wear red hats. By use of a magical hat, trolls can walk about invisibly; they also have the ability to bestow bodily strength on anyone, foresee the future, shape-shift into any form, and an array of feats beyond the power of man as needed in folklore. Only in ballads do the trolls have a king ruling over them; they do not in folklore or mythology.

On the Faroe Islands trolls are called foddenskkmaend, holder-folk, hollow-men, and underground-people. There it is believed trolls carry humans into their underground lairs and detain them there.

Trolls who dwell on the land are called Guild-Folk; they live beneath the green hills. The walls of their homes are said to be lined with gold and silver. Those trolls who live in the woods are called *SKOVTROLDE*; these trolls constantly seek to injure and torment mankind. Hill trolls ("bjerg-trolde") are the trolls living in the hills, sometimes alone or with their family.

It is said because of a racial memory from the time when the god of thunder, Thor, used to throw his hammer at them, trolls disdain loud noises. Trolls are believed to be virtually indestructible due to their hard skin and size; however, if they are exposed to sunlight they will retreat into the shadows or they will turn into stone.

Source: Keightley, *World Guide to Gnomes, Fairies, Elves, and Other Little People*, 63, 95–6, 162, 164; McCoy, *Witch's Guide to Faery Folk*, 322–23; Rose, *Spirits, Fairies, Leprechauns, and Goblins*, 316

Tronubeina

Variations: Tronnbeina

One of the hrymthursars (FROST GIANTS) from Norse mythology, Tronubeina ("crane legs") was born one of the daughters of THRAEL and THIR; she was described as being skinny, tall, and having bony legs.

Source: Crossley-Holland, *Norse Myths*, 20; Grimes, *Norse Myths*, 27, 304

Trooping Fairies

Variations: Aristocratic Fairies, Heroic Fairies, Trooping Faery

Throughout the British Isles there are two basic classifications of fairies, solitary fairies and Trooping Fairies. Large and small, benign and malignant, the trooping fay tends to wear a green jacket and live in social communities overseen by a monarch, although popular consensus seems to rule. Fairy raids are popular with trooping fairies, as it allows them to dress both themselves and their beloved horses in the finest of clothing and accessories; as they travel they create a fairy trail, a long path of dark grass; sometimes these paths are miles long. Trooping fairies are far more approachable than SOLITARY FAIRIES, although it is not always safe to get near them; on occasion one of the trooping fay will take a mortal human as its spouse.

Source: Briggs, *Encyclopedia of Fairies*, 412; McCoy, *Witch's Guide to Faery Folk*, 13–14, 23, 43, 68; Newcomb, *Faerie Treasury*, 70; Rosen, *Mythical Creatures Bible*, 259–61

Trow

Variations: Bannafeet (bannock feet), Creepers, Grey Neighbors, Night Stealers, Trowe, Truncherface ("trencher face")

On the Shetland Islands the trows are small GOBLINS dressed in grey. In many ways they are similar to the TROLL such as living inside earth mounds which are alleged to be filled with gold, precious metals, and silver; they serve only the finest drink and food upon their tables. Trows have a fondness for music and are not above kidnapping a musician and bringing him back to their home to play for one of their feasts. While only a few days may pass within the mound, years could pass in the real world. Trows are also known to kidnap human babies and leave a CHANGELING in their place. Descriptions of trows vary greatly in the specifics but generally they are described as being short and ugly.

Source: Avant, *Mythological Reference*, 196–97; Briggs, *Encyclopedia of Fairies*, 414; Emick, *Everything Celtic Wisdom Book*, 144–45; Frazer, *Golden Bough*, 169

Tsavoojok

A cunning GIANT from Paviotso folklore, Tsavoojok favored having young wives for himself even in his old age. He was said to cause fights between married couples and while they fought, he would abduct the wife. Tsavoojok, like other GIANTS and OGRES, was cunning but not intelligent; when the angry husbands banded together and constructed a pit trap, Tsavoojok literally fell for it.

Source: Gordon, *Encyclopedia of Myths and Legends*, n.pag.; Rose, *Giants, Monsters, and Dragons*, 367

Tsiatko

Variations: Sheahah, Snanaik, Steh-tathl, Timber Giants

A race of mountain-dwelling anthropoids appearing throughout Native American Indian folklore, descriptions of the tsiatko vary widely. To one tribe they are described as being extremely large, their feet, ursine (bear-like) in appearance, are eighteen inches long. They say, although the tsiatko do not wear clothes, their bodies are covered with doglike hair and they carry a noticeable and pungent smell. Making their homes in the caves deep in the mountains, the tsiatko usually only leave during the fishing season in order to carry off young girls, smother babies, and steal salmon. Another tribe may say these creatures are the size of a typical man but are noted for their constant gibbering to one another in an unintelligible language, making enough noise any two of them could pass as a party of a dozen or more. The Nisqually tribe say the tsiatko have the voice of an owl and use it to entrance people; anyone who hears them speaking will fall down in a swoon.

Source: *Oregon Historical Quarterly*, Volumes 56–57, 313–4; Penz, *Cryptid*, n.pag.; Varner, *Creatures in the Mist*, 75

Tsul 'Kalu

Variations: Judaculla ("he has them slanting"), Lord of the Hunt, Mooney ("he has slanting eyes")

According to Cherokee folklore Tsul 'Kalu was an ugly, slant eyed GIANT; fierce and frightening to behold, he was said to have hands like talons sporting seven fingers each and would leap from mountain to mountain in enraged pursuit of anyone who dared to hunt upon his lands. His thirst was so great he could drink up an entire stream in one swallow. For arrows, Tsul 'Kalu used lightning bolts; his home was called Tsunegun'yi.

Source: Conley, *Cherokee Medicine Man*, 26–30; Pitzer, *Myths and Mysteries of North Carolina*, 36–38

Tuatha de Danann

Variations: De Danaan, Feadh-Ree, Fir, Dea ("men of the goddess"), People of god whose mother was Dana, SÍDHE, Spirit Race

The Tuatha de Danann ("people of the goddess Dana") were the magical and mythological race who lived in Ireland and defeated both the FIR BOLG and FOMORIANS for control of the country. According to the *Book of Invasions*, which details the mythological history of the country, they arrived in Ireland on May 1 upon the mountains of Conmaicne Rein in Connachta having come from four northern cities—Falias, Finias, Gorias, and Murias. Dark clouds came with them and were said to hang in the air for three days. They were the fifth group of people to have settled the island.

For three thousand years the Tuatha de Danann ruled Ireland until the Milesians fought them for control. Neither side was able to gain the advantage so an accord was struck—the Milesians would rule the surface world and the Tuatha de Danann would have dominion over the rest. This bargain included the fairy mounds, the invisible islands, and the Underworld. Becoming a race of fairy people, these timeless immortals still interacted with the surface world, but only when the veil between the two realms was thin. When occasion permits, these TROOPING FAIRIES will parade, dressed in their finest, upon their magnificent horses. Described as being aristocratic, fair-skinned, perfectly physically fit, red-headed, and tall, the Tuatha de Danann were skilled in poetry, magic, and science.

The Tuatha de Danann were named after the goddess they are descended from, Danu. Many of the Tuatha de Danann were worshiped as gods in ancient Ireland. Each member of the race established his or her own fairy fort, some of which are well known to this day, such as Knockshegowna.

Source: Evans-Wentz, *Fairy Faith in Celtic Countries*, 27; Koch, *Celtic Heroic Age*, 245; McCoy, *Witch's Guide to Faery Folk*, 324–26; MacKillop, *Myths and Legends of the Celts*, 136; Marstrander, *Dictionary of the Irish Language*, 612; Monaghan, *Encyclopedia of Celtic Mythology and Folklore*, 475; Stepanich, *Faery Wicca*, Book One, 23

Tunnituaqruk

A type of anthropoid monster from Inuit folklore, the tunnituaqruk ("tattooed ones") of the Hudson Bay region in Canada are said to be humanoid in appearance but have an enormous head covered with tattoos. The tunnituaqruk and their female counterparts known as the KATYTAYUUQ scavenge behind humans on the trail searching out scraps. These creatures hide wherever they can and will terrify anyone who happens upon one or surprises it.

Source: Halpin, *Manlike Monsters on Trial*, 198, 205; Rose, *Giants, Monsters, and Dragons*, 368

Turehu

Variations: Heketoro, Korakorako, Nuku-maitore, Patu-pai-arehe, PATUPAIAREHE, Tahurangi

In Polynesian mythology the turehu was a race of fair haired and skinned fairies living in an underworld region known as Raro-henga. These fairies only ate uncooked food, were fond of dancing, and would on occasion take a human as a spouse. The turehu, when they landed on the island of New Zealand, conquered the residents, the Tutu-mai-ao, interbreeding and driving their species to extinction.

Source: Andersen, *Myths and Legends of the Polynesians*, 126, 288; Craig, *Dictionary of Polynesian Mythology*, 105

Tuurnngaq

Variations: Tuniq

A type of GIANT from Inuit folklore, the tuurnngaq from the Hudson Bay region in Canada are well-known for their construction of buildings out of living stone. Especially aggressive toward humans, these beings will kill any person they happen across.

Source: Laugrand, *Hunters, Predators and Prey*, 136; Rose, *Giants, Monsters, and Dragons*, 368

Typhoeus

Variations: Typhon

A monstrous, fire-breathing GIGANTE from ancient Greek mythology, Typhoeus was the husband of ECHIDNA the mother of monsters; together the couple produced CERBERUS, the CHIMAERA, the CROMMYONIAN SOW, the HYDRA, NEMEAN LION, ORTHOS, the SPHINX, and the eagle which ate Prometheus's liver. Typhoeus was conceived through the union between Gaea and Tartarus contrived by the goddess Aphrodite (Venus). Born during the

Titanomachy, he was encouraged to fight against the god by his mother; during the battle he was slain by Zeus (Jupiter), having each of his snake heads shot off with a thunderbolt. In another version of the tale, he was confined to eternity in Tartarus but before his confinement managed to mate with ECHIDNA.

Typhoeus was described as being enormous, larger than a mountain and so tall his head brushed the stars. Fiery eyes were upon each of the one-hundred snake heads issuing forth from his neck; the sounds they made varied between animalistic and human and each was horrific to hear. Other descriptions also added a beard, long hair, a serpentine lower body, and wings.

Source: Daly, *Greek and Roman Mythology, A to Z*, 129; Daniels, *Encyclopædia of Superstitions, Folklore, and the Occult Sciences of the World*, 1378; Roman, *Encyclopedia of Greek and Roman Mythology*, 507

Udaeus

In classical Greek mythology, Udaeus ("of the earth") was one of the five SPARTI who went on to become the progenitors of the five leading families of the city of Thebes who formed the military caste.

Source: Apollodorus, *Apollodorus' Library and Hyginus' Fabulae*, 22, 47; Dixon-Kennedy, *Encyclopedia of Greco-Roman Mythology*, 86; Hard, *Routledge Handbook of Greek Mythology*, 296

Udr

An ASYNJR from Norse mythology, Udr ("frothing wave") was one of the WAVE MAIDENS who were mother to the god Heimdall; she was the daughter of the god of the sea, Aegir. She, like her sisters, was said to have snow-white skin, blue eyes, and billowing blond hair; in one hand they carried a golden goblet filled with mead and in the other seashells filled with the finest foods. They wore long transparent robes of green or blue trimmed in white. When not serving food in the hall, they played on the shore in groups of three.

Source: Grimes, *Norse Myths*, 122, 274; Sturluson, *Prose Edda*, Volume 5, 219

Ulala

Variations: Walala

A female OGRE from Haida mythology, Ulala was an ancestral spirit called up and utilized during initiation ceremonies; during the event Ulala possessed the initiate, acting and speaking through him.

Source: Alexander, *Mythology of All Races*, Volume X North America, 247; Dixon-Kennedy, *Native American Myth and Legend*, 254

Ulfrum (OOLV-rum)

Variations: Ulfrun ("she who rides a wolf," "wolf runner")

An ASYNJR from Norse mythology, Ulfrum ("she wolf") was one of the WAVE MAIDENS who were mother to the god Heimdall; she was the daughter of the god of the sea, Aegir. She, like her sisters, was said to have snow-white skin, blue eyes, and billowing blond hair; in one hand they carried a golden goblet filled with mead and in the other seashells filled with the finest foods. They wore long transparent robes of green or blue trimmed in white. When not serving food in the hall, they played on the shore in groups of three.

Source: Anderson, *History and Romance of Northern Europe*, Volume 5, 1038; Daly, *Norse Mythology A to Z*, 47; Grimes, *Norse Myths*, 255

Ullikummi

A GIANT of stone, Ullikummi of Hittite mythology was the son of the god and personification of the sea, Kumarbi. According to the *Song of Ullikummi*, Kumarbi, the father of the gods but not the first god, was dethroned by Teshub, a god of storms, and sought revenge. Kumarbi, under the advice of the sea, "poured his seed" into a mountain which then gave birth to a son he named Ullikummi. Raised in the abyss beneath the oceans, upon the shoulder of the GIANT Upelluri (who held up the earth and heavens) Ullikummi grew a cubit a day until he was nine thousand leagues tall. Deaf and blind, Ullikummi was unable to be seduced into submission; Teshub, frightened, staged an assault against the GIANT, but to no avail. The god of wisdom, Ea, learned from Upelluri the source of Ullikummi's strength; another battle was staged and although this is where the text ends, its conclusion lost, it may be assumed Teshub is restored to power, Kumarbi and Ullikummi defeated.

Source: Fontenrose, *Python*, 211–12; Leick, *Dictionary of Ancient Near Eastern Mythology*, 106–7

Undine

Variations: Un'Dine

The Renaissance alchemist, astrologer, botanist, general occultist, and physician Paracelsus believed nature, both the visible and invisible, was inhabited by a host of beings aligned with the elements. On the invisible side he determined there were four distinct groups, the GNOMES of the earth, the salamanders (the hermetic symbol of fire) of fire, the sylphs of the air and the undines of the water.

The undines were water fairies or nature spirits who had the ability to control the element of water to a certain degree. Always depicted in art as being beautiful and nearly always in a female form, the undines of ancient folklore were said to resemble humans in appearance and size; the ones who inhabited smaller water sources were proportionally smaller but all were capable of assuming a human guise and intermingling with mankind. In Greek folklore undines resembled the goddess portrayed in statuaries; rising up from the water and draped in mist they could not retain solid form for very long out of the water. There are ancient Roman tales of an undine taking a mortal as a spouse but in all cases the call of the sea is too much for her to resist and she eventually returns to the water and the god of the sea, Neptune.

Generally it was believed these NYMPH-like fairies lived in coral caves under the oceans or in the reeds along the banks of rivers. In Celtic folklore undines lived under lily pads and in houses made of moss located underneath waterfalls. It is believed when the TUATHA DE DANNA retreated underground the undines also fell back to their homes where they remain to this day.

The ruler of the undines is named Necksa; she is honored, loved, and served untiringly by them. Emotional, friendly beings, they occasionally ride upon the backs of dolphins and other sea creatures.

Examples of species of undines would be CRINAEAE, DANAIDS, ELEIONOMAE, GWRAGEDD ANNWN, JENGU, KATAW, LIMNADES, MERMAID, MERROW, MORGAN, NÄCKEN, NECK, NIXEN, NOKKE, NYMPHS, OCEANID, PONATURI, POTAMEIDES, RUSALKA, SHELLYCOAT, SIRNES, STRÖMKARL, and SWAN MAIDEN.

Source: Hall, *Secret Teachings of All Ages*, 313–14; Evans-Wentz, *Fairy Faith in Celtic Countries*, 241; McCoy, *Witch's Guide to Faery Folk*, 328–29

Upelleru

Variations: Upelluri

A primordial GIANT from Hittite and ancient Hurrian mythology (ancient Anatolia), Upelleru is said to stand in the ocean holding the earth and the heavens apart with his outstretched arms. Upon his right shoulder the sea god Kumarbi placed his son ULLIKUMMI so the child could mature and prepare to wage war against Teshub.

Source: Leick, *Dictionary of Ancient Near Eastern Mythology*, 106–7; Lurker, *Dictionary of Gods and Goddesses, Devils and Demons*, 191; Rose, *Giants, Monsters, and Dragons*, 377

Urdr

Variations: Hurd, Urd, Urda, Urdar, Urdur, Urth

The eldest of the three NORNS from Norse mythology, the ASYNJR Urdr ("what was") personifies the past; SKULDR the youngest personifies the future and VERDANDI personifies the present; all of them are described as looking like old women spinning the threads of a person's destiny into a gigantic tapestry showing the lives of all people and the history of world—but only of the events fated to happen. She and her sisters live near Urdarbrunnr Well and see to the upkeep of Ygdrasil.

Source: Daly, *Norse Mythology A to Z*, 74, 110; Grimes, *Norse Myths*, 304

Útgarða-Loki

Variations: SKRYMER, Utgaard-Loki, Utgardaloki, Útgardarloki, Utgard-Loke, Utgard-Loki, Utgarð-Loki, Utgardr-Loki, Útgardr-Loki, Útgardur-Loki, Utgarthilocus, Utgarth-Loki

In Norse mythology, Útgarða-Loki ("wilderness Loki") was a clever JOTUN from Norse mythology and the master of Utgard (Útgarðr) castle; the god Thor once petitioned this crafty individual to become one of his followers and accepted a series of challenges to prove his worthiness.

The first was an eating contest against the JOTUN LOGE and the god Loki; the second test was to consume the contents of a drinking horn in no more than three gulps; the third was to lift Útgarða-Loki's cat. Having lost all events so far, Thor then requested a wrestling match. Losing that as well, he was presented with an ancient nurse-maid. Thor and his entourage left in the morning; Útgarða-Loki accompanied them to the border of his land where he confessed to having cheated by using his powerful magic to defeat Thor. Útgarða-Loki then advised Thor never to return to his lands as they would be over-protected with illusions and magic of his own making.

Source: Daly, *Norse Mythology A to Z*, 110; Grimes, *Norse Mythology*, 305; Thorpe, *Scandinavian Popular Traditions and Superstitions: Volume 2*, 63–5

Vættir (VAIT-ir)

Variations: De Underjordiske ("the subterranean ones"), Huldrefolk ("concealed people"), Maahinen, Vättar, Wight

In the Norse religion Vættir ("beings") are nature spirits; they are divided up into different groups, the Æsir, Álfar (elves), Dvergar (DWARFS), the gods, JOTUN (GIANTs), and the Vanir. The vættir consist of those among the dead, especially individuals in the Underworld, Hel.

Peasants were cautious about hurting or offending the vættir, as doing so would result in accidents occurring, disease spreading, or livestock dying. The vættir have the power of invisibility and carry about them a feeling of otherworldliness; they were described as being strikingly beautiful, clad in grey clothing, and living underground. In addition to having their own breed of cattle which gave tremendous amounts of milk these fairies could shape-shift into animals, making them difficult to observe; frogs were said to be their preferred form. After the introduction of Christianity the human-sized vættir began to shrink in size. Through Christian Europe tales of the Scandinavian vættir kidnapping unbaptized babies and leaving CHANGELINGs in their place began to spread. In some cases it was said the vættir themselves would remain behind in the infant's place.

Source: Croker, *Fairy Legends and Traditions of the South of Ireland*, Volumes 1–3, 68–69; Grimm, *Teutonic Mythology*, Volume 4, 1407; Norroena Society, *Asatrii Edda*, 56–59

Vafthrudner (VAV-throoth-nir)

Variations: Vaftheuthnir, Vafþrúðnir, Vafthrudnir ("strong in entangling [with questions]"), Valfthrudnir, Valthrudnir, Valthrupnir ("eminent but proud")

A proud JOTUN from Norse mythology, Vafthrudner ("mighty weaver") was the most witty and wise of his kind. The god Odin traveled to his hall, Vafthrudner, seeking advice, knowledge, and secrets of the past in the guise of Gangraaf (Gangrod, "weary wanderer"), and mortal wayfarer. After Vafthrudner asks his guest a few questions to see if he is worthy, Vafthrudner becomes annoyed by the laced insults he is answered with. Vafthrudner challenges his guest to a battle of wits on Norse mythology and promises him the loser shall forfeit their head. The god eventually defeated the JOTUN in the contest and used the knowledge he gain to consequently slay Vafthrudner and his entire household to the last.

Source: Anderson, *Norse Mythology*, 121–2; Grimes, *Norse Myths*, 305; Oehlenschläger, *Gods of the North*, lxvi; Norroena Society, *Asatrii Edda*, 389

Vagnhofdi (VAG-n-huhv-thi)

According to Saxo Grammaticus (circa 1150–1220), the Danish author, foremost advisor to Valdemar I of Denmark, historian, and secretary to the Archbishop of Lund, in his work *History of Denmark*, the JOTUN warrior Vangnhofdi ("wagon-chieftain" or "whale head") of Norse mythology was the foster father to the human hero Haddingr while he was still in hiding.

Source: Norroena Society, *Asatrii Edda*, 395; Waggoner, *Sagas of Giants and Heroes*, viii; *History of the Danes*, Books 1–9, 29

Valkyrie (VAL-ker-ya), plural Valkyries

Variations: Alaisiagae, Dises, Idises, Herjan's Disir, Valkyriar (plural), Valkyrie (plural: Valkyrior), Valkyrier (plural), Valkyrior (plural), Valkyrja (plural), Valkyrjur (plural), Valkyrjur (plural: Valkyrja), Valkyrs (plural), Vallkyr (plural), Valmeyar, Wælcyrgie, Walkyries

In Norse mythology the Valkyries ("choosers of the slain") are a select band of warrior maidens under the command of the gods Frejya and Odin. Some of them are born the daughters of Odin while others, such as the terrestrial humans, were the daughters of kings chosen from birth to become one of their number; some elected to join; all are virgins. There were two species of Valkyries, divine ones who numbered nine (or nine times nine; sources vary) and the half-mortal Vaetter maidens who were only visible to humans who had the gift of second sight.

Led by the NORN SKULD, they are dispatched in varying numbers to battlefields so they may oversee the conflict and at precisely the right moment snatch up the souls of the fallen warriors who have proven themselves worthy of an afterlife in servitude to Hel or in the Hall of Valhalla. These NYMPHS of battle are said to ride upon white horses with fiery manes and tails; the sight of meteors in the sky was said to be the Valkyries dispatched, an omen of an upcoming battle. The Valkyries do not make the decision of where the courageous warriors will ultimately reside, only if the combatant was worthy of being selected to serve in either place of honor. Should a warrior die a non-violent death the Valkyries may be dispatched to lead his soul to the path which leads to Valhalla. The Valkyries frequently flew to Midgard as SWAN MAIDENS, wearing their swan cloaks. If ever their cloak was stolen from them while they bathed, they were forced to do the bidding of the person who possessed the cloak.

When not delivering or guiding the souls of worthy warriors, the Valkyries work as serving girls, serving food and mead to those who were fortunate enough to become EINHERJAR. They also passed some of their leisure time working looms, weaving.

There are many Valkyries mentioned, named, and written of in Norse mythology; typically these names translate to be an expression of battle or something warlike in nature. Some of the Valkyries were better developed and utilized in the mythology than others; while there are those with long and well graphed stories, others are only a name said in passing among a horde of others; they are: ALAISIAGAE, ALVIT, BRUNHILDE ("bright battle"), GEIRAHODR ("spear-fighter," "spear of battle"), GEIRAVOR ("spear goddess"), GEIRDRIFUL ("spear thrower"), GEIROLUL ("spear waver"), GEIRONUL ("spear thrower"), GEIRROMUL, GEIRRONDUL, Geirskigull, GEIRSKOGUL ("spear battle"), GOLL ("battle cry," "loud cry," "noisy"), GONDULL ("enchanted stave," "magic wand," "she-WEREWOLF"), GUDR, GUDRUN ("battle rune"), GUNNR ("battle," "warrior-maiden"), GUTH, HERFJOTURR ("army ftter," "host fetter" or "war-fetterer"), HERJA ("Devastator"), HERVOR ("the all wise," "warder of the host"), HILDR ("battle"), HIORPRIMU, HJALMBRIMUL ("battle helm"), HJOR, HJORDRIMUL ("Battle-Sword"), HJORTHRIMUL, HLATHGUTH ("necklace-adorned warrior-maiden"), HLOKK ("battle," "din of battle," "lock," "noise"), HRIST ("shaker"), HRUND ("Striker"), Judur, KARA, Kára Hrist ("the shaker"), MGN ("host receiver"), MIST ("cloud"), ÓÐINSSEN, OLRUN ("one knowing ale rune"), Óðinssen, PRUDR ("power"), RADGRIOR ("counsel truce" or "violent counsel"), RAGRIDR, RANDGRIDR ("shield destroyer"), RANDGRITH, RATHGRITH, REGINLEIF ("heritage of the gods," "the mighty," "power trace"), ROSTGRIDR, ROTA ("creator of confusion," "she who causes turmoil"), SANG-RIDE ("true destroyer"), SIGRDRIFA ("victory blizzard," "victory urger"), Sigrun ("victory rune"), SIG-URDRIFTA, Sigurlinn, SKALMOLD ("sword age" or "sword time"), SKEGGJOLD ("axe age," "battle axe," "wearing an axe"), SKOGUL ("battle," "rager,"), SKULD ("debt," "necessity," "spinster," "what shall become"), Svafa ("sleep maker"), SVAVA ("sleeper"), SVEID ("clamor"), SVIPUL ("battle"), TANNGNIDR ("teeth grinder"), Thogn, THRIMA ("battle"), THRIMUL, THRUDR ("power"), and Thruth.

Source: Grimes, *Norse Myths*, 306; Oehlenschläger, *Gods of the North*, lxvi; Monaghan, *Encyclopedia of Goddesses and Heroines*, 294; Norroena Society, *Asatrii Edda*, 395

Var

Variations: Vara, Varr, VOR ("oath")

In Norse mythology Var ("beloved," "vow") was one of the ASYNJR and attendants of the goddess Frigg. Var was worshipped as a goddess of *varars* (marriage vows) and all betrothals, contracts, and oaths invoked her name.

Source: Grimes, *Norse Myths*, 306; Norroena Society, *Asatrii Edda*, 396

Veigr

In Norse mythology Veigr ("brew") was one of the rock DVERGAR (DWARFS) created by the DWARF DURINN.

Source: Grimes, *Norse Myths*, 260; Wagner, *Asgard and the Gods*, 311

Verdandi

Variations: Verdande, Verlandi, Verthandi

One of the three nornir (see NORN) from Norse

mythology, the ASYNJR Verdandi ("that which is") personifies the present; SKULDR, the youngest of the three, personifies the future and URDR, the eldest, personifies the past; all of them are described as looking like old women spinning the threads of a person's destiny into a gigantic tapestry showing the lives of all people and the history of world—but only of the events fated to happen. She and her sisters live near Urdarbrunnr Well and see to the upkeep of Ygdrasil.

Source: Daly, *Norse Mythology A to Z*, 74, 114; Grimes, *Norse Myths*, 307

Vestre

Variations: Vestri, Westri

In Norse mythology Vestre was one of the four DVERGAR (DWARFS) who were appointed by the gods to hold up the sky which they constructed from the skull of YMIR. AUSTRE held up the East, NORDRE held the North, SUDRE held the South, and Vestre held the West.

Source: Anderson, *Norse Mythology*, 183; Grimes, *Norse Myths*, 9; Norroena Society, *Asatrii Edda*, 398; Sturluson, *Prose Edda*, 26

Vidblindi

A JOTUN from Norse mythology, Vidblindi ("wide blind") was said to be able to draw whales out of the ocean as if they were fish.

Source: Lindow, *Norse Mythology*, 315

Vidyadharas

A race of fair complexioned beings appearing only in Hindu Puranic folklore, the Vidyadharas were said to have been gifted with supernatural qualities; they are not humans but rather humans who were once monkeys and monsters who through severe austerities came to possess magic and super-human powers. Generally, they are highly civilized and adhere to the vow of Ahimas ("the avoidance of violence"). Male and female alike, they are all described as being handsome, adorned with garlands, jewelry, and ornamentations; in light of their vow of Ahimas, they are often depicted in the sky and holding swords in their hands. The Vidyadharas were especially fond of flowers and garlands, gifting them freely on the success of anyone or for an auspicious occasion.

Source: Iyengar, *Asian Variations in Ramayana*, 81; Saklani, *Ancient Communities of the Himalaya*, 111–12

Vigs

A DVERG (DWARF) from Norse mythology, Vigs is named in the *Voluspa* part of the *Poetic Edda*.

Source: Daly, *Norse Mythology A to Z*, 22;

Vila

Variations: Veela, Vilia, Vilya, Vilishkis, Vily, Willi

In Serbian folklore, the vilas were the beautiful and young mountain NYMPHS clad in white; their voice was said to resemble the call of the woodpecker and was a warning of some mountain catastrophe, such as an avalanche. Vilas were known to carry off children whose mothers had, in a fit of anger, condemned them to the Devil or Hell. The vilas were said to injure those who interrupt their revelries as they dance beneath the branches of the ash or cherry trees, shooting them with deadly accuracy with their bow and arrows. Vilas would heal wounded deer, warn heroes of their imminent death, and had the ability to speak the languages of the animals. These fairies were said to bridle seven-year-old harts with snakes so they could ride them as mounts.

It is possible the vilas may have at one time not been a species of NYMPH but rather a singular goddess.

In Western Europe the vilia is a type of NYMPH or nature spirit; nearly always female they are described as being captivatingly beautiful. They will attract the attention and love of men but will eventually end the relationship; according to some tales, if a vilia ever found true love it would die a slow and terrible death. In Dalmatia, a man who is lucky enough to have the blessings of a vila is called *vilenik*.

As the vily, they are similar to Greek NYMPHS and found in the mountains of the European Alps and Poland; they are beautiful, female nature spirits who prefer not to become involved in human affairs. Although there are a few stories of the vily rescuing a person from an alpine disaster by guiding the team of rescue dogs it is not because the vily are inclined to help the human but rather because they love dogs over all other animals. The vily are believed to protect and watch over the Saint Bernard Monastery houses and train the much acclaimed rescue dogs.

Source: Keightley, *World Guide to Gnomes, Fairies, Elves, and Other Little People*, 491–2; McCoy, *Witch's Guide to Faery Folk*, 331–32; Porteous, *Forest in Folklore and Mythology*, 109

Vilmeidr (VIL-mayth-r)

A JOTUN from Norse mythology, Vilmeidr ("soothsayer," "wish tree") was the progenitor of evil *vitkar* (wizards).

Source: Norroena Society, *Asatrii Edda*, 399; Sturleson, *Viking Anthology*, n.pag.

Vindalf

Variation: Vindálfr

A DVERG (DWARF) from Norse mythology, Vin-dalf ("wind ELF") is named in the *Voluspa*, the first and best-known poem of the *Poetic Edda* (AD 985).

Source: Crossley-Holland, *Norse Myths*, 183; Daly, *Norse Mythology A to Z*, 22; Skyes, *Who's Who in Non-Classical Mythology*, 53

Vindloni (VIND-lohn-i)

Variations: Vindsval ("wind bringer"), Vindsvalr

A JOTUN from Norse mythology, Vindloni ("wind chill"), born the son of Vasad (Vasadr), is the father of Winter; he is described as having a cold heart, icy breath, and a gloomy and grim aspect. Vindloni is the father of Vetr.

Source: Grimm, *Teutonic Mythology*, Volume 2, 758; Norroena Society, *Asatrii Edda*, 399; Sturleson, *Viking Anthology*, n.pag.

Vindr

In Norse mythology Vindr ("wind") was a JOTUN; beyond a name, there is nothing else known.

Source: Norroena Society, *Asatrii Edda*, 399

Vingnir

Variations: Vingner ("winged")

A JOTUN from Norse mythology, Vingnir ("the strong") and his wife Hlor were the foster-parents to the god Thor; they took him in when he became too large and strong for his mother Frigg to handle. Thor's first hammer, Vingnir's Mjollnir, came from him; it was made of stone.

Source: Grimes, *Norse Myths*, 20, 194, 302; Norroena Society, *Asatrii Edda*, 399

Vingripr (VIN-grip)

In Norse mythology Vingripr ("clutcher," "friendly grip," "friendly hold") was one of the many named Jotnar (see JOTUN) named in the *Asatrii Edda*. Beyond a name, there is little or nothing else known.

Source: Norroena Society, *Asatrii Edda*, 399

Vinndalf (VIND-ahlv-r)

Variations: Vindalfr

In Norse mythology Vinndalf ("wind ELF") was one of the rock DVERGAR (DWARFS) created by DURINN.

Source: Grimes, *Norse Myths*, 260, 309; Norroena Society, *Asatrii Edda*, 399; Young, *Prose Edda*, 41

Virvir

A DVERG (DWARF) from Norse mythology created by DURINN, Virvir ("dyer") is listed as being one of DURINN's KIN. He, like the others created, paid particular attention to DURINN's leadership.

Source: Daly, *Norse Mythology A to Z*, 22; Grimes, *Norse Myths*, 260

Vit (Vit)

A DVERG (DWARF) from Norse mythology, Vit ("wise") is named in the *Voluspa* part of the *Poetic Edda*. Beyond his name, there is nothing else known of him.

Source: Daly, *Norse Mythology A to Z*, 22; Norroena Society, *Asatrii Edda*, 400; Young, *Prose Edda*, 42

Vodianoi

Variations: Vodianoi Chert ("water devil")

A particularly malevolent species of nature spirit or water fairy in Slavic folklore, the vodianoi exists only to drown swimmers, especially those who are boastful or proud by nature. Although they have the ability to shape-shift into a fish, descriptions of their true form vary; sometimes they are said to look like a bloated, hairy, naked old man covered in slimy fish scales while other times they are said to look like a simple bearded peasant wearing a red shirt. From time to time the vodianoi appeared looking like a hunchback with cow's feet and tail or as a MERMAN.

Living in deep pools with a mill, a vodianoi is created whenever an unbaptized child dies, someone commits suicide, or a person passes away without having received the Catholic sacrament of the Anointing of the Sick, more popularly known as Last Rites.

The female of this species is known as a VODI-ANIKHA; they are described as looking like women with large breasts. The vodianoi never come out of the water, emerging only as high as their waist; their spouses, however, will sit upon the rocks and comb out their hair in MERMAID-like fashion.

Source: Dixon-Kennedy, *Encyclopedia of Russian and Slavic Myth and Legend*, 145; Ivanits, *Russian Folk Belief*, 70–71; Rose, *Spirits, Fairies, Leprechauns, and Goblins*, 329

Vodni Panny

Variations: Bile Pani ("white women"), Vodui Panny

In Celtic mythology the vodni panny ("water NYMPHS") are pale, tall water-NYMPHS dressed in transparent green robes. Living in crystal palaces under the water, their gravel pathways are made up of bits of gold and silver. Sitting in trees these fairies sing SIREN-like, luring in young men. In the evenings, the vodni panny will go to local villages and partake in festival dances.

Source: Eberhart, *Mysterious Creatures*, 573; MacCulloch, *Celtic Mythology*, Volume 3, 271–72

Vor (Vuhr)

An ASYNJR from Norse mythology, Vor ("awareness") was so searching and wise no bit of information or secret could be kept from her.

Source: Daly, *Norse Mythology A to Z*, 117; Norroena Society, *Asatrii Edda*, 400

Vornir (VUHRN-ir)

In Norse mythology Vornir ("cautious") was one of the many named Jotnar (see JOTUN) of whom, beyond a name, there is little else known.

Source: Norroena Society, *Asatrii Edda*, 25, 400; Sturluson, *Prose Edda*, 98

Vorys Mort

Variations: Vorys Murt

A GIANT in Russian folklore, Vorys Mort was said to be so tall he could look down upon the tree tops; unlike others of his kind, he was not slow, rather he could run so fast he would create whirlwinds in his wake. A useful ally, Vorys Mort was helpful to hunters as he would drive game to them in exchange for a portion of tobacco.

Source: Barber, *Dictionary of Fabulous Beasts*, 151; Rose, *Giants, Monsters, and Dragons*, 385

Wasgol People

In the folklore of the Haida people of the Pacific Northwest Coast of North America, the wasgol ("sea wolf") people were one of the many supernatural ocean people who lived in underwater villages scattered up and down the shore. Since the ocean people were in control of a large part of the food supply, they not only were held in the highest of regard but were also appealed to for assistance with offerings of rare flicker feathers, grease, and tobacco.

Source: Goldenweiser, *Early Civilization*, 63

The Watchers

Variations: Benei Ha-Elohim ("sons of God"), GRIGORI, Irin

The *Book of Enoch*, where their story originates, names only twenty of the two hundred Watchers; however, over the years, various sources, texts, and grimoires have added to the list of names.

The Watcher angels were one of the seven orders of ANGEL created by God to oversee the first generation of humans and teach them how to properly survive. They were described as large, like GIANTS. They were made Chief of Tens, meaning each of them had ten ANGELS under his command. It was not so long after they went to work on Earth when the Watchers began to lust after human women. Under the leadership and instigation of the ANGEL Samiaza, they gathered together to form a pact amongst themselves. As a group they acted against the will of God and took human women as their wives, assuming God would not punish them all. They then taught their spouses and their families the arts of astrology, astronomy, botany, divination, healing, and magic as well as how to make cosmetics, mirrors, and weapons. The Watchers fathered the NEPHILIM, semi-divine offspring; they were generally violent, cannibalistic, and evil by nature. However, a few of the NEPHILIM became great artisans, poets, and priests. For their numerous sins, God punished all the ANGELS involved, casting them out of Heaven.

Source: Black, *Book of Enoch, or, I Enoch*, 27–35; *Book of Enoch the Prophet*, 11–21; *Journal of Theological Studies*, Volume 8, 444–7

Wave Maidens

The daughters of the JOTUN AEGIR and his wife (Ran-Gullveig), the nine wave maidens of Norse mythology were the collective mothers to the god Heimdall. The names of these women vary from source to source and in spite of all sources claiming nine was the total number of maidens, the names seldom matched; therefore the list of mothers to the god is much greater.

The Wave Maidens listed by the Icelandic historian, poet, and politician Snorri Sturluson (1179–1241) are: BLODUGHADDA ("bloody hair"), BYLGJA ("billow"), DROFN ("foam fleck"), DUFA ("pitching one"), HEFRING ("riser"), HIMINGLAEVA ("that through which one can see heaven"), HRONN ("welling wave"), KOLGA ("cool one"), and UDR ("frothing wave").

Rasmus Bjørn Anderson (1846–1936) the American author, diplomat, professor and originator of Leif Erikson Day, names the Wave Maidens as: ANGEYJA ("she who makes the islands closer"), ATLA ("the awful-grim maiden"), EISTLA, EYRGJAFA ("she who gives sandbanks"), GJALP ("yeller"), GREIP ("gripper"), IMD, JARNSAXA ("ironstone," "iron knife," or "she who crushes iron"), and ULFRUN.

Other named WAVE MAIDENS include ALTA, AUGEIA, AURGIAFA, Bara, EGIA, GIALP, GREIP, JARNSAXA, and SINDUR.

Source: Anderson, *Norse Mythology*, 440; Grimes, *Norse Myths*, 253; Sturluson, *Prose Edda*, Volume 5, 219

Werewolf

Variations: Bisclaveret (Brittany), Lob Ombre (Spain), Lob Omem (Portugal), Lobombre (Spain), Loup Garpou (France), Louweerou (France), Lupo Manaro (Italy), Lycanthrope (Greece), Slovalia, Versipellis ("turnskin," Ancient Greek and Roman), Vircolak (various Balkan states), Vlkodlaks ("wolf hair," Slovakia), Vookodlaks (Slovakia), Vulkodlak (Russia), Wawkalak (Byelorus), WEREWOLF (Germany), Wer-wold (Germany)

A WEREWOLF ("man wolf") is a person with the ability to transform into a wolf or a wolf-human anthropomorphic hybrid; this folklore is present in many cultures worldwide and dates back to man's earliest day. The ability to transform may be innate, a curse placed on the individual, or by magical means, be it an item or a spell. The first recorded story of a *lycanthrope* (one with the ability to transform into a wolf) was the Greek tale of Lycaon written by Ovid in his tale *Metamorphoses*, although older unrecorded oral traditions date back even further in Icelandic, Norse, Scandinavian, and Teutonic traditions.

In many cultures, there are physical manifestations present in the person's visage when not transformed which give them away for their ability no matter how they came about it; such tell-tale signs are eyebrows which have grown together; fanglike incisors; hirsute skin; the "Mark of Cain," a ruddy birthmark of no specific or set description; mismatched eye color; and short fingers with claw-like nails.

Werewolves are feared no matter how they came into being because of their panache for violence, ravenous appetites, and wanton destruction; there are many tales of a single werewolf slaughtering an entire herd of cattle or sheep in a single night; crashing into people's homes snatching up the children, and fleeing off into the night. In both instances the creature destroys anything and anyone who gets in its way. Typically, while transformed the creature is nearly indestructible and immune to most weapons. The means by which to prevent their attack or damage these creatures vary by culture, from region to region, and the time period from which the story originates; they are too numerous to list.

The idea of *therianthropy* ("wild animal man," were-creatures) also exists and is prevalent throughout the world and all along the time-line; popular were-creatures are were-bear (United States of America), were-boar (Greece and Turkey), were-cat, were-crocodile (Africa), were-cow (*Boanthropy*, ancient Greece), were-dog (*Kuanthropy*, ancient Greece), were-fox (China and Japan), were-hyena (Africa), were-jackal (Africa), were-jaguar (South America) were-leopard (Africa) and the were-mountain lion (United States of America).

Source: Baring-Gould, *Book of Were-Wolves*, 4–9; Guiley, *Encyclopedia of Vampires, Werewolves, and Other Monsters*, 316–8; Rose, *Giants, Monsters, and Dragons*, 391–3

Widenostrils

Variations: Gaffer Widenostrils, Wide-Nostrils, Widenostrils the Swallowers of Windmills

A GIANT from French folklore, Widenostrils was

said to have lived on the islands of Bohu and Tohu; his favorite food was windmills but once they were all consumed, he was forced to seek out other means of substance. Whenever food was prepared, Widenostrils would consume "every individual pan, skillet, kettle, frying-pan, dripping-pan, boiler, and saucepan in the land." Following the advice of his physicians, he consumed a lump of fresh butter in front of an oven, an act which proved to be fatal, as he choked and died while eating it.

Source: Daniels, *Encyclopædia of Superstitions, Folklore, and the Occult Sciences of the World*, 1378; Rabelais, *Gargantua and Pantagruel*, Volumes 4–5, 102, 170

Wild Man

Variations: Ooser, Wild Man of the Woods, Woodhouse, Woodwose, Wooser, Wudewasa, ("woodmen")

A hairy, bipedal anthropoid, the wild man of European folklore is an unfettered child of nature who is solely dependent on its ability to tap into those resources; it cannot be captured nor understood by civilized man. To the Dark Ages (476–800) minds which envisioned and popularized this being, the wild man was filled with dualities while keeping a balance between its fearsome aggressiveness and its natural benevolence. While these creatures had a kinship to the animals of the wilderness, some would even tend cattle, goats, and sheep of their own, acting more as their protector than he; however the wild man could easily fly into a full-blown rage and under the influence of their mad temper direct their violence toward man, woman, and unbaptized child, tearing their bodies to pieces and consuming their flesh. They were described as wielding a club and being large in size, wearing animal skins, and in many instances, having a head full of long and unkempt green hair. His female counterpart is simply called a wild woman.

By the early Medieval Ages (500–1000) the wild man began to be regarded more as a comical or grotesque figure than a fierce and savage keeper of the secrets of the wilderness. Its image was synonymous with abnormal and exotic races, the pre-Christian culture, the uncharted areas of Africa and Asia, and came to be the personification of emancipatory freedom based on its appearance and behavior. By the Early to Mid-Renaissance era (1300–1500) the wild man no long represented the non-agrarian life and the wildness of nature but rather a being who chooses to be wild and uncultured, a thorn in the side of the process of civilization.

Source: Lie, *Constellation Caliban*, 46–8; Monahan, *American Wild Man*, 11–12; Rose, *Giants, Monsters, and Dragons*, 394–6

The Wild Man of Orford

A WILD MAN of the sea, this creature was said to have been caught by several fishermen and taken to Orford Castle in Suffolk during the reign of Henry II (1154–89). Named the WILD MAN of Orford, he was described as being completely naked, having a full beard and a chest covered with hair, although his head had only patches of hair; no piscean characteristics or qualities were ever recorded or mentioned. At the time it was undetermined if the WILD MAN of Orford was a devil, an evil spirit possessing the body of a sailor lost at sea, a fish, or a MERMAN. A period of torture proved it was incapable of speech and while it would eat any food given to it, it seemed to prefer raw fish which it would squeeze between its hands, wringing it dry of all moisture. After several month of incarceration at Orford Castle, the creature was able to escape and made its way back into the ocean.

Source: Jones, *Myths and Legends of Britain and Ireland*, 77–8; Varner, *Creatures in the Mist*, 78

Windigo (WIN-dee-go)

Variations: "He Who Lives Alone," Upayokawitigo ("the hermit"), Weendigo, Wenbdigo, Wendigo, Wetikoo, Wiitigo, Witiko

The windigo is a demonic creature from Ojibwa and Saulteaux Manitoba folklore. Its name means "cannibal" and "evil spirit" in Algonquin. For a human to become a windigo they must travel into the creature's region and make offerings to it of flesh and prayers. The windigo will either consume the person, thereby ending his petition, or adopt him. Once adopted the man's heart will turn to ice, hair will grow all over his body, and the craving for human flesh will begin. Almost immediately he will chew off his own lips in a desperate act to consume flesh. Windigos created in this fashion are never as tall as those who are naturally born.

Typically male, these cannibalistic GIANTS are described as having a simian (ape-like) face, bloodshot eyes, huge jagged teeth, and a heart made of ice. They are addicted to human flesh and said to be as tall as pine trees with long hair covering their entire bodies. Their long and narrow feet have one toe each and pointed heels; they smell horrible.

Windigos hunt the subarctic forests in search of humans to consume. When it cannot find humans, it will eat parts of its own body; when it can no longer do that it will consume carrion, moss, and rotten wood. Eventually it will turn on its own family, eating its youngest children first. Blizzards accompany the windigo as it travels. On occasion they hunt in packs. These demons are known to run wildly through the woods, screaming in rage and tearing up earth and trees with superhuman strength.

These demonic creatures are impervious to all human weapons and the natural elements; it is speculated either decapitation or melting their heart may kill them. Their assaults can be prevented with shamanistic conjurations. If a person has become a windigo, they must be captured, bound up, and held over an open fire so the heat and smoke will drive the evil away and melt their heart of ice. If this method does not work, the person is typically slain.

Source: Gilmore, *Monsters*, 75–90; Jones, *Evil in Our Midst*, 43–6; Rose, *Giants, Monsters, and Dragons*, 119

Wood Wife

Variations: Green Woman, Skoggra, Swor SKOGSFRU ("wood-wife"), Wish Wife, Wood Maid, Wood Women

The wood wives of German and Swiss folklore were said to live in dense groves in old forests; these FAIRY-beings are described as being petite and beautifully dressed. These fairies were believed to be connected to the trees of the forest in a way similar to the DRYAD of ancient Greece; there was a belief if the bark of a tree was twisted off, a wood wife would die. In the oldest mythology, the wood wives made up the court of the ancient gods who dwelled in the forests.

Oftentimes these beings would approach people in the woods asking for assistance in baking bread or mending a broken wheelbarrow. Anyone one who assisted them was richly rewarded as wood chips in the area would turn into gold coins and remain thus so long as their origin was not revealed.

Wood Wives were the prey of the relentless Wild Huntsman; the only way these diminutive fairies could save themselves would be to find a tree a woodcutter had cut a cross into and dive into the center of the cross.

Source: Keightley, *World Guide to Gnomes, Fairies, Elves, and Other Little People*, 491; Porteous, *Forest Folklore*, 91–93; Siefker, *Santa Claus, Last of the Wild Men*, 183

Wrath

A GIANT from British folklore, Wrath was said to live in a cave along the seashore in Hayle known as the Giant's Zawn or Ralph's Cupboard; the people of nearby Saint Ives had given him a bad reputation although no one could ever remember him doing anything particularly evil. It was the opinion of the people of the area after Wrath's death that if

he was a cannibal he completely devoured his victims leaving no trace of any evidence behind. It was said of Wrath, only after his death, that if any sailing ship passed within a mile of his cave, he would wade out into the ocean, knock the fishermen and sailors out, and pull the ships back to the deep recesses of his cave; once there, he would toss the thin men overboard to fend for themselves and keep the plump ones for long-term provisions.

Source: Bottrell, *Traditions and Hearthside Stories of West Cornwall*, 46–7; Hunt, *Popular Romances of the West of England*, 76

Wrnach

A GIANT from Arthurian folklore, Wrnach possessed a magical sword; it was said this item was the only thing by which he could meet his death. Obtaining this sword was the last of the tasks assigned to Culhwch by the GIANT YSBADDADEN in the tale "How Culhwch Won Olwen" from *The Mabinogion*. Culhwch, knowing he would be unable to defeat the GIANT in one-on-one combat, pretends to be a swordsmith and offers to refurbish and sharpen the weapon. Wrnach believes the lie and eagerly hands over the blade; once he gives the sword a few practice swings, Culhwch easily beheads the unsuspecting Wrnach.

Source: Bruce, *Arthurian Name Dictionary*, 498; Fee, *Mythology in the Middle Ages*, 67–8; Rose, *Giants, Monsters, and Dragons*, 398

Wulver

A human and wolf hybrid from Scottish folklore, the wulver was something of a WILD MAN, living alone in the wilderness in caves and having as little to do with mankind as possible; however, in some tales these creatures would leave a gift of food on the doorstep of a needy person. Wulvers are described as anthropoids covered in short brown fur and having a wolf-like head.

Source: Monaghan, *Encyclopedia of Celtic Mythology and Folklore*, 475; Zell-Ravenheart, *Wizard's Bestiary*, 102

Xana

Variations: Xmas

In the Asturian mythology of northern Spain, the xana were a species of nature spirit or water-NYMPH of amazing beauty; they were said to have lived in forested regions with pure water, fountains, rivers, and waterfalls. These fairies were described as slender beings with curly, long, blond or light brown hair; they comb their hair with gold and silver combs made from moon- and sun-beams. Sometimes the xana are said to be a singular entity representing the balance of nature and acting as a moral trickster. If you pass her test she will reward you with a gift from her vast treasure hoard but if you fail she will publicly shame you.

The children of the xana are called *xaninos*; because the mothers cannot produce breast milk they will take their children and swap them out with a human child. When the xaninos is no longer dependent on milk and is weaned the xana will return and take her child back but will not necessarily return the human baby. Many stories say the xana drown the human infant as they do not have the means to properly care for it.

Source: Bahrami, *Spiritual Traveler Spain*, 139–40; Curran, *Dark Fairies*, 135; Mountain, *Celtic Encyclopedia*, Volume 5, 1109–1110

Xelhua

Variations: Xelhua the Architect

A GIANT from ancient Aztec mythology, Xelhua, along with six (or seven; sources conflict) others of his kind, survived the primordial flood by ascending Mount Tlaloc. To commemorate the event, Xelhua constructed an artificial hill and built the pyramid of Cholula to serve as an asylum for him and his people should they ever again need to take refuge. However, according to the folklore, before the work was completed the gods became angry with Xelhua's structure, as it dared to touch the clouds; hurling thunderbolts down from the heavens, they killed many of the workers and construction of the project ceased.

Source: Painter, *Ethnology*, 70; Rose, *Giants, Monsters, and Dragons*, 401

Xing Tian

Variations: The Headless One, Xingtian

A headless GIANT from Chinese folklore, Xing Tian ("he who was punished by heaven" or "punished one") was decapitated by the supreme divinity, Huang Di, in a battle for supremacy. Although he lost his head in the battle and it was buried in the Changyang Mountains, he fought on with sword and shield using his navel for a mouth and his nipples for eyes.

Source: An, *Handbook of Chinese Mythology*, 217; Gary, *Archetypes and Motifs in Folklore and Literature*, 32

Xtabay

A species of nature spirit from Mayan folklore, the xtabay were said to be beautiful, red-skinned women who lived in caves in the forest; they were also the consorts to the minor gods. Using their lovely SIREN-like voice they would sing out to the occasional human man passing their way, saying to him, "Stay with me and I will give you a child." If the man accepted her invitation, after he left it was prudent to return to his home and light incense to honor the god of the forest Kanank'ax; doing so would ensure future invitations from the xtabay. To linger too long or to not give thanks guaranteed to never see another xtabay again. Additionally, the place where the lovemaking occurred would turn barren or be covered with a boulder.

Source: Perera, *Last Lords of Palenque*, 159–60

Yara-Ma-Yha-Who (Ya-rah-Ma-Ya-Who)

The premier vampiric creature of Australian folklore, the yara-ma-yha-who looks like a short, red-skinned man with an exceptionally large head and mouth with suckers on its fingers and toes. What is most unusual about this carnivorous creature is it has no teeth whatsoever. Completely nocturnal and having a strong dislike of the sunlight, it spends its daylight hours in caves near a water source. An ambush predator, the yara-ma-yha-who hides in the branches of fig trees and attacks anyone who walks beneath. It grabs them up and, using the suckers on its fingers and toes, drains the blood from its victims. When it is finished, it swallows the body whole. A short while later it will vomit the person back up, whole and alive. A person who is repeatedly attacked by the yara-ma-yha-who will gradually become shorter and shorter until they are the creature's size. Then they will start to grow hair all over their body and become a yara-ma-yha-who themselves.

The spirit of the fig tree can kill a yara-ma-yha-who by climbing into its ear and making a noise which causes the creature's own soul to flee its body in the form of tree fungus.

Source: Reed, *Aboriginal Fables*, 142–44; Rose, *Giants, Monsters and Dragons*, 403–44; Smith, *Myths and Legends of the Australian Aboriginals*, 342–44

Yehwe Zogbanu

A forest dwelling GIANT of Fon folklore, Yehwe Zogbanu was described as having thirty horns over his head and body; extremely territorial and highly predatory, he was a threat to hunters who dared to enter into his domain.

Source: Lynch, *African Mythology, A to Z*, 85; Rose, *Giants, Monsters, and Dragons*, 404

Yeitso

Variations: Ye'iitsho La'I Naaghaii ("GIANT Ye'ii" or "One Walking Giant")

In the folklore of the Navajo people of the United States of America, Yeitso ("great genius" or "great God") was one of the ANAYE, a type of gigantic and monstrous supernatural being causing fear, misery, and wickedness throughout the world. The chief of his kind and born of the union between a wicked woman and a stone, scaly Yeitso lived by a lake; he was slain by the cultural heroes Nayanezgani ("slayer of alien gods") and Thobadzistshini ("child born of water") and with the assistance of Tsohanoai, was scalped.

Source: Cotterell, *Dictionary of World Mythology*, 220; Leviton, *Encyclopedia of Earth Myths*, n.pag.

Ymir (EM-ir)

Variations: Alvaldi ("all powerful"), AURGELMIR ("clay-roarer"), Blainn, Bolporn ("blae-thorn"), Brimir ("sea"), FORNJOTR, GANGR ("the faring"), Junner, Leirbrimir ("clay-Brimir," "clay-JOTUN"), Neri, Thirvald, Thrigeitr, Thorn ("thorn"), Ymer, Ymr

The JOTUN Ymir ("groaner") of Norse mythology was created when the extreme cold of Nifleheim ("land of mist"), the world of mist, and the intense heat of Muspelheim, the world of fire, combined in Ginnunga-Gap ("yawning gap"), the primordial abyss located in the center of space. Before the creation of the Nine Worlds he was nourished by the milk of the primordial cow AUDHUMBLA.

Ymir was the progenitor of his species and had several sons, BOLTHORN, Bor (counted among the gods), and THRUDGELMIR to name a few. He was also the progenitor of the HRYMTHURSARS (FROST GIANTS) and the Aesir. Ymir was slain by his own grandsons, the gods Odin, Ve, and Vili; his death caused a great flood as his blood flowed over the nine worlds. The body of Ymir was used to create Midgard ("mid-yard") the world of man; his blood and sweat became lakes, oceans, and rivers; his bones and shoulders were made into mountains; his brains were the clouds; his double teeth, splintered bones, and toes became pebbles and rocks; his eyebrows developed into flowers and grass; his eyes became the moon and the sun; his eyelashes were used to construct a hedge around Midgard to keep evil beings from entering; his hair became the plants and the trees; and his skull became the sky.

Source: Grimes, *Norse Myths*, 4, 254, 310; Oehlenschläger, *Gods of the North*, lxxi; Norroena Society, *Asatrii Edda*, 335, 339, 337, 348, 370, 391; Sheard, *Llewellyn's Complete Book of Names*, 318

Yngvi (ENG-vi)

Variations: Ynguni

A rock DVERG (DWARF) from Norse mythology created by DURINN, Yngvi ("prince," "warrior") is listed as being one of DURINN's KIN. He, like the others created, paid particular attention to DURINN's leadership.

Source: Daly, *Norse Mythology A to Z*, 22; Grimes, *Norse Myths*, 260; Norroena Society, *Asatrii Edda*, 401

Yoyo

A species of all male DWARFS, the yoyo of British New Guinea folklore are said to support the earth; it is believed when they put it down to rest, the movement causes earthquakes and volcanic eruptions.

Source: Seligman, *Melanesians of British New Guinea*, 649

Ysbaddaden (uss-path-AD-an)

Variations: Ysbaddaden Pencawr, Yspadadden, Yspadadden Penkawr, Ysbaddaden Penncawr ("first among warriors," "first among giants")

A GIANT from Arthurian folklore, Ysbaddaden ("chief giant") was the owner of a fortress in Cornwall and was the father of the beautiful Olwen; he was described as having eyelids so heavy they were propped up with spears. The father of the beautiful Olwen, Ysbaddaden was fated to die when she married. When the warrior Culhwch accompanied by King Arthur arrived at the castle to ask permission to marry Olwen, Ysbaddaden already knew he was going to refuse him but after an attempt to kill him first by poison and then in combat, he finally agreed to a compromise: if Culhwch could gather together thirty-nine *anoethur* ("things hard to come by") for the wedding feast of his choosing, he would finally relinquish his daughter. Among the items were a comb, razor, and scissors for his personal use which must come from the tusks of TWRCH TRWYTH, who can only be hunted down with the aid of a number of hand-picked heroes, horses, and hounds. With the assistance of Arthur, the warrior was able to achieve his goal. Shortly after Olwen was wed, Goreu, the son of one of his servants, beheaded Ysbaddaden and took control of his fortress and lands.

Source: Bruce, *Arthurian Name Dictionary*, 477, 501; Gerritsen, *Dictionary of Medieval Heroes*, 91–2

Ysja (ES-ya)

One of the hrymthursars (FROST GIANTS) from Norse mythology, Ysja ("harridan," "noisy," "sludge") was born one of the daughters of THRAEL and THIR. She, her parents, and siblings all lived a hard life of labor performing thankless tasks, such as cleaning, herding goats and swine, placing dung in the fields, and other varied unskilled labor; they were the progenitors of the serving folk and thrall.

Source: Grimes, *Norse Myths*, 27, 302; Norroena Society, *Asatrii Edda*, 401

Yu-Min Kuo Yan

A race of anthropoids in Chinese folklore, the Yu-Min Kuo Yan were believed to hatch from eggs with their bodies covered in feathers and having wings rather than humanoid arms; they were said to be shy as a people and would flee at the sight of a human.

Source: Rose, *Giants, Monsters, and Dragons*, 408

Yumbo

Variations: Bachna Rachna ("the good people")

On Goree Island, south of the Cape Verde Peninsula in Senegal, West Africa, the white-skinned, silver-haired race of fairies known collectively as the yumboes live underground in the hills located about three miles from the coast. Each evening they dress in their pangs (garments of two oblong cloths, worn over the upper and lower body) revealing only their eyes and sneak into the nearby villages. There the yumboes steal couscous and cornmeal by putting it into their calabashes and arranging themselves into a row by which to pass their loot downward. Fond of fish, yumboes will borrow canoes and take fire in order to cook their catch. Beating on their jaloff drums, these little fairies, standing only about two feet tall, will drink palm wine until they become intoxicated; they greatly enjoy dancing and feasting. Akin to the BANSHEE of Ireland, the yumboes will attach themselves to a particular family; when one of them dies the fairies are heard wailing and lamenting.

Source: Brewer, *Wordsworth Dictionary of Phrase and Fable*, 973; Keightley, *World Guide to Gnomes, Fairies, Elves, and Other Little People*, 496; Maberry, *Cryptopedia*, 119

Yurupari

In the folklore of the Tupiian people of Brazil the word yurupari has several meanings; some say it is a generic term for all demons and spirits while others claim Yurupari is a malicious individual being but are uncertain if he is a god, an OGRE of the forest, or a nature spirit.

Source: Coulter, *Encyclopedia of Ancient Deities*, 520; Graves, *Larousse Encyclopedia of Mythology*, 447

Zamzummim

Variations: Uzim, ZUZIM

An ancient race of GIANTS, the Zamzummim ("achievers," "Buzz-Buzzers," or "the people whose speech sounds like buzzing," "murmurers" or "stammerers") were said to have once lived east of the Jordan River but were eventually conquered by the descendants of Ammon. Moses described the Zamzummim as being the ANAKIM.

Source: Aichele, *Violence, Utopia and the Kingdom of God*, 52; DeLoach, *Giants*, 2, 293; Garnier, *Worship of the Dead*, 93–4

Zipacna

A GIANT from Mayan folklore, Zipacna ("one who throws up the earth," "mountain mover") was the older brother of CABRAKAN; they were born the children of the Mayan GIANTS and gods VUCUB CAQUIX ("seven macaw") and his wife, CHIMALMAT. Arrogant and boastful, Zipacna had the natural born ability to create and move mountains; every day he would dig up earth and construct mountains and then his brother, CABRAKAN, would shake the earth and knock them down flat. Because of the chaos he and his brother caused, it was decided they must die. The cultural heroes Hero Twins devised a cunning plan to kill Zipacna, burying him beneath a mountain; his body was crushed beneath its weight and his bones turned to stone.

Source: Bingham, *South and Meso-American Mythology A to Z*, 148; Spence, *Popol Vuh*, 12–14

Zméioaca

Zméioaca is a vampiric creature from southeastern European folklore. She is the mother and progenitor of the ZMEUS, a race of blood-drinking GIANTS.

Source: Bunson, *Vampire Encyclopedia*, n.pag.

Zmeu

A species of supernatural creature from Romanian folklore, the zmeu are said to be a type of dragon, GIANT, or OGRE who are prone to kidnapping young maidens; depending on the story the creature can be humanoid and may have the ability to breathe fire.

Source: Harrison, *Spiritualist Newspaper*, Volume 1–20, 198

Zuzim

Variations: ZAMZUMMIM

One of the races of GIANTS said to live in Palestine, the Zuzim were the descendants of the WATCHERS and the women of Canaan; they were described as being gigantic of stature and having great strength.

Source: Garnier, *Worship of the Dead*, 93–4

Bibliography

'Abd al–Raḥmān Ismā'īl. *Folk Medicine in Modern Egypt: Being the Relevant Parts of the Ṭibb Al-Rukka, or Old Wives' Medicine, of 'Abd Al Raḥmān Ismā'Īl.* London: Luzac and Company, 1934.

Acker, Paul, and Carolyne Larrington. *The Poetic Edda: Essays on Old Norse Mythology.* London: Psychology Press, 2002.

Ackerman, Robert William. *An Index of the Arthurian Names in Middle English.* Volume 10. Stanford: Stanford University Press, 1952.

Aichele, George, and Tina Pippin. *Violence, Utopia and the Kingdom of God: Fantasy and Ideology in the Bible.* New York: Routledge, 2002.

Aldington, Richard. *Larousse Encyclopedia of Mythology.* Lancaster: Prometheus Press, 1959.

Alexander, Hartley Burr. *Latin-American [Mythology].* Volume 11. Boston: Marshall Jones Company, 1920.

Alexander, Hartley Burr. *The Mythology of All Races.* Volume X, North America. Boston: Marshal Jones and Company, 1916.

Alexander, Hartley Burr. *North American [Mythology].* Boston: Marshall Jones, 1916.

Alexander, Skye. *Fairies: The Myths, Legends, and Lore.* Avon: F+W Media, 2014. .

American Anthropological Association. *American Anthropologist.* Volume 1. Berkeley: American Anthropological Association, 1998.

American Folklore Society. *Journal of American Folklore.* Volume 64. Cambridge: American Folklore Society, 1951.

American Museum of Natural History. *Memoirs of the American Museum of Natural History.* Volume 8, Issue 1. New York: American Museum of Natural History, 1909.

Amodio, Mark C. *The Anglo Saxon Literature Handbook.* Sussex: John Wiley and Sons, 2013.

An, Deming. *Handbook of Chinese Mythology.* Santa Barbara: ABC-CLIO, 2005.

Andersen, Johannes Carl. *Myths and Legends of the Polynesians.* New York: Courier Dover Publications, 1928.

Anderson, Rasmus Björn. *Norrœna: The History and Romance of Northern Europe.* Volume 5. London: Norrœna Society, 1906.

Anderson, Rasmus Björn. *Norse Mythology.* Chicago: S.C. Griggs, 1884.

Anderson, Rasmus Björn, and James William Buel. *The Volsunga Saga.* London: Norrœna Society, 1907.

Andrews, Tamra. *Dictionary of Nature Myths: Legends of the Earth, Sea, and Sky.* New York: Oxford University Press, 2000.

Anthon, Charles. *A Classical Dictionary, Containing an Account of the Principal Proper Names Mentioned in Ancient Authors and Intended to Elucidate All the Important Points Connected with the Geography, Bibliography, Mythology, and Fine Arts of the Greeks and Romans.* New York: Harper and Brothers, 1872.

Antoninus, Francis Celoria. *The Metamorphoses of Antoninus Liberalis: A Translation with Commentary.* London: Psychology Press, 1992.

Apollodorus, edited and translated by Sir James George Frazer. *Apollodorus: The Library.* Volume 2. London: W. Heinemann, 1921.

Apollodorus, translated by Michael Simpson. *Gods and Heroes of the Greeks: The Library of Apollodorus.* Amherst: University of Massachusetts Press, 1976.

Apollodorus, translated by Robin Hard. *The Library of Greek Mythology.* New York: Oxford University Press, 1997.

Apollodorus, and Hyginus, R. Scott Smith, and Stephen M. Trzaskoma. *Apollodorus' Library and Hyginus' Fabulae.* Indianapolis: Hackett Publishing, 2007.

Archibald, Malcolm. *Sixpence for the Wind: A Knot of Nautical Folklore.* Tonawanda: Dundurn Press, 1998.

Arrowsmith, Nancy. *Field Guide to the Little People: A Curious Journey into the Hidden Realm of Elves, Faeries, Hobgoblins and Other Not-So-Mythical Creatures.* St. Paul: Llewellyn Worldwide, 2009.

Ashkenazi, Michael. *Handbook of Japanese Mythology.* Santa Barbara: ABC-CLIO, 2003.

Ashley, Leonard R.N. *The Complete Book of Devils and Demons.* Fort Lee: Barricade Books, 1996.

Ashley, Leonard R.N. *The Complete Book of Vampires.* New York: Barricade Books, 1998. .

Ashliman, D.L. *Fairy Lore: A Handbook.* Westport, CT: Greenwood, 2005.

Ashton, John. *Curious Creatures in Zoology: With 130 Illus. Throughout the Text.* London: John C. Nimmo, 1890.

Auden, Wystan Hugh, and Paul Beekman Taylor. *Norse Poems.* London: Athlone Press, 1981.

Austen, Ralph A., and Jonathan Derrick. *Middlemen of the Cameroons Rivers: The Duala and Their Hinterland, C.1600-C.1960.* Cambridge: Cambridge University Press, 1999.

Austern, Linda Phyllis, and Inna Naroditskaya. *Music of the Sirens*. Bloomington: Indiana University Press, 2006.

Avant, G. Rodney. *A Mythological Reference*. Bloomington, AuthorHouse, 2005.

Bahrami, Beebe. *The Spiritual Traveler Spain: A Guide to Sacred Sites and Pilgrim Routes*. Mahwah: Paulist Press, 2009.

Balfour, Edward. *Cyclopædia of India and of Eastern and Southern Asia, Commercial, Industrial and Scientific: Products of the Mineral, Vegetable and Animal Kingdoms, Useful Arts and Manufactures*. Volume 1. Madras: Scottish and Adelphi Presses, 1871.

Barber, Richard W., and Anne Riches. *A Dictionary of Fabulous Beasts*. Sussex: Boydell and Brewer, 1996.

Baring-Gould, Sabine. *The Book of Werewolves*. New York: Cosimo, 2008.

Barthell, Edward E. *Gods and Goddesses of Ancient Greece*. Coral Gables, FL: University of Miami Press, 1971.

Bartlett, Sarah. *The Mythology Bible: The Definitive Guide to Legendary Tales*. New York: Sterling Publishing Company, 2009.

Bastian, Dawn Elaine, and Judy K. Mitchell. *Handbook of Native American Mythology*. Santa Barbara: ABC-CLIO, 2004.

Bechtel, John Hendricks. *A Dictionary of Mythology*. Philadelphia: The Penn Publishing Company, 1905.

Beckwith, Martha. *Hawaiian Mythology*. Honolulu: University of Hawaii Press, 1970.

Beckwith, Martha Warren, Vassar College and the Lucy Maynard Salmon Fund for Research. *Hawaiian Mythology, Volume 1940, Part 1*. Charleston: Forgotten Books, 1940.

Beech, Charlotte, Jolyon Attwooll, Jean-Bernard Carillet, and Thomas Kohnstamm. *Chile and Easter Island*. Victoria: Lonely Planet, 2006.

Beers, William. *Women and Sacrifice: Male Narcissism and the Psychology of Religion*. Detroit: Wayne State University Press, 1992.

Begley, Brandon. *The Faith of Legacy*. Morrisville: Brandon Begley, 2007.

Bell, John E. *Bell's New Pantheon; or Historical Dictionary of the Gods, Demi-Gods, Heroes and Fabulous Personages of Antiquity*. London: John Bell, 1790.

Bell, Robert E. *Women of Classical Mythology: A Biographical Dictionary*. Oxford: Oxford University Press, 1993.

Bello, Andres. *Dictionary and Grammar of the Easter Island Language*. Santigo: Prensas de la Editorial Universitaria, 1960.

Bellows, Henry Adams. *The Poetic Edda: The Mythological Poems*. Mineola: Courier Dover Publications, 2012.

Bennett, John, and Susan Rowley. *Uqalurait: An Oral History of Nunavut*. Montreal: McGill-Queen's Press—MQUP, 2004.

Berens, E M. *The Myths and Legends of Ancient Greece and Rome: Being a Popular Account of Greek and Roman Mythology*. London: Blackie and Son, 1880.

Berman, Michael. *The Shamanic Themes in Armenian Folktales*. Newcastle: Cambridge Scholars, 2008.

Bernal, Ignacio. *The Olmec World*. Berkeley: University of California Press, 1969.

Beshir, Mohamed Omer. *The Nile Valley Countries, Continuity and Change*. Khartoum, Sudan: University of Khartoum, 1984.

Besson, Gérard A., Stuart Hahn, and Avril Turner. *Folklore and Legends of Trinidad and Tobago*. Paria Bay: Paria, 1989.

Bharati, Agrhananda, editor. *Agents and Audiences*. Volume 1 of *Bharati, Agehanada: The Realm of the Extra-Human World Anthropology*. Chicago: Walter de Gruyter, 1976.

Bingham, Ann, and Jeremy Roberts. *South and Meso-American Mythology A to Z*. New York: Infobase Publishing, 2010.

Black, Matthew, James C. VanderKam, and Otto Neugebauer. *The Book of Enoch, Or, I Enoch: A New English Edition: With Commentary and Textual Notes*. Leiden: Brill, 1985.

Blackman, W. Haden. *Field Guide to North American Monsters: Everything You Need to Know About Encountering Over 100 Terrifying Creatures in the Wild*. New York: Three Rivers Press, 1998.

Blavatsky, Helena Petrovna. *The Secret Doctrine: Anthropogenesis*. London: Theosophical Publishing Company, 1888.

Blavatsky, Helena Petrovna. *The Theosophical Glossary*. London: Theosophical Publishing Society, 1892.

Blayer, Irene Maria, and Mark Cronlund Anderson. *Latin American Narratives and Cultural Identity: Selected Readings*. New York: Peter Lang, 2004.

Blunck, Jürgen. *Solar System Moons: Discovery and Mythology*. Berlin: Springer Science and Business Media, 2009.

Boas, Franz. *Anthropological Papers, Written in Honor of Franz Boas Professor of Anthropology in Columbia University: Presented to Him on the Twenty-Fifth Anniversary of His Doctorate, Ninth of August, Nineteen Hundred and Six*. New York: G.E. Stechert and Company, 1906.

Boas, Franz. *Race, Language, and Culture*. Chicago: University of Chicago Press, 1940.

Boas, Franz, and Henry W. Tate. *Tsimshian Mythology*. Washington D.C.: Government Printing Office, 1916.

Bolle, Kees W. *The Freedom of Man in Myth*. Nashville, TN: Vanderbilt University Press, 1968.

Bonvillain, Nancy. *Native Nations: Cultures and Histories of Native North America*. New York: Prentice Hall, 2001.

Bonwick, James. *Egyptian Belief and Modern Thought*. London: C. Keagan Paul and Company, 1878.

Book of Enoch the Prophet. London: Kegan Paul, Trench, and Company, 1883.

Bord, Janet. *Fairies: Real Encounters with Little People*. New York: Carroll and Graf, 1997.

Borges, Jorge Luis, and Margarita Guerrero. *El Libro De Los Seres Imaginarios*. New York: Dutton, 1969.

Borges, Jorge Luis, Norman Thomas Di Giovanni, and Margarita Guerrero. *The Book of Imaginary Beings*. New York: Penguin, 1974.

Boscaro, Adriana, Franco Gatti, and Massimo Raveri. *Rethinking Japan: Social Sciences, Ideology and Thought*. New York: Psychology Press, 1990.

Bottrell, William. *Traditions and Hearthside Stories of West Cornwall*. Penzance: William Bottrell, 1870.

Boulay, R. A. *Flying Serpents and Dragons: The Story of Mankind's Reptilian Past*. Palo Alta: Book Tree, 1999.

Bovey, Alixe. *Monsters and Grotesques in Medieval Manuscripts*. Toronto: University of Toronto Press, 2002.

Bower, Archibald. *Historia Litteraria: Or, an Exact and Early Account of the Most Valuable Books Published in* the Several Parts of Europe. Volume 2. London: N. Prevost, 1731.

Bowlby, Rachel. Freudian Mythologies: Greek Tragedy and Modern Identities. New York: Oxford University Press, 2007.

Boyce, Mary. Zoroastrians: Their Religious Beliefs and Practices. New York: Psychology Press, 2001.

Bray, Anna Eliza. The Borders of the Tamar and the Tavy. London: Kent and Company, 1879.

Breese, Daryl, and Gerald D'Aoust. God's Steed: Key to World Peace. Raleigh: Lulu.com, 2011.

Brewer, Ebenezer Cobham. Character Sketches of Romance, Fiction and the Drama. Volumes 1–3, 5–6. New York: Selmar Hess, 1902.

Brewer, Ebenezer Cobham. Dictionary of Phrase and Fable: Giving the Derivation, Source, or Origin of Common Phrases, Allusions, and Words That Have a Tale to Tell. Philadelphia: Henry Altemus Company, 1898.

Brewer, Ebenezer Cobham. The Reader's Handbook of Allusions, References, Plots and Stories: With Two Appendices. Philadelphia: Lippincott, 1880.

Brewer, Ebenezer Cobham. The Wordsworth Dictionary of Phrase and Fable. Hertfordshire: Wordsworth Editions, 2001.

Briggs, Katharine Mary. Abbey Lubbers, Banshees, and Boggarts: An Illustrated Encyclopedia of Fairies. New York: Pantheon Books, 1979.

Briggs, Katharine Mary. An Encyclopedia of Fairies: Hobgoblins, Brownies, Bogies, and Other Supernatural Creatures, Volume 1976. New York: Pantheon Books, 1976.

Briggs, Katharine Mary. The Fairies in Tradition and Literature. London: Psychology Press, 2002.

Briggs, Katharine Mary. Folklore of the Cotswalds. London: B.T. Batsford, 1974.

Briggs, Katharine Mary. Nine Lives: The Folklore of Cats. New York: Pantheon Books, 1980.

Briggs, Katharine Mary. The Vanishing People: Fairy Lore and Legends. New York: Pantheon Books, 1978.

Brinkley, Frank. Japan, Its History, Arts and Literature. Volume 5. Boston: J.B. Millet Company, 1902.

Brokenleg, Martin, and Herbert T. Hoover. Yanktonai Sioux Water Colors: Cultural Remembrances of John Saul. Sioux Falls: Center for Western Studies, 1993.

Broster, Joan A., and Herbert Bourn. Amaqqirha: Religion, Magic and Medicine in Transkei. Cape Town, Africa: Via Afrika, 1982.

Brower, Kenneth. Earth and the Great Weather: The Brooks Range. San Francisco: Friends of the Earth, 1971.

Brown, David. God and Enchantment of Place: Reclaiming Human Experience: Reclaiming Human Experience. Oxford: Oxford University Press, 2004.

Brown, Nathan. The Complete Idiot's Guide to Zombies. New York: Penguin, 2010.

Brown, Virginia Pounds, and Laurella Owens. Southern Indian Myths and Legends. Birmingham: Beechwood Books, 1985.

Bruce, Christopher W. The Arthurian Name Dictionary. New York: Routledge, 2013.

Bryant, Clifton D. Handbook of Death and Dying. Thousand Oaks: Sage, 2003.

Budd, Deena West. The Weiser Field Guide to Cryptozoology: Werewolves, Dragons, Skyfish, Lizard Men, and Other Fascinating Creatures Real and Mysterious. San Francisco: Weiser Books, 2010.

Bulfinch, Thomas. Bulfinch's Greek and Roman Mythology: The Age of Fable. Mineola: Courier Dover Publications, 2012.

Bullen, Margaret. Basque Gender Studies. Reno: University of Nevada Press, 2003.

Bunson, Matthew. The Vampire Encyclopedia. New York: Gramercy Books, 2000.

Bunyan, John. The Works of That Eminent Servant of Christ, John Bunyan: Minister of the Gospel and Formerly Pastor of a Congregation at Bedford. Volume 1. Philadelphia: J. Locken, 1832.

Burton, Richard F. Arabian Nights, in 16 Volumes. New York: Cosimo, 2008.

Bush, Laurence C. Asian Horror Encyclopedia: Asian Horror Culture in Literature, Manga and Folklore. San Jose: Writers Club Press, 2001.

Bynum, Edward Bruce. The African Unconscious. New York: Cosimo, 2001.

Callaway, Henry Canon. Nursery Tales, Traditions, and Histories of the Zulus: In Their Own Words. London: Trubner and Company, 1868.

Campbell, John Francis. Popular Tales of the West Highlands: Orally Collected. Volume 4. Paisley: Alexander Gardner, 1893.

Carlyle, Thomas. Complete Works. Volumes 1–2. Oxford: University Press, 1885.

Casey, Edward S. Remembering: A Phenomenological Study. Bloomington: Indiana University Press, 2000.

Chadwick, Nora Kershaw. Stories and Ballads of the Far Past. Cambridge: Cambridge University Press, 1921.

Chamberlain, Alex F. "Some Items of Algonkian Folk-Lore" from The Journal of American Folk-Lore. Volume 13, pages 271–77, edited by the American Folklore Society. Boston: American Folk-lore Society, 1900.

Chambers, William, and Robert Chambers. Chambers's Journal. Volumes 19–20. Edinburg: William and Robert Chambers, 1853.

Chopra, Ramesh. Academic Dictionary of Mythology. New Delhi: Gyan Books, 2005.

Clark, Ella Elizabeth. Indian Legends of the Pacific Northwest. Berkeley: University of California Press, 2003.

Codrington, Robert Henry. The Melanesians: Studies in Their Anthropology and Folk-Lore. Oxford: Clarendon Press, 1891.

Cohen, Jeffrey Jerome. Of Giants: Sex, Monsters, and the Middle Ages. Minneapolis: University of Minnesota Press, 1999.

Colburn, Henry, and Richard Bently, editors. "A Few Ghosts for Christmas," in The New Monthly Magazine. Page 77–80, Volume 25. London: Henry Colburn and Richard Bently, 1829.

Coleman, J.A. The Dictionary of Mythology: An A-Z of Themes, Legends and Heroes. London: Arctusrus Publishing, 2007.

Coleridge, Samuel Taylor. Encyclopædia Metropolitana; Or, Universal Dictionary of Knowledge: Comprising the Twofold Advantage of a Philosophical and an Alphabetical Arrangement, with Appropriate Engravings. Volume 23. London: B. Fellowes, 1845.

Colvin, S. "The Centaurs" in Cornhill Magazine. Volume XXXVIII, edited by the staff, pages 284–96. London: Smith, Elder, and Company, 1878.

Comay, Joan. Who's Who in the Old Testament: Together with the Apocrypha. London: Psychology Press, 2002.

Conley, Robert J. *Cherokee Medicine Man: The Life and Work of a Modern-Day Healer.* Norman: University of Oklahoma Press, 2014.

Conner, Nancy. *The Everything Classical Mythology Book: From the Heights of Mount Olympus to the Depths of the Underworld—All You Need to Know About the Classical Myths.* Avaon: Everything Books, 2010.

Converse, Harriet Maxwell. *Myths and Legends of the New York State Iroquois.* Issues 125–129. Albany: University of the State of New York, 1908.

Conway, Deanna J. *The Ancient Art of Faery Magick.* New York: Random House, 2011.

Conway, Deanna J. *Falcon Feather and Valkyrie Sword: Feminine Shamanism, Witchcraft and Magick.* St. Paul: Llewellyn Publications, 1995.

Conway, Deanna J. *Magickal Mermaids and Water Creatures: Invoke the Magick of the Waters.* Franklin Lakes: Career Press, 2005.

Conway, Deanna J. *Magickal, Mystical Creatures: Invite Their Powers into Your Life.* St. Paul: Llewellyn Worldwide, 2001.

Cook, Arthur Bernard. *Zeus: God of the Dark Sky (Thunder and Lightning).* New York: Cambridge University Press Archive, 1925.

Cook, John Douglas, Philip Harwood, Frank Harris, Walter Herries Pollock, and Harold Hodge. *The Saturday Review of Politics, Literature, Science and Art.* Volume 31. London: J.W. Parker and Son, 1871.

Cooper, Philip. *Social Work Man.* Leicester: Troubador Publishing, 2013.

Cotterell, Arthur. *A Dictionary of World Mythology.* New York, G.P. Putman's Sons, 1980.

Coulter, Charles Russell, and Patricia Turner. *Encyclopedia of Ancient Deities.* Jefferson: McFarland, 2000.

Courtney, Margaret Ann. *Cornish Feasts and Folk-Lore.* Penzance: Beare and Son, 1890.

Covey, Jacob. *Beasts!* Seattle: Fantagraphics Books, 2007.

Cox, Barbara, and Scott Forbes. *Wicked Waters.* New York: The Rosen Publishing Group, 2013.

Craig, Robert D. *Dictionary of Polynesian Mythology.* Westport, CT: Greenwood, 1989.

Craig, Robert D. *Handbook of Polynesian Mythology.* Santa Barbara, CA: ABC-CLIO, 2004.

Craigie, Sir William Alexander, translator. *Scandinavian Folk-Lore: Illustrations of the Traditional Beliefs of the Northern Peoplest.* London: Alexander Gardner, 1896.

Croker, Thomas Crofton. *Fairy Legends and Traditions of the South of Ireland.* Volumes 1–3. London: John Murray, 1828.

Cronin, Vincent. *The Last Migration.* New York: Dutton, 1957.

Crossley-Holland, Kevin. *The Norse Myths.* New York: Random House Digital, 1981.

Curran, Bob. *Dark Fairies.* New York: Open Road Media, 2012.

Custer, Stewart. *A Treasury of New Testament Synonyms.* Greenville, SC: Bob Jones University Press, 1975.

Dalal, Roshen. *Hinduism: An Alphabetical Guide.* London: Penguin UK, 2014.

Daly, Kathleen N. *Norse Mythology A to Z.* New York: Facts on File, 2009.

Daly, Kathleen N., and Marian Rengel. *Greek and Roman Mythology, A to Z.* New York: Infobase Publishing, 2009.

Damsté, Pieter Helbert. *Propertiana*: Volume 53 of *Mnemosynes: Bibliothecae Philologicae Batavae.* London: Cambridge University Press Archive, 1925.

Daniélou, Alain. *Gods of Love and Ecstasy: The Traditions of Shiva and Dionysus.* Rochester: Inner Traditions / Bear and Company, 1992.

Daniels, Cora Linn (Morrison), and Charles McClellan Stevans. *Encyclopædia of Superstitions, Folklore, and the Occult Sciences of the World: A Comprehensive Library of Human Belief and Practice in the Mysteries of Life.* Milwaukee: J.H. Yewdale and Sons Company, 1903.

Davidson, Gustav. *A Dictionary of Angels: Including the Fallen Angels.* New York: The Free Press, 1971.

Davis, Frederick Hadland, and Evelyn Paul. *Myths and Legends of Japan.* New York: Farrar and Rinehart, 1932.

Davison, Carol Margaret, and Paul Simpson-Housley. *Bram Stoker's Dracula: Sucking Through the Century, 1897–1997.* Toronto: Dundurn Press, 1997.

Day, John. *God's Conflict with the Dragon and the Sea: Echoes of a Canaanite Myth in the Old Testament.* Cambridge: CUP Archive, 1985.

Day, Peter. *Vampires: Myths and Metaphors of Enduring Evil.* New York: Rodopi, 2006.

Deck-Partyka, Alicja. *Poland, a Unique Country and Its People.* Bloomington: AuthorHouse, 2006.

De Claremont, Lewis. *The Ancient's Book of Magic: Containing Secret Records of the Procedure and Practice of the Ancient Masters and Adepts 1940.* Whitefish: Kessinger Publishing, 2004.

Dekirk, Ash. *Dragonlore: From the Archives of the Grey School of Wizardry.* Franklin Lakes: Career Press, 2006.

De Lafayette, Maximillien. *Akkadian-English Dictionary: Vocabulary and Civilization.* Raleigh: Lulu.com, N.d.

De Lafayette, Maximillien. *The New De Lafayette Mega Encyclopedia of Anunnaki.* Volumes 2 and 5. Raleigh: Lulu.com, 2010.

De Lafayette, Maximillien. *Sumerian English Dictionary, Volume 2: Vocabulary and Conversation.* Raleigh: Lulu.com, 2011.

de Las Casas, Dianne, and Zarah C. Gagatiga. *Tales from the 7,000 Isles: Filipino Folk Stories: Filipino Folk Stories.* Santa Barbara: ABC-CLIO, 2011.

DeLoach, Charles. *Giants: A Reference Guide from History, the Bible, and Recorded Legend.* Lanham: Scarecrow Press, 1995.

De Magalhães, Basílio. *Folk-Lore in Brazil.* Rio de Janeiro, Brazil: Imprensa Nacional, 1945.

Demetrio, Francisco R. *Myths and Symbols, Philippines.* Manila: National Book Store, 1981.

Dennis, Geoffrey W. *The Encyclopedia of Jewish Myth, Magic and Mysticism.* Woodbury: Llewellyn Worldwide, 2007.

de Rijke, Victoria. *Duck.* London: Reaktion Books, 2008.

de Rothschild, C. *The History and Literature of the Israelites According to the Old Testament and the Apocrypha.* London: Longmans, Green, and Company, 1872.

Dickens, Bruce. *The Icelandic Runic Poem.* Cambridge: Cambridge University Press Archive, 1915.

Dixon-Kennedy, Mike. *Encyclopedia of Greco-Roman Mythology.* Santa Barbara: ABC-CLIO, 1998.

Dixon-Kennedy, Mike. *Encyclopedia of Russian and Slavic Myth and Legend.* Santa Barbara: ABC-CLIO, 1998.

Dixon-Kennedy, Mike. *Native American Myth and Legend: An A-Z of People and Places.* London: Brockhampton Press, 1998.

Dooling, D.M., and James R. Walker. *The Sons of the Wind: The Sacred Stories of the Lakota*. Norman: University of Oklahoma Press, 1984.

Doty, W.G. *Mythosphere: Issue 4 of the Journal*. New York: Taylor and Francis United States, 2000.

Dowden, Ken, and Niall Livingstone. *A Companion to Greek Mythology*. West Sussex: John Wiley and Sons, 2011.

Dowson, John. *A Classical Dictionary of Hindu Mythology and Religion, Geography, History, and Literature*. London: Trübner and Company, 1870.

Doyle, Richard. *The Story of Jack and the Giants*. Scituate, Digital Scanning, 2009.

Drury, Nevill. *The Dictionary of the Esoteric: 3000 Entries on the Mystical and Occult Traditions*. Delhi: Motilal Banarsidass, 2004.

Du Chaillu, Paul Belloni. *The Viking Age: The Early History, Manners, and Customs of the Ancestors of the English-Speaking Nations. Illustrated from the Antiquities Discovered in Mounds, Cairns, and Bogs as Well as from the Ancient Sagas and Eddas. Volume 1*. Boston: Adamant Media Corporation, 1889.

Dumont, Jean-Paul. *Visayan Vignettes: Ethnographic Traces of a Philippine Island*. Chicago: University of Chicago Press, 1992.

Durrant, Jonathan, and Michael D. Bailey. *Historical Dictionary of Witchcraft*. Lanham: Scarecrow Press, 2012.

Dvornik, Francis. *The Slavs: Their Early History and Civilization*. Boston: American Academy of Arts and Sciences, 1956. .

Eason, Cassandra. *A Complete Guide to Faeries and Magical Beings: Explore the Mystical Realm of the Little People*. Boston: Weiser Books, 2002.

Eason, Cassandra. *Fabulous Creatures, Mythical Monsters, and Animal Power Symbols: A Handbook*. Westport, CT: Greenwood, 2008.

Eberhart, George M. *Mysterious Creatures: A Guide to Cryptozoology. Volume 1*. Santa Barbara: ABC-CLIO, 2002.

Edmonds, Radcliffe G. III. *Redefining Ancient Orphism: A Study in Greek Religion*. Cambridge: Cambridge University Press, 2013.

Eliade, Mircea, and Charles J. Adams. *The Encyclopedia of Religion. Volume 4*. New York: Macmillan, 1987.

Eliot, Alexander. *The Universal Myths: Heroes, Gods, Tricksters, and Others*. New York: New American Library, 1990.

Elliott, A. Marshal, Johns Hopkins University, and JSTOR (Organization), editors. *Modern Language Notes. Volume 16*. Baltimore: Johns Hopkins Press, 1901.

Ellis, Hilda Roderick. *The Road to Hel: A Study of the Conception of the Dead in Old Norse Literature*. Cambridge: Cambridge University Press, 2013. .

Elsie, Robert. *A Dictionary of Albanian Religion, Mythology, and Folk Culture*. New York: New York University Press, 2001.

Emick, Jennifer. *The Everything Celtic Wisdom Book: Find Inspiration Through Ancient Traditions, Rituals, and Spirituality*. Avon: Everything Books, 2009.

Esteban, Mari Luz, and Mila Amurrio, editors. *Feminist Challenges in the Social Sciences: Gender Studies in the Basque Country*. Reno: Center for Basque Studies, 2010.

Eugenio, Damiana L. *Philippine Folk Literature: The Myths*. Diliman: University of the Philippines Press, 2001.

Euvino, Gabrielle, and Michael San Filippo. *The Complete Idiot's Guide to Italian History and Culture*. New York: Penguin, 2001.

Evans-Wentz, Walter Yeeling. *The Fairy Faith in Celtic Countries: The Classic Study of Leprechauns, Pixies, and Other Fairy Spirits*. New York: Citadel Press, 1994.

Ezquerra, Jaime Alvar. *Romanising Oriental Gods: Myth, Salvation, and Ethics in the Cults of Cybele, Isis, and Mithras*. Leiden: Brill, 2008.

Facaros, Dana, and Michael Pauls. *Northern Spain*. London: New Holland Publishers, 2009.

Falola, Toyin, and Ann Genova. *Historical Dictionary of Nigeria*. Lanham: Scarecrow Press, 2009.

Fansler, Dean Spruill, editor. *Filipino Popular Tales. Volume 12*. Lancaster: American Folk-lore Society, 1921.

Fanthorpe, R. Lionel, Lionel Fanthorpe, and Patricia Fanthorpe. *Mysteries and Secrets of Voodoo, Santeria, and Obeah*. Tonawanda: Dundurn, 2008.

Farfor, Susannah. *Northern Territory*. Victoria: Lonely Planet, 2003.

Farrar, Frederic William. *Life of Christ*. New York: Dutton, 1877.

Fawcett, Melissa Jayne, and Melissa Tantaquidgeon Zobel. *Medicine Trail: The Life and Lessons of Gladys Tantaquidgeon*. Tucson: University of Arizona Press, 2000.

Fee, Christopher R. *Mythology in the Middle Ages: Heroic Tales of Monsters, Magic, and Might*. Santa Barbara: ABC-CLIO, 2011.

Fienup-Riordan, Ann. *Boundaries and Passages: Rule and Ritual in Yup'ik Eskimo Oral Tradition, Issue 212 of Civilization of the American Indian*. Norman: University of Oklahoma Press, 1995.

Finch, Ronald G. *The Saga of the Volsungs*. New York: Nelson, 1965.

Finlay, Hugh, Everist, Richard and Wheeler, Tony. *Nepal: Lonely Planet Travel Guides*. Victoria: Lonely Planet, 1999.

Fischer, Sibylle. *Modernity Disavowed: Haiti and the Cultures of Slavery in the Age of Revolution*. Durham: Duke University Press, 2004.

Fiske Icelandic Collection. *Mediaeval Scandinavia. Volume 15*. Odense: Odense University Press, 2005.

Flood, Bo, Beret E. Strong, and William Flood. *Micronesian Legends*. Honolulu: Bess Press, 2002.

Folklore Society of Great Britain. *The Folk-Lore Record. Volume 61*. Folk-lore Society, 1907.

Fontenrose, Joseph Eddy. *Orion: The Myth of the Hunter and the Huntress*. Berkeley: University of California Press, 1981.

Fontenrose, Joseph Eddy. *Python: A Study of Delphic Myth and Its Origins*. Berkeley: University of California Press, 1980.

Ford, Michael. *The Bible of the Adversary*. Raleigh: Lulu, 2008.

Ford, Michael. *Maskim Hul: Babylonian Magick*. Raleigh: Lulu.com, 2011.

Fornander, Abraham, and Thomas George Thrum. *Fornander Collection of Hawaiian Antiquities and Folk-Lore Gathered from Original Sources*. Honolulu: Bishop Museum Press, 1920.

Forth, Gregory. *Images of the Wildman in Southeast Asia: An Anthropological Perspective*. New York: Taylor and Francis, 2008.

Fossum, Andrew. *The Norse Discovery of America*. Minneapolis: Augsburg publishing house, 1918.

Fox, William Sherwood. *Greek and Roman [Mythology]*. Boston: Marshall Jones Company, 1916.

Frankel, Stephen. *The Huli Response to Illness*. Cambridge: Cambridge University Press, 2005.

Frazer, Sir James George. *Adonis, Attis, Osiris*. London: Macmillan, 1907.

Frazer, Sir James George. *The Golden Bough: A Study in Comparative Religion*. Volume 2. London: Macmillan, 1890.

Friedman, John Block. *The Monstrous Races in Medieval Art and Thought*. Syracuse: Syracuse University Press, 2000.

Fritze, Ronald H. *Travel Legend and Lore: An Encyclopedia*. Santa Barbara: ABC-CLIO, 1998.

Froud, Brian, and Alan Lee. *Faeries*. New York: Harry N. Abrams, 1978.

Garnier, J. *The Worship of the Dead or the Origin and Nature of Pagan Idolatry and Its Bearing Upon the Early History of Egypt and Babylonia*. Moscow: Ripol Klassik, 1997.

Garry, Jane, and Hasan El-Shamy. *Archetypes and Motifs in Folklore and Literature*. Edmonds: M.E. Sharpe, 2005.

Georgieva, Ivanichka. *Bulgarian Mythology*. Sofia, Bulgaria: Syvat Publishers, 1985.

Gerritsen, Willem Pieter, and Anthony G. Van Melle. *A Dictionary of Medieval Heroes: Characters in Medieval Narrative Traditions and Their Afterlife in Literature, Theatre and the Visual Arts*. Woodbridge: Boydell and Brewer, 2000.

Gilmore, David D. *Monsters: Evil Beings, Mythical Beasts, and All Manner of Imaginary Terrors*. Philadelphia: University of Pennsylvania Press, 2003.

Gimbutas, Marija. *The Living Goddesses*. Berkeley: University of California Press, 2001.

Goldenberg, Linda. *Little People and a Lost World: An Anthropological Mystery*. New York: Twenty-First Century Books, 2007.

Goldenweiser, Alexander. *Early Civilization: An Introduction to Anthropology*. New York: Alfred A. Knopf, 1922.

Goodfellow, Robin. *The History of Gog and Magog, the Champions of London*. London: J and C Adlard, 1819.

Goodman, Jim. *Guide to Enjoying Nepalese Festivals: An Introductory Survey of Religious Celebration in Kathmandu Valley*. Kathmandu: Kali Press, 1981.

Gordon, Stuart. *The Encyclopedia of Myths and Legends*. N.p.: Headline, 1994.

Grant, Michael, and John Hazel. *Who's Who in Classical Mythology*. New York: Psychology Press, 2002.

Grauer, Armgard, and John Kennedy. "The Dogri: Evil Beings of the Nile." *In Nubian Ceremonial Life*. ed. John Kennedy: 114–124. Berkeley: University of California Press, 1978.

Graves, Robert. *The Greek Myths: Classics Deluxe Edition*. New York: Penguin, 2012.

Graves, Robert. *The Larousse Encyclopedia of Mythology*. New York: Barnes and Noble, 1994.

Gray, Louis Herbert. *The Mythology of All Races*. Volume 2. Boston: Marshal Jones Company, 1964.

Greaves, Richard L. *Glimpses of Glory: John Bunyan and English Dissent*. Stanford: Stanford University Press, 2002.

Green, Thomas. *Arthuriana: Early Arthurian Tradition and the Origins of the Legend*. Louth: Lindes Press, 2009.

Grimal, Pierre. *The Dictionary of Classical Mythology*. London: Wiley, 1996.

Grimal, Pierre. *Larousse World Mythology*. Secaucus, New Jersey, Chartwell Books, 1965.

Grimassi, Raven. *Hereditary Witchcraft: Secrets of the Old Religion*. St. Paul: Llewellyn Worldwide, 1999.

Grimes, Heilan Yvette. *The Norse Myths*. Boston: Hollow Earth Pubishing, 2010.

Grimm, Jacob. *Grimm's Household Tales*. London: George Bell and Sons, 1884.

Grimm, Jacob Ludwig C. *Teutonic Mythology*. Volumes 2 and 4. London: George Bell, 1888.

Grimm, Jacob Ludwig C., and translated by James Steven Stallybrass. *Teutonic Mythology*. London: George Bell and Son, 1883.

Groves, Eric. *Baby Names That Go Together*. Avon: Adams Media, 2009. .

Guerber, H.A. *Hammer of Thor—Norse Mythology and Legends—Special Edition*. N.p.: El Paso Norte, 2010.

Guiley, Rosemary. *The Encyclopedia of Angels*. New York: Infobase Publishing, 2004.

Guiley, Rosemary. *The Encyclopedia of Vampires, Werewolves, and Other Monsters*. New York: Infobase Publishing, 2004.

Guiley, Rosemary. *The Encyclopedia of Witches, Witchcraft and Wicca*. New York: Infobase Publishing, 2008.

Guillermo, Artemio R. *Historical Dictionary of the Philippines*. Lanham: Scarecrow Press, 2012.

Gulmahamad, Hanif. *Stories and Poems by a Guyanese Village Boy*. Philadelphia: Xlibris Corporation, 2009.

Günther, comtesse Marie Alker. *Tales and Legends of the Tyrol*. London: Chapman and Hall, 1874.

Guppy, Shusha. *The Blindfold Horse: Memories of a Persian Childhood*. London: Tauris Parke Paperbacks, 2004.

Gypsy Lore Society. *Journal of the Gypsy Lore Society*. Edinburgh: The Society, 1964.

Haase, Donald. *The Greenwood Encyclopedia of Folktales and Fairy Tales*. Westport, CT: Greenwood, 2007.

Hacikyan, Agop Jack, Gabriel Basmajian, Edward S. Franchuk, and Nourhan Ouzounian. *The Heritage of Armenian Literature: From the Eighteenth Century to Modern Times*. Detroit: Wayne State University Press, 2005.

Hackin, J. Paul Louis Couchoud. *Asiatic Mythology 1932*. Whitefish: Kessinger Publishing, 2005.

Hail, Raven. *Cherokee Astrology: Animal Medicine in the Stars*. Rochester: Inner Traditions / Bear and Company, 2011.

Hajdú, Péter. *Ancient Culture of the Uralian Peoples*. Budapest: Corvina, 1976.

Halili, Christine N. *Philippine History*. Manila: Rex Bookstore, 2004.

Hall, Manly P. *The Secret Teachings of All Ages: An Encyclopedic Outline of Masonic, Hermetic, Qabbalistic, and Rosicrucian Symbolical Philosophy*. Charleston: Forgotten Books, 1928.

Hallen, Arthur Washington Cornelius, and John Horne

Stevenson. *The Scottish Antiquary: Or, Northern Notes and Queries*. Volumes 13–14. Edinburgh: W. Green and Sons, 1899. .

Hallenbeck, Bruce G. *Monsters of New York: Mysterious Creatures in the Empire State*. Mechanicsburg: Stackpole Books, 2013.

Halpin, Marjorie M., and Michael M. Ames, editors. *Manlike Monsters on Trial: Early Records and Modern Evidence*. Vancouver: University of British Columbia Press, 1980.

Hamilton, John. *Ogres and Giants*. Edina: ABDO, 2004.

Hansen, William F. *Handbook of Classical Mythology*. Santa Barbara: ABC-CLIO, 2004.

Hard, Robin. *The Routledge Handbook of Greek Mythology: Based on H.J. Rose's "Handbook of Greek Mythology."* London: Psychology Press, 2004.

Harrison, William H. "The Superstitions of Roumania: An Anonymous Post in the *Telegraph*" in *The Spiritualist Newspaper: A Record of the Progress of the Science and Ethics of Spiritualism*. Volumes 1–20, edited by W.H. Harrison, page 198. London: W.H. Harrison, 1881.

Hastings, James. *Encyclopedia of Religion and Ethics*. Part 23. Whitefish: Kessinger Publishing, 2003.

Hastings, James, John Alexander Selbie, and Louis Herbert Gray. *Encyclopædia of Religion and Ethics: Fiction-Hyksos*. Volume 6 *of Encyclopædia of Religion and Ethics*. Edinburgh: T. and T. Clark, 1914.

Hastings, James, Louis Herbert Gray, and John Alexander Selbie. *Encyclopaedia of Religion and Ethics*. Volume 3. Edinburgh: T. and. T. Clark, 1908.

Hendry, Joy. *Interpreting Japanese Society: Anthropological Approaches*. London: Psychology Press, 1998.

Hengstenberg, Ernst Wilhelm. *Dissertations on the Genuineness of the* Pentateuch, Volume 2. Edinburgh: T. and T. Clark for the Continental Translation Society, 1847.

Henriksen, Georg. *I Dreamed the Animals: Kaneuketat: The Life of an Innu Hunter*. New York: Berghahn Books, 2009.

Herbermann, Charles George, Edward Aloysius Pace, Condé Bénoist Pallen, John Joseph Wynne, and Thomas Joseph Shahan, editors. *The Catholic Encyclopedia: An International Work of Reference on the Constitution, Doctrine, Discipline, and History of the Catholic Church*. Volume 3. New York: Encyclopedia Press, 1913.

Herodotus, and translated by William Beloe. *The Ancient History of Herodotus*. New York: Derby and Jackson, 1859.

Herron, Thomas. *Spenser's Irish Work: Poetry, Plantation and Colonial Reformation*. Burlington: Ashgate Publishing, 2007.

Herskovits, Melville Jean. *The Myth of the Negro Past*. Boston: Beacon Press, 1990.

Hesiod, and translated by Hugh Gerard Evelyn-White. *Hesiod, the Homeric Hymns, and Homerica*. London: Harvard University Press, 1914.

Hesiod, Callimachus, Theognis, James Davies, Sir Charles Abraham Elton, Henry William Tytler, and John Hookham Frere. *The Works of Hesiod, Callimachus, and Theognis*. London: Henry G. Bohn, 1856.

Hiltebeitel, Alf. *Criminal Gods and Demon Devotees: Essays on the Guardians of Popular Hinduism*. Albany: State University New York Press, 1989.

Hines, Craig. *Gateway of the Gods: An Investigation of Fallen Angels, the Nephilim, Alchemy, Climate Change, and the Secret Destiny of the Human Race*. Grandville: Numina Media Arts, 2007.

Hollenbaugh, Henry. *Nessus the Centaur*. Huston: Alondra Press, 2009.

Hollengreen, Laura Holden. *Translatio, Or, the Transmission of Culture in the Middle Ages and the Renaissance: Modes and Messages*. Turnhout: Brepols, 2008.

Homer, edited by Robert Porter Keep. *The Iliad of Homer, Books 1–6*. Boston: Allyn and Bacon, 1883.

Homer, Bernadotte Perrin, and Thomas Day Seymour. *Eight Books of Homer's Odyssey*. Boston: Ginn and Company, 1897.

Honko, Lauri. *Religion, Myth and Folklore in the World's Epics: The Kalevala and Its Predecessors*. Berlin: Walter de Gruyter, 1990.

Hoops, Johannes. *Kommentar Zum Beowulf*. Heidelberg, Germany: Carl Winter, 1932.

Hopkins, Edward Washburn. *Epic Mythology with Additions and Corrections*. New York: Biblo and Tannen Publishers, 1968.

Howe, Leo. "Gods, People, Spirits and Witches: The Balinese System of Person-Definition." *Bijdragen Tot De Taal, Landen Volkenkunde* (1984): 193–222.

Howey, M. Oldfield. *The Horse in Magic and Myth*. Mineola: Courier Dover Publications, 2002.

Huffington, Arianna Stassinopoulos. *The Gods of Greece*. New York: Atlantic Monthly Press, 1993.

Hunt, Leigh. "The Sirens and Mermaids of the Poets" in *The New Monthly Magazine and Universal Register. [Continued As] the New Monthly Magazine and Literary Journal (And Humorist) [Afterw.] the New Monthly (Magazine)*. 273–283. London: Henry Colburn, 1836.

Hunt, Robert, editor. *Popular Romances of the West of England: Or, the Drolls, Traditions, and Superstitions of Old Cornwall*. London: John Camden Hotten, 1865.

Hurley, Vic. *Swish of the Kris, the Story of the Moros, Authorized and Enhanced Edition*. Salem: Cerberus Books, 2010.

Hyatt, Victoria, and Joseph W. Charles. *The Book of Demons*. New York: Simon & Schuster, 1974.

Icke, David. *The Biggest Secret: The Book That Will Change the World*. Scottsdale: Bridge of Love Publications, 1999.

Icon Group International, . *Sacrificing: Webster's Quotations, Facts and Phrases*. San Diego: ICON Group International, 2008.

Illes, Judika. *Encyclopedia of Spirits: The Ultimate Guide to the Magic of Fairies, Genies, Demons, Ghosts, Gods and Goddesses*. New York: HarperCollins, 2009.

Ingpen, Robert R., and Molly Perham. *Ghouls and Monsters*. New York: Chelsea House Publishers, 1996.

Ivanits, Linda J. *Russian Folk Belief*. M.E. Sharpe,: New York, 1989.

Iyengar, Kodaganallur Ramaswami Srinivasa. *Asian Variations in Ramayana: Papers Presented at the International Seminar on "Variations in Ramayana in Asia: Their Cultural, Social and Anthropological Significance," New Delhi, January 1981*. Delhi: Sahitya Akademi, 2003.

Jackson, James H. Jr. *The Mystical Bible*. Raleigh: Lulu.com, 2009.

Jakobson, Roman. "Slavic Gods and Demons" in *Selected Writings: Contributions to Comparative Mythology: Studies in Linguistics and Philosophy, 1972–1982* edited by

Stephen Rudy, pages 3–12. Berlin: Mouton Publishers, 1985.

James, Etter Robert. *A Devotional: Honoring Thor and Family*. Raleigh: Lulu.com, 2012.

The Japan Architect. Volume 42. Tokyo: Shinkenchiku-Sha Company, 1967.

Jennaway, Megan. *Sisters and Lovers: Women and Desire in Bali*. Lanham: Rowman and Littlefield, 2002.

Jennbert, Kristina. *Animals and Humans: Recurrent Symbiosis in Archaeology and Old Norse Religion*. Lund: Nordic Academic Press, 2011.

Jensen, E.A. *Manipulating the Last Pure Godly DNA: The Genetic Search for God's DNA on Earth*. Bloomington: Trafford Publishing, 2012.

Jernigan, Dennis. *Giant Killers: Crushing Strongholds, Securing Freedom in Your Life*. Colorado Springs: Waterbrook Press, 2005.

Johns, Andreas. *Baba Yaga: The Ambiguous Mother and Witch of the Russian Folktale*. New York: Peter Lang, 2004.

Jones, Charles W. *Medieval Literature in Translation*. Mineola: Courier Dover Publications, 2013.

Jones, David E. *Evil in Our Midst: A Chilling Glimpse of Our Most Feared and Frightening Demons*. Garden City Park: Square One Publishers, 2001.

Jones, Ernest. *On the Nightmare*. London: Hogarth Press, 1949.

Jones, Lindsay. *Encyclopedia of Religion*. Volume 1. New York: Macmillan Reference USA, 2005.

Jones, Richard. *The Medieval Natural World*. New York: Routledge, 2013.

Jones, Richard. *Myths and Legends of Britain and Ireland*. London: New Holland Publishers, 2006.

Jordan, Michael. *Dictionary of Gods and Goddesses*. New York: Infobase Publishing, 2009.

Jordan, Michael. *Encyclopedia of Gods*. New York, Facts on File, 1993.

Joseph, Frank. *Unlocking the Prehistory of America*. New York: The Rosen Publishing Group, 2013.

Journal of Theological Studies, Volume 8. Oxford: Clarion Press, 1907.

Joyce, Patrick Weston. *The Origin and History of Irish Names of Places*. Volume 1. Dublin: McGlashan and Gill, 1871.

Judson, Katharine Berry, editor. *Myths and Legends of Alaska*. Chicago: A.C. McClurg and Company, 1911.

Kalota, Narain Singh. *India as Directed by Megasthenes*. Delhi: Concept Publishing Company, 1976.

Kane, Alice, and Sean Kane. *The Dreamer Awakes*. Orchard Park.: Broadview Press, 1995.

Kanellos, Nicolás, and Claudio Esteva Fabregat. *Handbook of Hispanic Cultures in the United States*. Houston: Arte Público Press, 1994. .

Keel, John. *The Eighth Tower*. New York: New American Library, 1977.

Keightley, Thomas. *The Fairy Mythology Illustrative of the Romance and Superstition of Various Countries*. London: George Bell and Sons, 1905.

Keightley, Thomas. *The World Guide to Gnomes, Fairies, Elves, and Other Little People*. New York: Random House Value Publishing, 1878.

Kenkyūjo, Kokusai Shūkyō. *Japanese Journal of Religious Studies*. Volume 16. Tokyo: International Institute for the Study of Religions, 1989.

Kessler, E.H., and D.J. Wong-MingJi. *Cultural Mythology and Global Leadership*. Cheltenham: Edward Elgar Publishing, 2009.

Kewes, Paulina, Ian W. Archer, and Felicity Heal. *The Oxford Handbook of Holinshed's Chronicles*. Oxford: Oxford University Press, 2013.

Khanam, R. *Demonology: Socio-Religious Belief of Witchcraft*. New Deli: Global Vision Publishing House, 2003.

Khatri, Vikas. *Mysterious Monstors of the World*. New Deli: Pustak Mahal, 2006.

King, Jonathan C.H. *Thunderbird and Lightning: Indian Life in Northeastern North America, 1600–1900*. London: British Museum Press, 1982.

Kipfer, Barbara Ann. *The Order of Things*. New York: Workman Publishing, 2008.

Kline, Naomi Reed. *Maps of Medieval Thought: The Hereford Paradigm*. Woodbridge: Boydell Press, 2001.

Knappert, Jan. *African Mythology: An Encyclopedia of Myth and Legend*. Berkeley: Diamond Books, 1995.

Kng, Hans. *Tracing the Way: Spiritual Dimensions of the World Religions*. New York: A and C Black, 2006.

Knight, Brenda. *Goth Magick: An Enchanted Grimoire*. New York: Citadel Press, 2006.

Knowles, James. *The Nineteenth Century*. Volume 31. London: Henry S. King and Company, 1892.

Knox, Hubert Thomas. *The History of the County of Mayo to the Close of the Sixteenth Century*. Dublin: Hodges, Figgis and Company, 1908.

Knudsen, Shannon. *Fantastical Creatures and Magical Beasts*. Minneapolis: Lerner Publications, 2009.

Knudsen, Shannon. *Giants, Trolls, and Ogres*. Minneapolis: Lerner Publications, 2009.

Knudson, Nicolette, Jody Snow, and Clifford Canku. *Beginning Dakota—Tokaheya Dakota Iapi Kin: 24 Language and Grammar Lessons with Glossaries*. Saint Paul: Minnesota Historical Society, 2010.

Koch, John T., editor. *Celtic Culture: A Historical Encyclopedia*. Volume 1 and Volume 2. Santa Barbara: ABC-CLIO, 2006.

Koch, John T., and John Carey. *The Celtic Heroic Age: Literary Sources for Ancient Celtic Europe and Early Ireland and Wales*. Andover: Celtic Studies Publications, 2003.

Köprülü, Mehmet Fuat. *Early Mystics in Turkish Literature*. New York: Psychology Press, 2006.

Krensky, Stephen. *The Bogeyman*. Minneapolis: Lerner-Classroom, 2007.

Lake, Matt. *Weird England: Your Travel Guide to England's Local Legends and Best Kept Secrets*. New York: Sterling Publishing Company, 2007.

Lane, Edward William, and Stanley Lane-Poole. *Arab Society in the Time of the Thousand and One Nights*. North Chemsford: Courier Dover Publications, 2004.

Larrington, Carolyne. *The Poetic Edda*. New York: Oxford University Press, 2014.

Larson, Jennifer Lynn. *Ancient Greek Cults: A Guide*. New York: Psychology Press, 2007.

Larson, Jennifer Lynn. *Greek Nymphs: Myth, Cult, Lore*. London: Oxford University Press, 2001.

Laugrand, Frederic, and Jarich Oosten. *Hunters, Predators and Prey: Inuit Perceptions of Animals*. New York: Berghahn Books, 2014.

Laugrand, Frédéric, and Jarich Oosten. *Inuit Shamanism and Christianity: Transitions and Transformations in the*

Twentieth Century. Montreal: McGill-Queen's Press—MQUP, 2010.

Lawrence, Peter, and Mervyn J. Meggitt. *Gods, Ghosts and Men in Melanesia: Some Religions of Australian New Guinea and the New Hebrides.* Oxford: Oxford University Press, 1965.

Leach, María. *Funk and Wagnalls Standard Dictionary of Folklore, Mythology, and Legend.* New York: Funk and Wagnalls, 1972.

Leary, James P. *Wisconsin Folklore.* Madison: University of Wisconsin Press, 1999.

Leddon, Alan. *A Child's Eye View of Fair Folk.* Madison: Spero Publishing, 2011.

Lee, Jonathan H.X., and Kathleen M. Nadeau. *Encyclopedia of Asian American Folklore and Folklife.* Volume 1. Santa Barbara: ABC-CLIO, 2011.

Leeming, David Adams. *A Dictionary of Asian Mythology.* New York: Oxford University Press, 2001.

Leeming, David Adams. *The Oxford Companion to World Mythology.* Oxford: Oxford University Press, 2005.

Leick, Gwendolyn. *A Dictionary of Ancient Near Eastern Mythology.* London: Routledge, 2002.

Leland, Charles Godfrey. *The Unpublished Legends of Virgil.* New York: Macmillan, 1900.

Lemprière, John. *Bibliotheca Classica: Or, a Dictionary of All the Principal Names and Terms Relating to the Geography, Topography, History, Literature, and Mythology of Antiquity and of the Ancients: With a Chronological Table.* New York: William E. Dean, 1853.

le Roux, Deon. *The Myth of 'Roo.* Raleigh: Lulu.com, 2011.

Leviton, Richard. *Encyclopedia of Earth Myths: An Insider's A-Z Guide to Mythic People, Places, Objects, and Events Central to the Earth's Visionary Geography.* Norfolk: Hampton Roads Publishing, 2005.

Lie, Nadia. *Constellation Caliban: Figurations of a Character.* Atlanta: Rodopi, 1997.

Lim, David C.L. *The Infinite Longing for Home: Desire and the Nation in Selected Writings of Ben Okri and K.S. Maniam.* Amsterdam: Rodopi, 2005.

Lindow, John. *Handbook of Norse Mythology.* Santa Barbara: ABC-CLIO, 2001.

Littleton, C. Scott, and Marshall Cavendish Corporation. *Gods, Goddesses, and Mythology.* Volumes 1, 2, 4 and 11. Tarrytown: Marshall Cavendish, 2005.

LLC Books. *Native American Legendary Creatures: Aztec Legendary Creatures, Inuit Legendary Creatures, Maya Legendary Creatures.* Memphis: General Books LLC, 2010.

Loar, Julie. *Goddesses for Every Day: Exploring the Wisdom and Power of the Divine Feminine Around the World.* Novato: New World Library, 2010.

Lockyer, Norman. *Nature.* Volume 113. New York: Macmillan Journals, 1924.

London Encyclopaedia: Or Universal Dictionary of Science, Art, Literature, and Practical Mechanics, Comprising a Popular View of the Present State of Knowledge. Volume 11. Minneapolis: Thomas Tegg and the University of Minnesota, 1829.

Lönnrot, Elias, translated by Francis Peabody Magoun. *The Kalevala: Or, Poems of the Kaleva District.* Cambridge: Harvard University Press, 1963.

Lowie, Robert Harry. *The Test-Theme in North American Mythology.* New York: Columbia University, 1908.

Lurker, Manfred. *Dictionary of Gods and Goddesses, Devils and Demons.* London: Routledge Kegan and Paul, 1987.

Lynch, Patricia Ann, and Jeremy Roberts. *African Mythology, A to Z.* New York: Infobase Publishing, 2010.

Lysaght, Patricia, Séamas Ó Catháin, and Dáithí Ó hÓgáin. *Islanders and Water-Dwellers: Proceedings of the Celtic-Nordic-Baltic Folklore Symposium Held at University College Dublin, 16–19 June 1996.* Dublin: DBA Publications, 1999.

Maberry, Jonathan. *Vampire Universe: The Dark World of the Supernatural Beings That Haunt Us, Hunt Us, and Hunger for Us.* Secaucus: Citadel Press, 1996.

Maberry, Jonathan, and David F. Kramer. *The Cryptopedia: A Dictionary of the Weird, Strange, and Downright Bizarre.* New York: Citadel Press, 2007.

Maberry, Jonathan, and David F. Kramer. *They Bite: Endless Cravings of Supernatural Predators.* New York: Citadel Press, 2009.

Mabie, Hamilton Wright. *Norse Mythology: Great Stories from the Eddas.* Mineola: Courier Dover Publications, 2012.

MacCulloch, John Arnott. *The Celtic and Scandinavian Religions.* New York: Cosimo, 2005.

MacDermott, Mercia. *Bulgarian Folk Customs.* London: Jessica Kingsley Publishers, 1998.

Macdowall, Maria Wilhelmina, and Johann Wilhelm E. Wägner. *Asgard and the Gods, Tales and Traditions of Our Northern Ancestors, Adapted from the Work of W. Wägner by M.W. Macdowall and Edited by W.S.W. Anson.* London: W. Swan Sonnenschein and Company, 1884.

MacGillivray, Royce. "Dracula: Bram Stoker's Spoiled Masterpiece." *Queens Quarterly* 79 (1972): 518–27.

Mack, Carol K., and Dinah Mack. *A Field Guide to Demons, Fairies, Fallen Angels, and Other Subversive Spirits.* New York: Henry Holt and Company, 1998.

MacKillop, James. *Myths and Legends of the Celts.* New York: Penguin, 2006.

Macleod, Norman. *A Dictionary of the Gaelic Language, in Two Parts: I. Gaelic and English.—II. English and Gaeli.* Edinburgh: W.R. M'Phun, 1853.

Magnus, Leonard Arthur. *The Heroic Ballads of Russia.* London: K. Paul, Trench, Trubner and Company, 1921.

Malory, Sir Thomas. *The History of the Renowned Prince Arthur, King of Britain; with His Life and Death, and All His Glorious Battles. Likewise, the Noble Acts and Heroic Deeds of His Valiant Knights of the Round Table. In Two Volumes.* Volume 1. London: Walker and Edwards, 1816.

Mancing, Howard. *The Cervantes Encyclopedia: A-K.* Westport, CT: Greenwood, 2004.

Mandel, David. *The Ultimate Who's Who in the Bible.* Alachua: Bridge Logos Foundation, 2007.

Mandel, David. *Who's Who in the Jewish Bible.* Philadelphia: Jewish Publication Society, 2010.

Manguel, Alberto, Eric Beddows, James Cook, Graham Greenfield, and Gianni Guadalupi. *The Dictionary of Imaginary Places.* Boston: Houghton Mifflin Harcourt, 2000.

Manser, Martin H., and David Pickering. *The Facts on File Dictionary of Classical and Biblical Allusions.* New York: Infobase Publishing, 2003.

March, Jenny. *The Penguin Book of Classical Myths.* London: Penguin UK, 2008.

Marshall, Joseph. *The Lakota Way: Stories and Lessons for Living.* New York: Penguin, 2002.

Marstrander, Carl Johan Sverdrup, editor. *Dictionary of the Irish Language, Compact Edition.* Dublin: Royal Irish Academy, 1990.

Martinez, Susan B. *The Mysterious Origins of Hybrid Man: Crossbreeding and the Unexpected Family Tree of Humanity.* Rochester: Inner Traditions / Bear and Company, 2013.

Mason, Patricia F. *Indian Tales of the Northwest.* Vancouver: CommCept Pub., 1976.

Masters, Anthony. *The Natural History of the Vampire.* London: Hart-Davis, 1972.

Mathers, Samuel Liddell. *The Kabbalah Unveiled.* Pomeroy: Health Research Books, 2003.

Matson, Gienna, and Jeremy Roberts. *Celtic Mythology A to Z.* New York: Infobase Publishing, 2010.

Matthews, John Hobson. *A History of the Parishes of St. Ives, Lelant, Towednack and Zennor: In the County of Cornwall.* London: Elliot Stock, 1892.

Matthews, John, and Caitlin Matthews. *The Element Encyclopedia of Magical Creatures: The Ultimate A-Z of Fantastic Beings from Myth and Magic.* New York: Barnes and Nobel, 2005.

McClelland, Bruce. *Slayers and Their Vampires: A Cultural History of Killing the Dead.* Ann Arbor: University of Michigan Press, 2006.

McClintock, John, and James Strong. *Cyclopaedia of Biblical, Theological, and Ecclesiastical Literature.* Volumes 1, 9 and 12. New York: Harper and Brothers, 1891–1894.

McCloskey, Jason, and Ignacio López Alemany. *Signs of Power in Habsburg Spain and the New World.* Lanham: Bucknell University Press, 2013.

McConnell, Winder. *A Companion to the Nibelungenlied.* Columbia: Camden House, 1998.

McCoy, Edain. *Celtic Myth and Magick: Harness the Power of the Gods and Goddesses.* St. Paul: Llewellyn Worldwide, 1995.

McCoy, Edain. *A Witch's Guide to Faery Folk: Reclaiming Our Working Relationship with Invisible Helpers.* St. Paul: Llewellyn Publications, 1995.

McKinnell, John. *Meeting the Other in Norse Myth and Legend.* Cambridge: DS Brewer, 2005.

Mead, Margaret. *The Mountain Arapesh.* Piscataway: Transaction Publishers, 2002.

The Melbourne Review. Volume 10, number 37–40. Melbourne: George, Robertson and Company, 1882.

Meletinskiĭ, Eleazar Moiseevich, and translated by Guy Lanoue. *The Poetics of Myth, Volume 1944 of Garland Reference Library of the Humanities.* New York: Taylor and Francis Group, 1998.

Melton, J. Gordon. *The Vampire Book: The Encyclopedia of the Undead.* Michigan: Visible Ink Press, 1999.

Metallic, Emmanuel N. *The Metallic Migmaq-English Reference Dictionary.* Quebec: Presses Université Laval, 2005.

Meurger, Michel, and Claude Gagnon. *Lake Monster Traditions: A Cross-Cultural Analysis.* London: Fortean Tomes, 1988.

Meyer, Elard Hugo. *Mythologie Der Germanen.* Strazburg, Germany: Karl J. Trübner, 1903.

Middleton, Darren J.N. *Broken Hallelujah: Nikos Kazantzakis and Christian Theology.* Lanham: Lexington Books, 2007.

Miguel de Barandiarán, José, and Jesús Altuna. *Selected Writings of José Miguel De Barandiarán: Basque Prehistory and Ethnography.* Reno: Center for Basque Studies, University of Nevada, 2009.

Milbrath, Susan. *Star Gods of the Maya: Astronomy in Art, Folklore, and Calendars.* Austin: University of Texas Press, 1999.

Miller, Dean A. *The Epic Hero.* Baltimore: Johns Hopkins University Press, 2000.

Minissale, Gregory. *Framing Consciousness in Art: Transcultural Perspectives.* Amsterdam: Rodopi, 2009.

Mittman, Asa Simon, and Peter J. Dendle, editors. *The Ashgate Research Companion to Monsters and the Monstrous.* Burlington: Ashgate Publishing, 2012.

Monaghan, Patricia. *The Encyclopedia of Celtic Mythology and Folklore.* New York: Infobase Publishing, 2004.

Monaghan, Patricia. *Encyclopedia of Goddesses and Heroines: Revised.* Novato: New World Library, 2014.

Monaghan, Patricia. *Goddesses in World Culture.* Volume 1. Santa Barbara: ABC-CLIO, 2010.

Monaghan, Patricia. *New Book of Goddesses and Heroines.* St. Paul: Llewellyn Publications, 1997.

Monahan, Peter Friedrich. *The American Wild Man: The Science and Theatricality of Nondescription in the Works of Edgar Allan Poe, Jack London, and Djuna Barnes.* Ann Arbor: ProQuest, 2008.

Moore, Virginia. *The Unicorn: William Butler Yeats' Search for Reality.* New York: Macmillan, 1954.

Moorey, Teresa. *The Fairy Bible: The Definitive Guide to the World of Fairies.* New York: Sterling Publishing Company, 2008.

Morell, Sir Charles. *Tales of the Genii; or the Delightful Lessons of Horam, the Son of Asmar. Faithfuly Translated from the Persian Manuscript and Compared with the French and Spanish Editions.* London: Parernofter Row, 1810.

Mortensen, Karl. *A Handbook of Norse Mythology.* Mineola: Courier Dover Publications, 2003.

Mountain, Harry. *The Celtic Encyclopedia.* Volumes 1, 2 and 5. Aveiro: Universal-Publishers, 1998.

Mowat, Farley. *People of the Deer.* New York: Carroll and Graf, 2004.

Murakami, Kenji. *Yōkai Jiten.* Tokyo: Mainichi Shimbun Press, 2000.

Murray, Alexander Stuart. *Manual of Mythology: Greek and Roman, Norse and Old German, Hindoo and Egyptian Mythology.* New York: Scribner, Armstrong, and Company, 1876.

Murray, J. *A Classical Manual Being a Mythological, Historical, and Geographical, Commentary on Pope's Homer, and Drydens Aeneid of Virgil: With a Copious Index.* London: J. Murray, 1833.

Murrill, Rupert Ivan. *Cranial and Postcranial Skeletal Remains from Easter Island.* Minneapolis: University of Minnesota Press, 1968.

Nardo, Don. *The Gods and Goddesses of Greek Mythology.* San Diego: Capstone Press, 2011.

Newcomb, Jacky, and Alicen Geddes-Ward. *A Faerie Treasury.* Carlsbad: Hay House, Inc, 2008.

Newton, Michael. *Hidden Animals: A Field Guide to Batsquatch, Chupacabra, and Other Elusive Creatures.* Santa Barbara: ABC-CLIO, 2009.

Nicholas, Thomas. *The Pedigree of the English People.* Charleston: Nabu Press, 2010.

Nonnus (of Panopolis) and Levi Robert Lind. *Dionysiaca*. Volume 2. London: W. Heinemann, 1940.

Norroena Society. *The Asatrii Edda: Sacred Lore of the North*. Bloomington: iUniverse, 2009.

O'Connor, Frank, editor. *A Book of Ireland*. London: Collins, 1959.

O'Connor, Ralph. *Icelandic Histories and Romances*. Gloucestershire: Tempus, 2002.

Oehlenschläger, Adam Gottlob, and William Edward Frye, translator. *The Gods of the North: An Epic Poem*. London: W. Pickering, 1845.

Ogden, Daniel. *A Companion to Greek Religion*. West Sussex: John Wiley and Sons, 2010.

Ogden, Daniel. *Dragons, Serpents, and Slayers in the Classical and Early Christian Worlds: A Sourcebook*. New York: Oxford University Press, 2013.

Oinas, Felix. *Studies in Finnic Folklore*. London: Routledge, 1997.

Oliver, Douglas L. *Oceania: The Native Cultures of Australia and the Pacific Islands*. Volume 1. Honolulu: University of Hawaii Press, 1989.

Olrik, Axel. *The Heroic Legends of Denmark*. New York: American-Scandinavian Foundation, 1919.

Olsen, Brad. *Sacred Places North America: 108 Destinations*. San Francisco: CCC Publishing, 2008.

Olsen, Karin E., and L.A.J.R. Houwen. *Monsters and the Monstrous in Medieval Northwest Europe*. Sterling: Peeters Publishers, 2001.

Olupọna, Jacob Obafẹmi Kẹhinde. *Beyond Primitivism: Indigenous Religious Traditions and Modernity*. London: Psychology Press, 2004.

Orchard, Andy. *Cassell's Dictionary of Norse Myth and Legend*. London: Cassell, 2002.

Orchard, Andy. *Pride and Prodigies: Studies in the Monsters of the Beowulf-Manuscript*. Toronto: University of Toronto Press, 2003.

Oregon Historical Quarterly. Volumes 56–57. N.p.: W.H. Leeds, State Printer, 1955.

Osburn, William. *The Monumental History of Egypt*. London: Trübner and Company, 1854.

Ostling, Michael. *Between the Devil and the Host: Imagining Witchcraft in Early Modern Poland*. Oxford: Oxford University Press, 2011.

Ozeli, Motteux. *The Works of Francis Rabelais*. London: Lackington, Allen, and Company: 1807.

Page, Michael F., and Robert R. Ingpen. *Encyclopedia of Things That Never Were: Creatures, Places, and People*. New York: Viking Press, 1987.

Paine, Lauran. *The Hierarchy of Hell*. New York: Hippocrene Books, 1972.

Painter, John Thomas. *Ethnology: Or the History and Genealogy of the Human Race*. London: Bailliére, Tindall and Cox, 1880.

Pal, Pratapaditya. *Indian Sculpture: Circa 500 B.C.-A.D. 700*. Berkeley: University of California Press, 1986.

Parada, Carlos. *Genealogical Guide to Greek Mythology*. Lund C. Bloms Boktryckeri, 1993.

Paraiso, Salvador, and Jose Juan Paraiso. *The Balete Book: A Collection of Demons, Monsters, Elves and Dwarfs from the Philippine Lower Mythology*. Quezon City, Philippines: Giraffe Books, 2003.

Parker, Janet, Alice Mills, and Julie Stanton. *Mythology: Myths, Legends and Fantasies*. Cape Town: Struik, 2007.

Parmeshwaranand, Swami. *Encyclopaedic Dictionary of Puranas*. Volume 1. New Delhi: Sarup and Sons, 2001.

Pausanias, translated Arthur Richard Shilleto. *Pausanias' Description of Greece*. Volume 2. London: George Bell, 1900.

Pavitt, Robin. *The Ancient Symbolism Within the Heart*. N.p.: Robin Pavitt, 2012.

Peek, Philip M., and Kwesi Yankah. *African Folklore: An Encyclopedia*. New York: Taylor and Francis, 2004.

Pelton, Mary Helen White, and Jacqueline DiGennaro. *Images of a People: Tlingit Myths and Legends*. Englewood: Libraries Unlimited, 1992.

Pemberton, John. *Myths and Legends: From Cherokee Dances to Voodoo Trances*. Eastbourne: Canary Press eBooks, 2011.

Penard, A.P., and T.G. Penard. "Surinam Folk-Tales" in *The Journal of American Folk-Lore*. Volume 7 of *Bibliographical and Special Series of the American Folklore Society* edited by the American Folklore Society, 239–251. Lancaster: American Folk-lore Society, 1917.

Pentikäinen, Juha. *Kalevala Mythology, Revised Edition*. Bloomington: Indiana University Press, 1987.

Penz, Eric. *Cryptid: The Lost Legacy of Lewis and Clark*. Bloomington: Booktango, 2013.

Perera, Victor, and Robert D. Bruce. *The Last Lords of Palenque: The Lacandon Mayas of the Mexican Rain Forest*. Berkeley: University of California Press, 1982.

Perkowski, Jan Louis. *Vampires of the Slavs*. Columbus, Ohio: Slavica Publishers, 1976.

Perrault, Charles. *Histoires Ou Contes Du Temps Passé Avec Des Moralités*. Montpezat-en-Provence: AURORÆ LIBRI, Éditeur, 1982.

Pesznecker, Susan. *Gargoyles: From the Archives of the Grey School of Wizardry*. Pompton Plains: Career Press, 2006.

Peterson, Amy T., and David J. Dunworth. *Mythology in Our Midst: A Guide to Cultural References*. Westport, CT: Greenwood, 2004.

Phillips, Charles, and Michael Kerrigan. *Forests of the Vampire*. Amsterdam: Time-Life Books BV, 1999.

Pitzer, Sara. *Myths and Mysteries of North Carolina: True Stories of the Unsolved and Unexplained*. Guilford: Globe Pequot, 2010.

Placzek, B. "Arthropod Mythology," *Popular Science*. September 1882, Vol. 21, No. 37. New York: Bonnier Corporation, 1882.

Pliny the Elder, translated by John Bostock and Henry Thomas Riley. *The Natural History of Pliny*. Volume 1. London: George Bells and Son, 1890; Volume 2. London: Henry G. Bohn, 1855; Volume 6. London: Henry G. Bohn, 1857.

Pliny the Elder, translated by Philemon Holland. *Pliny's Natural History in Thirty-Seven Books*. Volumes 1–3. London: Wernerian Club, 1848.

Polynesian Society (N.Z.) *The Journal of the Polynesian Society*. Volume 27. New Plymouth: Polynesian Society, 1967.

Polynesian Society (N.Z.) *The Journal of the Polynesian Society*. Volume 68. New Plymouth: Polynesian Society, 1959.

Poole, Edward Stanley, ed. *The Thousand and One Nights, Commonly Called the Arabian Nights Entertainments: A New Translation from the Arabic*. Translated by Edward William Lane. New York: Hearst's International Library Company, 1914.

Popular Science Monthly. Volume 21 May to October. New York: D. Appleton, 1882.

Porteous, Alexander. *Forest Folklore: Mythology and Romance.* Whitefish: Kessinger Publishing, 2006.

Porteous, Alexander. *The Forest in Folklore and Mythology.* Mineola: Courier Dover Publications, 2001.

Porteous, Alexander. *The Lore of the Forest.* New York: Cosimo, 2005.

Powell, J.W., director, and the United States. Government Printing Office. *Congressional Serial Set. 11th Annual Report of the Bureau of Ethnology to the Secretary of the Smithsonian Institution, 1889–90.* Washington, D.C.: U.S. Government Printing Office, 1895.

Prahlad, Anand. *Encyclopedia of African American Folklore.* Westport, CT: Greenwood, 2006.

Prahlad, Anand. *The Greenwood Encyclopedia of African American Folklore: A-F.* Westport, CT: Greenwood, 2006.

Pughe, William Owen. *A Dictionary of the Welsh Language, Explained in English: With Numerous Illustrations, from the Literary Remains and from the Living Speech of the Cymry.* Volume 1. London: Williams, 1803.

Puryear, Mark. *The Nature of Asatru: An Overview of the Ideals and Philosophy of the Indigenous Religion of Northern Europe.* Lincoln: iUniverse, 2006.

Rabelais, François. *Hours with Rabelais.* Edited by Francis Griffin Stokes and translated by Sir Thomas Urquhart and Peter Anthony Motteux. London: Methuen, 1905.

Rabelais, François, and Peter Anthony Motteux. *Gargantua and Pantagruel.* Volumes 4–5. London: David Nutt, 1900.

Radcliffe-Brown, A.R. *The Andaman Islanders.* Cambridge: Cambridge University Press, 2013.

Raedisch, Linda. *The Old Magic of Christmas: Yuletide Traditions for the Darkest Days of the Year.* Woodbury: Llewellyn Worldwide, 2013.

Ragan, Kathleen. *Fearless Girls, Wise Women, and Beloved Sisters: Heroines in Folktales from Around the World.* London: W.W. Norton and Company, 1998.

Raleigh, Sir Walter, edited by Joyce Lorimer. *Sir Walter Ralegh's Discoverie of Guiana.* Burlington: Ashgate Publishing, 2006.

Ramos, Maximo D. *The Aswang Syncrasy in Philippine Folklore: With Illustrative Accounts in Vernacular Texts and Translations.* Quezon City, Philippines: Philippine Folklore Society, 1971.

Ramos, Maximo D. *The Creatures of Midnight: Faded Deities of Luzon, the Visayas and Mindanao.* Quezon City: Island Publishers, 1967.

Ramos, Maximo D. *Creatures of Philippine Lower Mythology.* Diliman: University of the Philippines Press, 1971.

Recinos, Adrián, and translated by Delia Goetz, Adrián Recinos, and Sylvanus Griswold Morley. *Popol Vuh: The Sacred Book of the Ancient Quicche Maya.* Norman: University of Oklahoma Press, 1950.

Reddall, Henry Frederic. *Fact, Fancy, and Fable: A New Handbook for Ready Reference on Subjects Commonly Omitted from Cyclopaedias; Comprising Personal Sobriquets, Familiar Phrases, Popular Appellations, Geographical Nicknames, Literary Pseudonyms, Mythological Characters, Red-Letter Days, Political Slang, Contractions and Abbreviations, Technical Terms Foreign Words and Phrases, and Americanisms.* Chicago: A.C. McClurg, 1892.

Redfern, Nick. *The Most Mysterious Places on Earth.* New York: The Rosen Publishing Group, 2013.

Reed, Alexander Wyclif. *Aboriginal Fables and Legendary Tales.* Chatswood, Australia: New Holland Publishing Australia Pty., 2006.

Reif-Hülser, Monika. *Borderlands: Negotiating Boundaries in Post-Colonial Writing.* Amsterdam: Rodopi, 1999.

Renner, George Thomas. *Primitive Religion in the Tropical Forests: A Study in Social Geography.* New York: Columbia University, 1927.

Rhys, Sir John. *Celtic Folklore: Welsh and Manx.* Volume 1. Charleston: Forgotten Books, 1983.

Riasanovsky, Nicholas Valentine, Thomas Eekman and Gleb Struve. *California Slavic Studies.* Volume 11. Berkeley: University of California Press, 1980.

Richardson, Maurice. "The Psychoanalysis of Ghost Stories." *The Twentieth Century.* vol. 166 (1959): 419–31.

Rigoglioso, Marguerite. *The Cult of Divine Birth in Ancient Greece.* New York: Macmillan, 2009.

Roberts, Jeremy. *Chinese Mythology, A to Z.* New York: Infobase Publishing, 2009.

Robinson, Fred C. *The Tomb of Beowulf and Other Essays on Old English.* Cambridge, Mass.: Blackwell, 1993.

Robisch, S.K. *Wolves and the Wolf Myth in American Literature.* Reno: University of Nevada Press, 2009.

Rodd, Thomas, editor. *History of Charles the Great and Orlando.* Volume 1. London: T. Rodd and T. Boosey, 1812.

Rodríguez de Montalvo, Garci, and translated by Edwin Bray Place and Herbert C. Behm. *Amadis of Gaul: A Novel of Chivalry of the 14th Century Presumably First Written in Spanish.* Volume 1. Lexington: University Press of Kentucky, 2003.

Roman, Luke, and Mónica Román. *Encyclopedia of Greek and Roman Mythology.* New York: Infobase Publishing, 2010.

Roof, George W. *Popular History of Noble County Capitals and Greater Albion: Growth, Resources, Surroundings, Facilities and Industrial Opportunities, Interesting Sketches and Reminiscences, with a Business and Professional Guide.* Albion: Unigraphic, 1908.

Room, Adrian. *Who's Who in Classical Mythology.* New York: McGraw-Hill Education, 1997.

Rooth, Anna Birgitta. *Loki in Scandinavian Mythology.* Lund: C.W.K. Gleerup, 1961.

Roraff, Susan, and Laura Comacho. *Chile.* Portland: Publisher Graphic Arts Center Publishing Company, 2001.

Rose, Carol. *Giants, Monsters, and Dragons: An Encyclopedia of Folklore, Legend, and Myth (In English).* New York: W.W. Norton and Company, 2001.

Rose, Carol. *Spirits, Fairies, Leprechauns, and Goblins, an Encyclopedia.* New York: W.W. Norton and Company, 1996.

Rose, H.J. *A Handbook of Greek Mythology.* London: Taylor and Francis, 1964.

Rosen, Brenda. *The Mythical Creatures Bible: The Definitive Guide to Legendary Beings.* New York: Sterling Publishing Company, 2009.

Ross, Margaret Clunies. *Old Norse Myths, Literature and Society.* Odense: University Press of South Denmark, 2003.

Roth, John E. *American Elves: An Encyclopedia of Little People from the Lore of 380 Ethnic Groups of the Western Hemisphere.* Jefferson, NC: McFarland, 1997.

Routledge, Katherine. *The Mystery of Easter Island*. New York: Cosimo, 2007.

Rowse, E.E. *In and Around Swansea*. E.E. Rowse: Swansea, 1896.

Royal Anthropological Institute of Great Britain and Ireland. *Journal of the Royal Anthropological Institute of Great Britain and Ireland*. Volume. 10. London: Royal Anthropological Institute, 1881.

Royal Anthropological Institute of Great Britain and Ireland. *Man*. Volume 23–25. London: Royal Anthropological Institute, 1888.

Rudolf, Winfried, Thomas Honegger, and Andrew James Johnston, editors. *Clerks, Wives and Historians: Essays on Medieval English Language and Literature*. Bern: Peter Lang, 2008.

Ruoff, Henry Woldmar. *The Standard Dictionary of Facts: History, Language, Literature, Biography, Geography, Travel, Art, Government, Politics, Industry, Invention, Commerce, Science, Education, Natural History, Statistics and Miscellany*. Buffalo: The Frontier Press Company, 1908.

Russell, Jeffrey Burton. *Lucifer, the Devil in the Middle Ages*. Ithaca, NY: Cornell University Press, 1986.

Rydberg, Viktor. *Norroena, the History and Romance of Northern Europe: A Library of Supreme Classics Printed in Complete Form*. Volumes 2 and 3. London: Norroena Society, 1906.

Rydberg, Viktor. *Our Fathers' Godsaga: Retold for the Young*. Lincoln: iUniverse, 2003.

Rzach, Aloisius. *The Sibylline Oracles*. New York: Eaton and Mains, 1899.

Saavedra, Miguel de Cervantes. *The History of Don Quixote De La Mancha. from the Span. to Which Is Prefixed a Sketch of the Life and Writings of the Author. Select Libr. Ed*. London: James Burns, 1847.

Sakihara, Mitsugu, Stewart Curry, and Leon Angelo Serafim. *Okinawan-English Wordbook: A Short Lexicon of the Okinawan Language with English Definitions and Japanese Cognates*. Honolulu: University of Hawaii Press, 2006.

Saklani, Dinesh Prasad. *Ancient Communities of the Himalaya*. New Delhi: Indus Publishing, 1998.

Sandars, N., editor and translator. *The Epic of Gilgamesh*. London: Penguin UK, 1973.

Sanders, Alan J.K. *Historical Dictionary of Mongolia*. Lanham: Scarecrow Press, 2010.

Sanderson, Ivan T. *Abominable Snowmen, Legend Come to Life*. New York: Cosimo, 2007.

Sardi, Francesca. *Psychological Activity in the Homeric Circe Episode*. Chicago: University of Chicago Press, 2003.

Savill, Sheila. *Pears Encyclopaedia of Myths and Legends: Chapter 7. Oceania and Australia. Chapter 8. the Americas*. Volume 4. London: Pelham, 1978.

Saxo (Grammaticus), and edited by Hilda Roderick Ellis Davidson and Peter Fisher. *The History of the Danes*. Books 1–9. Suffolk: DS Brewer, 1979.

Schmidt, Joël. *Larousse Greek and Roman Mythology*. New York: McGraw-Hill, 1980.

Schreiber, Charlotte. *The Mabinogion: From the Llyfr. Cocho Hergest, and Other Ancient Welsh Manuscripts. Part 3, Containing Geraint the Son of Erbin*. Volume 2. London: Longman, Brown, Green, and Longmans, 1849.

Schwartz, Howard. *Tree of Souls: The Mythology of Judaism: The Mythology of Judaism*. Oxford: Oxford University Press, 2004.

Scott, James George. *The Burman: His Life and Notions*. Volume 1. London: Macmillan, 1882.

Sebeok, Thomas Albert, and Frances Ingemann. *Studies in Cheremis: The Supernatural*. New York: Johnson Reprint Corporation, 1956.

Sedgefield, Walter John, editor. *Beowulf*. Manchester: Manchester University Press, 1918.

Segal, Charles. *Dionysiac Poetics and Euripides' Bacchae*. Princeton: Princeton University Press, 1997.

Selbie, John Alexander, and Louis Herbert Gray. *Encyclopædia of Religion and Ethics*. Volume 12. Edinburgh: T. and T. Clark, 1922.

Seligman, Charles G. *The Melanesians of British New Guinea*. Cambridge: Cambridge University Press Archive, 1975.

Senf, Carol A. *The Vampire in Nineteenth-Century English Literature*. Bowling Green, OH: Bowling Green State University Popular Press, 1988.

Sered, Susan Starr. *Women of the Sacred Groves: Divine Priestesses of Okinawa*. Oxford: Oxford University Press, 1999.

Shakespeare, William, and edited by Henry Chichester Hart. *The Merry Wives of Windsor*. London: Methuen and Company, 1904.

Shakespeare, William, and edited by Henry Chichester Hart. *Othello*. London: Methuen and Company, 1904.

Shalit, Erel. *Will Fishes Fly in Aquarius*. Carmel: Fisher King Press, 2011.

Shearar, Cheryl. *Understanding Northwest Coast Art: A Guide to Crests, Beings and Symbols*. Vancouver: Douglas and McIntyre, 2000.

Sheard, K.M. *Llewellyn's Complete Book of Names for Pagans, Wiccans, Witches, Druids, Heathens, Mages, Shamans and Independent Thinkers of All Sorts Who Are Curious About Names from Every Place and Every Time*. Woodbury: Llewellyn Worldwide, 2011.

Sherman, Josepha. *Storytelling: An Encyclopedia of Mythology and Folklore*. Armonk: M.E. Sharpe Reference, 2008.

Shoumatoff, Alex. *Legends of the American Desert: Sojourns in the Greater Southwest*. New York: Alfred A. Knopf, 1997.

Shuker, Karl. *The Beasts That Hide from Man: Seeking the World's Last Undiscovered Animals*. New York: Cosimo, 2003.

Shuker, Karl. *Mysteries of Planet Earth*. London: Carlton, 1999.

Siefker, Phyllis. *Santa Claus, Last of the Wild Men: The Origins and Evolution of Saint Nicholas, Spanning 50,000 Years*. Jefferson, NC: McFarland, 2006.

Sierra, Judy. *The Gruesome Guide to World Monsters*. Cambridge: Candlewick Press, 2005.

Sikes, Wirt. *British Goblins: Welsh Folk Lore, Fairy Mythology, Legends and Traditions*. Boston: James R. Osgood and Company, 1881.

Simek, Rudolf, and translated by Angela Hall. *Dictionary of Northern Mythology*. Cambridge: D.S. Brewer, 2007.

Simons, Geoffrey Leslie. *The Witchcraft World*. London: Abelard-Schuman, 1974.

Simpson, Jacqueline. *Icelandic Folktales and Legends*. Berkeley: University of California Press, 1972.

Simpson, Jacqueline, and Stephen Roud. *A Dictionary of*

English Folklore. Oxford: Oxford University Press, 2000.

Singer, Isidore, and Cyrus Adler. *The Jewish Encyclopedia: A Descriptive Record of the History, Religion, Literature, and Customs of the Jewish People from the Earliest Times to the Present Day*. Volume 5. New York: Funk and Wagnalls, 1916.

Skamble, Skimble (pseud.). *Fairy Tales*. Durham: Andrews, 1869.

Skyes, Edgerton, and Alan Kendall. *Who's Who in Non-Classical Mythology*. London: Routledge, 2002.

Slavic and East European Folklore Association Journal, Volume 3, Issue 2. Charlottesville: Slavic and East European Folklore Association, 1998.

Slusser, Mary Shepherd. *Nepal Mandala: A Cultural Study of the Kathmandu Valley*. Princeton: Princeton University Press, 1982.

Smith, Douglas B. *Ever Wonder Why?* New York: Ballantine Books, 2013.

Smith, Evans Lansing, and Nathan Robert Brown. *The Complete Idiot's Guide to World Mythology*. New York: Penguin, 2008.

Smith, George Adam. *The Book of Deuteronomy: In the Revised Version*. Cambridge: University Press, 1918.

Smith, Nigel J.H. *The Enchanted Amazon Rain Forest: Stories from a Vanishing World*. Gainesville: University Press of Florida, 1996.

Smith, Sir William. *A Dictionary of Greek and Roman Biography and Mythology*. London: John Murray, 1880.

Smith, Sir William, and Charles Anthon. *A New Classical Dictionary of Greek and Roman Biography, Mythology and Geography: Partly Based Upon the Dictionary of Greek and Roman Biography and Mythology*. New York: Harper and Brothers, 1862.

Smith, Sir William, and Charles Anthon. *A New Classical Dictionary of Greek and Roman Biography, Mythology and Geography*. Volume 1. Whitefish: Kessinger Publishing, 2006.

Smith, Sir William Ramsay. *Myths and Legends of the Australian Aboriginals*. London: George G. Harrap, 1930.

Snow, Edward Rowe. *Incredible Mysteries and Legends of the Sea*. New York: Dodd, Mead, 1967.

Society for the Diffusion of Useful Knowledge. *The Penny Cyclopaedia of the Society for the Diffusion of Useful Knowledge* Volumes 10 and 17. London: Charles Knight, 1838; 1840.

Sosnoski, Daniel. *Introduction to Japanese Culture*. Boston: Charles E. Tuttle Publishing. 1966.

Southey, Robert. *Southey's Common-Place Book*. Volume 4. London: Longman, Brown, Green and Longmans, 1851.

Speck, Frank G. "The Tale of Chahnameed" in *Journal of American Folklore*. Volume 7 of *Bibliographical and Special Series of the American Folklore Society* edited by the American Folklore Society, pages 104–107. Boston: American Folk-lore Society, 1902.

Spence, Lewis. *The History of Atlantis*. New York: Cosimo, 2007.

Spence, Lewis. *Legends and Romances of Brittany*. Charleston: Forgotten Books.

Spence, Lewis. *Legends and Romances of Spain*. N.p.: G.G. Harrap, 1920.

Spence, Lewis. *The Minor Traditions of British Mythology*. London: Rider and Company, 1948.

Spence. Lewis. *Mysteries of Celtic Britain*. Whitefish: Kessinger Publishing, 2004.

Spence, Lewis. *The Popol Vuh: The Mythic and Heroic Sagas of the Kiches of Central America*. Phoenix: David Nutt, 1908.

Sprague de Camp, L., and Willy Ley. *Lands Beyond*. New York: Barnes and Noble Books, 1993.

Squire, Charles. *Celtic Myths and Legend Poetry and Romance*. New York: Bell Publishing Company, 1979.

Stanley, David. *South Pacific Handbook*. Emeryville: David Stanley, 1999.

Stefoff, Rebecca. *Vampires, Zombies, and Shape-Shifters*. New York: Benchmark Books, 2007.

Steiger, Brad. *The Werewolf Book: The Encyclopedia of Shape-Shifting Beings*. Michigan: Visible Ink Press, 2011.

Stepanich, Kisma K. *Faery Wicca*. Book One. St. Paul: Llewellyn Worldwide, 1997.

Stevenson, Jay. *The Complete Idiot's Guide to Eastern Philosophy*. New York: Penguin, 2000.

Stookey, Lorena Laura. *Thematic Guide to World Mythology*. Westport, CT: Greenwood, 2004.

Stubbs, William. *Origines Celticae (A Fragment) and Other Contributions to the History of Britain*. London: Macmillan, 1883.

Sturleson, Snorri, Saemund Sigfusson, Saxo Grammaticus, and William Morris. *The Viking Anthology: Norse Myths, Icelandic Sagas and Viking Chronicles*. N.p.: Bybliotech, 2014.

Sturluson, Snorri, translated by Arthur Gilchrist Brodeur. *The Prose Edda*. Volume 5. New York: General Books, 2003.

Sturluson, Snorri, translated by Arthur Gilchrist Brodeur. *The Prose Edda: Norse Mythology*. Mineola: Dover, 2004.

Summers, Montague. *Vampire: His Kith and Kin*. Whitefish: Kessinger Publishing, 2003.

Summers, Montague. *Witchcraft and Black Magic*. North Chemsford: Courier Dover Publications, 2000.

Tada, Katsumi. *Edo Yōkai Karuta*. Tokyo: Kokushokan Kōkai, 1998.

Tate, Carolyn E. *Reconsidering Olmec Visual Culture: The Unborn, Women, and Creation*. Austin: University of Texas Press, 2012.

Taunton, Gwendolyn. *Northern Traditions*. Ocean Grove: Numen Books, 2011.

Taylor, Charles. *Calmets Great Dictionary of the Holy Bible*. Charlestown: Samuel Etheridge, 1812.

Taylor, W. Munro, and William Cooke Taylor. *A Hand-Book of Hindu Mythology and Philosophy: With Some Biographical Notices*. Madras: Higginbotham and Company, 1870.

Teachers' Curriculum Institute. *Ancient World History Activity Sampler*. Palo Alto: Teachers' Curriculum Institute, 1999.

Telesco, Patricia. *The Kitchen Witch Companion: Simple and Sublime Culinary Magic*. New York: Citadel Press, 2005.

Thomas, Neil. *Diu Crône and the Medieval Arthurian Cycle*. Cambridge: DS Brewer, 2002.

Thomas, William Isaac, and Florian Znaniecki. *The Polish Peasant in Europe and America: Monograph of an Immigrant Group*. Boston: Richard G. Badger Gorman Press, 1918.

Thompson, Charles John Samuel. *The History and Lore of Freaks*. London: Senate, 1996.

Thoms, William John. *Lays and Legends of Various Nations: Illustrative of Their Traditions, Popular Literature, Manners, Customs, and Superstitions.* Volumes 2–4. London: George Cowie, 1834.

Thorpe, Benjamin. *Northern Mythology, Comprising the Principal Popular Traditions and Superstitions of Scandinavia, North Germany and the Netherlands: Compiled from Original and Other Sources. In Three Volumes. Scandinavian Popular Traditions and Superstitions.* Volumes 1 and 2. London: Edward Lumley, 1851.

Thorpe, Benjamin, translator. *The Elder Edda of Saemund Sigfusson.* London: Norroena Society, 1907.

Tolley, Clive. *Shamanism in Norse Myth and Magic.* Issue 296. Helsinki: Academia Scientiarum Fennica, 2009.

Torchia, Christopher. *Indonesian Idioms and Expressions: Colloquial Indonesian at Work.* North Clarendon: Tuttle Publishing, 2007.

Tregear, Edward. *The Maori-Polynesian Comparative Dictionary.* Wellington: Lyon and Blair, 1891.

Triplette, Stacey Elizabeth. *Pagans, Monsters, and Women in the "Amadis" Cycle.* Berkeley: University of California, 2001.

Tripp, Edward. *The Meridian Handbook of Classical Mythology.* New York: Penguin USA, 1974.

Trzaskoma, Stephen M., R. Scott Smith, Stephen Brunet, and Thomas G. Palaima. *Anthology of Classical Myth: Primary Sources in Translation.* Indianapolis: Hackett Publishing, 2004.

Turner, Patricia, and Charles Russell Coulter. *Dictionary of Ancient Deities.* New York: Oxford University Press, 2001.

Twitchell, James B. *The Living Dead: A Study of the Vampire in Romantic Literature.* Durham: Duke University Press, 1987.

Ugresic, Dubravka. *Baba Yaga Laid an Egg.* New York: Grove/Atlantic, 2011.

Underhill, Ruth Murray. *Indians of the Pacific Northwest.* Phoenix: United States Department of the Interior, Bureau of Indian Affairs, Branch of Education, 1945.

Updike, John. *Picked-Up Pieces.* New York: Random House Publishing Group, 2013.

Urban, Sylvanus. "Ancient India and Ceylon as Described by the Edler Pliny" in *Gentleman's Magazine and Historical Review.* Volume 2, edited by the Magazine, pages 532–42. London: John Henry and James Parker, 1857.

Vālmīki, and edited by Rosalind Lefeber and Robert P. Goldman. *The Ramayana of Valmiki: An Epic of Ancient India-Kiskindhakanda.* Princeton: Princeton University Press, 1994.

van der Toorn, K., Bob Becking, and Pieter Willem van der Horst. *Dictionary of Deities and Demons in the Bible DDD.* Grand Rapids: Wm. B. Eerdmans Publishing, 1999.

van Deusen, Kira. *Kiviuq: An Inuit Hero and His Siberian Cousins.* Montreal: McGill-Queen's Press, MQUP, 2009.

van Scott, Miriam. *The Encyclopedia of Hell.* New York: Macmillan, 1999.

Varner, Gary R. *Creatures in the Mist: Little People, Wild Men and Spirit Beings Around the World: A Study in Comparative Mythology.* New York: Algora Publishing, 2007.

Varner, Gary R. *Mysteries of Native American Myth and Religion.* Raleigh: Lulu.com, 2007.

Varner, Gary R. *The Mythic Forest, the Green Man and the Spirit of Nature: The Re-Emergence of the Spirit of Nature from Ancient Times into Modern Society.* New York: Algora Publishing, 2006.

Vaughan, Robert. *The British Quarterly Review.* Volume 7. London: Hodder and Stoughton, 1848.

Vigfússon, Guðbrandur, and edited by Frederick York Powell. *Court Poetry: Volume 2 of Corpus Poeticvm Boreale: The Poetry of the Old Northern Tongue, from the Earliest Times to the Thirteenth Century.* Guðbrandur Vigfússon.

Vigfússon, Guðbrandur, and edited by Frederick York Powell. *Eddic Poetry.* Oxford: Clarendon Press, 1883.

Vigfússon, Guðbrandur, and translated by George Webbe Dasent. *Icelandic Sagas and Other Historical Documents Relating to the Settlements and Descents of the Northmen of the British Isles.* Volume 3. Cambridge: Cambridge University Press, 2012.

Viking Society for Northern Research. *Saga Book of the Viking Society for Northern Research.* Volume 25, 62.

Volta, Ornella. *The Vampire.* London: Tandem Books, 1963.

Voltaire. *Essays and Criticisms: Containing Letters on the Christian Religion; the Philosophy of History; the Ignorant Philosopher; and the Chinese Cathechism.* New York: Peter Eckler, 1920.

Wackerbarth, Athanasius Diedrich, translator. *Beowulf: An Epic Poem.* London: William Pickering, 1849.

Wagenwoorf, H. *Studies in Roman Literature, Culture and Religion.* Leiden: Brill Archive, 1956.

Waggoner, Ben. *Sagas of Giants and Heroes.* New Haven: Troth Publications, 2010.

Wägner, W. *Asgard and the Gods: Tales and Traditions of Our Northern Ancestors: Told for Boys and Girls.* London: W. Swan Sonnenschein and Allen, 1880.

Wallace, Kathryn. *Folk-Lore of Ireland: Legends, Myths and Fairy Tales.* Chicago: J.S. Hyland, 1910.

Walsh, William Shepard. *Heroes and Heroines of Fiction, Classical Mediæval, Legendary: Famous Characters and Famous Names in Novels, Romances, Poems and Dramas, Classified, Analyzed and Criticised, with Supplementary Citations from the Best Authorities.* Philadelphia: J.B. Lippincott Company, 1915.

Ward, William Hayes. "Light on Scriptural Texts from Recent Discoveries" in *The Homiletic Review.* Volume 26 edited by I.K. Funk, pages 508–10. New York: Funk and Wagnalls, 1893.

Warner, Charles Dudley, Hamilton Wright Mabie, Lucia Isabella Gilbert Runkle, and George H. Warner, editors. *Library of the World's Best Literature, Ancient and Modern.* Volume 20. New York: J.A. Hill and Company, 1902.

Warner, Marina. *Monsters of Our Own Making: The Peculiar Pleasures of Fear.* Lexington: University Press of Kentucky, 1999.

Washington State. *Report of the Governor of Washington Territory.* Washington, D.C.: U.S. Government Printing Office, 1884.

Watts, Linda S. *Encyclopedia of American Folklore.* New York: Infobase Publishing, 2006.

Weber, Henry William. *The Process of the Seuyn Sages. Octouian Imperator. Sir Amadas. The Huntyng of the Hare. Notes. Glossary.* Edinburgh: A. Constable and Company, 1810.

Webster, Richard. *Encyclopedia of Angels.* Woodbury: Llewellyn Worldwide, 2009.

Weinstock, Jeffrey. *The Ashgate Encyclopedia of Literary and Cinematic Monsters*. Burlington: Ashgate Publishing, 2014.

Westmoreland, Perry L. *Ancient Greek Beliefs*. San Ysidro: Lee and Vance Publishing Company, 2007.

Wheatley, Henry Benjamin. *Merlin, Or, the Early History of King Arthur: A Prose Romance (About 1450–1460 A.D.)*. London: Kegan Paul, Trench, Trübner, 1899.

White, John Tahourdin. *The Progressive Latin Reader*. London: Longman, Green, Longman, and Roberts, 1861.

White, Terence Hanbury. *The Book of Beasts: Being a Translation from a Latin Bestiary of the Twelfth Century*. Mineola: Courier Dover Publications, 1954.

Wichman, Frederick B. *Kaua I: Ancient Place-Names and Their Stories*. Honolulu: University of Hawaii Press, 1998.

Wiegele, Katharine L. *Investing in Miracles: El Shaddai and the Transformation of Popular Catholicism in the Philippines*. Honolulu: University of Hawaii Press, 2005.

Wiggins, Alison, and Rosalind Field. *Guy of Warwick: Icon and Ancestor*. Suffolk: Boydell and Brewer, 2007.

Wilde, Lady Jane Francesca Elgee, and William Robert Wilde. *Ancient Legends, Mystic Charms, and Superstitions of Ireland: With Sketches of the Irish Past. to Which Is Appended a Chapter on "The Ancient Race of Ireland."* Boston: Ticknor and Company, 1888.

Wildridge, Thomas Tindall. *The Grotesque in Church Art*. London: William Andrews and company, 1899.

Wilkinson, James John Garth. *The Book of Edda Called Völuspá: A Study in Its Scriptural and Spiritual Correspondences*. London: J. Speirs, 1897.

Williams, David. *Deformed Discourse: The Function of the Monster in Mediaeval Thought and Literature*. Montreal: McGill-Queen's Press, 1999.

Williams, Elena Arana. "Basque Legends in Their Social Content" in *Essays in Basque Social Anthropology and History* edited by William A. Douglass, 107–28. Reno: University of Nevada Press, 1989.

Williams, George M. *Handbook of Hindu Mythology*. Oxford: Oxford University Press, 2008.

Williams-Ellis, Amabel, and Frederick Jack Fisher. *The Story of English Life*. London: Coward-McCann, 1947.

Williamson, Robert W. *Religion and Social Organization in Central Polynesia*. Cambridge: Cambridge University Press, 2013.

Wilson, Sir Daniel. *Caliban: The Missing Link*. London: Macmillan, 1873.

Wilson, Laurence Lee. *Ilongot Life and Legends*. New York: Southeast Asia Institute, 1947.

Wood, Edward J. *Giants and Dwarfs*. London: Richard Bentley, 1868.

Woodgate, Fred. *Kamilaroi and Assimilation*. Canberra: National Library of Australia, 1995.

Worcester, Dean C. *The Philippine Islands and Their People*. New York: Macmillan, 1899.

Worth, Richard Nicholls. *History of Plymouth*. Plymoth: W. Vrendon and Son, 1871.

Wray, T.J., and Gregory Mobley. *The Birth of Satan: Tracing the Devil's Biblical Roots*. New York: Macmillan, 2005.

Wright, Elizabeth Mary. *Rustic Speech and Folk-Lore*. London: Humphrey Milford, 1913.

Yamaguchi, Kenkichi, Frederic De Garis, Atsuharu Sakai, and Fujiya Hoteru. *We Japanese: Being Descriptions of Many of the Customs, Manners, Ceremonies, Festivals, Arts and Crafts of the Japanese, Besides Numerous Other Subjects*. Japan: Fujiya Hotel, 1964.

Yamashita, Shinji, Joseph Bosco, and Jeremy Seymour Eades. *The Making of Anthropology in East and Southeast Asia*. New York: Berghahn Books, 2004.

Yasumura, Noriko. *Challenges to the Power of Zeus in Early Greek Poetry*. New York: Bloomsbury Academic, 2011.

Yoda, Hiroko, and Matt Alt. *Yokai Attack!: The Japanese Monster Survival Guide*. North Claredon: Tuttle Publishing, 2013.

Zell-Ravenheart, Oberon. *A Wizard's Bestiary*. Franklin Lakes: Career Press, 2007.

Zimmerer, Neil. *The Chronology of Genesis: A Complete History of the Nefilim*. Kempton: Adventures Unlimited Press, 2003.

Index

Aba 114, 119
Abaahy 9
Abaasy 9
Abarbarea 114
Abarbaree 114
Abarimon 9
Abassi 9
abassylar 9
Abasy 9
Abatwa 10
Abenaki Indians 17, 125
Abenaki mythology 9
Abgal 10
Abhaswaras 73
Abiku 10
Abishai 94
Abnuaanya 10, 11
Aboriginal Australian
  mythology 113
Abu Rigl Maslukha 11
Acamantis 54
Acamas 11, 128
Acephali 11
Acephalites 11
Acephalos 11
Acheloos 137
Achelous 13, 104, 105,
  126, 127, 147
Achilles 52, 84, 116, 128
Acis 128
Actaea 52
Acten 28
Actor 11
Actorid 11
the Actorione 11
Adam 24, 107
Adamastor, the Giant 129
Adiante 52
Adite 52
Adityas 73
Adlet 11
Admiraldus 69
Adokimus 121
Adroa 123
Aeda 33
Aegaeon 39
Æge 11
Aegean Sea 19, 27, 116,
  119
Ægeon 39
Æger 11, 97, 106
Aegina 114
Aegir 11, 12, 18, 27, 28, 29,

32, 35, 37, 42, 59, 60, 63,
71, 75, 79, 85, 87, 90, 95,
100, 131, 137, 154, 160
Ægir 11
Aegir 11, 12, 18, 27, 28, 29,
32, 35, 37, 42, 59, 60, 63,
71, 75, 79, 85, 87, 90, 95,
100, 131, 137, 154, 160
Aegius 53
Aegle 60, 114
Aegyptus 52, 53, 54
Aello 12, 44, 84, 120, 122,
  128
Aellopus 12
Aelous 124
Ænotherus 12
Aenotherus 12
Aepir 12
aes sídhe 136
Æsir 155
Aesir 7, 34, 38, 61, 64, 68,
  72, 73, 81, 90, 91, 110,
  111, 132, 138, 148, 164
Aethon 47
Aethra 91, 119
Aeti 12
Afghanistan 15
Africa 13, 14, 19, 20, 25,
  26, 27, 35, 37, 65, 83, 92,
  95, 106, 144, 160, 161,
  165
African mythology 14, 36,
  150, 163
Afro-Brazilian folklore 133
Afro-South American
  Suriname folklore 24
Aga 30
aganippides 113
Agaptolemus 53
Agatharchides (Agath-
  archus) of Cnidus 106
Agatho 11, 12, 22, 28, 39,
  45, 129
Agathodaemon 12, 43
Agathodaimon 12
Agathodemon 12, 13, 43
Agathos Daimon 12
Agave 52, 63
Agemor 141
Agenor 53, 54
Ägir 11
Aglaope 13, 104, 127, 138,
  147

Aglaopheme 13
Aglaophone 13
Aglaophonos 13, 111, 138,
  147
agloaopheme 137
Agnarr 89
Agogwe 13
Agreus 14
Agrotes 14
Agroueros 14
aguane 14, 133, 137
Ai 14, 61, 148
Aia 114
Aigaion 39
aigamuchas 14
aigamuxa 14
Aigeiros 83
Aigmuxab 14
Aino 96
Ainu 101
Ajshir-Baba 30
Akakanaza 99
Akephalos 11
Akkad 24
Akkadian-Babylonian
  mythology 103
aku 14–15
Agrios 13, 14
Agrius 13, 14, 87, 124, 148
Ahiman 14, 19, 136, 145
Ahani 20, 35
Agnes 21, 36, 37, 38
Aku-Aku 14
Akuaku 14
Akuan 15
Al 15, 115
Alaisiagae 15, 32, 71, 156
Alan 15
Alarabi 15
Alaska and British Colum-
  bia 20
Alaska, United States of
  America 11, 20, 151
Albadan 15
Albanian 36, 56, 58, 59,
  77, 95, 96, 98, 101, 136,
  144
Albanian and Balkan
  mythology 98
Albanian folklore 36, 136
Albanian mythology 56,
  58, 77, 95, 96, 101, 144
Albastor 15

Albasty 17
Albion 16, 34, 77, 92, 104
Albion the Giant 16
Albjofr 16, 60
Albnuaaya 17
Alboost 10, 17
Alces 53
Alcinoe 114
Alcion 16
Alcippa 17
Alcmenor 53
Alcyone 27, 124, 127
Alcyoneus 16, 17, 22, 26,
  59, 109, 125, 127, 129
Alcyonides 16
the Alcyonii 16, 17, 22, 26,
  59, 110, 125, 127
Alcyonis 16
Aleippe 17
Alexander the Great 9, 11,
  22, 28, 39, 45, 106, 129
Alexirhoe 114
Alf 16, 61, 141
Alfar 143, 155
Álfar 143, 155
Alfarin 16
Alfarinn 16
Alfgeirr 16
Alfheim 141, 142
Alfhild 141, 142
Alfrig 16, 34, 61, 79
Algebar 16
Al'gebar 16
Algonquin 161
Algroen Island 70
Alia 146
Alien Big Cats 36
Alien Gods 20, 164
Alifanfaron the Giant 16
Alii Menehune 17
Alipharon 16
Alipha-Ron 16
Alkippa 16, 17, 22, 26, 59,
  110, 127
Alkman 103
Alkyoneos 16
Alkyoneus 16
Alkyonides 16
Alkyonis 16
Allewyn 122
Allvaldi 123
almas 10, 17
Almast 10, 17

183

Index